RIGHTS REFUSED

Stanford Studies in Human Rights

RIGHTS REFUSED

Grassroots Activism and State Violence in Myanmar

Elliott Prasse-Freeman

Stanford University Press
Stanford, California

STANFORD UNIVERSITY PRESS
Stanford, California

Printed in the United States of America on acid-free, archival-quality paper

Library of Congress Cataloging-in-Publication Data

Names: Prasse-Freeman, Elliott, author.
Title: Rights refused : grassroots activism and state violence in Myanmar / Elliott Prasse-Freeman.
Other titles: Stanford studies in human rights.
Description: Stanford, California : Stanford University Press, 2023. | Series: Stanford studies in human rights | Includes bibliographical references and index.
Identifiers: LCCN 2022056354 (print) | LCCN 2022056355 (ebook) | ISBN 9781503634725 (cloth) | ISBN 9781503636712 (paperback) | ISBN 9781503636729 (ebook)
Subjects: LCSH: Human rights—Burma. | Political participation—Burma. | Government, Resistance to—Burma. | Political persecution—Burma. | State-sponsored terrorism—Burma. | Burma—Politics and government—21st century.
Classification: LCC JC599.B93 P73 2023 (print) | LCC JC599.B93 (ebook) | DDC 323/.04409591—dc23/eng/20221202
LC record available at https://lccn.loc.gov/2022056354
LC ebook record available at https://lccn.loc.gov/2022056355

Typeset by Motto Publishing Services in 10/14 Minion Pro

Cover design: Laywan Kwan
Cover painting: Dr. May Myanmar, *Three Fingers Painting with Pyit Taing Htaung Toy*, 2021, watercolor on paper, 21 × 29 cm, London, United Kingdom. The three-fingered salute is a symbol of pro-democracy movements across Southeast Asia. The Pyit Taing Htaung toy stands upright no matter how many times it falls, and is a symbol of the Burmese pro-democracy movement.

To the people of Burma amid their ongoing struggles for liberation.
အရေးတော်ပုံ အောင်ရမည်

Contents

Illustrations

Foreword

Elliot Prasse-Freeman's *Rights Refused* is a stunningly ambitious book, one whose contributions ramify throughout a wide range of disciplines, debates, and spheres of intellectual engagement, including contemporary regional studies of Myanmar and Southeast Asia; the anthropologies of social movements, law, power, and postcolonial governmentality; critical ethnographic methodology; neo-Foucauldian social theory; *and* critical interdisciplinary human rights studies. Indeed, *Rights Refused* serves as a potent reminder of how this latter topic—human rights and its discontents—continues to crystallize wider ethical preoccupations and uncover social, political, and economic aporia, even as the human tragedies and occasional triumphs at the heart of narratives like Prasse-Freeman's resist conclusive reduction to analytical categories or policy recommendations.

Prasse-Freeman's study unfolds across multiple registers, scales, and temporalities. He conducted longitudinal research in Myanmar over a decade between 2010 and 2019, a period that overlapped with Myanmar's putative democratic transition, during which the former political prisoner and Nobel Peace Prize–laureate Aung San Suu Kyi shared power with the country's military leaders. But since the political ascension of Aung San Suu Kyi, long imagined by Burmese democracy activists and international human rights campaigners alike, didn't formally take place until early 2016, Prasse-Freeman was able to chart the various landscapes of activism and resistance in Myanmar during a transitional period *before* the transition. Here, *Rights Refused* offers a beautifully rendered ethnography of the lives and interventions of Burmese who organize as part of long-term projects of what Prasse-Freeman describes as "refusal": the capacity to develop forms of nonsubjugation to the imperatives of sovereign violence as a strategy of subaltern empowerment.

In this way, *Rights Refused* takes its place alongside other major studies of everyday resistance, in which vulnerable and marginalized communities resist the Sauron's eye of state interpellation through creative practices of misdirection, mishearing, and a kind of studied—if potentially dangerous—absence from the ever-present demands of "blunt" biopolitical subjectification. And yet, Prasse-Freeman's provocative analysis also explores the realities of everyday resistance from a different direction: one in which the longtime victims of sovereign violence in Myanmar come to deploy various weapons of the weak as a form of interpellation in reverse, in which tactics like the pervasive turn to political cartoons might become a way to shape subjectivity *within* the apparatuses of state ideological power themselves. And among these tactics of interpellation from below, as Prasse-Freeman shows, Burmese activists mobilize human rights discourse in expansive and culturally nuanced ways.

But in the midst of this study of political resistance and what might be thought of as human rights *para*-activism, Prasse-Freeman's research was rocked by two historic events in destabilizing succession. First, in 2017, Aung San Suu Kyi, one of the world's most prominent living symbols of human rights and the struggle for dignity and freedom, "shamelessly defended" the genocide committed by the Burmese military against the Rohingya, Myanmar's long-beleaguered Muslim minority population. And second, in 2021, while Prasse-Freeman was analyzing his research data after having left the country, the Burmese military staged yet another coup d'etat, during which all the forces of state violence were openly brought to bear once again, including against Aung San Suu Kyi herself, despite the fact that she had engaged in an international act of moral and political self-immolation by trying to justify the Burmese military's ongoing atrocities.

So instead of an account of activism, mobilization, and political resistance within a period of democratic consolidation and social optimism, however tenuous, Prasse-Freeman was forced to keep the research envelope open for another year as he conducted "intensive digital ethnography" in order to shed some light on an "inexplicable coup" by a Burmese military regime that had enjoyed a "best-of-both-worlds position" for most of the prior decade. At the same time, Prasse-Freeman's digital ethnography in the aftermath of the coup was a source of tremendous anxiety as he followed the travails of his research interlocutors and comrades, who were by this point on the run, forced to go underground, and considering going into exile.

It is in the context of this dramatic shift from "democratic transition" to the "perilous milieu" of unremitting state oppression that *Rights Refused* must be read. Yet even in the darkest moments of social, political, and ideological closure, the language and practice of rights remained as tools to be used by the Burmese activists, many of whom had become something else, something more radical still—rebels. But as Prasse-Freeman's urgent study reveals with such convincing theoretical and ethnographic clarity, in mobilizing rights under the most difficult and indeed unlikely of circumstances, these heroic Burmese activists and rebels didn't simply stretch the boundaries of rights; they were compelled to remake the boundaries themselves.

Mark Goodale
Series Editor
Stanford Studies in Human Rights

Preface

After the Coup and the Killings

We all are now in the action.

The message came through the encrypted messaging app Signal on Thursday, February 4, 2021, at 11:57 a.m. Burma time,[1] from Ko Taw's number.

Three days earlier Myanmar's military had detained the country's elected president, Win Myint, and its state counselor, Aung San Suu Kyi, declaring a one-year state of emergency and preventing the recently elected parliament from being seated. The country was blindsided. After struggling through a decade-long democratic experiment, Myanmar citizens seemed stunned into sudden silence. More than just a betrayal, the military's decision seemed bizarre given the best-of-both-worlds position it occupied during the democratic transition it presided over from 2011 to 2021: it had enjoyed ongoing resource extraction opportunities and control of the means of violence while not having to attend to the hassles of everyday governance. Suu Kyi, despite her standing as a Nobel laureate, had even made herself the face of the 2017 clearance of nearly one million Rohingya from the country's Rakhine state, defending the country against accusations of genocide at the International Court of Justice (ICJ). Now she was back under arrest, reprising earlier incarcerations when she spent fifteen years during the 1990s and 2000s under house arrest. The people watched it all in shock.

But then, when night fell that same day, an eerie cri de coeur echoed throughout the country, as people joined together, tentatively at first but then in the millions, to bang on pots and pans, reprising a traditional practice of driving evil from villages. A cacophonous howl, feeble but present, haunted the country. Anticipating this call to action, Ko Taw, Thurein, Soe Aung, Teza, Thu Myat, and the rest of the Community Development Initiative (CDI) activists had already begun preparing. By the third day, they were taking action.

From where I sat in Singapore I watched the first tense days play out over the internet. I had worked with the activists in 2014 and 2015, and I had chatted weekly with Ko Taw since that time. Once the coup hit, he and the crew sent me updates, occasionally asking me to translate documents—including a handwritten note by 1988 protest leader Min Ko Naing—outlining the inchoate goals of the bourgeoning Civil Disobedience Movement (CDM) that they were helping to lead.

Such documents called for a general strike and nonviolent protests to shut down the country. By Saturday, Yangon teemed as tens of thousands of angry Burmese, hailing from all walks of life, took the streets. The CDI activists were on the run by this point: "We are in a dangerous situation. MI [Military intelligence] are trying to arrest us," Thu Myat wrote to me. By Saturday night, the country's internet was cut.

*   *   *

While the coup delivered its stunning death knell, Myanmar's democratic transition was already appearing moribund. Whether it was the intensifying neoliberalism undermining peasant livelihoods, the lack of progress in resolving protracted civil war with armed ethnic minority groups, or the putatively democratic government's own autocratic repression of free assembly, expression, and the press, the process had left many worse off and changed little for most. Still, Myanmar people were understandably devastated by the coup. Despite the transition's manifest failures, they still harbored reasonable hopes that conditions might improve—that through the strange alchemy of popular democracy the unenviable structural conditions of diarchic rule (in which civilian and military leaders uncomfortably shared power) could be overcome. Now it appeared that everything was back to square one, where Myanmar had been almost exactly a decade before this experiment began.

Except a genocide had occurred in the meantime. More than seven hundred thousand of the mostly Muslim Rohingya minority were driven across the country's northwest border into Bangladesh in the "clearance operations" of September 2017. More than ten thousand people perished at the hands of marauding soldiers who raped with impunity as they burned hundreds of villages. This well-equipped military force—known as the *Sit-tat* in local vernacular—unleashed this terror while ostensibly seeking a ragtag bunch of Rohingya militants who had led feeble attacks on local security installations. The country was brought before the ICJ based in part on evidence amassed during a UN-sponsored Fact Finding Mission (FFM) that Myanmar did not even permit to enter the country. At the ICJ, Suu Kyi, the Nobel Peace laureate, shamelessly defended the very military that had no compunction about imprisoning her again after its coup.

Many Rohingya, viewing the coup from refugee camps, hence interpreted the event as comeuppance for a coward who sold her soul for power and lost it anyway. As one Rohingya posted on Facebook, "Who stood with Rohingya in Myanmar when the Genocide took place? Now all stand with the one who ordered for Genocide!! Will remember all. . . . I hate both." This sentiment was shared by many from Myanmar's numerous ethnic nationalities, who laughed ruefully at the invocations of unity by the mainstream *Bamar* majority. To paraphrase one commenter, "Our armies are not marching down the hills to help you." Others highlighted that both Suu Kyi's party and the Bamar majority had ignored them for the transition's decade (and even before that) only to appeal to them in their own time of need. A Chin comrade, noting that Min Ko Naing's note (mentioned earlier) exhorted an implicit Bamar addressee to "Beg the 'Ethnics'" to join the revolution, erupted in derision: "When things are okay for themselves, they will forget us yet again." They observed lowland protesters' red shirts (for Suu Kyi's National League for Democracy [NLD]) and calls for freeing "Mother Suu" and shook their heads in contempt.[2] Some went so far as to declare an end to a shared future: "When we have to eat rice together, we will, but if our common destinies are over, we will go our own ways."

Schisms were highlighted along other vectors as well. Cartoonists, for instance, penned works that not only furiously condemned the coup but also articulated a trenchant overarching critique of the structures that made the coup possible and the conditions that perdured before and after it. In figure P.1, a smirking, self-satisfied general is juxtaposed against a peasant submerged in water—inadvertently evoking historian R. H. Tawney's famous metaphor in which peasants are always just about to go under with any false move.[3] The peasant, looking forlorn, says, "No matter the government, it does not concern us. We are having to search for our meals." This statement is formally juxtaposed with the general's comments: "No matter the misery the people fall into, it does not concern us. We are always working for our power."

FIGURE P.1.
Peasant (left): "No matter the government, it does not concern us. We are having to search for our meals." General (right): "No matter the misery the people fall into, it does not concern us. We are always working for our power." Source: Cartoonist Way-yan Taung-gyi, 2021.

While the focus is certainly on the general's callous indifference—he is literally foregrounded and delivers the punchline—the fact that the cartoonist describes peasant life as full of misery and sorrow *regardless* of who is in power is an implicit commentary on the previous "democratic" government as well. It focalizes a daily life that may not get much worse with the end of the democratic transition because that transition had not made things better in the first place.

Yet, even as the anticoup uprising struggled with these problems of solidarity—between ethnicities and across classes—there were innovations at the level of protest praxis that attempted to address and work through these challenges. Indeed, only a week after the coup, on Monday the eighth, red suddenly turned to black. Red shirts and flags became less prominent and calls for "Mother Suu" were subdued. They were replaced by black shirts, black flags, and black face coverings. Activists posted that black meant that the protests were for the whole country, not just Suu Kyi's NLD; they expressed that the country needed to look beyond the previous version of politics, as it was a dead end. Instead, they gestured toward transethnic solidarity and real federalism, trying to give Myanmar's ethnic people a reason to want to join them in a shared future.

✣   ✣   ✣

While Myanmar's military reinstalled itself after a ten-year interregnum of quasi-civilian rule, the uprising demonstrated that the country's people had other ideas. The work stoppages, consumer boycotts, and mass protests summarized under the CDM banner and led by workers, government employees, and youth brought normal state function to a halt. The radical activists whose lives are featured in the following pages were in the streets, fighting "to abolish the dictatorship entirely on this land," as Ko Taw put it in April 2021. As this book went to press, the military's grasp on power hence seemed both tenacious and tenuous—its willingness to deploy limitless violence against its population was matched by that population's seeming willingness to endure every assault. And thus the objectives that these activists had coveted for decades—ones that included not just demilitarization but also the end of economic exploitation and interethnic racism—seemed simultaneously tantalizingly within reach and yet never further away.

Given that this book is about those activists' lives, their contributions to the anticoup uprising will feature in every chapter that follows. Not least because the anti-coup movement is at times a perfect representation of activist practice, with the uprising distilling many of the themes that will be presented throughout the book: the arbitrary abuses and mass violence—including the murder of three thousand civilians (Irrawaddy 2022) as this goes to press in April 2023—but also the ludic commentaries and improvisational rebellions; and the movement's fragmentations and schisms as well as the unexpected successes and solidarities amid the staunch refusals lived in Myanmar after the coup.

And yet, given that the anticoup uprising has proven to be a moment of full mobilization, it conveys only one dynamic of activist life. In the theoretical language that will be developed throughout the book, a focus on moments of direct contestation against authority privilege what I will delineate as tactics of *resistance*, at the risk of eliding the longer-term strategies of *refusal* that make that resistance possible. Indeed, if resistance describes the encounter that pits the protester against the sovereign, refusal features refractions of that sovereign gaze, a turning away that enables modes of endurance of structurally violent environments. Resistance designates direct engagements, in which actors occupy public space and advance rejections of extant conditions and during which they invite and engage responses from sovereign agents (soldiers, police, and hired thugs as well as, often later, the law as wielded by venal officials and corrupt judges). Refusal defines strategies of movement building and consolidation under generalized conditions of hardship as well as practices of maneuver around the forms of biopolitics dominant in Myanmar, ones that I describe as "blunt." I use "blunt" here in three senses to describe this regime's dominant modality of governance: *uncaring* for the protection of life, *obtuse* in its forms of knowing that life, and reliant on *violence* ("blunt" as in "blunt force trauma"). Given this biopolitical milieu, Burmese activist practice is as much about attempting to redress the absence of care, evade obtuse and harmful forms of state knowledge, and blunt the effects of violence as it is about directly contesting unjust institutions.

Resistance and refusal thus operate quasi-dialectically, each enabling the other: acts of resistance mobilize followers and testify to a repressed population that alternative perspectives exist; strategies of refusal ensure that such actions are not pyrrhic. Indeed, resistance becomes enfolded as a tactic into a broader strategy or even habitus of refusal—one that is now becoming shared by millions more in Myanmar. In this context, invoking "rights" is just one technique in a vast repertoire of tactics, something that might work to intimidate officials and inspire new comrades but that also must be refused as concrete and metaphysical values in which one must be in fidelity.

✳   ✳   ✳

As a focus on refusal's longer-term temporal scales would suggest, we must look to before the coup to determine how the various aspects of this system articulate. I draw from my participant observation with the activists whose lives of resistance and refusal act as a latch that connects the subaltern peasants such as those represented in figure P.1 with the blunt biopolitical apparatus that violates them. By attending to activist life in 2014 and 2015, during the heart of Burma's "transition," the book seeks to make the coup comprehensible—both the state practices, desires, and logics that compelled the generals to seize power as well as the massive responses that sprung up to contest it.

And just as refusal encourages examinations of genealogies and previous experiences, it also opens up future horizons. At the time of publication, the coup is still being refused and its ultimate political and social meanings are still unfolding. While it seems perhaps inelegant from a narrative-arc perspective to begin in such an in-between place—within a struggle that is still being fought—it is actually quite appropriate for the following account of activist life in Burma. Because, despite their many failures and setbacks, the people featured in this book are successful by refusing to ever accept a struggle as finished, to ever accept an apparent loss as a final one.

Note on Language

When relaying texts or speech, this book attempts to clarify the predominant language used by speakers or authors, whether English (marked as [*Eng*] after the text snippet) or Burmese (marked as [*Bse*] after the text snippet). If the original text was Burmese, then the passage was translated; all translations have been completed by the author, unless clarified in footnotes. Certain important Burmese terms or expressions are given in Burmese orthography in footnotes. English overlain on several political cartoons featured in the book are the author's translations.

✻   ✻   ✻

Given the sensitivity of research on political activism in Myanmar, all legal names of individuals have been changed, except for those of well-known Myanmar political figures. These pseudonyms are kept consistent throughout the book, and there are no composite characters.

Acknowledgments

This book has been generously supported by several grants over the years, some formal and some informal. The National Science Foundation (DDRIG—AWDD02136) and the Wenner-Gren Foundation (#8990), respectively, supported my dissertation fieldwork in 2014 and 2015, while the National University of Singapore later supported this book in three distinct ways: with a research grant that allowed me to conduct follow-up research from 2018 to 2020; a book workshop grant in 2021 that allowed six colleagues from around the world to scrutinize the draft manuscript; and a book-publishing support grant that helped pay for costs associated with publication. When I first started doing Burma research back in 2004, a mentor, David Milloy, provided the support that helped me move to Yangon and start working there.

A similar mix of formal and informal support has characterized the non-monetary assistance this book has enjoyed, in ways that are too immense to adequately capture. But let me try. First and foremost, the people working as activists with CDI shared innumerable insights into Burmese lives. I am grateful that they permitted me to tag along and learn by observing and living with them. They are impressive and inspiring—I know on more than one occasion I have asked myself, while considering some (far less dire) political or social challenge of my own, "What would CDI do in this situation?" They are excellent guides for such questions particularly because of the joy with which they live their politics. Indeed, I hope to have captured and conveyed not just the pain and difficulty of life as a Burmese activist but the ebullience and love with which they live it. Ko Taw, CDI's leader, is first among equals here, and the book owes him an enormous debt for his patience, courage, creativity, and humor.

I have also relied on and learned from a robust and growing Burma Studies field over the last two decades. Phyo Win Latt, from and with whom I have been learning about Burmese politics for years, is an exemplary intellectual partner. In that same vein, Charles Carstens, Tharaphi Than, Tani Sebro, Elizabeth Rhoads, Ardeth Thawnghmung, Matt Schissler, Nay Chi, Chit Oo Lwin, Andrew Ong, Hilary Faxon, Michael Dunford, Courtney Wittekind, Siew Han Yeo, David Mathieson, Marshall Kramer, Rose Metro, Michael Edwards, Chu May Paing, Matt Walton, Zunetta Herbert, Wai Wai Nu, Lauri Nio, Jasnea Sarma, Carlos Sardiña Galache, Aung Soe Min, Kevin Woods, Seinenu Thein-Lemelsen, Thant Htet Zaw, John Buchanan, and Gerard McCarthy have all challenged and expanded my thinking in various ways. In particular, daily chats with comrades Geoff Aung and Stephen Campbell (in one chat group) and Shae Frydenlund and Kirt Mausert (in another) are interpersonal lifelines as well as platforms for learning and testing ideas.

Regarding Burmese language, Nance Cunningham, Kyaw Moe Tun, U Lay Lay, Justin Watkins, and the late John Okell were all cherished teachers. John is greatly missed, but his impact on Burmese language learning lives on.

Shannon Speed, James C. Scott, Lynette Chua, Stephen Campbell, Andrew Ong, Ken MacLean, Timothy Gitzen, Sayres Rudy, and Nick Cheesman read the entire manuscript and provided invaluable comments, both structural and substantive. Stephen, Nick, and Ken deserve special mention for their line-by-line close read, which corrected many embarrassing mistakes (the ones that remain are, of course, mine).

At NUS, Chitra Venkataramani, Jamie Gillen, Stuart Strange, Neena Mahadev, Canay Özden-Schilling, Tom Özden-Schilling, George Radics, Jen Estes, W. Nathan Green, Miles Kenney-Lazar, Matt Reeder, Nursyazwani, Carola Lorea, Vineeta Sinha, Eric Thompson, Kelvin Low, Kiven Strohm, and Maitrii Aung-Thwin have all engaged various parts of the manuscript and have been wonderful and supportive colleagues.

At Yale, Erik Harms, Paul Kockelman, and James C. Scott were inspiring and attentive mentors. Kalyanakrishnan Sivaramakrishnan, Louisa Lombard, Kamari Clarke, and Joe Errington were exemplary teachers and intellectual guides. All have remained incredibly supportive in the five years since I left. Andrew Carruthers has been a valued daily interlocutor on linguistic anthropology and sundry issues.

Timothy Gitzen, besides reading everything I have written over the last three years, has been a great friend. Sayres Rudy, my mentor during undergrad who has become my closest intellectual companion and one of my best friends, is in every page of this book, the interlocutor I am always writing with and for.

Colleagues at Stanford University Press deserve thanks for their dedicated work to vastly improve the manuscript. Dylan Kyung-lim White chaperoned this to completion and helped fix an earlier, quite disastrously convoluted title; Alison Rainey's insightful copyediting excised dozens of sneaky dangling participles and reminded me I barely know how to write; Gretchen Otto's production management was incredibly patient and flexible; and finally, massive thanks to Mark Goodale, the series editor, who believed in the book and encouraged me to take risks with it.

I want to thank my father for love and for staying alive, my brother for best friendship and brotherhood, and my mother for being the best person I've ever known. Finally, getting to go through life's adventure with the best adventurers I know—Andrea and our two daughters, who are suns, Soleil and Suriya—has been joy.

RIGHTS REFUSED

Introduction

The dogs nearly got us.

IT WAS APRIL 16, 2021, nearly three months into the uprising against Myanmar's military coup. During this period, Burma's masses had organized a Civil Disobedience Movement (CDM) against the country's armed forces. Mass protests had become a revolution and civil war. I had been in daily contact with Ko Taw, a grassroots political activist and my long-term interlocutor and friend with whom I worked and traveled extensively during fieldwork in Myanmar in 2014 and 2015. In periodic live streams and chat bursts in the two months since the February 1 coup, he and his comrades had been relaying details from the early days of their participation in the CDM, when their tentative sticker and pamphlet campaigns encouraging collective action gave way to massive protests and general strikes that effectively collapsed the state's normal functioning. But then came a brutal crackdown by the "dogs"—the ubiquitous term for both military generals organized under the newly formed State Administrative Council (SAC) and the ground-level police and soldiers. The dogs terrorized the country, having murdered by that point more than 750 people (including forty children),[1] maimed unarmed protesters, sexually assaulted imprisoned activists, shot at random into houses, destroyed cars, looted shops, and robbed citizens and even Buddhist temples for cash.

Ko Taw and the crew at the Community Development Institute (CDI),[2] their activist group, had reported on the pitched battles in the streets, the occupation of local governance institutions in peri-urban Yangon, and the arrest of members of their group. They described distributing funds smuggled into the country and extinguishing fires set by arsonists. They marveled at the courage of their countrymen and -women. But a week earlier Ko Taw's number had gone silent, text messages returning only red exclamation points.

On that day in mid-April, a "Hi" text suddenly arrived from an unknown number. And then, "It's Ko Taw." He went on to say, "We (Thu Myat, Teza, and Mya and me) were being checked on the way to the hide house. But the dogs didn't know who we really are. We pretended we were drunkards and there were two alcohol bottles we took for our cover story. They urged us to share one bottle with them. Ha-ha." Then, a pause. "But I think we can't hide for a long time. It has become hard to continue our activities—there are many explosions in many places. We have to go to the border (Liberated Area). Some of our members have already got there. They are now working and fighting together with EAOs [Ethnic Armed Organizations]."

Quitting the city was an agonizing choice. Both Teza and Ko Taw would leave behind young children who would wonder why their fathers were no longer there. "He won't understand why I discard him," Ko Taw said about his younger son. Ko Taw relayed how his wife had phoned him with a warning: "She will never forgive me if I die from this. She said she will beat my dead body severely." For the young members of their group, such as Thu Myat and Mya, the spatial rupture of going from city to jungle was an acknowledgment that the futures they had been expecting just three months earlier had vanished. Beyond this, they all felt that leaving was akin to throwing the city to the dogs: while recognizing the increasing futility of urban resistance, they felt like they were abandoning the people forced to continue life there. We connected briefly over video. Ko Taw panned over to Thu Myat and Mya, who smiled wearily. In the grainy rendering of their faces illuminated by the glare of the neon ceiling light, they looked much older than I remembered.

Rights Refused is an ethnography of these political activists' lives, attending to spaces such as the "hide house" and to the kinds of decisions debated and made there—when to protest, when to flee, how to mobilize others, how to withstand violence—that are then materialized on the streets, along paddy fields, in industrial zones, and eventually within jungle bases. It is based on eighteen months of in-country ethnographic fieldwork between 2014 and 2018 in which I worked, traveled, and periodically lived with this group of activists. I tracked how they advocated for workers and peasants across Burma during its time of so-called democratic transition, a period of massive, rapid political and economic change that was unceremoniously derailed by the 2021 coup, the aftermath of which I traced during a yearlong period of intensive digital ethnography following the military's seizure of power. The book has two main purposes: (1) investigating how activist practices constituted by what I will differentiate as *tactics of resistance* within longer-term *strategies of refusal* reveal a particularly novel form of postcolonial governmentality extant in Myanmar—helping to explain this inexplicable coup—and (2) providing insights into how people maneuvering against semiauthoritarian oppression generate and utilize unique perspectives on rights.

That moment in April 2021, as CDI members pondered leaving Yangon, felt like an inflection point. It seemed that a fundamental alteration of tactics had become necessary, that resistance was giving way to something else. Until this point—since the first quiet postcoup days had exploded into millions of demonstrators taking the streets, staging transgressive protests that rejected not just the generals but also the desire of those generals to monopolize the symbolic sphere (more on this in chapter 4)—setbacks and challenges had been met with courageous responses. When the regime seemed an implacable monolith, early defections by soldiers and bureaucrats made victory appear possible. Myanmar's ambassador to the UN inspired millions when, in a live speech in front of the General Assembly, he broke from the regime and delivered, his voice cracking as he broke into Burmese, the imperative to victory: "Ayay-daw-boun aung-ya-myee" (The revolution must be achieved).[3] When recruiting additional members to join the CDM had seemed to stall, various protests sabotaged public infrastructure. These acts prevented people from going to work, lending additional thousands the plausible deniability necessary to join the strike (more on this in chapter 3). When the first major violent crackdowns soon thereafter might have marked the dampening of demonstrations, protesters responded by bearing their own scarred and abused bodies in defiance, undercutting the regime's use of terror (more on this in chapter 1). When the concomitant collapse of the economy threatened to make continued resistance impossible for people who needed food to survive, networks of sharing emerged, diaspora remittance networks blossomed, and the taking of local government offices made distribution achievable (more on this in chapter 2). When the SAC tried to install its own government, the CDM enacted several substantive (albeit flawed) institutional improvisations, forming a parallel representative system called the CRPH that became in turn the National Unity Government (NUG). And when the *Sit-tat*[4] tried to court ethnic Burmese subjects into its regime, CDM members demanded that its elite representatives publicly self-examine and apologize for the failures of the implicit *Bamar* chauvinism that characterized the earlier democratic transition period (more on this in chapter 6).

Yet while the CDM had overcome each challenge, winning such battles nevertheless led simultaneously to a sinking feeling that the war was being lost: activists fleeing to the border meant they were no longer "keeping the streets" (Aung 2021). The protests had dwindled to flash mobs that vanished moments after materializing and which were pushed to the outskirts of Yangon, peri-urban areas known as the *hsin-kyay-boun*.[5] The SAC's leader, Min Aung Hlaing, and not the NUG, was invited to an Association of Southeast Asian Nations (ASEAN) peace summit in late April. Days later, the SAC attempted to normalize its abnormality, announcing the reopening of schools, banks, and local governance institutions that the CDM had shut down or appropriated. There was a creeping suspicion that the regime had absorbed the best the CDM had to muster, that through intimidation and indoctrination (Rio 2021), it had kept its ranks from breaking.

But even as the crew prepared to retreat to the hills, where they planned to join thousands to train for an imminent return, yet another activist campaign began to circulate on Burmese Facebook. Called the *buu*—or "no"—campaign, it deviated from earlier ones in an important sense. The litany of creative protests up to that point had seemed to escalate in semiotic density—going from the barely discernible moan of the banging pots (referenced in the preface) to the emphatic images of bodies brutalized in resistance. This acceleration betrayed a realization that the movement required not just reiteration but intensification of energy for it to persist. In fact, a campaign called #Sisters2Sisters, led by activist Thinzar Shunlei Yi, simulated the bludgeoned faces of female comrades, thereby risking accusations of fakery and inauthenticity as the cost of magnifying and circulating the arresting reality they represented (fig. I.1).[6]

The *buu* campaign, by contrast, was relatively subdued. Organized around the negating particle "buu," it articulated a simple and stark "no" to the coup, its slogan being, "If you carry a 'no,' the revolution must be achieved."

While the slogan's independent clause reiterated the CDM's refrain ("The revolution must be achieved"), the initial clause, about carrying a "no," invoked a Burmese proverb. Repeated in full by the male father figure in the cartoon in figure I.2, it reads, "Buu-ta-loun-saung oh-taung ma-sin-yeh" (If you carry a "no," you will not be poor even when you are old).[7] The verb *saung* has two simultaneous meanings here, "to carry" but also "to ward off evil." And

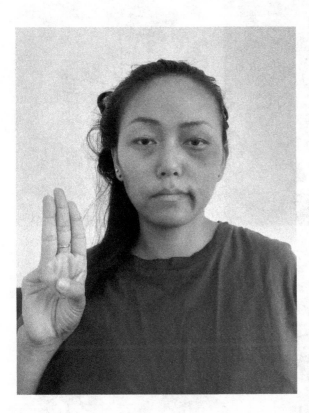

FIGURE I.1.
First photo in the
#Sisters2Sisters
campaign, mid-April
2021. Source: Thinzar
Shunlei Yi.

so carrying a "no" speaks to an imperative to constantly reject entanglement with others and their projects, to brandish "no" like a talisman to preempt even the consideration of an affirmative "yes." Rejection, denial, and refusal—according to the proverb—are the only ways to guarantee self-preservation in the daily precarity and violence that have long characterized life in Myanmar.

Given this foreclosure of the embrace of human sociality and the political transformation it might bring, the proverb is often considered cynical. It could stand as an emblem of what Ardeth Thawnghmung, in her recent book on daily Burmese survival (2019), describes as the destructive coping strategies on which many of Myanmar's poor are compelled to rely. Such strategies may assist individuals in the short-term, but by undermining collaborative action, they are deeply damaging to collective cooperation and survival over longer time frames.

Conversely then, by rejecting this classic injunction to turn inward, the *buu* campaign appropriated and resignified the "no," suturing negation to a wholly

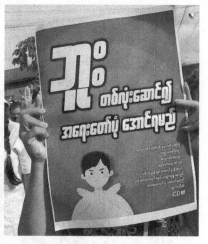

FIGURE 1.2. Clockwise from upper left: The first sticker deploys the slogan "If you carry a 'no,' the revolution must be achieved," against a soldier (source unknown). The second image, a photo of a protester holding a blown-up sticker, includes the same slogan and adds terse one-liners: "Overturn the age of fear; our world is not satisfied; our blood is not calm; do not retreat; if there is a fight, there must be a victory; the military dictatorship must fall" (source unknown). In the third illustration, the cartoon, the father intones the original parable, "If you carry a 'no,' you will not be poor even when you are old." The daughter figure, however, says, "I won't attend," while the wife says, "I won't carry [it]," which can be read as them rejecting the parable in favor of the inversion enacted by the *buu* protest. Source: Cartoonist OH, 2021.

different end: the revolution's victory. Hence, the campaign transmuted a self-defeating imperative to self-preservation into one for solidarity. The images in figure I.2 indexing the coup hence stand as "counter-negations," as historian Phyo Win Latt put it (pers. comm., October 8, 2021). Ko Taw concurred with this sentiment, saying, "The proverb means 'no joining' and 'no participation.' You should live alone. By this way no one can harm you. But it is just intended for individuals; the protest has another meaning. The protest is for the community" [*Eng*].

The CDM translated the demand into multiple rejections of any and all aspects of the new normal the SAC was trying to install. "The *buu* strike intends to choke the administration of the dogs [through] inclusive and continuous participation against the dogs. It also encourages the community and makes sense that we disobey the dogs' orders," Ko Taw asserted. As an April 2021 CDM tweet elaborated, "The 'NO' Strike: every #Myanmar can participate; - NO to paying taxes/bills - NO to businesses owned/affiliated by Junta - NO to #SAC's rules & regulations - NO to 'back to school, work, normal'; - NO to cash flow to #SAC; No one rules if no one obeys." This "no," however, yielded tragic acts of self-sacrifice. On August 11, 2021, a group of rebel youth hurled themselves from a four-story building rather than surrender to pursuing soldiers; it was believed that they chose group suicide—they held hands as they fell (Coconuts Yangon 2021)—so as not to betray comrades under ensuing interrogation (Irrawaddy 2021). More banal acts of sacrifice were precipitated by a public health infrastructure in revolt. A cancer patient, suddenly denied treatment by the absence of doctors, declared the following a week before his death: "I know I'm dying. But I will never blame the doctors, because young people are dying in the street after being shot by the police and soldiers. Compared to them, my death will be nothing" (Paddock 2021). This sentiment extended to the masses who chose to reject COVID-19 vaccinations delivered by SAC. The head of UNICEF in Myanmar was reported as averring that in her over two decades of work "in hot spots around the world," "she had never seen people so hostile to the authorities that they would refuse health care that they needed."

But just as importantly, such noes were also coupled with multiple yeses, as illustrated in figure I.3. In the cartoon, a woman calls out, "Hey Doctor," to a passing trishaw driver (whose vehicle is adorned with the CDM label); he responds with "Ha, Teacher!" They have left their offices (persisting in the general strike) but remain active as part of the social infrastructure, providing food and transport as part of CDM's mutual-aid support (Thawnghmung, Su Mon

FIGURE 1.3. This cartoon depicts members of how people, such as doctors and teachers, participate in the revolution. The woman says, "Hey Doctor!," and the man on the bike answers her with, "Ha teacher!" Source: Cartoonist Halman, May 2021.

Thazin, Moo Moo Paw, and Boughton, forthcoming). Veteran Burmese writer Ma Thida (2022) renders the affirmative effervescence in the present tense: "Young doctors and nurses eat lunch from anonymous donors on the street while waiting for anyone who needs medical care. Some street boys and girls are enjoying a variety of free meals and drinks. . . . Rich people politely collect rubbish from poor protesters and they appreciate each other's roles" (29).

The *buu* movement marked a reinvestment in popular opposition—after all, "every #Myanmar [person] can participate," as the earlier tweet put it. It displaced the centrality of direct challenges in the streets to recenter a diffuse and all-encompassing rejection of military rule always present in the CDM. But it went further. By resignifying the parable's original atomizing negation—where *buu* was a rejection of everything, even hope in something better—it encouraged connection and collaboration. The *buu* campaign thus evoked social theories, such as Tina Campt's, that stress the generativity of negation (2019, 25) and its ability to create new political possibilities (see also Hartman 2018, 470).

Simultaneously, however, the *buu* protest's original referent—the cynical parable—was not obliterated; *buu* could not so easily be irrevocably reformulated.

Instead, the parable lurked as the condition that would reemerge if the revolution collapsed—or that would reemerge to collapse the revolution. It stood as an ever-present reminder of the fine line separating "no" as rejection of power's prerogatives and "no" as rejection of solidarity and collaboration. As such, the *buu* distills the challenges of activism in a place such as Myanmar. Contentious action is necessary to beckon masses, who have been habituated to pursue self-preservation to the point of pathology, to see their conditions differently. The "no" must be robust and public enough to interpellate them. Yet direct resistance to the state will court annihilation (Shah 2021, 78). The "no" must be calibrated and strategic enough to not be suicidal. How can activism operate within such a perilous milieu, and how can its specific operations be understood?

Resistance/Refusal

To give names to these different tactics just outlined, the direct challenge of the first months of the anticoup movement can be called "resistance," whereas the multiplication of rejection in the *buu* protest can be described as "refusal." Discourse on the latter concept—as recently theorized in anthropology (Simpson 2014; Weiss 2016), in Black studies (Hartman and Moten 2018; Hartman 2018; Campt 2019; and inspired in part by Glissant 1997), and at their intersection (Sojoyner 2016; Shange 2019a, 2019b)—has generated significant interest in adjacent fields as well.[8] Scholars find inspiration in the promise of reorganizing political potentialities that is contained within wholesale preemption of an institution of authority's paradigms of dominance or rule. "Another life is possible," as Damien Sojoyner (2016) puts it. For this reason, refusal's theorists distinguish resistance and refusal by their respective ontologies of power: these authors argue that resistance implies contesting *superior* power, while refusal insists upon the *equality* of two opponents. For instance, Carole McGranahan holds that while "theories of resistance presume a hierarchical relationship in which a subordinate resists a superior power," refusal "works differently by professing a relationship between equals" (2018, 368). Campt describes refusal as entailing "thinking beyond hierarchal structures of power/resistance as the primary schematic for representing the relationship of black subjects to power" (2019, 26).

And yet many of these claims appear to elide the necessity of attending to the *effects* of acts that position refusers as equal to their opponents and hence of the potentiality for such acts of refusal to fail to achieve their intended results. Take Audra Simpson's insistence that "refusal comes with the *requirement* of having one's political sovereignty acknowledged and *upheld*" (2014, 11; emphases added). In this definition, for refusal to exist at all, institutions of authority are required to act in a particular way, not only recognizing a subjected group as sovereign but materializing that acknowledgment—upholding it, as Simpson has it—through, say, enacted policies and delivered resources. But this entails a near paradox: if one's demands were *initially* acknowledged and upheld, then refusal as a set of *ensuing* actions would be unnecessary. Refusal, in the moment of its very enactment, would in that same moment have rearranged political relations to such an extent that refusal would dissolve away.

That conception of refusal would seemingly endorse a theory of action that relies on a "metaphysics of presence," as outlined in Derrida's (1988, 15) famous critique of unmediated relationship between action and outcome.[9] He argued instead that not only is failure the condition of possibility for any successful action but that such successes are also dependent on myriad exchanges and encounters that came far before and after the apparently determinative act.

Such a dismissal of refusal, however, would be shortsighted. Let us examine McGranahan and Campt's respective quotes again. McGranahan claims that refusal "works differently by *professing* a relationship between equals" (emphasis added); for Campt, refusal entails "*thinking beyond* hierarchal structures of power/resistance as the primary schematic for representing the relationship of black subjects to power" (emphasis added). Glissant, for his part, "*clamors* for," rather than presupposes the existence of, "the right to opacity for everyone" (1997, 194; emphasis added). Highlighted in these emphases on stances taken and new horizons considered—irruptions of the putatively immediate and unequivocal enactment or material realization of one's sovereignty—is that refusal is consciously processural or semiotic: its effective meaning relies on the responses that it generates. This would acknowledge that signs are co-constructed by the interpretants they create (Kockelman 2007a), despite refusers' protestations to the contrary. Indeed, refusers articulate absolute repudiations even as they maneuver because of them in the penumbra that those repudiations create. Enunciated rejections give them the space, perspective, time, strength, and wherewithal to navigate. So, when Simpson (2014, 118–22) clashes with casually racist US border guards and asserts her Mohawk sovereignty, she ultimately uses various identification documents issued by the United States and Canada, *not* her Iroquois Confederacy papers, to pass through the checkpoint. What would have been gained had she had remained at the border for hours to insist on Iroquois mobility rights? Instead, she writes about it, telling us that "in documenting the interaction, I realized that ethnography in anger can have a historically and politically productive effect" (119).

Therefore, given that desired ends often do not immediately materialize and so cannot be presumed, as opponents may respond in any number of ways, it may be more productive to consider the contours of engagements with those adversaries more closely. It seems instead that what distinguishes resistance and refusal is how they describe different *forms of encounter* across often repeated encounters.

Understood thus, I theorize resistance as defining encounters in which sovereign power encroaches upon subjects[10] who oppose that assault head-on or on its own terms, rejecting the sovereign demand, contesting its incursion, and so on. Whether with vassals before kings or citizens before the law, two forces contest each other directly, thereby *defining* each other as opponents and co-constituting one another as subjects: the resister enacts a subject position that must declare itself, thereby reproducing the same mode of sovereign legibility. Whether each part of the dyad accedes to the other's claims is not relevant in the first instance; it is rather their mutual imbrication in the relationship of contestation that matters.[11] Yet, simultaneously, by conceiving of the contest this way, resistance theorists perceive a bifurcated power terrain in which sovereign and subject are monadic, internally coherent and mutually external to one another. Therefore, subjects are capable of retreat—both subjectively and physically—to zones in which "hidden transcripts" can be cultivated (Scott 1985, 1990).[12]

Refusal, by contrast, both rejects that form of sovereign "recognition" and denies the separability of the subaltern subject from the field of power with which it interacts (Spivak 1988). First, refusal to answer the sovereign's demand (Rudy 2014) enacts a *turning away* that creates an alternative subject position (Deleuze 1997, 73). Refusal describes the attempt to maintain such a subjective "opacity" (Glissant 1997) that deflects recognition, therein carving out a space outside of the dyad full of potentiality (Agamben 1999). Second, though, refusal recognizes that subjects remain within the field of power; unable to completely escape, they must negotiate biopolitical inclusions and exclusions at perpetual risk of interpellation and absorption by those power fields. Therefore, rather than a smooth "infrapolitics" connecting subalterns and enabling rapid and efficient mobilization at appropriate conjunctures

(Scott 1990, chap. 7), political work is necessary to resignify collective understandings of power relations.

Consequently, subjective opacity—the turning away from direct contestation—cannot be so great that the refuser dissolves completely; the distance cannot be so vast that the subject vanishes (Bonilla 2015). Otherwise, there is a risk—especially when flight remains a privilege inaccessible to many—that refusal becomes effectively undifferentiable from pacification (Honig 2021, 1). As we will see in lower-class coping strategies featured throughout the book, this kind of refusal can be a turning so far away as to no longer trouble that which is being refused. What's more, such actions send signs to others that are more likely to be read as acquiescence. As with the *buu* parable—say "no" to everything—by preempting solidarity, such absolute rejection becomes autophagic: self-devouring.

Slippery Sovereign Power, "The State," and Activist Mimesis

Thus far our discussion has considered the challenge of horizontal mobilization (convincing masses to contest a brutal regime) amid sovereign repression. But there is an additional problem. As elaborated explicitly in chapter 1, the country's security apparatus can be described as a sort of "slippery sovereign" in the sense that it often refuses a position of legibility against which Burmese could even resist. Yet it also retains the capacity to act with a brutality that demands particular strategic maneuvers for those dealing with it to remain alive at all.[13]

Regarding illegibility, while scholarly research on Myanmar stresses how subjects escape the state, and they certainly do, I observe something different than evasion.[14] Evasion implies a response to pursuit: one eludes that which attempts to entrap. Evasion can hence be said to exist only if a state agent or institution is reaching out: surveilling, investigating, enrolling subjects into projects, managing them through regulation, and so forth. While people do get entangled by Myanmar's state, such outcomes are somewhat exceptional. Instead, Burmese often encounter problems because they are *ignored* by state institutions and yet choose not to seek them out (such as by attempting redress through legal institutions), as they fear their problems will consequently become calamities.[15] Daily life for Myanmar people at the margins is defined not by state pursuit and subjective evasion but by *mutual rejection*; rather than the gaze of joint recognition described by anthropologists and sociologists of the state, we see a field of vision refracted at both ends, such that subjects and the state turn away from each other.

Average subjects thus perceive the state as a bifurcated apparatus: the front line agents that are encountered occasionally (for example, the official who administrates the household list in a ward and effectively grants a child the ability to attend school, the policeman who demands bribes for protection, or the judge who declares guilt or innocence) are seen as only contingently connected with the other actors understood as existing "behind" or "above" and who sporadically insist on the implementation of their own imperatives. For instance, Nick Cheesman's (2015b) research on the justice system illustrates how frontline officials are free to extract rents from clients involved in court cases provided that the specific cases do not implicate security or business concerns of those "above"—at which point local-level machinations must be relinquished. Jangai Jap (2021), in her study of average subjects' interactions with street-level bureaucrats, relays these citizens' conception of this split: "When a street-level bureaucrat requests additional documents or tells them that he (the agent) needs to consult with those in the higher ranks, clients often assume that they are being given a hard time" (124–25).

Given that both zones (the local and the "higher ranks") are seen as parts of "the state,"[16] what distinguishes them? Burmese subjects "disaggregate the state" (Slaughter 2004) based on degrees of sovereign force, specifically the ability to execute decisions and make exceptions to rules. On one hand, local-level officials are somewhat free to make decisions. To illustrate, much was made of the fact that according to the 2008 constitution, the military would control the General Administrative Department (GAD), the backbone of the state apparatus, connecting wards and villages to the commander in chief of the military. The generals, however, made the stunning choice—one less commented on—to abdicate control of the agency (Arnold 2019), *voluntarily* severing their sustained connection with, and responsibility for, the grassroots. On the other hand, even if local-level officers (police officers, land department officials, and home affairs administrators) can make decisions, these have diminished sovereign force, as such officers are subject to supersession from those above.

There are several consequences of this system. On one hand, local officials are susceptible to activist intimidation or negotiation, affording activists time and space to make incursions into public space. On the other hand, officials' inability or unwillingness to act means that, pace resistance paradigms that presume a stable, legible object for activists to protest against, contentious Burmese politics runs the risk of creating signs that do not signify. Therefore, when those decision-makers are absent or illegible—ignoring complaint letters, not delivering services, or occasionally turning a blind eye to demonstrations—activists must try to make them appear, demanding response either in the moment or by circulating and mediatizing that demand in order to reiterate it later.[17]

And yet, when these institutions then become present, they often operate with an "extreme violence" that, evoking Etienne Balibar (2016), approaches "an *annihilation of all possibility of resistance*" (131). As apparent in both the Rohingya genocide and protracted wars against the country's ethnic villagers, violence ceases to be purely instrumental—Burma's security forces indulge in rituals of excess (Bataille 1993). Hence, in response to this utilization of violence, subjects have no access to what Partha Chatterjee calls the "calculative, almost utilitarian" violence that he identifies as "part of performative strategies" (2011, 229) that would enact what Nusrat Chowdhury calls protesters' "rehearsed spectacles of presence" (2019, 10). When the state destroys villages, ways of life, and futures, and when it rapes, maims, and slaughters, refusal is necessary as a maneuver away from such dire ends. Even when less extreme outcomes are at stake—such as the ever-present threat of reincarceration—activists are constantly aware of the potential for violent sovereign reaction and are cognizant of the risks and potential benefits tied up in various scenarios of potential encounter.

Absent Presence

Therefore, attention to Burmese activism enables a conceptualization of refusal as neither complete *absence* (either as abandonment of space or as subjective quietude) nor assertive *presence* (implacable, interminable, incorrigible resistance that could prove suicidal against excessive sovereign power). Refusal is rather an *absent presence*, as illustrated in the particular moment of the anticoup uprising considered here, defined temporally by evanescent occupations (those fleeting flash mobs) and then spatially (the flight to and return from the hills)—all buttressing the resounding *buu* of Myanmar's masses.

A focus on oscillation, movement, and flux—something with a long lineage in Burma studies (Leach 1959; Robinne and Sadan 2007; Ong 2020)—also destabilizes conceptions of social actors as monadic, whether the coherent resisting subject ("the people") or the solid resisted object ("the state"). Further, and if we return to Derrida's critique of presence, it becomes clear that activist power comes from the play between positions—the oscillation within presence/absence.[18] Burmese activists must become present to conjure

the sovereign into existence; then they must dissolve away lest they invite annihilation. Indeed, while in one sense the Burmese state is saturated with sovereign power—whether run by generals or Aung San Suu Kyi, state elites are
committed to an aesthetics of power that cannot abide resistance (Prasse-
Freeman 2019)—it takes a significant amount of work for those moments of
encounter to be constructed, for those who would resist to even become part
of the "political society" (Chatterjee 2004) that could advance claims. *Rights
Refused* examines the effort put into transforming groups of peasants and
workers into collective subjects who can resist, groups whose claims might
be legible to and whose calls may interpellate responses from generals, elites,
and publics.

This dangerous game played between activists and the military-state,
which has unfolded in different iterations over generations (Boudreau 2004),
is one in which social power itself becomes a rhizomatic pursuit of asymmetry.[19] This contrasts with an "arborescent" model of power, in which actors
pursue capture of hierarchical structures but in so doing make themselves
vulnerable to attacks (in terms of physical violence or political claims). Indeed, if one way to define sovereign power is as "a capacity to engage" as well
as "a right to resist" (Slaughter 2004, 188), we might consider the dialectical relationship between the two: *greater* capacity to enact control may render that
entity *less* able to resist contestation. In a rhizomatic model of power, conversely, control is forfeited as political strategy, undermining the ability of
counterclaims to be advanced.

Hence, rather than mirror one another in mutual recognition, in Myanmar both activists and regime attempt to maximize absent presence. Activists use tactics of resistance to presence the state when it is absent and then
withdraw away to refuse sovereign reaction. Such withdrawal is both physical (flight to safe houses or the border, or refusal to even hold a protest or participate in a rally) and subjective (refusing the temptation to contest when
the outcome of direct resistance is likely to produce effective self-destruction).
This seems similar to Michael Taussig's definition of mimesis (1993): the attempt to copy so as to pillage the power of the alter without being dominated
or captured by it. Both entities—regime and activists—are in a continual fight,
a tug-of-war, a battle of becoming ill/legible.

As this suggests, resistance and refusal are inextricably bound, an idea that
is immanent within the refusal literature as well. Iroquois refusal, so power-
fully traced by Simpson (2014), also involves moments of direct contestation as

well as acquiescence when assertions of refusal are ignored (112, 150). Likewise, the Israelis silently avoiding army conscription (Weiss 2016) have their refusal clarified by those who *explicitly* resist service. Savannah Shange (2019a), writing about Black girls' refusal of their simultaneous hypervisibility and invisibility in the contemporary United States, describes how an interlocutor in a single moment—"She watched me watch her, her Black girl opacity demanding to be seen but refusing to be seen through" (16)—insists on being seen (a direct confrontation definitive of resistance) but also turns away from being seen the wrong way (refusal). Because, as Ko Taw put it, at the level of tactics, "*buu* is not the primary one—it is just a kind of protest. And it is hard to abolish the military dictatorship entirely by only the *buu* strike." He continued by highlighting all the other aspects necessary: should people "continue nonviolent protest? Or armed struggle? Or make handmade bombs or kill [collaborators], or [set] fire [to] the dogs' building or . . ." He trailed off at the number of resistance tactics that all seemed necessary and that could harness and magnify the dispersed orientation of refusal committed to by the population.

As this helps clarify, refusal should not be thought of as a set of tactics but as a disposition, habitus, or even ontology, where habitus is the sedimented and ultimately embodied ensemble of patterned responses to stimuli shared by members of a community of practice,[20] and ontology is the embodied experience of reality itself. And in the same way that sovereign power does not disappear within regimes of governmentality (Foucault 2007, 4–8) but can be reanimated and reinvigorated as one constituent modality of that regime's functioning (Butler 2006, 61), we might say that, homologously, resistance nests as a constituent practice within activist lives devoted to refusal. Hence, refusal as a form of survival expands the spatial-temporal domain of consideration from that of classic resistance, stressing longer time scales and broader domains of engagement (Sobo 2016; Ahmann 2018, 342). Refusal envelops resistance: it comes *first*, producing possibilities for resistance, and continues *after*, focusing on the ways that struggles persist after encounters with state security forces, judges, prison officials, mafia thugs, and so forth. Hence, resistance and refusal can be delineated in terms of specific processes even as they must be thought of as intertwined, operating in a quasi-dialectical relation: subjects, through the interplay of direct confrontation and self-management of themselves as populations, can fortify stronger positions from which they can persist. These describe complex and unavoidable entanglements, akin to taking up residence in a system without becoming subsumed by it (Kockelman 2013).

The refusal paradigm then directs focus on all the work—enduring, mobilizing, waiting, rehabilitating, planning, and evading—that happens in the shadow of resistance (protest and contestation). As that list suggests, refusal seems attuned to highly mediated modes of governmental rule and biopolitical regulation that are difficult to contest directly, as they are realized through the interacting effects of myriad policies, plans, and projects (Prasse-Freeman 2022b). Refusal thus requires maneuvering within, against, and with governmental forces: surviving structural violence and elaborating an alternative to it, recovering from violence's effects, quietly organizing comrades and gradually transforming erstwhile bystanders into militants, and biding time until the moment for direct action appears more fortuitous.

Unsurprisingly, this quasi dialectic or oscillation between resistance and refusal outlined here and enacted during the anticoup resistance did not emerge spontaneously. Its seeds were sewn in refusal of the military dictatorship that ruled from 1962 to 2011 (Tran 2020). But it also drew direct inspiration from the intense days of the transition (2011–2021)—an era an interlocutor once referred to as "the time of protests," defined by struggles over access to livelihoods, environmental sustainability and local resource control, education reform, fair energy prices, and, above all, land access. By tracing the projects that the activists supported then, *Rights Refused* shows how Burmese subjects were forced to both directly and indirectly maneuver this era. They faced a neoliberalizing reform project that exposed them to both the opportunities and dire consequences of increased market access and legal formalization, one buttressed by unpredictable state coercion defined by direct violent repression and maddening absence. How then, more specifically, do activists forge responses to these multiple demands?

Anticipating Victory

As the CDM's demand that "revolution must be achieved" echoed across Myanmar in 2021, it also echoed across time. Six years earlier, on May 14, 2015, six defendants had emerged from Dagon Township courtroom near downtown Yangon having just been sentenced to a fifty-two-month prison term. The crime for which they were to spend nearly a half decade behind bars? Holding an unauthorized protest in front of the Chinese embassy in Yangon four months earlier. During that demonstration they had burned a Chinese flag to punctuate their opposition to Chinese investment in a copper mine in Letpadaung, located in central Burma eight hundred kilometers away. The project had displaced hundreds of farmers, and police had repeatedly brutalized protesters.

This severe sentence was no surprise—the dozens of reporters, family members, and supporters (not to mention an equal number of police) gathered in the court compound that day had already learned of the impending verdict through official rumor conveyed by court officials. What was extraordinary, however, was what transpired as they exited from the courthouse itself and met this crowd. Flanked by ushering police, the six halted, raised the three-fingered salute that would come to define the CDM a half decade later, and burst into song, leading the audience in a spontaneous rendition of Burma's national anthem. The crowd surged forward to meet them, holding cell phones aloft to capture the scene. At this point, San San, who had clearly anticipated her own conviction, attempted to unfurl a banner condemning the outcome. The police chief, recognizable by his special uniform insignia and officious disposition, grabbed the banner and tried to wrest it from her.

As they struggled for the banner, other prisoners entered the fray; other police officers met them in turn. A riot of motion and sound ensued as bodies flung about, screams sounded, and arms and legs entwined—a throng of limbs locked in a violent dance that churned and eddied. A female supporter was ejected and slid across the dirt. A video journalist collapsed a folding table he had perched on, crashing both to the ground. Relatives screamed; recently convicted Htin Htut Paing exploded in rageful, sobbing denouncements; young women wailed.

I held my phone above the fracas and, like dozens of others gathered there, filmed the strange proceedings, waiting for some sort of external intervention—the riot police or the army—that never came. Instead, the central protagonists gradually disentangled as comrades comforted the prisoners, many of whom continued to denounce the injustice. The police officers nodded compassionately at them, remaining close but not interfering with the convicts as each retreated to respective corners of the compound to meet with family and hold interviews with the assembled press.

As I wandered around the compound to commiserate with the now incarcerated activists—passing on the greetings of the CDI crew, with whom I had been doing research for six months at that point—the sudden lull provided time to process this event in broader context. While the protest for which the convicts were arrested had been held in immediate response to a crackdown on protesters in which a police officer's stray bullet had killed local farmer Khin Win, the fact that it was held outside the Chinese embassy was telling. By choosing the Chinese embassy, the protesters, themselves an eclectic mix of classes, generations, ethnicities, and orientations—Nay Myo Zin, the former military officer turned activist; Naw Ohn Hla, the simultaneously stately and fiery Karen ethnic minority matron; Htin Htut Paing, the brash youth leader; among others—appeared to intentionally avoid making a narrow commentary on the authoritarian brutality that persisted after Myanmar's ostensible transition from military rule that had begun in 2011. Instead, the group reproduced the message of their activist colleagues leading protests in Letpadaung itself. These organizers had taken the joint venture between state-linked businesses of both Myanmar and China that had displaced villagers from their lands as well as destroyed a sacred mountain to establish a copper mine and turned it into an emblem of the transition itself.

Letpadaung had become emblematic only when protest leaders recruited Buddhist monks into the protests, and security forces retaliated with white phosphorous bombs that left dozens of monks severely burned. Images of revered holy men with skin peeling off their bodies initiated a countrywide uproar. Villagers had persisted in their rejection of the land grab, responding with land reoccupations and even occult cursing ceremonies that condemned the thieves to perpetual torment by ghosts and ogres. A Burmese colleague at a legal aid firm told me she returned to Myanmar from a private-sector job in Singapore to "work for the country's future" because of the injustice that had transpired in Letpadaung. The standoff had become so severe that Aung San Suu Kyi, then a backbencher in parliament, had herself chaired a commission to address the land grabs; when she traveled to the region in 2014 to convey the outcomes, which insisted that locals would have to sacrifice their livelihoods for the country's future, she was berated by her audience and effectively driven out of the villages.[21] The activists in Yangon were carrying that message forward, objecting not simply to the militarist past but to a dawning authoritarian neoliberalization of Myanmar that appeared to be the country's future.

Back in the present, San San, the protester who had tried minutes before to unfurl her banner, began bellowing again, beckoning the crowd to re-form. She then removed her shawl, displaying it so the crowd could read the words "2008 Constitution." The constitution, drafted by the military and ratified by

FIGURE I.4. San San declaring that victory has been achieved while burning her shawl in the Dagon Township court compound. Photo by author.

a plebiscite that was neither free nor fair, legally codified persistent military rule, reserving 25 percent of the parliamentary seats for the *Sit-tat*. San San paused and called for a lighter, and as she slowly ignited the garment, a dozen photographers crouched in a semicircle at her feet like supplicants. With her comrades beside her and the police lingering awkwardly around the periphery (fig. I.4), San San dangled the ignited shirt before her and thundered, "The three branches of government are destroyed, burned up. We are victorious. The constitution is totally destroyed. *Victory has been achieved! Victory has been achieved! Victory has been achieved!*" The crowd cheered as she repeated "Aung-bi, aung-bi, aung-bi" (Victory has been achieved)[22] in succession, a fist pump accompanying each roar. San San then stood, silent, smiling contentedly at her handiwork until she let it fall to the dirt. Photographers continued to film the smoldering remains as the police chief entered the circle and stomped out the embers, gesturing angrily at his minions who had allowed this scene to play out.[23]

What had just occurred? Would this mean an additional sentence for San San? And to what did her declaration that "victory has been achieved" refer?

Those lines remained with me, given their ambiguous content. Declaring that victory was achieved even as she condemned her incarceration as unjust could be read as a sarcastic statement implicating Burma's so-called political transition. The claim of victory seemed to say that although the country was then four years into this transition—often hailed as a victory by many liberals and international observers—its economy remained dominated by extractive neighbors such as China, it still had draconian laws imprisoning citizens for peaceful expressions of discontent, and so forth.

Another interpretation, however, takes the referent of "victory has been achieved" quite differently. To call a clear setback (imprisonment for more than four years) a victory constitutes a moment of refusal of the entire paradigm of judgment and incarceration. Whether it is radical or only desperate is difficult to determine, but it does refocus the audience on the agents interpreting *their own* fate; more importantly, by calling what appeared to be a blatant loss a victory, the activists pried back open a cycle of contentious engagement that appeared to close with the judge's verdict.

A third interpretation reinforces this point about activist persistence of refusal through escalation of resistance tactics but argues that it does so by simultaneously drawing on political resources derived from the esoteric realm. When I later showed my video of San San's performance to a dozen or so Burmese interlocutors, most suspected that she was invoking astrologically informed magical practices that initiate a string of potential outcomes. The images of cursing protests in Letpadaung that had splashed across Burmese journals and newspapers in previous months immediately came to mind. My informants pointed out that the same exclamation—"Victory has been achieved"—had been used by Burmese kings, anticolonial political activists, and even the Buddha himself upon reaching enlightenment (Matthews 1998, 7, 19–21). Several pointed out that San San wore the clothes of a yogi (an acetic holy person), which in combination with the burning of the shawl suggested that she was enacting a destructive ritual reliant on darker arts.[24] Here, rather than enacting victory only in the moment of its enunciation, victory was also an attempt to condition the future to come, an omen enacted in real time to impact the unfolding of fate.

Although grappling with state agents, leading unscripted public singing, and lighting things on fire are extreme examples, the fifteen minutes in the Dagon court compound can be seen as distillations of Burmese activist techniques, especially when read as parts of larger political engagements and when anticipating the anticoup protests to come. Whether in courtrooms, paddy fields, factories, or peri-urban slums, Burmese activists continually improvise based on situational context to alter that context and influence future contexts, creating opportunities for action. Indeed, in this trial's penultimate court date a month earlier the activists had set the stage for this very confrontation, announcing a challenge and invitation to their adversary: "President Thein Sein, if there is real democracy, we will be innocent on the 14th." In addition, the activists' families had set up a cold-drinks stand in the corner of the court compound, offering *zi-thapanya* (Asian prune) juice to "everyone coming from all directions"—as one family member put it—even inviting the police, whom I had noted demurred with bemused contempt (recognizing that the activist supporters were insulting them with their hospitality given that it came as part of a brazen occupation of state space). During that earlier court date, a boisterous celebration was more appropriate than the shirt burning that occurred on the day of the conviction.[25] But it is not difficult to surmise that this earlier episode—the recodification of a state space through effective invasion—increased the likelihood of the latter, more explicitly oppositional event.

But why must activists operate in these improvisational ways? I had once asked Ko Taw how he engaged Burmese villagers who were facing injustices for which they sought redress. By that point (it was 2018), I had observed his engagements of such villagers dozens of times over several years, but I was curious how he would describe this work. We sat on the balcony of the one-bedroom apartment, which doubled as the CDI office, tucked away on a side street in peri-urban Yangon. As we chatted, university student volunteers taught free lessons to high-school children from the surrounding area. The single oscillating floor fan, switched on for my benefit, carried the call and response chants that reverberated from teacher to students—central to the rote memorization methodology—providing a soothing cacophony over which Ko Taw spoke, in Burmese: "The first time I go to a new place and meet the villagers, I cannot say 'one has to protect one's own rights' [*goh.-akwint-ayay-goh gah-gway ya meh*].[26] If I talk that way, they will drive me off! 'Who is this guy?!' they will say." Ko Taw had then been subdued by an undiagnosed respiratory illness and vertigo symptoms, which he attributed to his long-term stint in prison years earlier, but he became more animated when describing the scenario. He lighted a *cheroot*—a short Burmese cigar—and proceeded.

Those who "do not understand the situation" might use "rights" in their appeals, he said, but Ko Taw insisted on a different route. He switched to English: "You shouldn't say 'rights,' not the first time. They [the villagers] need someone to protect them. So, I have to boast, and they get the mental security from this. [I must be seen] as a protector, one who will defend them against dangers, someone who will protect their property, someone standing with them who can impress [others]." How is this done? In Burmese again, he said, "We make them impressed. If we cannot do any act to make them impressed," such as intimidating a local official, "we then tell them about something: 'I fought the military regime, and I got the life sentence,' to make them impressed."

He also acknowledged that using his political prisoner résumé was ultimately unsustainable: "I can't stay all the time in their region; they have to try to solve their problems." But, he said,

> after three or four months of activities, we eventually tell them, "*You* are also the heroes of your life. You can protect yourself; you can promote yourselves." Sometimes the farmers phone me when I'm in Yangon, and I tell them what to do—this and this and this. But they have no confidence to do so, and so then we encourage them. Then they do it. And then sometimes after two or three activities, they don't have to phone me anymore. They go ahead and do it on their own. We encourage them and then they imitate us. [*Eng*]

Ko Taw, evoking a 1946 speech by martyred independence leader Aung San,[27] presented the register of heroic protection as a way of attaining entry into communities, the ultimate goal of which was to get the marginalized to eventually "be their own protectors." Such a progression could not be achieved through rights talk. To come to an unprivileged community and invoke rights presupposes and then relies on a quasi-contractual relationship secured by an entity external to the situation, typically the state. But in Myanmar that entity is the problem, not the solution. To invoke it as savior—as the guarantor of goods that have never been forthcoming—struck Ko Taw (and villagers) as bizarre. Relying on some guarantor even further external to the situation (international law or the nebulous "international community") was simply unthinkable. The problem hence could not be solved by correcting a gap in *knowledge*—villagers coming to "know their rights," as it were. While most Burmese people certainly did *not* know about rights, gaining such knowledge would not act as a catalytic agent sparking an ineluctable flow of those rights to them.

Being a protector, however, presented a different political model to the villagers. Under this model, rights were not worth invoking unless conditions of possibility existed for them to be enacted; having a protector could create that context in which they might begin to mean something. Only at that point

could one begin to talk of rights—and not, it would seem, as things presupposed but as things that might be performed into being.

As introduced through these vignettes, San San, Ko Taw, and other activists featured in the coming pages direct us to ask how people conduct politics
when they lack the legally and symbolically stabilizing force of rights to guarantee their incursions against injustice. What forms, idioms, and norms do
they employ and generate when they eschew rights as the particular technology and imaginary securing their justice claims? Moreover, their actions in
turn encourage an examination of the forms of power—both directly coercive
(police and military brutality from the transition to the coup) and more subtle
(as with the symbolic injunction delivered by Suu Kyi for the peasants to sacrifice for the country's political-economic future)—that they encounter and
must maneuver against. How to characterize the mix of belligerent neglect
punctuated by exceptional violence in Myanmar's governance assemblage?

Perceiving Blunt Biopolitics through Rights and Refusal

By way of further elucidating the "slippery sovereign" concept introduced earlier, the book concerns itself with sharpening accounts of postcolonial governance and the operations of power therein by focusing on the particular
kinds of improvisational state tactics that play out in Myanmar. I summarize
these tactics and the regime into which they coalesce with my term "blunt
biopolitics," before elaborating how they animate the particular kinds of refusal available to Burmese activists and how in turn the broader assemblage of
power inflects the subaltern understanding of "rights."

A Biopolitics "Blunt" in Three Ways

I define blunt biopolitics as a mode of regulation that deviates from classical
accounts of biopolitical governance in three principal ways: it neither actively
protects nor intensively *knows*, but rather uses *violence* to govern, the bodies
and sometimes populations—but never individual rights bearers—it takes as
its object.

To clarify, biopolitics as developed by Michel Foucault (2003) describes a
form of governance committed to the protection of population groups rather
than individuals—or, rather, it promotes the lives of individuals-as-members-
of-population-groups (a distinction whose importance will be revealed later).
These governmental systems, devoted to the indirect "conduct of conduct"
(Foucault 2007), are able to attend to these populations through aggregated

knowledge—in which, for instance, "the ratio of births to deaths, the rate of reproduction, the fertility" (Foucault 2003, 243) are known so as to be best intervened in and enhanced, inciting greater aggregate productivity while also securing a more stable political-economic order.

The story of the population group in the postcolony is, however, different. In the West studied by Foucault (2007), biopolitics does not displace the individual and its rights-based paradigm; the two commingle in the same regime. By contrast, Partha Chatterjee argues (2004, ch. 2), polities formed under colonial domination were from the beginning structured through population groups rather than through citizen rights. Postcolonial states, according to Chatterjee, have reproduced these structures, promulgating a politics that is mediated through these populations. Therefore, to the extent that those stipulations hold, in the postcolony it could be said that all politics is (a form of) biopolitics.

But do all forms of biopolitics treat "life" and the population groups through which life is amassed identically? No. I observe in Myanmar a blunt biopolitics that proceeds by alternative logics, diverging from the standard kind articulated by Foucault along three dimensions. First, blunt biopolitics is not a politics motivated by the imperative to protect life; indeed, it attends neither to life's defense nor to its promotion. Or, to be more specific, while Myanmar's military rulers have discursively asserted desires to protect and promote the prosperity of "the people," this group remains an undifferentiated mass whose flourishing (or suffering) is never assessed, let alone actively promoted. The people's collective prosperity is never conceived as a direct concern of governance, as something that could, let alone should, be enhanced through the dedication of scarce resources by the governing apparatus.

Second, while many biopolitical regimes reject the rights-bearing individual as the object of governance (Chatterjee 2004, 2019), instead governing by massifying and then dividing polities into subpopulations (ethnic groups, class groups, and so on), blunt biopolitical ones do not devote resources or political will toward building sophisticated apparatuses of knowledge and power to deeply know and regulate those subpopulations. Third, violence is used instead to compensate for absent knowledge, made a governmental technique that supplements the reactive violence of sovereign force ("making die and letting live," as Foucault put it (2003, 247) and the structural violence of calculated withdrawal ("making live by letting die") with a proactive violence that *makes live by making die*. It uses violence to cleave the polity apart, demarcating particularly derogated parts: explicit violence for ethnic minorities or activists and "structural" violence for poor peasants and workers.

While this refraction of classic biopolitics may appear to devolve into what Achille Mbembe (2019) calls necropolitics, blunt biopolitics does not conform to the simple enactment and management of death. The opposite of *bios* is not necessarily *necros*; that binary obscures more than it reveals because fixating on death elides how the different ways of producing that death also inflect how those *not* killed continue to *live*. Indeed, given the state's aggregate bluntness—absence, obtuse knowledge, violent practices—the polity takes on a key role not just in reproducing life but in arranging and rearranging it biopolitically. When the state does not know or define groups, people themselves construct meanings and practices, coproducing biopolitical groups and contributing to their differential exposure to violence.

Attending to these interactions and interpretations, I hence seek to trace the semiotics of violence,[28] in which actions become encoded and identified as violent to divergent degrees depending on the reactions of those subjected to them. Blunt biopolitics thus sees Mbembe's necropolitics not as an outcome, one that devours meaning and politics itself, but as one force among others, creating a "tension between the *principle of destruction* . . . and the *principle of life*" (2019, 118). Indeed, Mbembe shows how governance through violence has bifurcating effects: on one plane it arranges, defines, and differentiates population groups—particularly those targeted as that life that must be *made* to die. But those not subject to such direct violence—those *left* to live or die—somewhat naturalize the brutality of their own structurally violent conditions against the observed mass violence deployed against others. This is because structurally violent treatment does not rise to the level of intersubjective typification as a violence that can be named so as to be opposed. In other words, because members of the social community do not define, discursively and symbolically, certain acts as beyond the pale of expectation and desert, structural violence exists somewhere between natural condition and violence authored by an identifiable and responsible actor. Consequently, structural violence is not politicized, and communities are left atomized and fragmented.

Noteworthy here is the particular form of structural violence in which the state is "strong" enough to create a system of discretionary citizenship in part by disciplining the economy and supporting richer classes but "weak" enough to foster identity battles without accountable legibility. In other words, it is strong in neoliberal terms—not in the sense of privatizing public goods, as people long have had to fend for themselves—but in the sense that land is grabbed, the wealthy are favored, and so forth. But it is weak in the sense that it provides no center for other claims, so various subjects have to fight out, often literally, access to their own social reproduction. In such an authoritarian neoliberalism, subjects are permitted and encouraged to battle for the spoils of the market, but the "rules" regulating that market are improvised and radically fungible.

Taken together, blunt biopolitics refers to "the state" dividing into a form of radical presence (neoliberal reterritorialization, sovereign exception, and racialized differentiation) and radical absence (permitting its various subjects to fight among themselves over identity and survival).[29] Indeed, this is a kind of state that can conduct genocide and stage a coup d'etat—some of the most definitive sovereign acts imaginable—but also disappear from grasp. In contrast to accounts of other postcolonies, such as in India when a crowd "forces the state to represent itself in a concrete manner" (Chakrabarty 2007a, 53), Myanmar's state will not respond to complaint letters; its agents will tell protesters to finish up a plow protest (where farmers reoccupy their stolen lands) quickly so as to not make a scene. It will not, as we saw, rearrest a protester when she removes her shirt and burns it in a court compound. This is a kind of state that would have administrative forms and not actively apply them, ethnic classifications but not know them, and ID cards that it does not insist anyone carry. It is a state whose racial categories can not only be maneuvered away from but refigured at the level of the category itself.[30] It will wage civil wars, imprison protesters, and disregard elections, but it will also relinquish certain localized state functions to right-wing politicoreligious organizations. It is unprincipled, inconsistent, brutal, willfully divisive, and improvisational—even to the point of violating its own putative neoliberal focus on state regulation and capital accumulation to carry out a genocide and orchestrate a needless coup.

While such state plasticity can be difficult to perceive, it materializes through attention to activist practices and their effects. For one, in the penumbra of blunt biopolitics, activists (but also monks and ethnic armed leaders) draw on resonant cultural idioms to advance critiques of state violence and articulate alternative (bio)politics. For another, activists reveal the shape of the slippery sovereign because they come to perform a kind of mimesis of the state as outlined above, in which they navigate and thus trace this larger labile apparatus.

Rights and Refusal

It follows that marginalized Burmese, living under such an arbitrary system, understand a vast array of practices as susceptible to going wrong or as processes whose success proves difficult to confirm. Elite Burmese, often living stable and predictable lives, do not share that understanding of reality (Prasse-Freeman 2015a, 99), but the subaltern Burmese communities with whom I worked live with a certain vulnerability and peril that lends itself to an attitude of uncertainty regarding the efficacy of most acts.

As will be elaborated in chapter 5, these people thus rarely demand "rights." Instead, Burmese subjects take a semiotic or pragmatic approach to rights: they assess and reassess rights as a category based on its affordances—what rights actually do or could do for them—by adducing the material opportunities and constraints that define their existences. As will be demonstrated through textual examples, interviews, and, most importantly, observations of social practices, rights are understood not, as they are in the liberal tradition, as *inalienable* possessions. Instead, when rights are lost, Burmese people do not talk about them like they would body parts or kin—as still possessed after dispossession (Kockelman 2007b, 2009). This is because relations between the average Burmese and governance apparatuses have never stabilized into contractual forms describing standards of care to which subalterns have legible and predictable entitlements (rights). Rather, "rights"—synonymous, as we will see, with "opportunities"—are accessible only to those who perform them adequately; they emerge only if there is an *opportunity* for their realization.

While the villagers that Ko Taw invokes in his soliloquy above may chase off those misspeaking about rights, that is an extreme response. Most of the time people seem to listen, consider, reflect on the claim ("You have rights!"), and decide if it applies to them. Mostly they decide that it does not. Because how many times, or in what kinds of ways, must a performative (such as "You have rights!") fail before the performer sees that failure not as an exception or a mistake but as a reflection of reality? How many times must a rule be broken before it breaks, indelibly? We can describe this phenomenon in terms of semiosis, because actors experience a rule's breaking as a process: realizing that one does not have a status tends to be recursive and iterative—when a rule does not work that failure must be interpreted. The first time may be a mistake, and the second may be another exception, but what about the third time that a rights holder cannot enact her rights? Or the fourth? Or the fifth?[31]

Hence the refusal in *Rights Refused* points in two directions. Rights, if considered transcendent guarantees either to opportunities or standards of care, are certainly refused *to* Burmese subjects by the state—if "refused" is meant in the general sense of "denied" or "rejected." But given this rejection, rights are also refused *by* Burmese subjects, at least in keeping with the technical conceptualization of refusal developed throughout the book. Under the refusal paradigm, tools are rarely outright fully rejected. After all, any tool is a weapon if held right.[32] But weapons can misfire or not fire at all; or they can cut both ways, harming the holder more than the enemy. Refusal permits any tool to be turned away from, its presuppositions questioned, its attendant logical ligatures loosened.[33] This allows subjects to occupy a space to maneuver, one in which they can engage the potential of a concept such as rights without becoming captured by its prerogatives. In this sense, the dialectic in which rights claims (as aspirations) could somehow come to produce rights (as resources delivered) remains open as potential. But until then, rights are refused with a lateral slide away from the imperatives and circumscriptions that would come with a full endorsement of and commitment to the rights paradigm. This helps explain a common subaltern Burmese response to rights appeals: a smile that seems to assent but actually demurs, conveying an effective "I would prefer not to," given success is so unsure and the risk so great.

I hence describe the villagers and workers described in the chapters that follow as exemplars of "subaltern" political thought. A word here on my interpretation of this term: "Subaltern," following Gramsci (1971; see also Crehan 2002) and Spivak (1988), describes those subjects who are only partially inscribed in a field of ideological-material hegemony. Gramsci, understanding the concept in class terms, held that while some nondominant classes may come to identify with the ideology, goals, and dispositions of the dominant class's civil society, others remain unenveloped and hence in fidelity to their interpretations of their own material experiences.

Because of what he saw as the determining nature of class relations and the existence of a single civil society (as part of what he imagined as a *national* economy), Gramsci could describe individuals as fully inhabiting the category of subaltern. But in contemporary Burma there are multiple civil societies—there is a global cosmopolitan one (Sanyal 2007, 76), from which they are entirely excluded, and a national one, which they are a part of in some ways and not in others. Hence, a Burmese NGO leader may endorse liberal imaginaries—as observable in Lynette Chua's (2019) account of human rights–devoted

LGBT activists. Conversely, a Burmese villager or worker may find the descriptions of herself as someone who has had her rights denied to be incomplete, inaccurate, and unhelpful—as conveyed in Ward Keeler's (2017) account of Burma's Buddhist-influenced social hierarchy. Keeler and Chua appear to research two wholly different places. Keeler depicts all social action in Burma as deriving from a vast system of hierarchy in which everyone knows their place. In this account, there is no resistance or refusal per se but instead desires to maneuver within the system: to move up the ladder by acquiring wealth, prestige, and clients. Chua, however, describes a vastly different universe, in which for her Burmese LBGT activists "human rights is a way of life." *Rights Refused* attempts to synthesize these two positions through attention to the activists, as they exist in a space between the elite and the subaltern. They are sympathetic to local idioms and conceptions of political morality, but they are also aware of cosmopolitan rights talk and at times beckoned by it. They must decide whether to embrace the latter value or to remain uncommitted to it, refusing it and retaining it as a tool rather than a value, a tactic rather than a strategy.

Ethnographic attention to various subalternities also provides a comparative lens for reflections on rights and movements at the centers of political liberalism in the West. It asks if the Burmese experiences are more like those in the West than we may presume: are rights elsewhere (the ostensibly liberal West) similarly dependent on opportunities for their realization? Ultimately, then, the book begins by marking an apparently fundamental difference between the hegemonic liberal West and Burma's Other, only to collapse that clean division by showing that the liberal West is different in its assumptions about itself and that only a recognition of its similarities to the Other can uncover the potentialities within seemingly deviant forms of politics. Indeed, more than merely deconstructing the human rights regime, and the human in "human rights," Burmese activist praxis rendered here also interrogates the perpetually unexamined presuppositions attending rights themselves. *Rights Refused* hence takes Burmese subaltern ontology—perceived through interrogations of political economy, governance, and activism—and uses it to generate empirical political theory, thereby compelling a reconsideration of how rights operate everywhere.

Activist Practices: Bodily Performativity amid the Perpetual Possibility of Failure

But how, given a sociopolitical field that denies actors the stabilizing ground of rights on which to secure their interventions, do activists operate at all?

While social action in Myanmar means that victory can never be assured, it also means, conversely, that defeat is never final and that opportunities can be created out of situations that might otherwise appear bleak. A refined understanding of the fundamental necessity of activist improvisation emerged for me only at the end of my fieldwork period, a half year after the events in the courtroom. It was the day of the 2015 elections, the first national ballot since 1990 that looked to be free and fair, and the activists were in their neighborhood in peri-urban Yangon working to ensure that it would be so for their community. I was apprehensive about my presence during this tense time and became more concerned when I saw the CDI crew attaching their video camera to its tripod. "What kind of permission or authority do you have to take video?" I asked Teza, in Burmese. "What do we always say?" he replied with a smile. "It depends on the situation" (*Achay-anay aya mu-tii-day*).[34] I had been perceiving this ever-present phrase in a circumscribed way—as if "the situation" is only the constellation of variables of power that were *already* there. No, the situation in the activists' world is always in the process of becoming.

Returning to the critique of presence introduced earlier, and following Judith Butler (1997, 141–159), the performatives relevant for activist praxis must *create* the very conditions that make themselves possible. This is because the permission for the activists to act is not prefigured; it is not presupposed by anyone. Where a rights holder—according to rights ideology—need only point to those rights as the authorizing structure securing his enactment of those rights, the Burmese activist cannot rely on such transcendent guarantees. An individual rights holder must confirm his status as a member of the set of rights holders, but the job of the activist is far more complex. She must assess every situation for its potentialities: what is the immediate participant framework that constrains and animates the encounter—what kind of security forces may restrict us? What kind of publics may observe us, thereby potentially constraining the security forces? What about the broader context—have various state agents been receptive to such advocacy in the past? Whose interests are vested and at stake in the contentious action? She then must decide how to act—is an aggressive show of force recommended? Or is cajoling, begging, or playing on the vanity of the official the appropriate move?

But before any such assessment of how to navigate the situation occurs, the activists must create it. If they do not, it will not come to exist. So they have to go—to the village, to the industrial zone, to the police station, to the courtroom—always conjuring the conditions that people might then use to alter the situation. Let us return here to San San. She was victorious in burning the icon of the 2008 constitution—itself a rebellious act within a court compound. That act was seen as both a *representation* of how the state had been acting (thereby "exposing it as a sham," as two separate informants put it) and an *enactment* of an ongoing sequence of political events, themselves influenced by the application of esoteric power. The different meanings at play seem to both buttress and mitigate each other; indeed, as "Victory has been achieved" is split, becoming both a spatiotemporally circumscribed act (burning the shawl) and a series of forward-looking objectives (justice for the convicted activists, for the farmers for whom they were ultimately fighting, and for the country), the two versions implicate each other. The enunciation of "victory" exposes the fact that victory was not yet achieved (undermining it) and is also precisely that which makes the ultimate victory imaginable.

Ultimately the vulnerability and hazards—even the contradictory dimensions—of San San's performance bear an iconicity to the political environment she is engaging, making her actions resonant (if not perfectly clear) to political participants and observers. In contrast to many rights claims, by using an idiom of historical resistance and religiopolitical significance, by invoking a set of powers beyond the strictly secular, by taking a risk (to burn her shawl and potentially garnering additional prison time) that is somehow both brazen and humble, she creates a field of joint understanding that enables, saturates, and activates the attendant political demand. This is the kind of performative available to those who occupy a marginalized position in a power structure. In contrast to a judge who declares a couple married—or who, in this example, declares a "guilty" verdict and a fifty-two-month punishment—the subaltern performative cannot enact the new reality all at once but rather lays down a set of conditions that if fulfilled might lead to an alternative future and lays them down in such a way as to increase the likelihood that others feel called to fulfill them.[35] As we will see, in everything from cartoons to curses, the effects are not immediate but build gradually as acts continue to unfold, providing an alternative framework with which to interpret forthcoming events. If a group of farmers curses a tycoon for stealing farmland, that curse does not necessarily work immediately. But if the farmers get enough people to believe in the potential of the curse, and perhaps the tycoon starts to believe it, and then maybe the tycoon asks the farmers to remove the curse as a precondition for negotiation—*aung-bi*! The curse has worked! Victory has been achieved.[36]

And yet while the possibilities are many, they are not necessarily liberatory. *Rights Refused* uses such reliance on contingent and contextual performativity in Burmese politics to also explain reactionary devolutions—specifically, to illuminate what I call Burma's current "devernacularization" of human rights even by elites who had earlier espoused it, exemplified by Suu Kyi's effective repudiation of the concept in the context of her defense of ethnic cleansing against Burma's Rohingya minority. The book concludes by examining failures by the marginalized minority group to perform rights to political belonging in Burma: the Rohingya inhabit a position so far outside of Burmese society that passage into legibility and acceptance through the typical modes of citizenship performance and through the aid of activist brokers appears impossible. Hence the Rohingya rely on rights as an act of *desperation*—a way of performatively installing precisely what they lack.

Biopolitics and the Body

Because an abstracted individual rights bearer is unimaginable for lower-class Burmese, subjects cannot simply invoke their standing as citizens or human beings and expect entitlements to follow. But neither are population groups— who can make collective claims and mobilize threats in the space of exception—necessarily potent forces, at least in the sense that they do not come preformed as they seem to in other postcolonies. To put this in Partha Chatterjee's terms (2004, 2011, 2019), if "civil society" is the domain of rights holders, and "political society" is that of population groups demanding exceptional entitlements, peasants and workers in Burma exist in a field *outside* of political society, itself largely illegible and thus politically impotent. Activists help these subjects reformulate themselves, performing themselves into population groups, brokering a "politics of passage" into the domain of political society.

To the extent that these performatives transform performers into members of population groups who can make demands—farmers, workers, coethnics, coreligionists, activists, all subsets of "the people"—the process requires the politicization of the body. This is borne out in right-wing mobilizations of average people to fortify their bodies as Buddhists by avoiding polluting foods (such as beef)—a move that, not coincidentally, has the additional political benefit of undermining slaughtering businesses, a sector dominated by Muslims. The quotidian act of eating becomes a way of performing oneself as Buddhist and as a contributor to the nation. Relatedly, Buddhist nationalist desires are mediated through the female body and its reproductive potential, as the biological act of reproduction becomes politicized as propagating and defending the faith (Chu May Paing 2020).

Similarly, as activists can point to neither rights nor law as justifying or legitimating political interventions (just as citizens and noncitizens alike cannot invoke rights to secure daily existence), they must foreground their own physical bodies as the only foundation on which claims can rest. When standing in front of security officials or thugs, they oscillate between different bodily arrangements: they puff out their chests, demanding that their enemies assault them, or inversely, they remain calm and impassive, unperturbed by their enemies' threats. Such interventions often rely in turn on mobilizing the *history* of their bodies—during incursions on public space they bear the scars of previous struggles and incarcerations,[37] narrating how earlier actions resulted in literal or psychological markings of their special status.

Finally, while direct and potentially violent contests with officials are not daily occurrences, everyday existence does play out within public spaces suffused with structural violence stitched into institutional and built environments and punctuated by sovereign prerogatives of arbitrary injunctions and diffuse despotism, from bureaucratic agencies denying services to police officers abusing powers. In this context, daily activist praxis is a pedagogy of the body in which followers and publics are instructed on how to traverse the grassroots domains of quotidian abuses and humiliations; it is a set of instructions that recognizes their opportunities, respects those who live in them, and refuses a politics of mere survival.

Notes on Methods: Uses of Theory and Language

The introduction has outlined the book's three novel contributions. First, it retheorizes refusal as a way of deflecting violent and destructive kinds of sovereign recognition to instead maneuver against (bio)political violence. While most subalterns suffer, avoid, or are simply neglected or ignored by this form of perverse mis/recognition, opponents who actively weaponize refusal against such regimes enact a form of absent presence in which they conjure the sovereign into existence, making it vulnerable to contestation on their own terms, to then evaporate away before ensuing sovereign annihilation. Second, the book theorizes the particular regime of power that subalterns endure and activists oppose: blunt biopolitics, like the classic kind, organizes the political economy by enabling elites and taking populations rather than rights-bearing individuals as its object. But it neither cares for nor knows those populations, liquidating them into mass only to redivide them through violence. Third, the effects on daily life of this regime produce novel conceptions of rights—

a formulation that is lived as undifferentiable from opportunities. Without the overarching and transcendent quasi-contractual guarantees that rights (seem to) provide, activists are compelled to improvise creative tactics, including relying on their own bodies as mobile archives of rebellion to politicize daily structural violence and contest Myanmar's slippery sovereign power.

Given these objectives, the following subsections outline how the book uses theory and language to pursue these tasks.

Theory

Since the advent of military rule in 1962, Burma has been significantly undertheorized in the social science literature, with critical exceptions.[38] This does not mean that theory has not been projected or transposed onto the space—researchers cannot operate without an implicit theory through which to organize data.[39] In fact, this is precisely what I mean by undertheorized: external theories have organized materials on the ground rather than the inverse, in which ethnographic milieus would become sites for generating theory that better describes Myanmar and that could illuminate other postcolonial (and otherwise!) settings (Chatterjee 2019, xii). I consider this latter project "abductive theorization," following Peirce's sense of hypothesizing from, rather than drawing dispositive conclusions about, empirical materials (Frankfurt 1958).

But that raises the question, advanced by Chakrabarty (2007b), of the extent to which Euro-American concepts hegemonize the tools through which we could theorize. The tension is apparent in this book as well. While it seeks to deconstruct the rights paradigm and the presuppositions about personhood and the state that undergird it, it also relies on social theory arguably of the same episteme (Mbembe, Foucault, Butler, and even the Subaltern Studies Collective) to do so.

Perhaps the lessons from Subaltern Studies, itself a project of hybrid theorization incorporating Gramscian West and the lessons from peasant insurgencies in the East, can assist here, in two ways. First, Subaltern Studies transformed Gramscian hegemony by attending to how the concept morphed through application elsewhere. Second, Subaltern Studies showed, in this transformation, how hegemony may be even less intense (compensated for by domination), producing even more dissonance with dominant ideologies (Guha 1997). This insight can be applied to the broader epistemological conundrum raised by Chakrabarty (2007b): hegemony is rarely totalizing. As Lisa Wedeen adds, "It is not clear who or what owns any conceptual system"

(1999, 130), meaning that concepts cease to be purely "Western" when they are appropriated and resignified as they travel (Said 2014). An imperative here is to take seriously local conceptions of politics—themselves forms of theorization—without immuring them in hermetically sealed worlds (which smacks of neo-Orientalism); rather, by juxtaposing these conceptions with common sense understandings elsewhere, we might generate more capacious understandings of politics (Graeber 2015, 6–7). Therefore, I endeavor to use extant terms ("refusal," "biopolitics," and "rights") to enter debates and conversations that rely on those theories, to then innovate new concepts that hew more closely to realities on the ground.

Language

As suggested by the preceding discussion (particularly of rights and their devernacularization in Burma), the movement or translation of concepts across various domains is a critical object of interest in this book. Therefore, some description of the treatment of language is warranted.

As a work of ethnography, the book's fieldwork privileges interactional texts—the social engagements and intercourse that show rather than tell how concepts are understood, deployed, and lived. Yet, as identified long ago (Clifford and Marcus 1986), such seemingly spontaneous moments are not pristine portals into unmediated, pure "culture" available for observation as it unfolds. Instead, such moments require interpretive labor of many kinds, work that was in this book distributed across multiple interlocutors and that involved elements of failure that, somewhat paradoxically, both undermined and enabled the construction of possible meanings.

For instance, for several reasons, including security concerns, I tape-recorded only a few of the conversations relayed in the pages to come. This meant that I was often left trying to make sense of Burmese idioms and slang along with unfamiliar vocabulary and syntax, often delivered at speeds uncomfortable for me. But my own limitations in Burmese language competency became an opportunity of sorts as well—when possible I sought to clarify specifics with speakers or overhearers afterward, and often this led to my acquisition of written texts (for example, pamphlets, manifestos, and published interviews) that clarified (or complicated!) matters. Other times, such moments in turn allowed interlocutors to reflect on, refine, and work through issues that emerged in those interactions, engagements that enrolled them as co-constructors of meanings. Further, the use of English also provided unexpected insights, as I was able to observe dissonance as concepts traveled across linguistic frontiers. For example, Ko Taw once told me, "Tonight, you have the right to meet with Soe Aung," even though Soe Aung was not an eminent figure but a friend whose availability that evening had simply been unclear. Ko Taw's use of "right" where "opportunity" would be more apt provided a window into his own translation practices: thinking in Burmese, he picked out the term *akwint-ayay*[40] (opportunity/right), but then, forced to choose only one in English, his brain supplied "right." We then reflected on these dynamics together, discussing related cognates in Burmese. The broader point here is that the activists were active interpreters of what we experienced and observed, even if errors in ultimate interpretation rest with me.

To supplement these ethnographic examples, I also collected, read, and translated significant amounts of Burmese vernacular literature—especially a range of weekly journals and hundreds of political cartoons.[41] When I encountered a local media article in English (from *Democratic Voice of Burma*, say), I attempted to track down the original Burmese version to observe how words were translated; if no original existed on the web, I emailed the editors to ask if Burmese-language interview transcripts existed. I analyzed how laws and policies—from Myanmar's 2012 land laws to its 1947 constitution—translated *akwint-ayay* into English and "rights" into Burmese. In all these tasks I read texts with interpretive communities that included but also went beyond the activists; in particular, by regularly posting cartoons to Facebook along with my attempts at translation and interpretation, I recruited a wider range of opinions. Combining these texts with my reconstructed transcripts of interactions allowed me to build a corpus for analysis.

Given these many languages, registers, and interpretive communities, the book tries to make as clear as possible the language(s) used in those interactional spaces—whether in Burmese (marked as *Bse*), English (marked as *Eng*), or a mix. (Additionally, it puts into endnotes the orthography of Burmese terms commonly used.) But the book also acknowledges alternative interpretations of the statements rendered; indeed, if any moment must be re/constructed ethnographically, it can be done so differently.

Finally, these notes on Burmese language remind me to clarify that this book is very much a "lowland" study, in which the spaces and norms are structured by a "Bamar Buddhist" hegemony (Campbell and Prasse-Freeman 2022). Hence, the concepts developed and idioms described may not travel well: they may not apply well or at all to Myanmar's many ethnic peoples, who not only employ different languages and cultural scripts but have different experiences with Myanmar's state.[42]

Progression of the Book

The book is divided into three parts—Part 1: Blunt Biopolitics, Part 2: Lives of Refusal, and Part 3: Rights as Opportunities. Part 1 consists of chapter 1, which outlines the blunt biopolitical apparatus and the way power flows through it to influence both the state's slippery sovereign power and the activists' mimetic responses, thereby serving to introduce the broader system that activists and citizens must maneuver. While it utilizes illustrative ethnography through-out, it is undoubtedly the book's most theoretically dense chapter, as it seeks to generate concepts that can be applied beyond Burma. Readers less interested in these dimensions may skip it without losing the book's central arguments, which are reiterated throughout.

Chapter 2 begins part 2, the book's three-chapter-long ethnographic core. Chapter 2 describes how activists construct a life of refusal, tracking the dif-ferent aspects of their existence—from moments of radicalization, the near-universal political prisoner experience, and the effects on social reproduc-tion (such as finding gainful employment or raising a family). The second part of the chapter is devoted to understanding activist tactics for engaging both those they defend and those they oppose. Chapter 3 focuses on a common ac-tivist intervention—opposition to land grabs—describing how activists assist in specific peasant tactics for reclaiming stolen land while also exploring the forms of ownership that can persist amid dispossession. Chapter 4 uses eth-nographic accounts of occult cursing ceremonies to demonstrate how Bur-mese political activists use bodily and speech acts together to etch out spaces from which to conjure publics and shame state actors into considering polit-ical changes.

After adducing alternative ways of thinking about rights in the previous chapters, part 3 directly explores how subaltern Burmese think about the dis-juncture between rights discourse and power's realities. Chapter 5 shows how the terms "rights" and "opportunities" that English keeps separate are a sin-gle expression in Burmese, demonstrating how rights are considered discrete, alienable possessions. Chapter 6 illustrates how rights have been devernacu-larized in Myanmar, examining the ways in which human rights have been rejected by Burmese partisans. The chapter reads the polity's endorsement of Rohingya expulsion as a dialectical outcome in which violence against the

Rohingya shores up the nation by making palatable less extreme structural violence endured by non-Rohingya subjects.

Finally, the conclusion reflects on the theoretical concepts developed in
the book—particularly refusal and "rights as opportunities"—assessing their
applicability in terrains beyond Burma. It considers to what extent the deteriorating biopolitical commitments and intensifying neoliberalism in domains
of entrenched political liberalism—such as Euro-America—enable a transpo-
sition of the analysis from Burma to the West.

PART I

BLUNT BIOPOLITICS

CHAPTER 1

Variegated Violence

Head shot. Dead. Now I am crying friend. He is just 14. How many people and youth will be killed to abolish the junta? In Thaketa, North Okkalapa, Tamwe, Insein, everywhere many people are being killed, arrested, beat. We are also Human. We are not animals. We are valuable. And they don't deserve the name of dogs. Dogs are better. [*Eng*]

KO TAW'S LAMENT CAME a week after the Community Development Institute (CDI) had buried another of its own, this time twenty-four-year-old Chit Min Thu, who left a young child and pregnant wife. CDI collected donations for the family and presented them with a certificate of heroism that quotes the fallen: "Even if I die, it was worth it. If people like me don't go out [into the streets] like I am, I am worried that we may not get democracy" [*Bse*].

And it was not just that the bodies were piling up but that they were killed so brutally. "A poet doused in gasoline, burned to the ground. A girl shot dead while sitting on her father's lap. Bodies in a temple, piled high" (Sharma 2021). A young man from Magway, Hlyan Phyo Aung, became what local media referred to as "an emblem of his generation" after enduring a sadistic dismembering in which soldiers taunted him while they blew off his hand (Myanmar Now 2021a). Female protesters returning from detention reported on sexual torture (Radio Free Asia 2021), while thousands of others, mostly young men, have been disappeared (Milko and Gelineau 2021). Civilians suspected of supporting the revolution have been killed in mass executions (Myanmar Now 2021b), and entire villages have been razed to the ground as collective punishment (Myanmar Now 2021c). Perhaps most unendurable have been the slain children—at least forty within the first three months—who were seemingly directly targeted, such as the six-year-old shot while running to her father inside her Mandalay home (BBC 2021).

A human rights report (McDowell and Mason 2021) argued that such signs of brutality were not simply outcomes of security tactics. Rather, officials intentionally emplaced dead bodies in public space, calculatedly turning them into "tools of terror." The research identified "more than 130 instances where security forces appeared to be using corpses and the bodies of the wounded to create anxiety, uncertainty, and strike fear in the civilian population."

Yet, such attempts to circulate signs of violence to intimidate others, while consistent with practices of Myanmar's previous military-state regimes (Prasse-Freeman 2019), were coupled with their seeming opposite: the bodies and their ultimate causes of death were often removed from sight. The same human rights report highlights how authorities have conducted cremations and exhumations of the deceased "secretly in the middle of the night." It notes that the parents of a boy whose murder by a police sniper was evidenced by a gaping hole in his neck were forced to sign "a paper saying their son died of head injuries from falling off the motorbike"; it describes how bodies were burned to hide evidence of trauma: one man's "sister said they were allowed to look at his bruised face, but not his entire body, and then authorities took him away for cremation over [the family's] objections" (McDowell and Mason 2021). In a separate analysis, Nick Cheesman (2021) scrutinizes a video in which a *Sit-tat* commander instructs his subordinates on the official cause of death of a murdered protester, a video that becomes not "of what they did, but of what they did not do," thereby sowing "seeds of doubt about what happened and who was responsible."

The switch here from brazen displays of wounded bodies to various attempts to conceal signs of harm invites reflection. At first glance it appears that if the State Administrative Council (SAC) was indeed using bodies to terrorize, then removing them and obscuring signs of brutalization would seem to dampen the effect of terror. But, alternatively, the oscillation between presencing the body only to then disappear it could work to produce a different kind of terror, one more consistent with the Myanmar state's slippery sovereign power. Here sovereign prerogative, best projected through excessive and ostentatious enactments of violence, vertiginously dissolves into illegibility, leaving only haunting traces—in memories, in bystanders' shaky cameraphone videos—in place of clear transcripts of abuse.[1]

Motivated by these subtle dynamics and calibrations of violence observable in the coup, this chapter is devoted to theorizing the overarching apparatus of power that animates Burma's state. The chapter focuses on how the state engages with life and death such that bodies become a particular object of intervention and how this in turn structures subjectivities of the governed.

Using violence as a point of departure seems apt because from the moment armed militants entered Yangon's Secretariat building on July 19, 1947, and gunned down Burma's independence leader, Aung San, and seven members of his cabinet, Myanmar's postcolonial history has been defined by political violence. Within months of the assassination, communists and ethnic minorities had taken up arms; ensuing military coups have precipitated protracted armed conflicts that, as we have seen, persist to this day and have not only extinguished the lives of thousands but structured the realities of millions more. Indeed, spectacular episodes of physical violence dominate the imagination of Myanmar's postcolonial history, whether the slow-burning "four-cuts" counterinsurgency campaigns—in which civilians are targeted to undermine insurgents—waged against the country's recognized ethnic minorities whose homelands in the hills surround Burma's central Ayeyawaddy Valley (Mac-Lean 2022); the slaughter or repression of popular protesters in the lowland urban centers (Fink 2009); or the protracted genocide against the Rohingya minority in the country's northwest (Farzana 2017; Wade 2017).

But there is also a concern here that in rehearsing the litany of violences suffered by Myanmar subjects over the last eighty years, spectacle displaces everyday suffering. The challenge is to keep both in view, exploring how they might relate—how the everyday violence enables the spectacular and how the spectacular inflects the interpretation of the everyday. To this end, it is incumbent on us to theorize the variegations of violence—attending to how they affect institutions and produce subjectivities. To wit, the definitive moment of Aung San's assassination—Burma's bloody baptism—drew lineages from the colonial period, during which the British administered through a martial law (Callahan 2003; Michael Aung-Thwin 1985) that executed at whim (Maitrii Aung-Thwin 2011, 19), destroyed local governance institutions (Taylor 2009), crushed (Huxley 1988) or corrupted (Lammerts 2018, 181) indigenous legal structures, and extracted resources mercilessly (I. Brown 2013). The period *before* the colonial encounter, however, was defined by forms of violence and their evasion that cast light on the way violence inflected political-economic relationships between subjects and governing apparatuses. As James Scott (2009) has argued, because dynastic Myanmar states greedily exploited peasant rice paddy cultivators, subjects were perpetually fleeing capture, literally running to the hills—or to other competing patrons (Lieberman 2010)—where they could craft political economies defined by relatively diminished coercion. Burmese kings then led wars that were relatively nonsanguinary slave-gathering efforts to replenish human stocks (Beemer 2009). In other words, governance itself was a violent endeavor, one that formed the backdrop for more extraordinary violence.

This chapter incorporates governmental and political-economic factors into the analytical frame—enabling an articulation of easily perceptible mass violence with what we might call the more structural violence endured in daily existence. Particularly, the specific forms of governmentality (how subjects are known and regulated), and the affordances of the political economy (how peasants and workers are able to reproduce themselves) have drastically changed from the dynastic period to today. This chapter seeks a synthesis out of the different forms of violence, illustrating the state's biopolitical unwillingness to care for, let alone compensate, those left unable to reproduce themselves. Examining both collective and individualized responses to these phenomena illuminates the regime that the activists, and average people too, must navigate.

Taking inspiration from other accounts of postcolonial governance, in particular the respective interpretations of Michel Foucault forged by theorists Partha Chatterjee and Achille Mbembe, I develop a theory of "blunt biopolitics" below. This form uses tools similar to those used in classic biopolitical systems—Myanmar's state has pursued a mode of ethnic categorization and regulation and has articulated developmentalist state rhetoric putatively directed at uplift of governed populations—but refracts those modes and incorporates other dimensions of de facto governance in ways that produce significantly different outcomes.

Specifically, I articulate blunt biopolitics as operating thorough three declensions from the standard. First, blunt biopolitics is unmotivated by protection and promotion of individuals' lives. Whereas Chatterjee (2019) describes postcolonial states as committing "to ensure that the poor have the minimum means of subsistence" (144), Myanmar's regimes—authoritarian or democratic—have never subscribed to such an imperative. Their version of biopolitics takes "the people" as a mass population whose flourishing is considered not in itself—not measured in individuals' leading longer or more enriching lives—but as the axiomatic outcome of the fulfillment of other variables. These are the preservation of "order," the maintenance of the Buddhist sangha, and the perpetuation of sovereignty against external enemies. Second, while Myanmar's regime does govern population groups rather than individual rights-holding subjects, because it is unwilling and unable to know these population groups intensively, subjects exist outside of the realm of "political society," the domain where "population groups with distinct traits and propensities" (64) "negotiate selective and often exceptional terms of benefit" (144–45). Third, this regime instead governs through violence—physical, symbolic/discursive, and structural—that produces deeply ambiguous effects.

This system will be introduced through an exploration of daily life in peri-urban Yangon, showing how the activists try to intervene against its more brutal and arbitrary aspects.

Deluge

In June 2015 massive floods resulting from Cyclone Komen hit Burma, leaving thousands displaced. As media reports began highlighting how monsoon rains had left much of Myanmar inundated, the outpouring of giving in Yangon was immediate, spontaneous, and enormous—a deluge in itself. Roaming bands of youth went from street to street collecting donations. Anyone walking downtown was interdicted by various groups of young people shaking donation buckets; some wore T-shirts they had printed to describe their shared endeavors. The mood in all these activities must be described as festive, and the incursion upon public space took a unique tenor: people beckoned others to get involved, not with a tone of sorrow attending a tragedy but with the exuberance of announcing a *pwe*—a festival or party. The call was to collective action, exclamation marks punctuating every word: "Donate! Donate! Donate!"

CDI put its normal activities—which included its supplemental education program, civic education, public health outreach, worker organization, and leadership of various protest campaigns—on hold and sent members to assist in the nearby hard-hit townships of East Dagon and Hle-gu. Some of the high-school-aged CDI volunteers then proposed doing a money collection drive, and CDI's leadership—Ko Taw, Thurein, and Teza—agreed to "take the responsibility" for implementing it. They were joined by about thirty-five youth volunteers, who wore their white school-uniform shirts and dangled tags around their necks identifying them as CDI volunteers.

I was invited to join the team, and we began the day at a street corner near the Kaba-aye Pagoda in northern Yangon. We stood along the sidewalk taking donations from passing cars, chanting, "Donate for the citizens who have been affected by dangerous water" [Bse], a call that I repeated hundreds of times that day, to the delight or at least amusement of CDI members and passersby. After an hour the decision was made to walk through the nearby neighborhoods, and we made our way north through Mayangone Township

FIGURE 1.1.
The congratulatory letter awarded to donors giving over 5,000 kyat. Photo by author.

toward North Okkalapa and the office. These communities were very poor—one-room shacks on stilts hovered above drainage ditches, bamboo poles operating as bridges over the muck. While walking we encountered several other groups also requesting donations, and we joked that we were competitors. Given the poverty, I imagined that residents here were struggling quite a bit with these continual requests to give. Even though most of the donations received were small—from one hundred to two hundred kyat (eight to sixteen cents)—the team brought along certificates of donation to recognize donors who gave 5,000 kyat or more (fig. 1.1).

The following day, CDI held another collecting session. I met them at noon and was told that an officer from Special Branch (the secret police, referred to by its English initials *SB*, who despite the putative transition remained unaccountable and hence quite intimidating) had visited the office the previous night to inquire about the project. Ko Taw had explained the donation drive and asked him if he cared to donate; the SB officer gave 10,000 kyat. Thurein and Teza watched for my reaction at the chutzpah on display here, in which SB officers, tormentors of the people, were presupposed as being on the people's side. As if this was not enough, Thurein added that they had also gone to the local police station to ask for donations. This was an act that no one else would dare to do, he boasted mischievously. "The police asked me, 'Who are you?'" Thurein announced with satisfaction and to laughter from all.

The rains were already hitting hard when we set up at a road intersection in North Okkalapa that Sunday, but our group of twenty or so volunteers stood in the downpour with signs and boxes for several hours. Before the signs disintegrated in the downpour, senior CDI members picked their way through cars and buses stopped at the traffic light, meeting hands sticking out of windows handing over bills. Those in the buses often could not reach those receiving on the ground, and so the money fluttered down to Thurein or Aung Baing waiting below.

Later at the office, after a two-mile walk back, the volunteers ate egg curry, while others deferred their meal to sort and count the money. Teza set up the projector and showed photos that he had taken of the activities. The students were enraptured seeing themselves in action. After the video concluded, Ko Taw made a quick announcement: the funds would go to the Free Funeral Society, a large NGO that pursued ostensibly apolitical activities and had significant networks in the flood-hit area.[2] Ko Taw congratulated everyone on their efforts. Enthusiastic applause ensued, and all agreed to collect donations again the following weekend.

The pedagogy of the activity became clear as I watched the young people watch themselves on the screen. I recalled how during the walk through the wards, the girls and boys were yelling slogans, but when we reached a monastery or an old person's housing complex, the activists shushed everyone, and all noise ceased. At one point, Ko Taw pointed out a local administration post he had helped bomb during the uprising in 1988; then he turned and bellowed at their group to move to the side of the road to allow motorcycles to pass. Later, the same deference was given to a girl on a bike selling snacks along a neighborhood's dirt lane. This attentiveness to how to read social signs when making intrusions into public space was a lesson in being a good activist, a strategic activist: one who would "stand in front of the people"[3] only after first respecting those people. Thurein told me that many of these youth had never yelled in public in such a way. Ko Taw, referencing his own background, described such initial activities as the way of gradually fostering leadership and comprehension of what could be done with social action—specifically how to perceive the everyday challenges as objects for activist intervention.

Most of the younger members had come to CDI to avail themselves of the free classes on offer—this was CDI's initial gift, both to the students and to the community. Such "tuition classes" are effectively essential, as public education in Burma does not provide enough substantive content for students to pass annual exams.[4] Given that "tuitions" are private enterprises, poor students are excluded and hence have reduced opportunities to pass exams, diminishing their life prospects. CDI thus provided free tuition to needy students by hiring certified teachers in mathematics, English, science, and so forth (and hence the rote memorization technique featured in the introduction: the tuition was designed specifically for passing the state tests that demanded perfect mimicry of formulas inscribed in textbooks). Critically, such classes pulled in youth from the community and built trust that CDI was attentive to families' material concerns. And during the first formal session (June 2015) enrollment exceeded capacity, with forty students filling each of five classes; tuitions remained consistently popular after that. CDI's ulterior motives were obvious: the tangible benefit of tuition classes provided plausible deniability for youth to spend time at the office, giving them a chance to learn more about CDI and its work.[5]

As we ate and watched the photos circulate across the screen, I asked the youth about the day. Most were shy and murmured things about the need to help people suffering from the bad weather; or they were happy their parents let them join the event (CDI insisted on parental permission). But months later, I had a chance to speak with Thu Myat and Khin, two of the more committed youth members who had begun to join more politically oriented forms of activism, such as civic education seminars and even worker-organizing sessions in the nearby industrial zones. Thu Myat cited earlier experiences like the donation drive as giving him the self-confidence and motivation to "raise his voice" in the later ones: "Before I was afraid to talk with people, but I got experience with so many different kinds of people, that I realized I could organize them" [Eng]. Khin nodded, "When I realized I had helped others I felt my education [had] worth." She got choked up while adding, "And I felt like I did well for my family" [Bse]. The community and its challenges constituted a laboratory, the domain in which activists engaged potential recruits in low-stakes projects (for example, public service awareness campaigns and charity drives for flood victims) that allowed young people to practice public advocacy before participating in higher stakes engagements.

Everyday Death, Desperation, and Responsibility

While the collection rituals were a micropractice that gently introduced young people to activist life, the events were also motivated by a broader concern: the necessity of private mobilizations to address public problems such as floods. Burma's state, which had long devoted resources to building up its apparatus of coercion and organized violence—not to mention to aggrandizing generals and connected elites—had neither the capacity nor the will to attend to such disasters (more on this later). But focalizing such disasters risks eliding *everyday* catastrophes that befall average subjects, individuals made responsible for surviving such hazards. This section attends to everyday death, the desperation produced by political-economic dislocations that enhances risks of it, and the ways that the system of blunt biopolitics makes the governed responsible for their own maneuvers through such a perilous environment.

Everyday Death

Almost exactly a year after CDI mobilized to help support the flood-affected, a young worker died from electrocution in Yangon. He had stepped into a monsoon-fed puddle that had been electrified by fallen power cords. The next day the English-language newspaper headlines condemned the gross, and incorrigible, negligence: "One Day after Teen Electrocuted on Yangon Street, Site Not Blocked Off or Secured," one read (Aung Naing Soe 2016). Yet even as the same cords that killed the youth had still not been removed, *local* newspapers struck a different tone, featuring political cartoons mocking the death. These were not inflammatory texts written by misanthropic provocateurs; rather, they were run in mainstream newspapers by cartoonists who often penned uncompromising social critiques. More importantly, they were received (if Facebook comments are any indication) as ultimately lighthearted commentary on a quotidian reality of Myanmar life.

The cartoon in figure 1.2 plays on a Burmese proverb: "Don't step in every puddle you encounter," which effectively means "Don't pursue every woman you see." The violation of the injunction to remain faithful here takes on life-and-death consequences. Figure 1.3, for its part, makes a rueful commentary on municipal services: electricity that is too often cutting out can suddenly come back to kill. The character here is presented as shocked, literally and figuratively, at the abrupt return of the current; his use of "Damn" [lit. "Oh mother"] strikes a comedic tone—both mordant and morbid—of exasperation, a dissonant interpretation of the event given his apparent death.

How to make sense of such texts? They could be interpreted through a psychoanalytic framework as using humor to displace real anxiety and despair over the ever-present and randomly distributed death that suffuses daily life in Myanmar. I want to entertain that reading while also acknowledging that it is noteworthy that neither newspaper columns nor public campaigns using a serious or moral-panic register to rally collective opinion against such events attended these macabre cartoons. No movements, let alone complaints, were forthcoming at this kind of abandonment to violent death. While the *absence* of consistent electricity is the constant bane of urban existence—it

FIGURE 1.2. "Don't step in every puddle you encounter!" Source: Cartoonist Poe Zaw, 2016.

FIGURE 1.3. "Damn! The power only comes when I'm crossing the road." Source: Cartoonist Ko Kit, 2016.

is much commented on (Kyaw Hsu Mon 2014, 2015) and publicly lamented (Aung Shin 2014), and it has even been the object of protests that have landed many activists in prison (Prasse-Freeman 2019)—death from its sudden presence generated a perverse laughter, one that simultaneously marked the reality as both excessive and all too normal.

Everyday Desperation

Indeed, there was a sense that the electrocuted youth's day-worker profession and peri-urban provenance made death a natural outcome for him, particularly because he was from the *hsin-kyay-boun* (the peri-urban outskirts). Returning to the observation at the beginning of this chapter about fleeing to the hills, while peasants could once escape the exploitation of kings and lords and were later able to move to more productive ecologies through state assistance or coercion (whether that meant the British relocating thousands to open the delta's paddy frontier from the 1880s through the 1920s or the military government in 1958 and 1990 relocating the poor and politically inclined to areas that would become industrial zones), those options gave way during the transition era to an abandonment in which movement to find laboring opportunities became relatively perpetual, as persistent job opportunities evaporated and environments became exhausted.

Indeed, Myanmar's economy has been gradually inserted into circuits of transnational capital since 1990, the point at which the capitalism of the Burmese Socialist Programme Party (BSPP) gave way to the authoritarian neoliberal version (Campbell 2022). The period of democratic transition saw an intensification of this process that undermined many livelihoods. The most significant driver of this precarity has perhaps been land's commodification, which has transformed land from a means of production to an investment vehicle (Levien 2013) that requires few or no laborers. This has been particularly concerning in Myanmar, a country that is 70 percent rural and where landlessness is highly correlated with poverty (Boutry et al. 2017). Bodies are no longer as necessary in many capitalist processes, particularly those of the extractive variety. Whether for agribusinesses, for real estate development, or as a speculative site for overaccumulated capital such as gems and drugs moneys or for Chinese capital using Myanmar real estate as a way to evade corruption investigations in China (Bo Bo Nge 2020), land is more "productive" without peasant labor. Moreover, while agrarian households can decreasingly support all members of the household on the farm, forcing many to migrate to find labor opportunities (World Bank 2015), the opportunities for reabsorption into urban labor markets are unstable and fleeting.

Scholars of Myanmar have been increasingly attending to processes of reincorporation in capitalist circuits, their ethnographic work demonstrating how the terms of trade enjoyed by those forced to move are often drastically degraded. Going from owning the means of production to being proletarianized (finding regular wage work in a factory) is bad enough, but what most of these subjects encounter are the kind of violent, temporary, and often even unfree laboring opportunities that support other productive processes: former farmers harvesting worms from open fields in Yangon's slums to supply eel farms (Campbell 2022) or Rohingya women occasionally laboring for

FIGURE 1.4. "We are making the Peasant's Day celebration in here. . . . Even more of us in here than out there; hey hey!" Source: Cartoonist Htoo Gyi, 2016.

brick-making factories and leather tanneries in Sittwe (Frydenlund 2020) are some of the contingent laborers who define precarity in Burma. Moreover, many of these laborers ultimately or directly end up in spaces of resource extraction, where they take all sorts of materials (gold, ruby, amber, sand, and jade) from the earth, before the ground and their bodies are exhausted (Prasse-Freeman 2022a).

Commentaries on these degraded and degrading socioeconomic conditions abound. Political cartoons regularly feature peasants incarcerated within, or associated with, prisons. Figure 1.4 features the common phenomenon of protesting farmers being imprisoned. Land has long been seized from Myanmar's peasants, and the various modalities and actors will be discussed in chapter 3. For now, let us focus on how commentaries note that these patterns of

FIGURE 1.5.
Peasant (on left):
"This land got taken,
so where do we live?
What can we do so
that we can work and
eat?" MP (on right):
"Ah, don't you worry.
The current project
will build a new
prison." Cartoonist
Naing Lin, 2015.

farmer incarceration were continued, rather than reversed, under the democracy of transition. For instance, the Burmese-language journal article "For Farmers' Downtrodden Lives, When Will the Bridge to Prison Be Closed?" (San Moe Htun 2016) tells the story of four farmers, two of whom are octogenarian women who had lived on their land for decades, given prison sentences for refusing to acquiesce to the state's eminent domain claims. Author San Moe Htun makes sure to highlight the consistency of their treatment across military and civilian regimes.

More complex cartoons and commentaries provide a structural critique—in the sense of going beyond legal violations (land being grabbed) to focus on the deteriorating condition of peasants, redress for which seems evasive. Figure 1.5 portrays a farmer complaining that without his land he will not be able to forge a sustainable livelihood. His interlocutor is an MP (so marked with his *kaung-baung* headpiece) who tells the farmer not to worry, as a prison will be built on the land. A simple reading is that the farmer can get employment in the construction sector. A deeper implication, however, is that in the midst of the country's enclosures, peasants themselves are endangered: extruded from the sociopolitical order, the prison is one of the only spaces in which they can be reinscribed. This evokes Hannah Arendt's famous insight (1973, 286, 296) that a stateless person can be recognized by the political order only by breaking the law, becoming a legible figure only as a criminal. Farmers are hardly stateless—they are exalted as the heroes of the nation—but the continual substantive betrayal of such respect renders the other conclusion also imaginable.

Commentaries by farmers themselves demonstrate that the cartoons echo their reality; for instance, a farmer who spent time in prison for attempting to get his land back told CDI activists: "I have read in the book that farmers are the benefactors [*kyay-zu-shin*][6] of the country. They said that 'farmers are the benefactors, farmers are the benefactors.' But those benefactors were arrested and sent to prison with such minor cases. It is nonsense!" [*Bse*]. The book the farmer is referencing here could be any number of texts. Cheesman relays how in primary school textbooks the country's "mighty farmers" (2002, 152), who "provid[e] the nation with agricultural wealth" (135), are presented as the nation's *kyay-zu-shin*—a category of estimable figures that includes monks, parents, and teachers to whom an unrepayable debt is owed.[7] Juxtaposed with this ideal is the quotation from the farmer in which he recognizes his political-economic degradation and how discourse on his contributions to the country has become hollow amid an evolving political economy in which peasants no longer play a part. In a recent survey of how average people think about "rights" (Lall et al., n.d.), a striking finding is that the only feature that Burmese people will point to as even approximating a right is basic territorial belonging within the borders of the nation-state. But given the political-economic dislocations, that "right" is becoming undermined, as people must go to where they can survive—which is not always even within the country's confines.

The *hsin-kyay-boun*—peri-urban edge zones (Harms 2011)—become a liminal confluence space that provides (often temporary) refuge for variously extruded people while they are still in the country. One morning in March 2015 I sat with Teza in his ice shop, which was just around the corner from the CDI office, outside of Myauk Okkalapa's Number-2 Market. Two men, one young (perhaps eighteen) and the other old (fifty), pulled slabs of ice from Teza's flatbed truck and slid them across the dirt street in front of the shop; they then descended on the ice with long hand saws, cutting the slabs into blocks. The elder one was shirtless and donned a classic peasant *kamaut* hat, a chinstrap keeping it affixed; he wore a simple star tattoo on his right arm. The boy was in longyi and a blue tank top. Both were in sandals. Trishaws rolled up every few minutes to take ten-pound blocks off to destinations presumably nearby. The sound of the saw on ice was bracing, like metal on metal. Teza's wife, dressed in a blue T-shirt and multicolored knee-length shorts, filled orders, stoic expression set against fatigue. A middle-aged man entered for a single can of strong beer (a "Diablo"); a woman lugged in a rice bag filled with empty bottles, her body bowed against the weight, free arm out to stabilize herself.

Teza gestured toward a large sign affixed to a pole outside the market entrance across the street: three large portraits of monks arranged side by side stared serenely at passersby. Teza commented that Myauk Okkalapa was one of the few places where one could observe a *taya-pwe* (a lecture given by a senior monk that requires wealthy people to sponsor it) as well as crushing unemployment and significant crime. The township boasts a huge amount of new construction and two growing industrial zones but also massive squatter communities living in shacks along the river. And then there are people like Teza, the day laborers, the garbage pickers, and the morning beer drinkers somewhere in between. Those leaving city centers are fleeing the city for one reason or another: to escape insurmountable debt or exorbitant real estate price pressures or to speculate on land or start businesses—in those latter cases, fleeing lower-class lives. People coming from the countryside, conversely, are mostly displaced from destroyed or insufficiently productive economies and are looking for opportunities of any kind.

Whether expelled from the countryside or the city, masses generally do not find consistent work in Myauk Okkalapa and other *hsin-kyay-boun*: formal labor opportunities are fleeting (Campbell 2020, 2022), and wages in general are subject to downward pressure produced by a glut of job seekers, such that rates do not even outstrip rural wages (World Bank 2014). CDI members relay that many people either are incapable of securing jobs or manage to find only short-term, low-skilled work. Given that circulating symbols of new wealth understandably spur desires for commodities (Prasse-Freeman and Phyo Win Latt 2018), many turn to get-rich-quick schemes, often in the criminal underground economy: the illegal and unregulated "two-digit" lottery, the narcotics trade, robbery, and even human trafficking (Boutry, Htike, and

Wunna 2014; Campbell 2022), heightening both material and affective experiences of precarity. Teza highlighted how this strange mix of wealth (evinced by the monk events) produced frequent eruptions of violence. Violence played a persistent role in the identity of the *hsin-kyay-boun*—even its name, "protector of the elephant's foot," invoked the first lines of defense, the cannon fodder, in ancient wars. In the centuries since, the name has been refracted, turned against what it was originally meant to protect: when I first met Ko Taw, he promptly announced Myauk Okkalapa as his home, asking if I knew that it took an actual air force bombing to subdue it during the 1988 uprising. It was not surprising that the *hsin-kyay-boun* became the site of the most intense resistance to the coup (Nadi Hlaing and Haack 2021; Frontier 2021; Boutry 2021).

Everyday Responsibility

Remaining with the precarity of life in the *hsin-kyay-boun*, we can now return to the topic of electrocution. Two years after the cartoons mocked the dead laborer, during the 2018 monsoon season, a child biking through a puddle charged by a live wire was similarly killed. This death was captured on closed-circuit camera, making it more visceral for the thousands able to watch it circulate across Facebook. His death was not mocked, likely because he was not old enough to be held responsible for his life. But still, his death provoked no mobilization; memes merely lamented the tragic waste. The point for now, if we take the two cases together, is that these respective youths' senseless deaths became an object of comedy or pity rather than demands for action, demonstrating that such events were understood as neither governance failure nor political obscenity. Neither were they considered situations in which rights had been violated by a responsible party. Responsibility fell elsewhere.

I encountered similar interpretations in interactions with Burmese colleagues and friends. In early 2015, for instance, I stopped in at the downtown office-cum-home of my friend Nway to find the typically ebullient activist-turned-political-operative despondent. He told me why: "Yesterday we were on the Yangon-Mandalay highway and our car flipped over, rolled over three times. We called 1880 [the number to call if there is an accident]. After forty-five minutes they called back and told us they had called the police station and the police were coming" [*Eng*]. He paused to let this seep in: a medical emergency was displaced by a law-and-order imperative to assign blame and determine fault. Nway continued: "While we were waiting the driver died in my embrace. Fifteen minutes later the police finally arrived. The first thing they asked was to see the driver's license. I told them that they can ask the driver if they like, but he is dead. One of the women in the car got very angry and started yelling at the police. So they had to apologize to her. . . . They told the foreigner from Oxfam and me that we had to go the police station [instead of to the hospital]."

All of this occurred because the officials in charge, both at 1880 and the police, were simply following protocol. I asked Nway if any of this struck him as strange. "Of course not. It is to be expected." But he added that it would be different for a VIP, who would be able to get service very quickly, bypassing the law. There is even a separate number to call, he said ruefully. The driver's death, by contrast, is one to which, as Mbembe might put it, "nobody feels any obligation to respond. Nobody even bears the slightest feelings of responsibility or justice toward this sort of life or, rather, death. . . . Such death has nothing tragic about it" (2019, 38).

As these stories suggest, the extent to which one is responsible for one's own life is often dictated by those "following procedures" and is even codified in law. "Negligent arson," perhaps the most noteworthy statute of this kind, is an often enforced Burmese law that holds citizens *criminally* liable if their domicile accidentally causes a fire. As a result, all tenants must flip the switch on the breaker panel to cut the power to the house or apartment whenever leaving. The logic is as follows: if there is a power cut to the entire grid (a very common occurrence), when power reconnects this can cause a spark (given the state of disrepair of many circuits and appliances), which in turn could lead to a fire that the denizen is not there to extinguish. In such a situation Burmese law holds the tenant culpable for the consequences.[8]

Non-Burmese expatriates living in Myanmar who learn about the law find it highly unreasonable: fires derive not from personal negligence but from a noteworthy abdication by the state of basic duties, such as providing access to consistent electricity as a public utility and regulating electrical grids to prevent them from dangers secondary to their degradation. In other postcolonial contexts, similar issues have become the objects of massive mobilizations, with masses either demanding water, for instance, as a social *right* (Von Schnitzler 2013, 26–29) or, more generally, "recasting . . . social provisioning in the language of human rights" so as to "[reconceive] state care" (172).

While, as mentioned earlier, basic goods delivery is a potent issue in Burma as well, the form of appeal is different and not based on rights demands. This is because a rights claim would presuppose the state as the duty bearer; indeed, *abdication* implies the state accepted responsibility in the first instance, only to at some point foist it off on the people, who would in response mobilize against that relinquishment. By contrast, Burmese collective response and commentary suggests the Burmese state has never been assumed to bear responsibility.

Instead, the responsibilization of normal people—to access goods while preventing harms to themselves and others—has been naturalized. Indeed, Burmese citizens are often surprised at foreigners' surprise at, and fascination with, the negligent arson statute. As Nway might say, "It is to be expected." Also to be expected are the corollaries that this law is applied discretionarily[9] and that elites use fires to eliminate records of misdeeds. Even more insidiously, given the existence of an arcane law that returns privately held land to state ownership in the event of arson, state agents have used arson to force unwanted people—such as those perceived as unsympathetic to the military regime—from their homes (Rhoads 2018). As with floods, fire is a "natural" force that becomes a weapon that harms the poor.

Further, while buildings can go up in smoke they can also fall down on residents. One street sign I once observed declaimed lack of liability: "Windows are being installed on the 21st floor. If things become detached and fall, we take no responsibility" (Coconuts Yangon 2016). It should be added that it would be difficult to attend to those rare announcements or to look up to watch for falling debris when the roads themselves are pulsating and liquid—solids melting into air or, rather, into open sewers below. Zay-Kone Street, in downtown Yangon's Latha Township, for instance, is simultaneously a fully functional wet market and a street open for auto traffic. It works like this: there are two lanes for foot traffic, and three lanes of goods (one of which is the narrow strip that bisects the road) so that shoppers or passersby can walk north and south and browse goods. When cars come down the street, they orient their tires to tread along the foot lanes, straddling the goods that are in the narrow middle swathe. The vendors tending wares in that middle tranche move out of the way temporarily when a car passes, and of course they must ensure that their goods are not piled so high as to impede the auto's clearance. The road thus flexes and bends like an accordion.

Myanmar's urbanites so deeply internalize the mutating nature of urban spaces that one rarely sees collisions or conflicts over their use—or, at the very least, fewer than might be expected. Various speeds, purposes, objectives, and even paths intersect on the same terrain. The fairly harmonious intermeshing of these projects must be at least partially attributed to the injunctions (learned through semiotic interpretation of others' acts) that everyone is responsible for themselves: for not walking in the wrong space when the debris falls, for not being too heavy when the sidewalk breaks, and certainly for not having left the power on when the electricity finally returns. One can observe this in watching what follows when rare but inevitable collisions in space do occur: people apologize to each other before they blame; they look embarrassed at falling into a ditch rather than annoyed or indignant that some putatively responsible actor (the city, the state, the corporation, the neighbor) would allow that to happen to them. There is no responsible actor but themselves.

Zooming out from these examples, we can observe from several recent studies of daily life in Myanmar how such self-reliance is incumbent for survival (Thawnghmung 2019). Tactics abound, whether residents are developing local support systems to alleviate deteriorating economic conditions (Leehey 2016; Griffiths 2020); CSOs are begging officials for permission to provide assistance to the poor (Prasse-Freeman 2012); communities are funding public infrastructure through their own resources (McCarthy 2016); individuals are pursuing extralegal "understandings" to access essential public services (Roberts and Rhoads 2022); laborers are fortifying their bodies with medicines so as to survive labor's harms (Kramer, forthcoming; Yuzana Khine Zaw 2022); or desperate workers are engaging in dangerous labor arrangements that often end in death (Prasse-Freeman 2022a) and that even approach voluntary self-enslavement (Campbell 2022). All these examples reflect what appears to be an absence of biopolitics, if biopolitics is conceived of as governance directed at enhancing life. As McCarthy puts it about the transition era, "The ubiquity of 'self-reliance' initiatives in [that era's] more democratic context highlights how a minimalist reconfiguration of state social responsibility ha[d] taken root" (2019, 328). Consequently, in the shadow of neglect, local collectives provide alternative biopolitical supplements: free funeral societies (Hsu 2019), lay meditation movements (Jordt 2007), Buddhist monks (Rozenberg 2010), and armed collectives (Brenner and Tazzioli 2022; Buscemi 2022) all articulate life-promoting projects despite and against state disregard. Even spaces of daily consumption, such as Burma's ubiquitous tea shops, are enrolled into reproducing life of the marginalized, as child laborers recruited from impoverished families are supported in a way that resembles collective patron-client welfare. Not only does the proprietor treat the tea shop "as something in between a business, a charitable service, and a kind of national service, a kind of liminality that sustains this discourse of child labour as a kind of benevolence and welfare" (Nyunt Nyunt Win 2021), but patrons tacitly endorse and materially underwrite the same model. Activists, for their part, provide similar kinds of life and livelihood support, but they also intervene in the conventional wisdom about biopolitical expectation—as we will see.

Unsurprisingly, given the contingent nature of care provision in Burma, the issue of responsibility (*taa-wun*)[10] is a continual topic of discussion in the domain of cultural critique—from the politically charged to the relatively quotidian. *Taa-wun* emerged not just in protest signs or in grassroots journals (Saung U, n.d.; *Worker Journal*, n.d.) but in military magazines and popular periodicals as well (U Hla Win 2015). It was also a constant source of anxiety and angst in scores of political cartoons I collected.

And as indicated earlier, when I recounted how the activists declared they would "take responsibility" for the fundraising drive, *taa-wun* was a constant concern of activists as well. When I asked Ko Taw in June 2015 about *taa-wun*, inquiring if his and others' (meaning activists and nonactivists) use of the term had increased during the transition compared to the previous era, he insisted that it had. But then I pressed him, asking him if things were actually *better* before, during the military period, especially during its phase of putative socialism. "No!" he replied emphatically. "But during that period the military was *supposed* to take the responsibility," he added. He elaborated:

> They didn't, but they *should* have. But now, who will take it? The parliament? The president? They say land will be given back and then it is not given back, and they do not take the responsibility to make sure that it is. And then the Farmland Investigation Commission—they make recommendations, but they cannot do anything. And then the *letpatni*—who is responsible for them? Before we knew: it was the government who called them in. But now, no one has any idea—is it the local government or the generals or who? [*Eng*]

The *letpatnii*[11] (lit. "arm around red") thugs—so named after the red armbands they wore that declared their *taa-wun* and *sii-gan* (discipline)—beat protesters in two separate February 2015 incidents (Swe Win 2015a). Ko Taw's search for accountability actually anticipated the state's response, in which a national government spokesperson not only denied knowledge of who organized the *letpatnii* but suggested that democracy meant that the responsibility of finding out no longer belonged to the central state. The spokesperson acknowledged the earlier existence of the *Swan Arr Shin*,[12] a paramilitary group organized by the military state in the first decade of the twenty-first century (Fink 2009; Cheesman 2015b, 205), but insisted this group belonged to a previous era; in the current era, conversely, "That word 'Swan Arr Shin' does not exist nowadays. . . . You should ask [the Rangoon Division government] which groups the men in civilian clothing belong to, and what kind of policy determines their operation" (Shwe Aung 2015). Ko Taw's commentary hence identified the system during the "transition" as one wherein procedures and processes were invoked to conceal the sovereign. The example highlights the difficulty in finding efficacious ways to rally people when it is the system of quasi-democracy, however superior in many ways to military rule, that similarly obscures visibility of itself.

What is more, this illegibility impacts responsibility itself, allowing elites to resignify it into its opposite: unaccountability. In the run-up to the 2015 election, Suu Kyi responded to demands by local constituents to choose their own representatives by telling her supporters that their only choice was to "just vote for our party," adding, "We will take the responsibility" (Radio Free Asia 2015b [*Bse*]). Ironically, by doing so she arrogated the "responsibility" to decide on political trajectories, ones that entailed displacing demands for actual representation. Worse still, at least according to a meme circulating in 2017, she then foisted real responsibility back on the people, telling them, in the meme's construal, "Don't rely on the government for everything. If you just rely on the government, why are you asking for democracy? Why don't you live under [a] dictatorship? Dictators do it all for you."[13]

And yet, the state's general absence (of services, of provided care, of presence itself) and attendant prosaic responsibilization of its subjects does not tell the entire story. After all, Myanmar's postcolonial state has waged war on its minorities for as long as it has existed. As alluded to earlier, since Aung San's assassination, ethnic armed organizations (EAOs) have fought for either independence or autonomy, pitted against a *Sit-tat* that gradually became the state's dominant institution (Callahan 2003). The *Sit-tat*'s legacy among ethnic civilians is one of attacks (including summary execution and torture), displacements and forcible transfers, destruction and pillage of property, enslavement, rape, and persecution (MacLean 2018; Prasse-Freeman and Ong 2021). These horrific effects, diffused across decades, were also concentrated into a paroxysm of carnage in August and September of 2017, when the *Sit-tat* torched hundreds of villages of its Rohingya minority, raping en masse, slaughtering children, and forcing seven hundred thousand into Bangladesh (UNOCHR 2018).[14] The analytical observation relevant here is that such violence could be construed as a project of biopolitical destruction par excellence: the Rohingya are an entire *population* distinguished from standard subjects through both legal and symbolic exclusions and then targeted for death or expulsion as a way to enhance opportunities for less abused and derogated populations (Prasse-Freeman 2023b). Taking these phenomena together, we then must ask: how to make sense of the coexistence of what appears to be a simultaneous *rejection* and *intensification* of biopolitics?

Blunt Biopolitics

Taking daily neglect and exceptional mass violence together, I theorize this system and its production of death as a sort of biopolitics, but as a "blunt" kind defined by three key features: a disregard for life (blunt as in uncaring); an obtuse relationship with knowledge and the power that is tied up in it (blunt as in unsophisticated, fumbling); and governance achieved through violence (blunt as in the intensity and immediacy of blunt-force trauma that eschews the precision—even blunting the intensity—of other methods of enacting conduct).

Why call this biopolitics at all? Indeed, Foucault elaborated biopolitics as a novel form of power that both displaced and absorbed earlier forms operating in Western Europe in the fifteenth through eighteenth centuries (2007, 4–8). Specifically, where *sovereign* power "makes die and lets live"—sporadically and violently reacting to acts by members of the polity who defied legally defined contractual relationships with the ruler—and *disciplinary* power works to habituate and train individual bodies, *biopolitics* operates on a broader object and seeks a different objective. Biopolitics takes, which is to say creates, entire populations as the subjects to be governed—not by "individualizing but . . . [by] massifying" (Foucault 2003, 243)—with the purpose of "not only manag[ing] life"—protecting it—"but mak[ing] it proliferate" (254).

In the postcolony, however, biopolitics of this type is mostly adduced as existing in highly capacitated and relatively ambitious governance regimes: South Africa's Basic Income Grants, Brazil's AIDS care programs, and India's biometric identification project stand as emblems.[15] Outside those contexts, the biopolitical paradigm has been dismissed as inapplicable to the postcolony's "failed states."

Mariane Ferme, questioning the abandonment of the biopolitical analytical lens, acknowledges that "biopolitical regimes appear very distant from" places such as Sierra Leone that she studies. But in such contexts, where "a regulatory and governing apparatus has failed to such a spectacular extent . . . that one can invoke neither governmentality nor older contractual, juridical models of sovereignty," the state persists "as an apparatus of capture, integrated more as a network than an organism" (2004, 89). In such a context, biopolitics, according to Stephen Collier (2009), should not be seen "as a logic of government" but rather "as a problem space in which diverse topologies of power may be observed" (80). Conceptualizing biopolitics as a "problem space" directs focus on how power relations are an *outcome* (Foucault 1997, 167) of the interaction between various logics of government (expressed by state institutions, local community-support organizations, activist groups, and so on). These interactions produce biopolitical tendencies: particular ways of managing life and death, deploying violence, and using knowledge. When state knowledge about and administration of the polity is so weak, and the state's ability to circulate that knowledge so meager, the polity appropriates the ability to construct meanings and practices. Biopolitical outcomes—for example, how life is promoted or ignored, how individuals are amassed and sorted into population groups, and how violence is interpreted and hence reproduced—are coproduced by multiple institutions and actors.

Following Ferme and Collier, I use Foucault's critical vocabulary to then track different biopolitical features than those that he advanced. Specifically, while life in Burma is neither promoted nor enhanced, it is still taken as the object of governance—such that bodies imagined as parts of populations rather than as rights-bearing individuals are the materials of interest. As we saw in the description of the coup, it is the body that is grabbed and rearranged by the state. And yet, because blunt biopolitics does not entail an imperative to know and thus order life but still retains some of the modalities (such as censuses and citizenship ID cards on which a holder's ethnicity is inscribed) of the biopolitical paradigm, it thus structures its object of governance differently: as neither the rights-bearing individual nor always the population group in its absence but the masses that live *outside* what Partha Chatterjee (2004, 2011, 2019) calls "political society." Finally, blunt biopolitics stands in a different relationship to violence, articulating explicit violence *and* "structural" violence (the latter as the unmarked normal, the background soundtrack to daily life) into a single mode of governance. The following subsections will describe each arm of the theory through a continuing discussion of life and politics in Myanmar.

Blunt Biopolitics' First Characteristic: Unexalted Life

It is important to note, as we return to the story of necessary self-reliance, that elite rhetoric endorses rather than displaces this injunction to survive on one's own. And we need not refer to the callous comments of Burma's generals—such as when, after the devastation of 2008's Cyclone Nargis, which left 140,000 dead, the state mouthpiece declaimed that survivors did not require aid because they could survive by scavenging frogs and fishes found in ponds (Bell 2008). Instead, similar messages came during the transition from the democratic government of Aung San Suu Kyi.

For example, on June 22, 2020, sustained rains that had been battering the jade-mining Hpakant region of northern Myanmar for days unleashed a massive landslide within one of the area's many "trash-rock quarries." These makeshift mountains are constructed of mounds of stone that mining companies deposit as detritus. Peasants from all over Myanmar, however, displaced from homes due to the violent land grabs or silent compulsion of intensifying market forces described earlier, see in these rock piles more than refuse: these "pickers" sift through the falling rocks, hoping to identify jade overlooked by the companies. Even in normal conditions these moments of rock dumping can produce death, as bouncing boulders buffet bodies. But on this day, like so many others in the past (Tar Yar Maung 2019, 37), the combination of monsoon rain and additional rock loosed thousands of tons of earth from the mountain, unleashing a landslide on the pickers below, enveloping 174 and leaving another 100 missing.[16] In the wake of yet another landslide disaster, Myanmar's government finally appointed an investigatory commission. It should be noted that pickers themselves did not demand this—a survey found that they did not hold the state responsible for their plight (Lin 2019). This commission formed instead in response to international pressure, and its chair immediately foreclosed inquiry into either interested parties or structural causes by attributing responsibility for the deaths to the "greedy" pickers themselves (Radio Free Asia 2020a). While such caricatured callousness made headlines, democratic leader and erstwhile human rights heroine Suu Kyi's comments were more illuminating, and perhaps more troubling. In remarks that earned the ire of Burmese labor advocates (Radio Free Asia 2020b), Suu Kyi intoned, "Among those who lost their lives yesterday, most were illegal scavengers. [That] means that many of our people could not find jobs legally. We must accept and face this reality" [Bse]. Suu Kyi's three terse sentences offer a provocative rumination on Myanmar's biopolitical pretenses. First, by demarcating the dead pickers as a particular population of illegal laborers (thereby evoking the "floating" or "dangerous" populations reviled in bourgeois discourses the world over)—she seems to draw a line between the life that must be "let to die" (Foucault 2003) to protect the polity's privileged life. Drawing such a line appears to illustrate Roberto Esposito's (2008) observation that biopolitics emerges from an immunitary paradigm in which a polity divides itself internally, demarcating that which must be sacrificed, abandoned, or killed to preserve and promote that which must live.

But more important is her ensuing line, in which Suu Kyi then assimilates the plight of the *particular* population (the illegal scavengers) to a *general* condition that laborers in Myanmar face, in which "many of our people [cannot] find jobs legally." The forthcoming recognition of the demand immanent to this situation—"We must accept and face this reality"—hence produces an ambiguous effect. Is hers a call to political action (and, if so, what might such politics entail?) or a sigh of acquiescence to this spreading condition in which the entire population has been given over to the carnage of the quarry?

To assess the ambiguity, it must be stressed that this quotation distills rather than distorts Suu Kyi's approach to the mines and her general engagement with the biopolitical: during her time in office, she "face[d] this reality" by repeatedly taking *no* action, ignoring legal-juridical, legislative, and political tools available to her. Suu Kyi neither regulated the industry's consumption of human lives (Frontier 2021) nor sought to capture and redirect its largesse to Myanmar's desperately underresourced population (as an exposé of the industry points out, the annual jade revenues are forty-six times the amount the government spends on health [Global Witness 2015, 6]). More generally, Suu Kyi ignored calls for land reform that would prevent the dispossession of laborers (Herbert 2020) and eschewed the development of a political platform (McCarthy 2020) that would address these populations' abandonment. Indeed, Suu Kyi's term in office (2015–2020) was defined by a neoliberal alliance with the military-business elites (Prasse-Freeman and Phyo Win Latt 2018) who benefited from the mines' rapacious consumption of human lives.

In articulating blunt biopolitics, it is important to differentiate here between life as *object* and life as *imperative* and hence biopolitics as *modality* (a way of seeing its object) and as *motivation* (the objective sought by way of that sighting). As mentioned, biopolitics takes the mass as its object, and in the cases Foucault (2003) studied, this dovetailed with a governance imperative to continuously intervene—stimulating, encouraging, and modifying aggregates such as mortality rates, life expectancies, and birth frequencies—to promote this population's flourishing (246). Immediate consequences followed; by making the population's life the object of government, subjects who previously could have been unproblematically either destroyed or ignored with no consequence were *considered* as objects of concern—as either responsibilities or threats. This change did not alter their capacity to be destroyed or ignored, but such acts became considered for how they affected the life meant to be defended and promoted. Most infamously, certain subpopulations (for example, the diseased, the poor, and the degenerate "races") came to be considered infesting of the good life and therefore were isolated for destruction (Foucault 2003, 256; Esposito 2008). Consequently, attending to life's proliferation and threats to it installed a new economy in which there came to be equations, equivalences, and commensurations between those "made live" and the ones "let die" (Foucault 2003, 247).

But I would like to suggest that if biopolitics as a concept is provincialized, then taking life as an object need not entail the imperative to defend or promote it—or even to intervene in it at all. A Burmese inflection of biopolitics is not indifferent to life but sees in populations an instrument to, or index of, other objectives. Following Emanuel Sarkisyanz (1965), we can observe how Burmese rulers have taken a robust and prosperous population as "guaranteeing the economic basis" (56) for the preservation of "order," the defense of sovereignty, and the maintenance of the Buddhist sangha (80).[17] If such conditions are secured, then the masses will be drawn to the leader—their presence itself indexing the dynasty's flourishing.

Without an imperative to promote the "good life," both the bar dividing good life from bad, and the concern that such a line could be breached by the latter to infect the former, disappear. Returning to Suu Kyi's words about abject laborers in mines and Myanmar subjects generally, we can observe how she inadvertently dissolves any division between life that must be left to die (on one hand) to secure the life that must be saved (on the other) when she slides from "the illegals" to "our people" tout court. The protection of any life—not simply "the *people* as a subset and as fragmentary multiplicity of needy and excluded bodies" but also "the *People* as a whole and as an integral body politic" (Agamben 2000, 31) presumably meant to be defended—is abdicated. In this sense, she advances a quiet renunciation of any life-promoting compulsion.

TABLE 1.1. Biopolitics in classic and 'blunt' formulations

	Form of Biopolitics	Division of Population
Classic	Made to live	Let to die
Blunt	Let to die	Made to die

Within this paradigm, we can thus distinguish between those who are *made* to die (Rohingya, ethnic villagers across the country) and those who are *let* to die (the miners, the flood victims, those left on the side of the road after car accidents). Foucault (2003) himself collapsed this distinction, differentiating making die and letting die only through the modality (killing versus abandoning) in which death is produced (256). But the modality has symbolic and semiotic effects. Blunt biopolitics draws two lines, just as does standard biopolitics: the first around the population as a *whole* (against those populations beyond the sphere of regulation) and the second *within* the population to be divided. But whereas regular biopolitics differentiates that which must be let to die so as to allow the good life to both survive and flourish, blunt biopolitics divides that which must be killed so that the other can be let to die, be left to survive on its own, and feel privileged by comparison (table 1.1).

Blunt Biopolitics' Second Characteristic: Desultory Knowledge/Power

In this context, citizenship becomes divested of much material purchase. Other affiliations become more important for securing life. And the blunt biopolitical system divides the governed population in such obtuse ways that the governed themselves are afforded the opportunity to refigure themselves.

The desultory forms of governance derive from the way Myanmar's military occupied the nexus of political economy and organization of violence as it captured the state (Callahan 2003). Consequently, the Burmese state, heavily reliant on rents from natural resource extraction, has neither delivered services to nor taxed its masses (Prasse-Freeman 2012); instead, it effectively outsourced social welfare and human development to the private sector (McCarthy 2016) and to those masses themselves (Prasse-Freeman 2012). A secondary effect of this brutal bargain, in which the state ruled but did not govern (Bünte 2022), was that the state abdicated any potential for generating knowledge about its population. Indeed, it had not taken a census in thirty years before the one held in 2014, and the ones held in 1973 and 1983 did not incorporate significant areas outside of government control (Ferguson 2015, 12–15). Not only has it not distributed biometric identification documentation, but nearly one-third of the population lives without the state's rudimentary ID card (Myanmar Census 2015). And because such cards are formally "necessary for buying and selling property, enrolling in higher education, opening a bank account, accessing formal employment, travel, and [some] political participation" (Roberts and Rhoads 2022), the fact that ten million survive without them indicates the proportion of daily existence lived beyond the regulatory reach of the state while also suggesting the existence of informal work-arounds for those without cards (Brett 2021, 350). Further, because Burmese individuals have no surnames, they can hold multiple nicknames and noms de guerre (Selth 2010), which has enabled activists to evade state security (Houtman 1999, 29)—Ko Taw (his activist name, literally meaning "jungle brother")[18] has two other names that I know of. The resources the state did devote to knowing its population addressed security threats, as Andrew Selth's recent study (2019) of Military Intelligence has shown.

Therefore, while governance has certainly *not* taken an individual rights-bearing subject as its normative interlocutor, the population groups it takes as objects are hollow shells, so poorly known as to barely exist as substantive categories. To wit, regarding *lu-myo*[19] (often translated as "race" or "ethnicity"), when the state did promulgate a citizenship law (most recently in 1982), it operated as a monologic decree more than a fine-tuned project of knowing—the law's effects have derived from extralegal state *violation* of its statutes rather than from the law itself (Cheesman 2017). Moreover, an inspection of the 135 ethnicities made official following that 1982 law shows them to be arbitrary and confused, asserting phantom ethnicities while eliminating ones actively lived (Gamanii 2012; Ferguson 2015, 15–16; Sai Wansai 2017). Although the 2014 census collected ethnic information, those data have not been publicized.

This has produced the deeply contested and divergently understood nature of critical categories—race, socioeconomic status, citizenship, and so on—that other postcolonial contexts have made significantly more legible, durable, and immutable. In India, the state and related apparatuses govern through categories such as tribe, caste, and poverty: members of these categories know themselves as such, in part because they receive entitlements as a result. Their standing as members of these population groups and their inclusion in larger categories such as citizen are not in irreconcilable tension; much to the contrary, the former is reinforced by the latter in voting rituals, when they are mobilized as voting blocs by elites.[20]

In contrast, there is no mutually reinforcing system of recognition between state and polity in Myanmar. Deviating from the unmarked Bamar standard generates no resources and only negative recognition, if any recognition at all. For instance, Muslim Burmese report that the state refuses to grant them identification documents (Gravers 2021, 22). Contra racist biopolitical states that manage subpopulations through administrative categorization, we witness here a *denial* of direct bureaucratic violence. Instead, discrimination is channeled through exclusion, creating the Muslim as nebulous and unmarked outside category.

This lack of administrative rigor effectively empowers Burmese subjects to coproduce biopolitical realities. For instance, the law may delineate certain affordances or circumscriptions, but as we will see, *let-dwe t'-myo*[21] ("reality is another way"), meaning that on-the-ground negotiations based on knowledge gleaned from previous interactions dictate substantive opportunities. The state may declare which ethnicities "belong" (Cheesman 2017), but members of a derogated group—such as Burmese Muslims generally and Rohingya particularly—find their ability to realize the substantive entitlements of citizenship preempted by extralegal mobilization by members of the polity. Peggy Brett (2021), relaying how Kaman Muslims lost their citizenship status after local Rakhine Buddhists called for their scrutinization, writes "that popular opinion of who should be a citizen had the power to influence the legal citizenship status of those concerned" (350).

Moreover, this muddiness of state categories permits the existence of varying and competing ontologies of categorization. Rather than people simply shifting and maneuvering between different ethnicities—because the state cannot ascribe specific ones to those individuals—the way categorization itself is conceived is also mutable. As an example, I return to the phrase *lu-myo*, which literally means "kind of person." The common translation of the term as "ethnicity" smuggles in the presuppositions about that term that deviate from the understandings held by Burmese people. The state has not monopolized the understanding of the term, narrowing the term's semantic range to ethnicity; rather, it remains broadly understood, in that the term "Myanmar" can be synonymous with the Bamar ethnic group, a marker of *civic* national identification having little to do with ethnicity/race, or a way to *generally* define inclusion as one or many of the country's authentic inhabitants (regardless of citizenship status).[22] More interestingly still, people describe their *lu-myo* as "Muslim," "Buddhist," or even "Hindu-Buddhist" (see also Boutry 2016, 100; Carstens 2018; and EMReF 2019, 12 for similar findings)—circumventing the question of ethnicity entirely. These answers suggest not only that religious practice is the key marker of social identification for many but also that ethnicity as conceived elsewhere—as an ontological category that defines what someone "is"—is not operative in Myanmar.

So, even as ethnicity has over the years hardened as a category "at the top"—as it was symbolically represented and circulated in discourse—it has remained fluid "on the ground," to the point of being categorically reimagined. On one hand, subjects are barely interpellated (as the field of governmentality is weak), and on the other they are *mis*interpellated (the field gets them so wrong that they can maneuver within it with more ease). Modifying a term coined by James Martel (2017), I describe "misinterpellation" as a form of metapragmatic awareness generated by situations in which discourses misdescribe subjects to such a degree and with such obtuse tools that these subjects recognize the disjuncture and are then able to strategically maneuver with and within labels and categories. Hence, while population groups such as ethnic identities are administratively and symbolically real in Burma, they cannot be easily ascribed to subjects from the outside. Subjects can navigate between identities with comparative ease by modifying their particular bodily and dispositional indices (for example, clothes, language and accent, and religious performances).

Without intensive administrative power, ethnogenesis has become influenced by the silent compulsions of the political economy. Bamar, the dominant majority, should be understood as a class-inflected hegemonic category, produced through biopolitics insofar as the capital accumulated from independence through "socialist" state capitalism to the militarized capitalism that persists today—and the emblems of "development" that were generated attendant to that accumulation—were spatially and symbolically coded as "Bamar" and led by figures likewise coded. "Bamar" came to be linked with ideas of national progress, modernity, and development within the country, even as, in the context of armed insurgency, the non-Bamar minorities became seen as separate and distinct groups militating against the country. Thus, while distinctions exist at the level of the group (Bamar versus Shan, for example), given the absence of knowledge and power apparatuses delineating populations biopolitically, the category Bamar has remained relatively open for entry for those individuals who could pass as such (those who look South Asian or Chinese, conversely, are largely barred).[23]

Blunt Biopolitics' Third Characteristic: Governing through Violence

In the absence of fine-grained knowledge and power used to differentiate populations, governance through violence is deployed instead—violence meant in the dual senses of *modes of acting* and *outcomes effected*.

Regarding modes of acting, rather than interpellating subjects, "conducting their conduct" to coparticipate in their own regulation, governance under blunt biopolitics is enacted without consent: it is foisted on its recipients in a monological key, achieved through fiat. It rejects the possibility of dialogue— qua interchange of discourse over collective values—and interprets any such attempts at that participation as threat. Such approaches, that "do not recognize otherness," that "abhor difference" (Holquist 1990, 52), can be assimilated to Arendt's definition of violence: "Acting without argument or speech and without counting the consequences" (1970, 64). In Jennifer Leehey's (2010) commentary on military state–era propaganda, the authoritarian state betrayed a metapragmatic recognition of its own sovereign will such that propaganda was neither "particularly persuasive" nor "really intended to persuade;" instead, and similar to the dead bodies with which the chapter opened, signs are used to "display the regime's control of the symbolic realm, a control that need not produce legitimacy to be valued politically" (52–53; see, comparatively, Wedeen 1999, chap. 3). To reiterate the theme in which state and polity seek to maximize their own illegibility, if in the subsection earlier we saw how subjects evade the way they are categorized, here the state not only is aware that its own propaganda is untrue but seeks to *communicate* that awareness.

Blunt biopolitics also operates through violence *effected*—meaning the recent torture of protesters after the coup and the atrocities distributed across decades of counterinsurgency and repression should be considered, in part, as a mode of governance, with impacts on both its direct and indirect objects. Here we can address Mbembe's work, which has been devoted to interrogating the relationship between violence and governmentality. Mbembe is often invoked for his neologism *necropolitics*, the politicization of death-making that works through but beyond biopolitics, making the latter "insufficient to account for contemporary forms of the subjugation of life to the power of death" (2019, 92). But Mbembe's work also, often simultaneously, finds violence *productive*, able to create something new or at least leaving something leftover that escapes the abyssal pull of death-making apparatuses. Indeed, while necropolitics foregrounds death, Mbembe admits that the violence that produces it also differentiates "populations [that] are then disaggregated into rebels, child soldiers, victims, or refugees, or civilians" (86). I incorporate this observation to show how, in blunt biopolitics, violence becomes a proactive way of splitting masses apart, of carving up population groups (such as rebels and refugees in this quotation, groups that are reproduced in Myanmar through ongoing war) for ensuing regulation or abandonment. This optic allows us to inquire into the kinds of political structures and social lives that are possible in such spaces.

For instance, indiscriminate killing of the Rohingya has *massified* together various tokens—those killed, wounded, or observing such attacks—into a common type: some who had not necessarily understood themselves as Rohingya before the violent campaigns of 2012 or 2017 came to see themselves as such afterward (Prasse-Freeman 2023b). Indeed, while respective Rohingya communities across Rakhine state demonstrate noteworthy ethnolinguistic and cultural differences, being excluded *as the same type* has helped cohere them, massifying them into Rohingyas in a literal life-and-death way: as individuals and communities became aware that people more or less like them were being targeted for death or expulsion under the sign "Rohingya," they became interpellated by the category. But even as this occurred, others relinquished or rejected the identity, quite understandably passing into other identity categories not targeted by the state and polity—a maneuver that was relatively available (see Wade 2017; Sardiña Galache 2020) despite their South Asian physiognomy because of the obtuse state governmentality mentioned earlier. Still others, however, seem to exist somewhere in between—both refusing Rohingya and refusing the Myanmar state's disavowal of Rohingya (Prasse-Freeman 2022b).

The Rohingya case is perhaps a particularly extreme example of the double move that has affected other Burmese groups, where even as individuals were assembled into population sets, those *objects* were eviscerated as political *subjects*. Take the Buddhist sangha (community of monks). As an expansive, if diffuse, social institution in which most Burmese Buddhist men spend at least a short time at one point during their lives, the sangha is a definitive social identity. It has also been the object of unrelenting assault and co-optation by the postcolonial military state, which has succeeded in significantly curtailing its ability to operate autonomously (Jordt 2007, 52). This outcome was attained by institutionalizing the sangha under a state-controlled council, by patronizing and promoting key abbots, and by viciously attacking politically active monks, both physically and symbolically (Elgee 2010).[24] It is not surprising that the sangha, historically a robust political opponent of tyranny (active in anticolonial uprisings, for instance), has gradually become less politically mobilized over the years (Schober 2011). Neither is it surprising that Thidagu Sayadaw, the country's most revered abbot, who we will reencounter in chapter 6, provided soteriological absolution for soldiers committing the 2017 Rohingya genocide and accompanied *Sit-tat* leader and coup architect Min Aung Hlaing on weapons-acquisition trips to Russia after the putsch. The same pattern of massification and evisceration can be found in how peasants, students, and workers as population groups have been treated: amassed and then gutted through centralization, co-optation, and violence.

Population categories are hence available, and they are arguably necessary vehicles through which subjects must convey demands, as it is only during immense political crises that being an unmarked governed Burmese subject is sufficient for collective mobilization. (At such moments, as scholar Phyo Win Latt put it about collective violence waged by the *Sit-tat* during the coup, "*Sit-tat* becomes a *lu-myo* of its own, and it assumes any group of people who rebel against them as *th'pon lu-myo*[25] [rebel-kind]" [pers. comm., September 2021], even those who are not directly implicated in rebellion.) But because of the assault on these groups, they exist as collective *objects* even as they are undermined as collective *subjects*.

These population groups were not co-opted, policed, and targeted equally, of course. Where monks were co-opted, farmers neglected, and students and workers pacified, ethnic groups were targeted for violent incorporation or expulsion differentially (Prasse-Freeman and Ong 2021). Hence, diverse Burmese subjects reassessed their specific identities in this broader context of violence, therefore allowing us to observe in blunt biopolitics a similarly recursive relationship between those two separate populations within the standard biopolitical field: where those "made to live" could do so by observing those ignored ("let to die") or sacrificed, in Myanmar those *merely* let to die observe their relative privilege when compared to those destroyed without consequence. They simultaneously observe how the discursive rendering of the explicit violence obscures the suffering they must endure, a fact that spurs revanchist anger against the more marginalized ethnicities (as we will see in chapter 6). In this sense, blunt biopolitics homologously circumscribes the whole population such that a specific subpopulation considers another sub-population's treatment, thereby compelling each to interpret their own lives by comparison.

Slippery Sovereign Power and Responses

Now that blunt biopolitics has been elaborated, "slippery sovereign" power can be brought into sharper analytical focus. Recall, as adumbrated in the introduction, how the standard resistance paradigm relies on a dialectic of recognition between sovereign and subject in which the legibility produced through attempts by the state at unmediated domination permits the objects of that attempted domination to respond with direct confrontation. The three declensions from standard biopolitics elaborated earlier pervert that recognition dialectic, allowing the state to recede from grasp, thereby undermining resistance.

First, rather than being defined, as with other postcolonial states (see Sanyal 2007, 78), by an imperative to promote the life of the population, Myanmar's postcolonial regimes have been saturated by a motivational deficit regarding the lives of the governed. Therefore, claims on the state must then take the form of demanding not simply that responsibilities are discharged but that life itself should be an object of responsibility in the first place. Indeed, the ubiquitous responsibility discourse is an attempt at broadening the field of objects of accountability and therefore an attempt to conjure the sovereign into presence.

Second, the blunt biopolitical regime has not translated its surfeit of force into a sophisticated knowledge and power apparatus. The key point here is how its disinterest in knowledge of the governed make it inscrutable in turn, leading to a culture of rumor whereby people speculate on state intent, operations, and goals (Schissler 2015). Contrast that with an elaborate biopolitical state in which censuses deployed lead to laws written and policies enacted, revealing a series of objectives—even when not explicitly stated or actually achieved. In Myanmar, conversely, it is difficult to adduce will or intention from the biopolitical trappings (censuses, laws, and policies) that the regime retains. Indeed, Myanmar has again begun taking censuses, but like the colonial censuses before them (McAuliffe 2017), these do not seem to know what they are asking (Callahan 2017a). The blunt biopolitical regime has laws, but those under the BSPP regime, implemented as they were through diffuse people's courts, were arbitrarily interpreted;[26] legal institutions eventually became subsumed by the military state's law-and-order obsession (Cheesman 2015b). During the transition, lawyers were often unaware of the law and were forced to track it down (Beyer 2015). This context left space for much variation in interpretation when laws or policies were operationalized; moreover, this space for arbitrary enactment led to opportunities for negotiations throughout the apparatus that have produced highly contingent norms. Izzy Rhoads and Jayde Roberts (2022) have studied such arrangements, described in the vernacular as *nahlehmu* (understandings) that provide all parties with plausible deniability when conditions inevitably change. Rather than *nahlehmu* standing outside of law, as law's shadow or underbelly, it invests and infests the state itself. Hence, rather than in nearby China, where scholars show how activists use tactics described as "rightful resistance" (O'Brien and Li 2006) to hold the state to its word, in Myanmar making claims for accountability is difficult, because laws, policies, pledges exist without principals (Goffman 1981) who could be accountable to them.

Finally, violence under blunt biopolitics is semiotically ambiguous (Daniel 1996) in the sense that while purpose and intention can be adduced from specific acts (the policeman firing the gun leads to the dead protester), a vast array of potential "ultimate meanings" (Kockelman 2007c) that redound on various objects ramify from such events. For example, Myanmar's military has operated with impunity for decades, which even during the transition persisted in the habituated conduct of state agents, as Cheesman perceptively argues (2019). What is more, while at least during the period of explicit military rule there was a presumption that state apparatuses and military institutions shared the same leaders, during the transition fragmentations pullulated, and not simply between civilian leadership and the military but even within that military. During the 2011–2016 period, a former general, Thein Sein, was formally in charge, and in 2015 he ordered his own military to cease hostilities against the Kachin. Instead, in direct defiance of the order, bombing proceeded. Who could be said to be acting here? The military—divided as it was between Min Aung Hlaing (the commander in chief) and Thein Sein? The state? The air force commander who literally pulled the trigger? What does the event mean politically in a context of such deep illegibility? Did it represent to Kachins an assault by the Myanmar state, associated with the majority lowland people, the Bamar? Or was this an example of a rogue army operating with impunity? Or a mixture of both?

A similar confusion emerges in the violence waged against Myanmar's Muslims—whether the ethnic cleansing of Rohingya in western Myanmar or the extralegal violence conducted against various communities spread across the rest of the country—since the time of transition. The state has made no attempt to intervene to stop right-wing populist groups from mobilizing local exclusionary violence—of the explicit physical and exclusionary symbolic varieties—against Myanmar's Muslims. In fact, these groups have captured specific state legal and policy tools to weaponize the legal system against religious minorities, drafting and then successfully pushing through parliament four Race and Religion Protection Laws that police Muslim procreation, marriage, and religious conversion of Buddhists (Crouch 2016). These laws call for the deputization of state institutions at the local level, transforming right-wing vigilantes into quasi-agents of the state. While military and civilian elites use discourse to make some sense of this violence (Prasse-Freeman and Ong 2021), confusion and illegibility generally dominate. And hence when activists are shot, when villagers are bombed, when monks are given platforms to endorse genocide, the governed become an audience forced to consider the ultimate intention—*was this a capricious local commander or an order that came from the top?*—and hence whether they may become not just an audience to but also an object of violence.

How, then, can people respond to this system?

Responses (1): Formulating Populations

Burma's reality hence calls Partha Chatterjee's "political society"—a domain in which subjects do not make rights-based claims but amass as population groups to generate corporate appeals for resources or opportunities—into question. In "most of the world" (2004, 3), Chatterjee argues, individuals cannot present themselves before the law as rights-bearing citizens and expect associated privileges to ineluctably follow, but they can negotiate strategically within the state's field of governmentality, presenting the *benefits* they can offer and the *threats* they can conjure. I see much to recommend in this assessment. But while Chatterjee's work has been critiqued by many who see the tidy division between civil and political societies as inadequate,[27] I advance a critique from the other side. Rather than, as Chatterjee does, presuming that subjects exist within political society and can advance legible, if exceptional, claims at the state, Burma's masses seem to exist in a space *outside* political society, ignored and neglected by the state and incapable of becoming legible subjects.

Across Chatterjee's India, state elites and their distributed agents can be described as internalizing "a public obligation to look after the poor" (2004, 40). Further, feedback loops from electoral outcomes bring experiences of re-subjectivization that alter perceptions on democracy. And instrumentally organizing oneself with others can secure real benefits. For all these reasons, Chatterjee's focus on the *exceptional* nature of Indian citizens' negotiations elides the *foundation* on which they are based: the outcomes of negotiations may be aleatory and contingent, but they are animated by the negotiators' status as citizens and the substantive entitlements that follow therein. In India, citizens are tethered, however fragilely, to the state through an ideology of obligation, even if access to citizen privileges is refracted through the contingencies of political society maneuverings (see also Herzfeld 2016, 23 passim).

In Burma, by contrast, there has long not been any obligation binding citizens to the state: power flows between state and subject based not on foundations of rights or on obligations to populations but on the power of what Mbembe calls *commandement*, the absence of which is neglect. As Mbembe notes bleakly, "The basic question, of the emergence of a subject with rights, remains unresolved" (2001, 93). We might ask, pace Chatterjee, if this space is the rule, in the postcolony and otherwise, and whether "political society" would be an ideal space in comparison.

To simply gain access to public services—such as paved roads or electrification—a Burmese community must provide a significant amount of the material costs and labor, something that "proves its worthiness to receive state support" (McCarthy 2019, 331), substantiating them as a group legible to the state. Relatedly, for resistance to register—for protests to solicit responses—collections of people must become legible groups. As later chapters will demonstrate, activists act as "political brokers," chaperoning the masses into political society while empowering them with the skills and dispositions to remain there.

One problem here is that even if these populations are forged, they may contest one another. To wit, after the coup there was a burst of transethnic solidarity that identified the *Sit-tat* as Burma's common enemy. The Bamar (the majority ethnicity) claimed ignorance of the violence that ethnic nationalities—even including the Rohingya—had endured for decades (Kyed 2021). There were pledges to end Bamar privilege—explicit and unintended alike—and there were endorsements of substantive federalism. Simultaneously, however, counterdiscourses and affects wove themselves into these discussions. Ethnic nationalities questioned the very possibility of forging a multiethnic union, accusing the Bamar of willful ignorance of their suffering. Bamars in turn responded by arguing that impoverished Bamar villagers earned no privilege from their ethnicity.[28] Debates threatened to devolve into unresolvable frission; in Burma's blunt biopolitical context, where oppression and violence take such different forms across the space, suffering was incommensurable. Those surviving the violence of being "made to die" and those surviving being "let to die" found little with which to, as one partisan to the debate wrote me, build "common ground that we can share together."

Responses (2): Simulating Slippery Sovereign Power

This chapter opened with the SAC using bodies and their disappearance to terrorize the Myanmar public. But this is not the end of that story. Because even as such acts demonstrated the regime's arrogation of the prerogative to rearrange bodies—whether through rape or maiming—Burmese people responded by using their bodies in response. In addition to the bodily protest performances on display on the streets featured in this book's first pages, other anticoup tactics similarly weaponized the body. For instance, various sticker campaigns plastered the streets with pictures of the commander in chief, capitalizing on the taboo against placing feet near human faces, even their visages. Burmese social media reveled in the absurdity of soldiers and police pausing their inhumane counterinsurgency campaign to stoop over in the oppressive April heat to peel paper off pavement. Similarly, female protesters hung their sarongs in public spaces, weaponizing traditional misogynistic beliefs, particularly strong in military culture, that women's garments had enervating effects (Hue 2021). Photos circulated of exasperated commanders ordering the offending garments removed; the SAC went so far as to ban the hanging of the skirts, revealing the practice's relevance.

Even more compellingly, perhaps, were the ways that protesters treated their own brutalization. In mid-March 2021 the regime released on state television pictures of young protesters it had arrested and brutally beaten. As with its message a week earlier that it was shooting to kill ("in the head and back" [Reuters 2021]), this act was interpreted as a threat to all participating about the bodily violence they would endure. But rather than acquiescing after their torture, upon release the youths began circulating their own images. Other

FIGURE 1.6. #Sisters2Sisters campaign explanatory sticker. Source: Thinzar Shunlei Yi.

images followed, showing the before and after status of the activists' bodies, memes that were picked up by local and global mainstream media (see Al Jazeera 2021).

As mentioned in the introduction, in yet another cycle of creative troping the well-known activist Thinzar Shunlei Yi posted her own picture of brutalization, which she revealed in its accompanying text to be only *symbolic*—and the apparent blood and bruises only makeup—of the generalized abuse suffered by her national sisters. She rallied other women to participate in the campaign, called #Sisters2Sisters (in Burmese, "Revolutionary Sisters 2 Revolutionary Sisters"), using her status as a popular Bamar-majority woman to connect with the suffering endured by ethnic minority women across the country for decades. TSLY encouraged others to also "stage torture photos in solidarity with women in interrogation centers," and dozens of images began to pullulate (fig. 1.6).

#Sisters2Sisters played loose with a certain version of truth, eschewing archival veracity of specific bodies wounded to convey shared realities of both material and psychic wounds borne by women across Myanmar. In so doing, it mimicked the SAC's approach: similar to how the military presented bodies to generate shock only to then withdraw them, denying audiences a full and coherent story about those abuses, #Sisters2Sisters stirred affect through the staging of various scenarios of suffering—including not only the aftermath of abuse but also renderings of actual moments of their own (sexual) assaults too graphic to reproduce here[29]—that through their representational capacity also served to protect those who suffered real blows. In other words, rather than capitulating to a knowledge and power regime in which assaulted bodies must risk retraumatization to establish the authenticity of their suffering, a truth deeper than facts was distributed and magnified by comrades.

When Mbembe describes how subjects attempt to navigate slippery (ludic, excessive, vulgar, and violent) sovereigns, he suggests they pursue "a form of reason that would make everyday existence readable, if not give it actual meaning" (2001, 143). This is indeed the case. But as the maneuvers by Burmese protesters introduced here indicate, activists are not simply detectives trying to discern the specific physics of the regime—the different legibilities, the rhythms to the vacillations between legible and spectral, and so on. Instead, activists themselves mimic this illegibility, asserting themselves to then dissolve, becoming liquid and equally unaccountable. The following chapter will explore those activist tactics and strategies.

Conclusion: Blunt Biopolitics Beyond/Within the Nation State

As alluded to above, the atomization and division entailed by structural violence often leads to anger toward, resentment of, and contempt for those victims who experience clearly identifiable violence. What produces such anger has much to do with the way the two populations articulate in the same biopolitical field. But the apparatus enacting blunt biopolitics cannot be reduced simply to the Myanmar state. Rather, because the Myanmar state nests within the larger Westphalian sovereign order, various populations that in the precolonial era existed in the interstices of various mandala polities (Wolters 1999; Thongchai 1994; Prasse-Freeman and Mausert 2020) or outside their remit entirely (Scott 2009; Lieberman 1984) were emplaced within Myanmar, the spaces in which they lived becoming inscribed within (as well as bisected by) its borders. This emphatically does not mean that the Myanmar state came to care for these populations or even see them as full and equal subjects. Rather, it means that no one else would or even *could* care for them. This point was driven home forcefully in Aung San Suu Kyi's defense against the accusation of genocide at the International Court of Justice in December 2019. There she essentially argued that the Rohingya may not be *citizens* of Burma, but because they are *populations* emplaced within Burma's borders, Burma has the sovereign prerogative to treat them as it wishes. This economy of neglect is defined as follows: the multiple ethnic cleansings of Rohingyas since 1978 and their subsequent (sometimes forced) repatriations back into Myanmar show that Myanmar cannot simply exchange its populations for ones it prefers, but it can do whatever it wants with them when they are within its borders, even as discourses ascribed to the international community or that emanate from interpretations of international law insist they must not. The overlap of these two fields—the neglect of the Myanmar state and the minimalist biopolitics (Redfield 2013) of the international order (that declares that populations must not be killed even while providing no mechanisms for enforcing that injunction) carves a paradoxically inclusive line around populations such as the Rohingya that the state disavows (Prasse-Freeman 2023b).

But even as these populations are incorporated into the same geo-body, they are held apart by an apartheid-style regime that for decades has kept the Rohingya immured in northern Rakhine state near the Bangladesh frontier. Their position along the border of a state that has been perpetually narrativized as the most overpopulated in the world, combined with the absence of sophisticated knowledge/power that could identify the population of the Rohingya with certainty, means that uncertainty regarding the Rohingya has metastasized into phantasmagorias of invasion and annihilation (Arraiza, Phyu Zin Aye, and Shakirova 2020).

For example, in Myanmar, specifically, while the *Sit-tat* has enacted mass violence against the Rohingya for decades, the active endorsement of their suffering by Myanmar's polity is a relatively new phenomenon, seemingly spurred by other factors (Prasse-Freeman 2021). The explanation may come from how blunt biopolitics simultaneously incorporates both the massifying power of mass violence (that produces ethnic groups such as the Rohingya as objects of destruction) and the dividing power of structural violence, which partitions those subject to it into atomized units struggling to survive. This division undermines solidarity among the polity to differing degrees, such that poor ethnic groups and poor Burmans alike are treated like degraded members of the in-group, while the Rohingya are the constitutive outside who are not treated as belonging at all. Indeed, in the context of increasing precarity, in which households cannot reproduce themselves as easily as in the past (although the state never helped them out, such help was not necessary in the past), and in the context of new wealth that seems up for grabs but tantalizingly out of reach, the Rohingya present not just as an expanding population who might snatch those resources but as a group that lies about their standing as victims of mass violence in order to gain those rights (qua opportunities).

PART II

LIVES OF REFUSAL

CHAPTER 2

Living Refusal

KO TAW AND I SAT in the bed of Teza's flatbed truck as we sped across the highway to Mandalay. It was early June 2016, and the monsoon had not yet arrived. Teza was at the wheel and Mawsi accompanied him in the cab. The lush greens of lower Burma's foliage that guarded each side of the highway, unperturbed by the hot-season sun, were giving way to the browns and oranges of upper Burma's drier climes. The truck's canopy covered us from the sun's rays, but the breeze swept away only some of the heat emanating from the vehicle's engine and conducting through the car's body and into ours. Ko Taw fished through the Styrofoam icebox and offered me water, but I demurred. He took a pull, and as he did, a chemical smell struck me. I looked over to a stricken Ko Taw; he leaned over the edge and spat the contents out onto the road. "It's not water," he groaned, searching for something to rinse his mouth. "B.E.?" I asked. Ko Taw nodded, directing an exasperated look at the back of our driver's head. "What a crazy Teza," he exclaimed, but he smiled too: Teza had filled the water bottles with B.E., short for Burmese Engineering, the government agency that also clandestinely brewed moonshine during the Burma Socialist Program Party (BSPP) era.[1] The agency is no more, but the drink, a local favorite, lives on, which is no doubt attributable to its dangerously low cost.

I had brought along an anthology of 1950s- and 1960s-era political cartoons by the famous cartoonist U Ba Gyan, and Ko Taw and I scanned them as we bounced along. He lingered on one about the BSPP, which had ruled the country under General Ne Win from 1962 to 1988. Ko Taw told me his father had been the local head of the party in Thingangyun, an exurb of Yangon where Ko Taw was born. Seeing my shock, he added that his older brother had, until his early death, held a similar role in nearby Shwepyitha under the military-backed State Peace and Development Council government that controlled Burma from 1988 to 2011.[2] In fact, when Ko Taw had come to lead a labor protest in Shwepyitha a decade before, in 2005, he got a call from that same brother. Ko Taw relayed the conversation as follows: "'Little brother, I will arrest you,' he told me. 'Your job is to arrest, my job is to get arrested,' I replied." Ko Taw then added, "I hadn't spoken with him for the last seven years before his death last year." Then he turned back to the cartoons.

That Ko Taw's family was divided by this strange division of labor, in which two men were pitted against a third, was not as odd as it might seem—as later examples attest. Ko Taw, in fact, attributed his radicalization in part to the access and perspective his father's position afforded him. They were not wealthy—Thingangyun, where Ko Taw grew up, was a peri-urban zone of Yangon to which the family was extruded from earlier dwellings closer to downtown, as is the common trajectory of social descent in Yangon under ever-deteriorating socioeconomic conditions. "We needed money for many things. So, my father sold his house in Tamwe and bought a house in Thingangyun, which is rather cheaper," Ko Taw explained. Nevertheless, in contrast to a great swath of Burmese, who, as Ardeth Thawnghmungh (2019) argues, are fixated on daily survival in ways that circumscribe political consciousness, his father's stable salary gave Ko Taw time as a youth to "participate in social welfare activities," as he put it, and be active in his school council; his father's position also gave him the latitude to access township-level BSPP authorities. "Sometimes authorities beat the poor without reason. I argued against them and asked them why they beat them." Ko Taw was able to use his connections to a corrupted system to contest its corruption. Of course, "because I was just a kid, sometimes they did not pay attention to me," he admitted.

But others did pay attention. In his local tea shop, as in any of the ubiquitous tea shops across the country, underemployed men and women chatted for hours as they sipped the unlimited and free plain tea, provided by custom even to noncustomers. Some of the chatting men, however, had knapsacks filled with books and pamphlets, which they lent to Ko Taw. He devoured and returned each one, the texts becoming increasingly radical in their analyses and implications. The tea shop became a library and these men his tutors. "Before they gave me the books, they had already inquired about me. They knew that I was very willing to work for the community and loved to do those activities. That is why they decided to organize me like that." Ko Taw described these men as communists working as underground agents to foment revolution, or at least spur in the people an awareness that a different future was possible through political action. The communist organizers also warned Ko Taw about what he should look forward to as someone living the life of a political struggler: "They told me to expect prison and maybe death there."

When the 1988 mass uprisings—against military-state authoritarianism and mismanagement of the economy—erupted, Ko Taw was thus somewhat prepared. Many activists describe how they got caught up in political events swirling around them at key moments (1974, 1988, 1996, 1998, 2007 are the critical touchstones, coming to define the mini "generations" of activists who self-associate with key events that occurred in each respective year). While these flows effectively carried those activists into entirely new identities and life trajectories, Ko Taw was ready for 1988 when it came. "The activist" had already been presented to him as an intelligible social type, complete with ideas to engage and espouse, literature to read, role models—in the form of book-toting organizers—to emulate, and comrades to imagine as doing the same thing in the country's countless tea shops. Activism, in which refusal to the status quo saturated existence, materialized as a legible life to be led.

As our truck rambled north to Mandalay, I reflected on the bemused smile he had directed at Teza, and I considered how Ko Taw inhabited his role—how he executed the duties of his "job," as he had put it to his brother—as an activist. This vocation included leading farmers and workers but also teaching comrades such as Teza, and even more so the much younger university students described in chapter 1, about the ways of activism, just as he had been taught before them. These trajectories, and the labor put not only into traversing them but also into enabling others to follow similar paths, evokes recent ethnographic work on the ethics of activism, such as Naisargi Dave's research on sexual rights activists in India. Dave identifies the "ethical practice" of activism as "an effect of three affective exercises: the problematization of social norms, the invention of alternatives to those norms, and the creative practice of these newly invented possibilities" (2012, 3). This triumvirate—of challenge, innovation, and praxis—all braided together through affect, applies nicely to Burmese activists. But in tracking how activists forge lives that can be defined through refusal, this chapter also illuminates the particular contours of activist affect in the Burmese context—specifically, how it manifests in interpersonal ties forged around the activist habitus and how refusal becomes not just inscribed in but sedimented upon the body. This produces both intense interpersonal identifications and bitter ethical divisions over how refusal should be articulated, what alternatives are both reasonable and just, and what practices—particularly how much risk, and borne by whom—are efficacious.

In this chapter, I expand on the brief descriptions of CDI in the introduction and chapter 1. I will describe how activists navigate these paths and the ethical challenges tied up in them, an exploration that will also serve as a way to outline how the system of blunt biopolitics sketched in chapter 1 is negotiated. The following section will explain how the system and activist existence articulate by describing refusal, which functions as a hinge linking the two domains of governmental structure and activist behavior. The chapter will then proceed by delving further into the various histories—both of individuals and of Burmese political events—that have defined activist life to then focus on specific activist tactics through which they refuse the injustices of governance in Myanmar.

Refusal and Resistance as Illustrated through Activist Lives

Refusal has recently enjoyed a noteworthy uptake across the social sciences (see Prasse-Freeman 2022b for a review). Its point of departure, endorsed by most of its proponents, lies in its demarcation of a break with classic resistance paradigms. As I explained in the introduction, Carole McGranahan holds that "theories of resistance presume a hierarchical relationship in which a subordinate resists a superior power" (2018, 368). What does this mean in practice? One initial instinct is to examine scenes of contentious encounter. Do those making impassioned demands—moves that we can characterize as classic resistance—in so doing actually recognize the latter's authority, hence insidiously reinstalling it? Does refusal, by contrast, describe ways of forging contentious events that somehow avoid the resistance hierarchy trap?

While some scholars advance this argument (Bhungalia 2020, 394), close examination of actual encounters exposes ambiguity. In activist events in Myanmar, bodily arrangements display perpetual oscillation between transgressive defiance (resistance) and stoic denial (refusal). They also partake of the domain that we might call performed obeisance. For instance, in 2014 a group of land-grab victims, whom Ko Taw helped organize, from the Michaungkan section of Thingangyun occupied Mahabandoola Park in downtown Yangon and set up a protest camp, where they lived for nearly a year. I visited them during the months of November and December 2014, observing their periodic rallies and quiet times in between. When protesting, the group of mostly elderly women would pump their fists in synchronicity, chant slogans castigating the injustice of the government, and even hold cursing ceremonies in which they condemned the thieves to multiple hells (more on this in chapter 4). After the rallies, however, the protesters arranged themselves in tidy rows for observing publics; when a parliamentarian visited, they kept their bodies nearer to the ground, as befits the supplicant in Burmese culture, and reached up to touch their patron. When the protesters escalated tactics and occupied the entrance to city hall in December 2014, state officials rolled out four-foot-tall stereo speakers and blasted dance music in attempts to drown out the protesters' messages. The protesters were unshaken by this, however, and immediately pivoted to different tactics: as darkness settled over Yangon, they lit candles and put their heads down in prayer. Their bodies silhouetted by the flickering light and sonically framed by the pulsating music created a stunning spectacle for the hundreds of passersby. The protesters amended their signboards to read, "Thank you for playing loud music; now more people will know about our cause" [*Bse*].[3]

As this example demonstrates, it is difficult to describe micropolitical encounters through refusal alone. What's more, a focus on the encounter displaces from view the work that makes the encounter possible and the work that comes after the encounter ends. I focus on that labor, thereby clarifying refusal as a way that collective subjects turn away from sovereign encounter, refusing to capitulate to its precise way of structuring the relations of rule. Rather than only *resisting* direct domination (sovereign power, following Foucault's schema),[4] these groups often *refuse* such contests and instead manage and respond to biopolitical administration by disavowing, rejecting, and maneuvering with and away from diffuse and mediated forms of power (governmentality). In so doing they refuse consequences that violate their conceptualizations of their collective identity and ways of life.

Attending to the specific contours of governmentality—what I have described as blunt biopolitics in chapter 1—helps us understand what forms refusal will take. In contexts such as Canada and the United States that Audra Simpson studies (2014), for example, Mohawks must refuse intensive biopolitical regulation—the way they are demographically enumerated, taxed, legislated, symbolically represented, and so forth, as these factors redound both on the way being Mohawk is lived and on the future of their collective existence. In Myanmar, where Ko Taw and other grassroots activists mobilize around land, livelihood, and labor issues, the forms of mediation are different. Engaging a state both rapacious and indifferent—as we saw in chapter 1, it has raided natural resources while delivering no meaningful social services—activists resist by reoccupying stolen land, unionizing workers, organizing peasants, protesting all matter of social injustices, and training youth in all of the above. In so doing, they sometimes encounter a state suffused by sovereign power—seemingly constitutionally incapable of strategically ignoring their defiant acts. But creating such encounters requires them to forge a life of refusal and to mobilize others to become part of the "political society" (Chatterjee 2004) that could elicit sovereign response. As mentioned earlier, in this sense refusal envelops resistance: it foregrounds the resistance to come, and then it continues after the encounters subside, enabling struggles to persist. This latter kind of survival was particularly relevant during the five years of Aung San Suu Kyi's democratic rule (2015–2020), a time when activists had to alter their approaches because of a transition that foreclosed contentious action. When the 2021 coup came, however, the activists were able to rapidly re-form, incorporating into their civil disobedience campaigns many of the youth who until then had only led trainings. The following descriptions of the life cycle of activism will further illustrate how this spectrum of refusal is lived.

Doing One's Time: Political Prison

"We are supposed to forgive but never forget. I have heard that, and I understand it; it is good. But I will never forgive the generals who put us in prison. If I had the chance, I would kill them" [Eng]. Ko Taw held my gaze after delivering this pledge. I eventually looked away. We were in Myo-Tha, an area outside of Mandalay, and had just repaired to a roadside cafe after a meeting with villagers opposing their dispossession at the hands of an encroaching industrial zone project. Beneath a majestic banyan tree constellation fifty feet in diameter, Ko Taw talked about his health, specifically about a liver disease that he attributed to mysterious injections he was administered by Military Intelligence during torture sessions or that he possibly contracted from the contaminated food and water he was compelled to consume in the notorious Thayawaddy Prison. He described, with anguish, his son's poor health. Doctors believed that Ko Taw had transmitted the disease to his boy. It made sense that Ko Taw could not forgive, because the prison was still with him—not just in his own body but living on through his child.

Amid this rage, though, Ko Taw paused and then sighed. He continued in a different tone: "Life is more meaningful in the prison. You don't have to worry about money. Only being against the regime."

✳   ✳   ✳

By 1988, Ko Taw described himself as a communist. At sixteen this did not mean much, he admitted. But as for many participants in the mass protests that shook the country and forced the military-state to reconsolidate under a different set of leaders and orientations, the events of 1988 solidified his still-nascent choice of activist life.

He was active during the uprising, organizing other students and youth in Thingangyun, but perhaps due to his youth, he was not arrested immediately after the military regained control, and he did not flee to the border as so many others had. Still, given that three thousand protesters were killed, several of whom were his mentors from the tea shop, and many others arrested (Cheesman 2015b), Ko Taw also "did not want to return to a normal life." Instead, he became consumed with the desire "to revolt against the junta." The trauma of this moment, combined with the feeling that the regime's toppling for good was imminent, drove him underground ("U.G." in activist parlance). Rather than continuing social welfare activities, which we saw in chapter 1 acted as a bridge between civilian and activist worlds and supplied plausible deniability for subtly political work, Ko Taw joined two explicitly revolutionary organizations, becoming an internal operative for the All Burma Students' Democratic Front (ABSDF), the student-led armed group that had formed on the Thai-Burma border, and the president of the All Yangon Student Union. Activities with these groups involved leading protests against the 1988 coup, distributing pamphlets decrying the military's annulment of the 1990 election won by the opposition National League for Democracy (NLD), and publishing journals encouraging widespread uprising. He was allowing himself to get pulled further into the U.G. life, but access to normal life trajectories was not irrevocably severed until he was arrested for these activities, for which he was given a life sentence in 1991. After spending a year in Insein Prison, he was sent to Thayawaddy in Bago Division.

Constructions of Political Prisoners as a Distinct Population

As the transition to a quasi-democratic system commenced in late 2011, Burma's president, Thein Sein, responded to calls to free political prisoners by reiterating that this was an impossible task, as there were none.[5] According to the former general turned president, those who had used an unregistered fax machine or joked about the regime's mismanagement had *not* actually been incarcerated, or they were criminals of the same *type* as those who murdered or stole.[6] But this was merely an external narrative, directed at Burmese publics and perhaps not to instantiate Burmese justice as just or to discredit political dissidents as morally compromised national security threats as much as to demonstrate that those in power could still assert narratives that most everyone knew to be false (as discussed in chapter 1), maintaining the public face of dissimulation and prevarication definitive of slippery sovereign power. Regardless, inside the prison, the state did indeed recognize political prisoners as a distinct population.

A decade before meeting the CDI activists, I lived in Yangon and co-taught a clandestine class on politics for former political dissidents organized through a foreign embassy. I spent several afternoons talking at length with Myo, a friend from that course, about his time in prison. Myo always laughed when discussing awful things, and so he chuckled when he described how the hardest times in prison involved the murder and sodomy of prisoners. Seeing me blanch, he added, "No, not on me! This was guards and *regular* prisoners. It made us protest for our own cell" [*Eng*]. "Us," he clarified, consisted of *political* prisoners, a separate group that had not earned the punishment of casual rape.[7] They found the conditions unacceptable enough to warrant demands for different treatment, and the prison managers capitulated to that argument, moving "the politicals" to their own block. Myo thus did not talk about torture or poor conditions but rather the intermixing with normal criminals as his most degrading prison experience. It seems that politically active Burmese could expect to relinquish their freedom as the logical exchange for doing politics in a state in which opposition was clearly anathema; they could even expect to endure terrible conditions as political prisoners. But that they were political prisoners was key—this status allowed them to militate for the opportunity to be treated as such.[8]

Bo Kyi, the founder of the Assistance Association for Political Prisoners (AAPP), the central advocacy organization not just for political prisoners but for the count of those murdered in 2021's anticoup uprising,[9] reiterated this theme when I interviewed him in 2010 in Mae Sot. In English, Bo Kyi described his time in several prisons and how the prisoners fought for what he described as "rights." This struck me as odd. They had been put in prison for demanding rights that did not exist, but once in prison, in this place *beyond* the law, they appealed to the nonexisting rights they had demanded outside? Bo Kyi clarified: "This is only *prisoner* rights, not *political* rights, that we were asking for." Both Myo and Bo Kyi were drawing on a long history of similar mobilization, dating back to at least 1939 (see Development Ko Ko Lay 2013, 31). Their militating demonstrates the layers and mechanics of refusal, in which new contexts demanded and provided opportunities for new tactics. They worked to build connection and community with other prisoners:

> We had to keep up [the political prisoners'] morale, their motivation. We needed to keep them together. We started to fight each other, so much tension, about small things, so we directed the fight against the authorities instead of with ourselves. . . . We were very aggressive with the guards. If the food has gravel in it, we throw it away and say, "This food is not made for a human. We should report it to the prison authorities and request for change. . . ." In many cases we can discuss like this, within our own room obviously, sometimes with other rooms. We could use English because we were educated and the prison guards were not.

Part of the need for such actions was the paradoxical absence of sovereign power in Burmese prison: there was little work directed at "turning" political prisoners, at inducing them to change; at the most, sentences were meant to punish and hopefully deter. Hence here Bo Kyi describes political prisoners *seeking out* engagements with guards so as to build solidarity with other prisoners. It warrants mentioning comparative contexts in which political prisoners, as Lena Meari (2014) puts it about the Palestinian context, are "constituted as they resist" the prison's crucible of pain (554) but are also constituted where the contest between sovereign and struggler drags "the whole community into the interrogation encounter" (573). By contrast, and consistent again with the theory of refusal developed here, Burmese political prisoners did not develop their subjectivities through contestations with the sovereign. Rather, those encounters were brief moments enveloped by their broader refusal to acquiesce to the arbitrariness of incarceration. Bodily pain and existential boredom were sustained through moments of resistance that refocused energies and objectives. Refusal entails that subjectivities are developed *horizontally*, with other political prisoners, rather being directly mediated by sovereign contestation.

The instances of resistance the activists created led, ironically yet understandably, to experiences with prison guards that seemed to contradict the activists' antagonism. As Bo Kyi put it,

> When you stay in there for a long time, you know many prison guards, and many of them know you. They all are human beings. We requested their help—after we gave them coffee or cake, they ate with us. We then make requests; they know we are good men, and we are different than the other criminals. We are students, we are educated, we care about our families. We are rich compared to them, and they needed help. If they needed money, we would pay money. All the prison guards are good to me; one of them is very close to me, [and] I don't have to pay any money. Whenever he was assigned to my cell block, he always slept in front of my room. 2:00 a.m. for night shift they got rice; he would give me half, wake me up. . . . I don't know why he was so close with me.

Bo Kyi did note that his experiences were hardly universal. He relayed brutal treatment too: a prisoner on hunger strike to protest his delayed release was allowed to die; another had his back broken and now lives permanently supine (see also Ma Thida 2016; Win Tin 2012). He cited Min Ko Naing, who had experienced two different situations, adding that, "Some prisons are good, some are bad."[10] Most were good and bad simultaneously (Win Tin 2012).[11] But the love on display in Bo Kyi's situation is striking. Does it suggest that the guards whom Bo Kyi tormented with demands knew he was performing and respected him for it? Simultaneously, does the love also suggest that his demands, while annoying to the guards, were also *legible* to them, that the performance also acted by using a vocabulary of participation agreed on by both guard and prisoner?

Political Prison as Zone of Existential Quarantine?

In his story about providing the guards with loans, Bo Kyi highlights the political economy that operated within the prisons, showing how the relatively privileged political prisoners could leverage class status.[12] This also demonstrates how the guards, meant to perfectly replicate the generals' law-and-order will, were compelled to evade it because of the miserable material conditions that the generals themselves helped enact. By attempting to presence the state, the prison protests rearranged relationships with its agents, thereby also reconstituting the state, albeit at the minor scale of its frontline embodied representatives.

These relationships refract the ways in which prisoners were detached from "the outside"—the prison was certainly not, as was universally presented in advocacy literature, completely isolated from the rest of Burma. The existence and critical importance of connections with kin and comrades outside Myanmar prisons has been identified in recent literature (Jefferson and Martin 2020) and was reiterated to me after the coup, when Ko Taw's father publicly renounced him in an advertisement in *Kyay Moun* (a military-backed newspaper). Ko Taw was nonplussed: "My father discarded me as his own son. But I have phoned them already, and I said I already realize the situation. Because during my prison life from 1991 to 1999, they didn't blame me and regularly [came] to the prison to meet me and provide me some food. [Now], it is because of pressure from the dogs."

And yet, despite those ligatures binding prisoners to their previous lives, Myo and Bo Kyi's descriptions do suggest that the political-prison block was seemingly the heart of the Burmese state and yet somehow *outside* of its logics and some of its key practices. It emerges as "heterotopic," Foucault's (1984) term for spaces in which social relations are sustained, lubricated, and secured but also innovated, tested, improvised, imagined, and reimagined. In the Burmese political prison, a culture of dissent and defiance was reinforced and multiplied such that prison time became essential for building an activist's credibility. In fact, *Taungt Ayatha* (A Taste of Prison), a prison memoir comprised of contributions by many of the nationalist student leaders of the 1930s anticolonial struggle, contained an editor's introduction that explicitly labeled the text as a *guidebook* for future activists: "All the political devotees had to have gone to prison. If one had not yet gone, I believed their qualification in political business was not yet completed, and it was my obsession to improve and secure them" (Thakin Ohn Myint 2013, 8). As prison was necessary, activists had to acquaint themselves with its realities. Thus, in 2008 four former political prisoner friends told me that they did not trust a mutual acquaintance, Maung, because even though he was a loyal member of the opposition, Maung had not "done his time yet." During this same conversation, these friends spent fifteen minutes arguing about whether a different comrade of theirs—one who had been incarcerated with them—was or was not an informer.[13] One explained that "he was a strange guy. Even though he was in jail for seven years, we thought he might be [a] spy. Maybe he had been loyal for six years, but in the seventh they turned him?" [*Eng*]. In other words, prison was a *dangerous necessity*. It was unclear whether his time in prison was an asset or a detriment: seven years is enough time to prove you are committed to the cause, but it is also a long time to be away from life's prosaic pleasures. Everything was on the margin: one had to be able to read the signs to determine if a comrade was going to flip. That conversation then moved into a discussion of what informing could mean: one defended the "strange guy" by suggesting that he was actually just *pretending* to flip. After all, you have to tell the Special Branch (SB)[14] *something*; but, he added, "you can tell them something and not the *important things*," thereby putting officials off the scent. Informers can end up being triple agents of sorts: first an opponent in hiding, then a double agent (a spy for the regime), and then a fake spy (who gives the wrong information).

Their disdain for Maung as frivolous and reckless became clearer to me after this byzantine conversation. Maung could not read the signs, could not ponder potential triple agents, because he had not entered this zone of intensity, this existential crucible. Such a crucible either flings one off (those who flee to normal life, turning their back on politics, or those who become state spies), concentrates them down into struggle's essence (those who become durable opponents, albeit often of a dogmatic and rigid type), or burns them in incomplete and unstable ways (forging mutated and continuingly mutable radicalizations defined by trauma, anger, hope, and confusion). The four friends could not know which direction Maung might go. All they knew is that Maung could not speak their same language, because he had not yet been incarcerated.

This generates a question: if there was so much potential in this space for political radicalization and bond formation, why did the military state permit it? Surely it understood the solidarity built in these spaces. One interpretation is that whether it intended to or not, the state effected a situation of political *quarantine* (a model of containment for the political dissident in the country more broadly, as we will see). Indeed, political prisoners were initially incarcerated with normal criminals, but when the political prisoners militated for their own space, asserting their group identity, they were moved. Thus, their demands were assuaged, and they were removed from the larger masses of criminals who might be radicalized as a result. Bo Kyi argues that the decisions were conscious: "Sometimes prison authorities don't want [political prisoners] to be among the criminals because they will organize them."

Exile at Home

The long prison terms were not, curiously, merely for pacification through immurement, because the punished often enjoyed early amnesties, decades before their full sentences had been served. Ko Taw spent eight years in Thayawaddy Prison before being offered one of these conditional pardons, a kind of sovereign *gift* for which the recipients were meant to give thanks. Note how the language in the pledge that prisoners were forced to sign underlines how the state imagined its own beneficence:[15] "I am aware that if I commit the same type of offence in the future, I will be subject to action in accordance with the law. I was arrested because of an offence. I am being released because the state has leniency. I pledge that if summoned, I will come at all times" (quoted in Cheesman 2015b, 213 [*Bse*]). The state calls attention to its own magnanimity—its own leniency is to thank for freedom—while keeping the threat of reincarceration ever present.[16] Ko Taw, however, refused to sign, as did many others who were imprisoned. He had inquired with other political prisoners about it: "Some were released after signing. But not all." He was not willing to capitulate, especially when release was not ultimately predicated on the pledge.

In one sense, however, they were not really released, as the quarantine lingered in postprison life. This became apparent on a night in 2017, when five members of CDI sat together on the office's floor in Myauk Okkalapa, snacking on barbeque and singing along to Thurein's guitar. With enough B.E., songs inevitably became political ballads. *Thachinmya Neh Lu*, literally "the person of songs," told the many stories of lives destroyed directly or indirectly by the regime's oppression. Teza then sang *Yadana*, another famous tune about a girl beaten during the 1988 uprising, as narrated by the male comrades who could not save her (Teza got choked up while singing it). When it concluded, Ko Taw made the connection between the themes of the song and the time in prison. There, "the prisoners love each other and have love and respect. One makes a guitar and we all play it; another makes a *chinlone* [a volleyball-type game played with a rattan ball] and we all kick it. It doesn't matter your education or how much money your family has—only how much you work for the community. One activist from Mandalay only had [a] second [grade education] but he is always ready to fight" [*Eng*]. Then Ko Taw paused and said, "I don't think I will ever feel that way again." The prison continues to be a presence in the lives of the activists, reactivated through self-descriptions, felt in pains remaining in the body, and invoked in songs they sing together on Thursday evenings decades after their confinement.

In this sense, *Yadana* is worth lingering on. As an abused female body, Yadana is a potent indexical icon, pointing to a number of highly gendered anxieties felt by the prisoners. Thurein averred that she represented all the women (and presumably the heterosexual love and companionship) that the prisoners were denied in prison. Relatedly, her presence in the song calls attention to her absence within the company of those singing about her, evoking the destabilization of the heteronormative life cycle: as other boys are becoming men, the political prisoner remains without his own Yadana. Finally, her abused female body also stands as symbolic representation of "the nation," which the heroic male is compelled to save; his failure evokes his impotence.

Yadana is one of many phenomena indexing the miseries and hopes that the prisoners were forced to engage. But because these challenges were shared and because the prisoners shared the same spaces both before and after prison, they dealt with them together, processes of coping that bred intense affective bonds that are continually referenced and reactivated throughout postprison life, especially given that the quarantine described in prison can continue upon release. According to Bo Kyi, AAPP found that before the transition a smaller percent than they would have expected remained directly committed to the cause; this is perhaps because of the difficulty of being "free" but having to remain within the quarantine zone.[17] The Burmese military state was particularly skilled at immuring resistance within underground cells that had few linkages to society (Boudreau 2004). Hence activists went from prison to NLD offices or into the U.G. networks (which were meant to be organizing communities), or they fled the country to Mae Sot or beyond. For the NLD and Mae Sot networks in particular, the spaces effectively constituted quarantine given the activists' inability to connect with average Burmese lives. For instance, as we huddled clandestinely in a safe house in Yangon in January 2010, a member of the NLD Central Executive Committee told me that "we really want to raise issues, but we cannot operate in township and regional levels. Only when the democratic government comes to exist could we connect; now we cannot do anything" [*Eng*]. Essentially the party at that point was reduced to waiting for a messianic delivery of democracy—either from a "spark" that was continually invoked as an imminent deus ex machina or from military intervention by the West;[18] they had turned outside the country for sustenance rather than gleaning it through interactions with Burmese subjects. That the elite opposition remained unaware of and therefore unresponsive to people's material realities may help explain why many of them ignored socioeconomic issues (such as electricity, water, education, and health) that may have better resonated with constituents.[19]

And not even those running the U.G. programs were clear about whether the state's intelligence services were unaware of them or whether they knew about them and simply *chose* to allow them to continue. Regarding the latter possibility, the state could have been content for dissidents to keep as quiet as they were, repairing to the safe houses and stealing away with information transmitted in code, for that meant the activists were not projecting the message to the masses; they were not organizing communities to demand services. As for the underground activists such as Ko Taw, Thurein, and Soe Aung, while they began to immerse themselves in the daily challenges of average people through service delivery projects—particularly for organizations such as the Free Funeral Service Society that dealt with life and death situations— that they had earlier eschewed when revolution appeared nigh, they were incapable of broadcasting key messages about the political causes of daily immiseration. The organizing work through service delivery was painstakingly slow and left a residue of existential frustration, in which those who had been incarcerated shared experiences that were difficult to communicate to humanitarian co-volunteers.

As might be expected, this turn to daily challenges cuts both ways—meaning that even as it allowed some to remain underground organizers under the aegis of plausible deniability (because they were doing "nonpolitical" humanitarian work), it demobilized many. Bo Kyi says that while a handful who exited politics did become state spies, most of those who left did not repudiate the struggle as much as attempted to return to "normal" life "until the time [was] right." This comment was made before 2011's transition, but it remains relevant after the coup. "They stay away and wait for the time; they are always looking at the situation. They want to be arrested again only if there is something big." But until then, "it is very difficult to reenter the family life. Especially the income: if you can't find regular income no one will think you are a man. You can get a job, but you have no capacity. If you are in jail for fifteen years, [since] you were twenty, you have no chance to officially study, no certificate; when you apply for a job, what is your qualification? If you are famous, even though you have capacity, businessmen are afraid of hiring you. Even UNDP is reluctant to appoint former political prisoners" [*Eng*]. Bo Kyi here highlights how even those who eschewed oppositional politics could not reenter society, themselves remaining somewhat quarantined. Many dealt with the dissonance of having postprison lives that seemed enervated of both opportunity and meaning after their lives in the political prison block had promised so much, even in their pain.

Activists tell stories of their mentors that bear this out. Of Ko Taw's three most important mentors—those who originally "organized him," as he put it in English—"one has become a homeless drunkard, one went into acupuncture and withdrew from politics, [and] one died in Mae Sot on the street." Bo Kyi and Ko Taw both pointed to their surprisingly supportive families as helping them avoid such outcomes. Ko Taw attributed his ability to find a different postprison path to his father: "Even though he is a government party official and doesn't approve of politics, he asked me what I learned in prison. 'English, astrology, et cetera,' I told him. 'Keep learning English,' he told me. He encouraged me. But I reapplied to university and was not accepted. I would have to write a letter admitting guilt and that concerned my dignity; I would not do it. So [my father] encouraged me to go into business. I am so grateful for that."

Ko Taw's appreciation for his father's words have more to do with the encouragement than any specific focus on business, certainly. This is because any "business" Ko Taw pursued was only to enable his political activities. "I did so many jobs to get money," he explained. "[I operated a] satellite dish . . . , sold shoes, [and] made popsicles at night and sold them during the day." In fact, after the 2021 coup CDI returned to selling popsicles to support the strike.

Ko Taw and other former political prisoners pursued such miscellaneous tasks rather than taking advantage of more lucrative opportunities available to them. Even after exiting prison, SB officers offer activists material benefits in exchange for signing the pledge: "They tried to persuade me to stand [with] them. If I had signed, I would have some opportunities for my private life. But I would have to give info [on] my comrades. I refused" [*Eng*]. Ko Taw's invocation of refusal allows us to return briefly to the theoretical concept outlined earlier and use it to assess activists' postprison activities. These various activist stories of prison life and postprison trajectories demonstrate how refusal is continually reanimated in the existential and political-economic choices forced on activists. Whereas *resistance* was assisting a former political prisoner comrade to flee to the border in 2002 (for which Ko Taw was rear-rested), and *resistance* was also pasting posters at Dagon University that read "We are against the military education" in 2005 as a member of the 88GS—the "88 Generation Students" activist collective (again rearrested); *refusal* was selling popsicles rather than accepting the pledge and becoming part of the extortionary state.

But let us consider the issue of returning to university by signing the pledge. Refusing to sign is obviously refusal, but signing and returning while retaining subjective rebellion, while remaining uncaptured by the political-economic logics within a military regime, would *that too* have been refusal? For Ko Taw, the answer then was no. But when two young CDI members were swept up and sent to Insein Prison during the anticoup uprising in 2021 and were offered release the next day contingent on their repudiation of politics, they signed and immediately returned to the streets. The point is that refusal depends on the situation and that in activist life, while resistance popped up here and there, when necessary and sometimes perhaps when unnecessary, re-fusal was the molecular flow that saturated life, the ligatures allowing one day of struggle to turn into the next, the bedrock on which resistance could rest. The related point is that there are specific moments, such as in the early anti-coup protests, when direct resistance is essential and long-term strategies of refusal can be put on hold.

Becoming MDC(F) and CDI

After his first release in 1999, Ko Taw rejoined the student movement but was arrested again in 2002. After a brief forty-five-day detention in what he called a "torture camp," he was released again.[20] From 2005 to 2007 Ko Taw began working with the 88GS in the run-up to what would become the Saffron Rev-olution—somewhat misnamed because thousands of Buddhist monks came out to defend peaceful protesters *already* leading rallies responding to the military state's desubsidization of fuel,[21] and the attendant economic pain wrought therein, that occurred in August 2007. At this point Ko Taw's trajec-tory came to intersect with those of many other eventual CDI members.

Thurein, CDI's effective vice president, took a different path to activism from Ko Taw. He is a quiet, exceedingly attentive, immediately likable man of about forty with short yet somehow shaggy hair and thin whiskers on his up-per lip that give him a diffident feline appearance. When I met him, he and his wife ran a curry shop out of the front of their house in Myauk Okkalapa. They

FIGURE 2.1. MDC rally, Yangon, early 2007. The sign in the middle reads, "For reducing the goods' prices." The sign on the right reads "To get full 24 hours of electricity." Photo by Ko Taw.

rented out upper-floor rooms, one of which was donated pro bono as CDI's office. Thurein also took the responsibility for most of CDI's logistics. Given his mild manner and excessive humility, it was shocking to learn that Thurein had previously made his living in the underground economy, running an illicit two-digit lottery scheme for an organized crime syndicate in the early 2000s. When I discovered this he shrugged, blushing; one has to survive.

Thurein's life began to change when, in 2003, Saya Nyo, a local schoolteacher who had grown up in Myauk Okkalapa, began to organize local men and women around the area's deteriorating economic conditions and the broader causes of these deteriorations. They formed a group called the Myanmar Development Committee (MDC), whose name partook of the quasi-apolitical nature of socioeconomic uplift.

Saya Nyo did not mind Thurein's occupation—everyone was hustling to survive and Thurein's money helped support the fledgling organization, which began holding public rallies in early 2007 protesting the rising prices of daily necessities (figure 2.1). Returning here to the discussion in chapter 1 of structural violence—perceived by Burmese masses as morally wrong and objectionable but not politically resonant as an object of intervention—I note here that MDC engaged in a "politics of the daily" (Prasse-Freeman 2012) that attempted to politicize those moral objections, resignifying conditions that had been taken for granted. And under the anodyne name, MDC members like Thurein became radicalized: "We had political discussions: what should we do for the community? It was different than respect, what I had for Saya Nyo," said Thurein. "If he said die, I would die."

While mostly unacknowledged in representations of the massive "Saffron" protests that erupted later that year (but see Schrank 2015, 59–60), MDC rallies anticipated and partially inspired the later events. When activists Ko Ko Gyi and Min Ko Naing of the 88GS group began their campaigns soon after, they borrowed from these early MDC rallies for basic necessities. MDC held small rallies every month in 2007, delivering the same message about rising prices, sending only those willing to be arrested, and not sending too many at a single time lest the entire movement get immediately repressed in a single sweep of arrests. Of course, repression came, precipitating in turn what Thurein called "the tragedies of MDC." He elaborated: "Aung Gyi, a DVB reporter, was MDC and he died; Ko Gyi Aye died; Ma Man Nweh became insane—she got sucked into the moment. Saya Nyo had organized us to go in waves so if one group was arrested then the next could replace them, and so it would not be snuffed out all at once, before anyone even noticed. Ma Man Nweh's duty was just to get the experience, but when she saw the protest she participated in it, was arrested and tortured, and has not recovered" [Bse].

Thurein also participated in that first protest but then pretended to be a drunkard to avoid arrest. Eventually, however, he was detained and tortured. The SB would come to him often after that, wanting to make him an informer. But his other sources of income insulated him from material need and suspicion from others.

Thurein met Ko Taw, Teza, and Soe Aung during Saffron, and they continued working together afterward. Saya Nyo soon became too old and ill to continue leading the group, and the most active MDC member, Htin Kyaw, took over; he formed MDCF, Movement for Democracy Current Force, the addition of the word "force" indexing a more confrontational approach than its predecessor. But when Htin Kyaw was incarcerated for leading the 2007 protests (Cheesman 2015b, 208), Saya Nyo transferred the group to Ko Taw, the latter's bona fides confirmed by mutual comrades. In January 2009 they

FIGURE 2.2. Police intercept the MDC at Sule Pagoda, Yangon, 2007. Photo by Ko Taw.

officially formed the MDC Youth, bringing in younger members to organize local *hsin-kyay-boun* communities around similar material issues, all while keeping a low profile. "If we are arrested we can't always continue our activities, so we avoid [arrest]" [*Bse*], Thurein reflected. In 2010 Htin Kyaw was released from prison and retook the reins of MDCF, and while Thurein, Ko Taw, and others remained part of MDCF, they also formed the group now called CDI.

How did these groups differ? In November 2014, during our very first meeting, Ko Taw introduced himself as being from MDCF. Hearing the word *in-ah-su*[22] (force), I struggled to fit the group into the institutional paradigms laid down by that current moment of transition. "Are you an NGO? Are you a political party?" I asked in Burmese. Ko Taw retorted, flatly, in English, "We are a force." I laughed, and after a pause, so did he, but I came to understand the insight in this name: MDCF, like many of what might be called grassroots activist groups, refused to be labeled and inscribed into (and hence contained by) the funding frameworks, silos of project management, and narrow cause-based work of transition-era NGOs; likewise, its members did not want the compromises and the distance from grassroots concerns that they felt political party membership entailed. Ko Taw then continued, by way of explanation, "There are many in Myanmar who are not activists, just NGO people. Things like amending the Constitution—that is not the real fight. Those holding plow protests dare to fight and die. Those NGO leaders do not. They are *yay-baw-hsi*."[23] This was the idiom for "elite," literally "the oil on top of the water," which evokes both spatial hierarchy and a refusal to mix with the people (the water).[24]

While MDCF was a force—an organization of veteran activists working all over the country (although many of them were often in prison) who were devoted to disrupting and contesting the status quo—CDI was a different type of organization. It was based in Myauk Okkalapa, and its objective was to address the challenges for poor people there. Where MDCF would fly off to the site of national conflagrations, CDI was a drop-in center for local people and a place where, as introduced in the previous chapter, youth could get support in their studies.

But, of course, CDI members were *also* MDCF members. When the members introduced themselves, it was often as *who* they were and what they had *done* rather than the particular group they were with at that moment. Thurein, for instance, talked about how he not only was in Saffron but had been involved in the much more difficult and dangerous work that spurred it. Ko Taw used his political prisoner status and his membership with ABSDF more than anything else, as the former indexed sacrifice and the latter his longevity in the movement.

Seen this way, the groups were often less like coherent entities (encompassing individuals) than labels that individuals could affix to themselves when convenient and could shed when less efficacious. Indeed, the formal name of a group tends to shift so often as to become far less meaningful than who participates and what actions they are conducting.[25] MDCF was a label that one had to earn and that one used when communicating to intimidate, impress, and index connections; CDI was a label that stressed fidelity to local challenges and was a way of recruiting younger people who might eventually become seasoned activists ready to join a group like MDCF. When an activist would use one over the other would "depend on the situation," as I was always reminded.

Activist Actions

"But as you know there are few experienced people inside the country. . . . Especially the youth (GenZ) do not know the technics of the protest not to be arrested—how to have a scout, to inquire where they are and how we flee when the dogs get the place, to switch hide house every 10 days. They have no experiences about those type of protest[s]." Ko Taw sent me this text in April 2021, after the coup, and it demonstrates the micropolitics—of the body in space—involved in contentious action. Hence far the actual activities of activists have been alluded to but not explored. The following section will draw out some patterns in my observations of their engagements with grassroots communities, showing how these actions partake in direct contests (resistance) as well as more subtle maneuvers and negotiations with fields of blunt biopolitical governmentality (refusal).

Build Movements through Plausible Deniability

The CDM that sprouted up to shut down the Myanmar state after the military executed its coup seemed to have reached a peak by the end of the second week, as some normalcy appeared to be returning after the effervescence of street protests across the first fortnight. But at the start of the third week, cars in Yangon began mysteriously breaking down, completely gridlocking traffic. The day before, a military tank had malfunctioned in the middle of downtown Yangon, provoking mockery both in the streets and online. Perhaps a plague was afflicting Burmese vehicles? And to be fair, cars breaking down in the middle of the road is eminently plausible, because Burmese cars for decades existed largely in a state of rampant disrepair. But bikes and even trishaws got in the act as well.

The "Why you break down, car?" protests (Frontier 2021; fig. 2.3) were also a wonderful iteration of the age-old tactic in Burma of protesting through plausible deniability, evoking the 2007 Saffron protests during which, in response to government desubsidization of fuel, Ko Taw, Min Ko Naing, and others led people in "walk to work" protests; when interdicted by officials, they were able to reply, "We're just going to our jobs. . . . You guys made it so the only way we can get to work is by walking" (Prasse-Freeman 2012, 389).

The broken-down car protests had exponential effects, enabling other plausibly deniable protests. A Burmese friend pointed out that the blockades were not just annoying and humiliating for police (who had to push cars out of the way in the hot sun) but also good cover for those who had not *yet* participated in the CDM because of coercion or fear. They could say, "Sorry, I couldn't make it into work today, sir. The road was totally blocked." The next day the military brought bulldozers to move cars, but people decided that— for *health's sake* (the risible reason the military had given for shutting off the

FIGURE 2.3.
In his cartoon, the driver thinks, "Only if I'm able to pretend it's broken down... hee hee." The police officer wonders what happened. Source: Cartoonist Ayeyawadi DeeMo, February 2021.

internet every night)—they should drive very, very slowly, achieving much the same objective. Some cars crawled around the same traffic circle for hours in pursuit of such healthy outcomes. Masses of youth found themselves with shoelaces untied as they crossed the street and were horrified to realize that no matter what they did, the shoes would not become tied again (Thawda Aye Lei 2022, 128).

Politicizing the Daily

MDCF posted its seventeen-point "Policy for the People" on its office wall (fig. 2.4). Some of its goals—for example, lowering the costs of basic goods and getting twenty-four-hour electricity—were the same as MDC's a decade before. But it also added new goals, including eradicating unemployment,

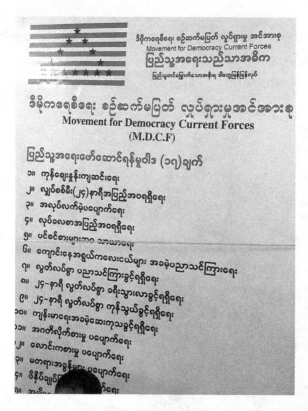

ဒီမိုကရေစီရေး စဉ်ဆက်မပြတ် လှုပ်ရှားမှု အင်အားစု
Movement for Democracy Current Forces

FIGURE 2.4.
Movement for
Democracy Current
Force's seventeen-
point Policy for the
People, posted at its
Yangon office. Photo
by Ko Taw, 2018.

corruption, gambling, and unjust taxes; getting a full salary (which could be translated as a "living wage"); obtaining free education for children; getting the right/permission to travel freely twenty-four hours (per day); being able to trade freely twenty-four hours (per day); and obtaining free health care services.

All these goals are grounded in material realities that have been accepted by most Burmese citizens but that the activists insist should not be accepted. Hence, when the activists make broader political claims, these demands emerge from and remained linked to these daily conditions. Critically, they are all claims that resolutely would not be resolved by resistance to and ultimate displacement of a military state—the specific sovereign force—but that are tied up in a broader constellation of authoritarian capitalism that demands redress. Indeed, the life of refusal lived by activists finds a perfect homology in this form of politics, given that it participates not in binary contests against a sovereign for political power (as with the NLD and its leader Suu Kyi, who long confronted the military over control of the country) but in a long march to the alteration of material conditions and to how those material conditions are perceived.

Systematizing Nascent Campaigns

While MDCF's actions were animated by values grounded by, for instance, the just-mentioned seventeen points, the specific campaigns that MDCF, CDI, and other networks became involved in were more demand driven. Typically, farmers or workers, after having organized on their own (writing letters to relevant officials), might encounter inefficacy if not outright rejections: their letters would go unreturned; their protests were ignored or permissions to hold them were rejected. Those who did not disband at these moments inquired through informal word-of-mouth channels or local political party offices (mostly NLD) to obtain referrals to the activists.

If the activists felt they were able to assist in a specific grievance, they would travel to the site, assess the situation, and then engage in a series of actions that could be called political brokerage.[26] Activists began without fail by assisting local groups in getting their affairs in order. The first step was redrafting complaint letters: establishing the chronology of events, acquiring and collating the correct documents, and ensuring that each letter in the next round was directed to the most relevant recipients in government (and that all recipients were inscribed on the bottom of the message as copied). This mimicked the state's official (and officious) register (Hull 2012), parasiting on bureaucratic affect; it also created joint attention among officials at various levels such that everyone's bosses and subordinates also knew of the complaint.

Reading complaint letters occupied literally dozens of hours of each trip, as villagers would pour in from surrounding regions with individual letters, or—more commonly—groups of villagers would come present their letters to the activists and work with the activists on revising them (see fig. 2.5).

For example, during a trip to Mandalay in late March 2015, a group of farmers from far north in Sagaing Region (Htigyaing Township) came with their case to U Gyi's compound, where the activists were staying. Ko Taw and U Gyi looked over the farmers' letter, and after about five minutes declared the verdict: the letter was very good for media, but it was not good legally, and it had to be both. It then had to be sent to the relevant parties. The content of the letter needed to answer the following four questions: (1) Who owned the

FIGURE 2.5. CDI members visiting farmers north of Mandalay spend one of many afternoons getting papers in order. Photo by Daniel Ginsberg, November 2014.

land and what did they do on it? (2) Who stole the land and when? (3) What happened to the farmers after—was any compensation given?, and (4) What are the farmers doing now? U Gyi made sure to stress that while the legal path alone would not get them their land back, it could play a part in how the broader negotiation played out.

After revising the letters, the activists then advised locals on how to build and sustain their movements; this often meant linking them with other village- or factory-based groups already connected to the activists, thereby plugging new members into, and further building, networks that could assist with logistical aspects of specific campaigns. Perhaps most critically, if locals did decide to hold escalations, the activists would outline the risks while guiding them on how to intensify their engagements. The activists often suggested strikes, occupations, and plow protests, and they outlined the set of tactics necessary for executing such actions successfully.

As an illustration, during a single day during a June 2015 trip to upper Burma, the activists deployed all of these tactics. During the day they visited Mattaya to advise one group of farmers on how to *sustain* a plow protest and another group on how to *launch* one. Ko Taw gave three pieces of advice to the first group: "One, ongoing success depends on your solidarity. Don't look at other farmers' problems and think they are not your concern. Two, have a network that you can use if/when [the word is the same in Burmese] things go bad; and three, the situation in the country will be changing, so the opportunities can change. The [2015] election is near, and after it, keep your eyes and ears open" [*Bse*]. As they were going through the documents, I followed up on the first point, asking what it means, in more specific terms, to have solidarity. Ko Taw said that "farmers have to be taught how to protest—to know that if they all come out together the police will not charge at 100 people" [*Bse*]. Aye Than, his Mandalay-based colleague, added that one way to accomplish this was to form a farmer's union.

In the evening we returned to the NLD office in Kyaukse. Its local chairperson, who most everyone just called "Okkada" (chairperson), was more comrade than NLD cadre, and hence he was a critical node in the broader activist network. Two middle-aged men entered the office looking for advice from Okkada and the activists. They described how in 2006 the Mandalay Region chief minister had confiscated their lands on the grounds that a state biotech college would be built there. Ko Taw asked to see their complaint letter, presuming that they had it with them. They did not and exited on motorbike to retrieve it. In came a group of four labor activists, young men in their midtwenties who worked in a nearby cement factory. They were considering holding a strike for better wages and treatment, and Ko Taw and Okkada jointly gave advice. Much of their lecture was hortative, encouraging the young activists to have confidence, therein modeling the disposition the young men would need to lead hesitant workers. The middle-aged men returned shortly with their complaint letters. Ko Taw advised them to rewrite the letters to describe their specific sufferings, including the effects of the land grab on their families' daily existence, and to outline the fact that the chief minister's project has not actually helped the public.

Know Law as a Tool

Across these engagements, a set of patterns emerged regarding the general tactics and dispositions necessary for mitigating risk of failure. On one hand, activists described law as essential and delivered trainings on relevant statutes and those statutes' specific bearings on the current situation, so farmers would at least know the law when it was being weaponized against them. Such effective weaponization of the law came up repeatedly during my fieldwork. For instance, during a trip to Shan state in January 2015, the plan was that the CDI crew would sleep at the local NLD office where they would be giving a training, and I would sleep at the only local guesthouse in that entire region that was registered to accept foreigners. Monday afternoon we traveled by minibus through the night across a rutted path more uncomfortable than harrowing, arriving in Shan state on early morning Tuesday; we napped at the office until the beginning of the training. As attendees filled in for the training, some men arrived on motorbike. Their sunglasses, jeans, and demeanors indicated they were clearly not there for the training.

The men, revealed as SB officers, asked for my passport and other documents, and after some discussion about where I would be staying, left to make photocopies. Later that afternoon we got a call saying that I could not stay at the guesthouse because it was "full." Ko Taw rolled his eyes. He suspected those SB put pressure on the guesthouse proprietors to say they were full so I would have nowhere to stay. He complained that the SB was causing problems so that they would not have to take responsibility, even though we were in accordance with the law (in that we gave the authorities the correct materials, and so on). Further, while getting me to leave would rid them of responsibility, they were also able to exert leverage over me (and CDI) by effectively *making me break the law* (by sleeping at the NLD office) if I chose to stay. As it did not seem reasonable to turn around and travel eight hours back to Mandalay, I just slept at the office with everyone else. CDI had no intention of mobilizing locals to protest, for example, but by illegalizing me, the local officials made it less likely that the out-of-state activists would do anything while there; and, the officials also would have been able to build a better case against us if they needed to present the situation to their superiors.

For these kinds of reasons, the activists also simultaneously said that law is *not* important; the constant refrain was "the law is just on paper. . . . Reality is another way."[27] In response to my queries about what the law said, how a case would go, or whether someone would get arrested during a protest, the reply was often the same: "It depends on the situation." Having the perspective that everything depends on the situation means that the law becomes valuable as a part of one's maneuvering of that situation. Indeed, only a lawyer or activist's own power and skill animate the law; only his or her ability to wield it in an argument (and often as part of numerous other strategies—including using the media, negotiating, and encouraging tactical payment of bribes) makes it relevant.

"Knowing the law" was more than simply having knowledge about the law per se: it was a way to intimidate local officials or businessmen into relenting or at least negotiating. For example, one day at CDI's office, which was still then Thurein's extra room, I encountered Koko, who I had seen many times before but never spoken with. Koko was visually captivating: he had ear gauges (circular disks inserted into his ears in punk style) and long hair, typically pulled into a ponytail, which that day fell loose on his shoulders. He was often shirtless, exposing a muscular physique covered in elaborate cascading serpent tattoos. He moved fluidly and with an exceeding lightness; he was simultaneously menacing and gentle.

Koko and I chatted about something banal—his unique longyi pattern. He gave polite, if terse, answers and then retreated back downstairs. When Ko Taw returned I inquired about Koko—what was his story? Ko Taw explained: "He was a *lu-maiq* [thug]. He was hired by some gangsters to beat us because we were encouraging people to not use drugs and [not] do the two-digit lottery—and that affected [the gangsters'] business. But when Koko came to us, we talked to him and explained what we do. He decided to join us instead of beating us" [*Eng*]. Ko Taw smiled broadly at this outcome, a microcosm of the transformation he wanted to effect everywhere.

"Koko is a very skilled driver, but he did not have an ID card," Ko Taw continued. It is quite common for people in peri-urban Yangon to not have national identification cards; the 2014 census found that 30 percent of residents in Yangon lacked them. This has been attributed to, inter alia, debt flight—in which families incapable of repaying loans will flee a ward, leaving behind their ID card, which had been held as collateral by the lender (Trautwein 2016).[28] Koko never got a card in the first place, an outcome attributed to a lack of fixed address on the part of parents who were moving around continually. CDI informed him that he was eligible for one—the process required a combination of filling out forms and paying fees. But Koko felt that he did not know how to navigate this process himself, a problem of not knowing what the process formally required *and* not knowing how to negotiate with authorities. Ko Taw relayed that Koko also wanted to avoid courting trouble: "These *lu-maiq* might be afraid to approach the authorities." He then added, "Or they might feel embarrassed not knowing how to negotiate" [*Eng*]. CDI intervened on Koko's behalf, brokering the application to the immigration department officials, pointing out that they knew the law, a performative presenting themselves as those with superior knowledge, as those who get what they want (rather than, they told me, the law having any power itself). Koko got his ID card after paying merely 30,000 kyat (then USD 23); he then got the driver job he had sought.

As this demonstrates, legal knowledge was perhaps a way of communicating the *ability* to access such rarefied domains: wielding the knowledge was wielding the networks of power that allowed someone to learn the knowledge for wielding. Moreover, knowing the law acted as a coordinating device, a way to get the entire community aligned with the same narrative about how they were wronged. Returning to refusal, we see here how law becomes a terrain to be maneuvered within rather than being a site of binary resistance, as negotiations, postures, and performances dictate outcomes as much as the sovereign rule of decision.

All of this is, of course, at first glance much the same as in other legal situations: law is always a competitive and unequal terrain where statutes and procedures are tools that skilled jurists manipulate to best their opponents. But in many of those systems (for example, those in the West from whence so many so-called Rule of Law reformers descended on Myanmar from 2011 to 2020) there is a sense that such lawyerly improvisations are mere momentary deviations from a normative procedure that is fundamentally just (despite repeated evidence to the contrary). Burmese actors understand their situation differently.[29] When the law is improvised it *may actually change* in the process, and it may never functionally return to what the statute originally said or to what people may have considered just. Hence, whether in a court negotiation or paddy field protest, lawyers and activists often simultaneously present the law as a normative goal to be aspired to *and* as pure tactic whose rules one must master. The necessity of seeing the law as nothing more than a tool gnaws away at the idea of any pure and perfect law, thus leaving open the broader question of whether law is the appropriate tool for delivering justice (Prasse-Freeman 2015a).

Tactics over Strategies

As this treatment of the law suggests, for those in positions of relative powerlessness, everything must be assessed for potential benefits and costs. As laws are perceived as containing a double edge, activists and their clients do not commit to them either as strategy or as morality. Law remains open as an option. Moreover, failures to achieve demands can work to further mobilize support rather than risk enervating movements. For instance, protest signs—such as "Deliver the rule of law"—that seem to assert substantive values remain only tactically endorsed. Protesters are strategically uncommitted to such demands—leaving meanings ascribed to the rule of law open—such that while

FIGURE 2.6. Ei Thinzar Maung, the exiled NUG's deputy minister of women, youths and children affairs, poses with a sign telling the UN to "please ignore us," April 2021. Source: Ei Thinzar Maung.

the achievement of the rule of law (as a set of material resources or affordances) might be desirable, its failure to materialize would further confirm the stance of the enemy (those who will not deliver rule of law) and helps recruit more people to the cause.[30] An identical maneuver was pursued during the anticoup uprising but vis-à-vis the international community: activists invited help from abroad, but if such aid was not forthcoming, then that rejection became inscribed into the updated political reality and was used as a way of persuading and mobilizing to action those otherwise waiting for an external savior.

The lone member of the NUG who can be called an activist, Minister of Women's Affairs Ei Thinzar Maung, brilliantly deployed this dual tactic with her contribution to the #Sisters2Sisters campaign introduced earlier, in which women called attention to the abuses, often sexual in nature, wrought by the *Sit-tat* and suffered by women throughout Myanmar for decades. While many women called explicitly for the UN to help them, Ei Thinzar Maung, featured in figure 2.6, refracted that demand, holding up a sign reading, "Myanmar women are being committed sexual assaults [*sic*] by the Military and UN Women keep ignoring it. 'UN Women, please ignore us.'" As with activists using the law, Ei Thinzar Maung was still *using* the international: she kept the hope for international intervention alive by maintaining the international (the UN and other English-reading publics) as the explicit addressee of the speech act, one perhaps encouraged to feel shame at its inaction. But as with the law ("It is just on paper. . . ."), Ei Thinzar Maung repudiated that same tool, redirecting her message to other Burmese, insisting that they not wait for saviors who may never come (Prasse-Freeman 2023a).

Project Superior Commitment

Even as activists taught the law as a potential resource, they also stressed that laws would likely work against them and that if villagers wanted to get their land back or if workers wanted to get a wage raise, their leaders would likely have to go to jail (even if they were legally in the right). It goes without saying that being prepared to go (back) to prison was also a prerequisite for activists. This did not mean, of course, that they were always seeking out prison, for obvious reasons; instead, they cultivated sophisticated sensibilities for when an altercation would likely precipitate arrest. For instance, in 2015 they visited Letpadan, where university students were engaged in a standoff with the government over education policy, but the activists left before hired thugs broke up the protest camp and dozens were arrested. "That was not our fight," Teza said. "It was not our time to get arrested" [*Bse*]. Six years later, in the first days after the February 2021 coup, the activists planned their first protest the following day (February 5th) partly by deciding who was willing to get arrested. Included with the usual suspects—Thurein, Teza, Soe Aung—were the youngest members, Thu Myat and Mya, both of whom had never had altercations with the state's coercive arm. I asked, over Signal, how CDI leaders prepared them for those encounters. "We don't need to tell them much," Ko Taw said, nonplussed. They had been around the elder ones for long enough that they had become "the bravest," so much so that "they are leading the activities," he insisted. And indeed, days later when they phoned me on Signal in the middle of a protest, Thu Myat was on the megaphone barking the call-and-response chants of "A military government?" "We don't want it!" [*Bse*]. In terms of preparation, there was a sense that they had been with the older activists for so long that they did not need any pep talks. But the previous day (February 4), Ko Taw had posted a message directed to the next generation of leaders:

Your generation is superior, ours is inferior. In the time we are thinking to avoid, you are trying to come face to face. Our leaders are over there. Coming behind these leaders in these fucked up times you guys are starting to lead campaigns to oppose the military dictatorship. At the time when we are composing poems, you are thinking about all the methods of opposition. When we deviate in all the ways from our expectations, you are out on the street. . . . I am ashamed that up until this point we have lived as the military's slaves. . . . I'm proud of all of you! . . . If I get a chance, I'm willing to sacrifice my life in this battle we're facing. [*Bse*]

There will be more said about this post in chapter 4—specifically for how it was meant for Ko Taw's age-cohort comrades as well as the younger ones to whom it was explicitly directed—but the point for now is not only the way it projected superior commitment (stated willingness to die) even while imparting that same commitment in his followers but also how it accomplished the latter by inverting his position, putting those followers in the lead.

Projecting superior commitment, of course, does not always involve sacrificing one's life, let alone going to prison. Here MyoTha Industrial Park—introduced at the beginning of this chapter and which I visited a half-dozen times from 2014 to 2016—is worth revisiting. The activists saw MyoTha as a distillation of the sham nature of the transition—a land grab accelerating at a time when peasants were supposed to finally be receiving their lands back. Thus, the activists directed significant support to the local movement. Of course, Myanmar MyoTha LTD's publicly filed prospectus (MMID 2013) declared that the area on which MyoTha Industrial Park (MIP) sat was chosen because it was scrubland home to few peasants. The prospectus claimed that all displaced farmers were given adequate compensation and were happy to have the project. The document includes photos testifying to these facts.

But farmers living in their villages in the middle of the gated-off zone who refused to leave told a different story (FIDH 2017). During one visit we found them sleeping in shifts in tents alongside the road near the company's quarters to guard against its looming bulldozers (see fig. 2.7). If a bulldozer engine fired up in the middle of the night to plow their lands under, watchmen and watchwomen called other villagers to come stand in front of the bulldozers (which they had done on numerous occasions and which had led to the imprisonment of their leaders—charged, preposterously, with inducing the public to violate the state).

FIGURE 2.7. A villager from MyoTha stands outside of the villagers' makeshift camp, established to prevent their fields from being bulldozed under. Source: Daniel Ginsburg, 2015.

Once in mid-2015, when the activists were in the village meeting with the local monk who had helped organize the villagers, the owners' representatives interdicted Ko Taw: "They approached in seven Land Cruisers and took so many photos. All of those cars, like a mafia! 'What is your name?' they asked. But then I said to them, 'You tell me *your* name first. *I* am the former political prisoner. I got the life sentence. That was a very bad situation, and that did not make me stop. So this will not make me stop. You cannot intimidate me,' I yelled at them" [*Eng*]. He smiled mischievously relaying this performance, which had the added advantage of being intensely real. Indeed, observing real-time interactions with officials always made me nauseated from the flood of adrenaline and affect, even though I was a mere bystander. Even when Ko Taw merely relayed that he was "a former political prisoner and not afraid to die," the air bristled with emotion, harkening up histories of struggle. As discussed in chapter 4 on the use of the activist body, these were not just speech acts but full bodily enactments in which muscles flexed, teeth clenched, and hair stood on end.

In MyoTha the next day, the industrial zone's chairman, his followers having failed at intimidation, called Ko Taw and complained that "the farmers are very greedy." Ko Taw relayed the rest of the conversation: "'Ok, they may be, they are human beings—they may be greedy just as human beings are greedy—but they don't deserve to be treated like this.' The chairman told me, 'You can be the negotiator and get them to accept, and you can organize the farmer. In that case I can support you.' But I said, 'I cannot do that, as they trust me because I do not hurt their livelihood. If you want to resolve, you have to compromise'" [*Eng*].

Noteworthy here is how Ko Taw's initial recalcitrance compelled a different tactic by the company, at which point Ko Taw adjusted his stance as well: he went from aggression to negotiation. While rejecting the chairman's overture to swindle the villagers, Ko Taw then provided counsel, advising him on what he could do: "Come forward a bit." This suggests that he could get the farmers to back off some in their demands in exchange for an equitable settling of the conflict. Superior commitment translated into pragmatic negotiation. (The crony refused and instead had his thugs deliver death threats to Ko Taw, which he mostly shrugged off, although he did get a new SIM card for his phone.)

While Ko Taw did not go back to prison during the years I was with him, his comrades often did. In March 2015 we visited Oh Boh Prison, a facility surprisingly close to downtown Mandalay: after ten minutes of driving straight north from the palace compound, cows and their herders start to muscle out cars for space on the road, and the low-slung shops (pharmacies, mechanics, tea shops, and beer stalls) characteristic of peri-urban Burma begin to dominate the roadside. We parked in the prison lot, and Teza lugged out a bulging plastic bag full of snacks from the flatbed. He augmented these by purchasing more from one of the many stalls across the street from the prison, their wares arranged seemingly as a cruel reminder of the deliciousness of freedom. We then waltzed over to the registration desk, where Teza gave the name of the incarcerated—Thein Aung Myint—as well as Thein Aung Myint's father's name, and ultimately his own. I stood there waiting to be rebuffed or at least asked to explain myself. ("I am doing research on the rule of law . . . , and prisons are a part of that," I practiced in my head. It sounded even worse in Burmese.) But the guard just looked at me—a look neither of annoyance nor of surprise—and waved me on.

We passed through the barbed-wire gates and crossed an actual moat by way of a wide dirt bridge. Facing an inner walled area that marked the cell blocks from the wider grounds, I read a pleasantly colored sign: "If you please, this is a space for children, thank you" [*Bse*]; and to the immediate right as we faced the walls was a play area with jungle gym. "There are children here?" I asked. "Yes, the guard's children," Teza answered. Turning right and walking past the playground, we came to the destination: a large open-air shed, much like a covered area for recreational activities, taken over that day by people waiting to see their relatives. It was largely women and children—which made sense, given that most prisoners are men. A huge open-bed truck—similar to a garbage truck—was being filled with clear plastic bags such as Teza's to be delivered to those incarcerated. Ko Taw, Lay Gyi, and Teza then went in to see Thein Aung Myint; they decided that my joining would be pushing my luck, so I just sent my regards. But moments later they returned, arguing with a walkie-talkie-carrying man in plainclothes. Never a good sign. I was asked to show them my phone—to show that I had no photos of the grounds—and then I was politely asked to leave, which seemed reasonable. A boy in prison guard uniform escorted me out.

Later when they emerged, all were subdued. Thein Aung Myint was in good health, he was happy that we visited, and so forth, they relayed. As we pulled away, Ko Taw pointed back and said, with a mixture of pride and sadness, "I have lived inside those walls." One never really leaves prison.

Cultivate the Public . . . and the State's Agents

As alluded to earlier in the discussion of the Michaungkan protesters' oscillation between defiance and respect, activists seemed always cognizant that as their performances could reach broader publics (through signs, videos, and mediatized performances), their messages should be disciplined and respectful and invoke conceptions of justice that could enroll new participants. They even modeled this approach in the arrangement of their protesting bodies (a point to which we will return in chapter 4). Specifically, most protest marches during the transition era brought their own cordons—a rope that the organizer at the front and the one at the back would hold to demarcate the protesters from others. It served several purposes; as Ko Taw put it, "We bring the rope so that the dogs cannot accuse us that the protest disturbs the public transportation or public rights. And the rope also can hinder the fake protestors who are sent by authorities. If the protestors mingle with ordinary people, [it is] difficult to control and manage them."

Activists also used a call-and-response structure that mimics the traditional Burmese call-and-response practice called *thanja*—observable during village festivals and New Years' celebrations—in which a seven-syllable call is met with an eight-syllable riposte (Keeler 2009, 3), which could beckon new members and audiences. Ko Taw relayed that activists played with the structure (it did not need to retain the eight/seven construction), thereby making a recognizable cultural script even more welcoming: "Chanting [like this] is just the easiest one. Chanting must be clear and it needs to [encourage] inclusiveness." In other words, the simple responses could be bellowed by anyone: "This is our cause" (*Doh-ayay*); "We don't want it" (*A-lo ma-shi*); "Give it to us now" (*Chet-chin pay*).[31]

And even as the activists intimidated local officials with their stories of prison and the locals' unity, they not only often diffused tension and avoided direct confrontation with frontline members of the state security apparatus but attempted to recruit the lower-level officials as well.[32] For instance, before an action the activists would almost always show lower-level SB agents the respect of calling them first and letting them know the action they would take, even when this action was likely to break the law: that is, "We are doing this. If you would like to arrest us, you can." While calling the SB was brazen, especially given that the proceeding tactics were adversarial (particularly when they directly or indirectly escalated into cursing ceremonies, riots, and, in one instance, taking policemen hostage), the activists also effectively made those lower-level officials part of the broader public to whom they were appealing (separating them, as with the prison guards mentioned earlier by Bo Kyi, from the state they were speaking against). This became clearest when Aye Than received a call *from* an SB informing him that he would soon be arrested and hence should go into hiding. The reason for this call, it was explained to me, was that Aye Than had continually highlighted in his public demonstrations how the lower-level police and SBs were abused by the corrupted system of which everyone was a part.

Hence, while it would be a stretch to argue that the activists were able to capture local-level officials, they were able to occasionally generate enough ambivalence to create the conditions of possibility for recurring cycles of social action. For example, in Mattaya (Mandalay division), the activists met with farmers and advised them on how to carry out a plow protest. When the farmers finally held the protest, the police reportedly came, observed, and then quietly told the farmers, "Finish this up quickly and we can go home." As a plow protest is not simply a symbolic event but depends on a material component (actually seeding a field), the farmers saw the completion of their protest not simply as a public performance against authority but also as getting one step closer to harvesting crops. There was clearly risk and ambiguity here: were the farmers simply being silenced under the pretext of police solidarity or acquiescence? The farmers found out during harvesting season, when they were able to reap what they sowed without interference from the authorities. This does not officially guarantee their renewed ownership of the land, but they knew that, for that time being at least, the police were not against them.

Conclusion

This review of the activists' lives has illustrated how resistance and refusal operate in a quasi-dialectical relationship in which stances of refusal and moments of resistance together constitute a "politics of maneuver." For Antonio Gramsci, who coined the terms "war of position" and "war of maneuver," those deploying the latter naturally acknowledge that strategies that rely on direct confrontation with sovereign power will likely fail. Wars of maneuver hence involve, as we have seen, resistance strategies that instigate sovereign power into responses that provokers can mediatize and circulate to other publics (more on this in chapters 3 and 4) all while they leverage tensions and contradictions within the broader governmental assemblage (such as by cultivating local agents) to constrain sovereign vengeance.

Moreover, my reformulation of refusal focalizes longer time scales that in turn emphasize survival, endurance, and maneuver with evolving contexts. Refusal not only "often begins well before . . . utterance[s] or act[s], and extends far beyond the moment of behavioral or verbal proclamation" but by looking beyond "overt power contests" (Sobo 2016, 342) incorporates new spaces and subjects. In the interregna of resistance engagements, activists fortify their own positions (by which I mean sustaining their lives as refusers) by building solidarity through living together and enduring marginalization (rather than building that solidarity only through heroic affect-laden protests).

The next two chapters will delve more deeply into specific tactics—plow protests and cursing ceremonies. The following chapter will focus more on direct action, through the case of the plow protests; chapter 4 looks at the inverse, the cosmological time scales invoked by occult cursing ceremonies, while also showing how they nest into broader strategies of refusal.

CHAPTER 3

Plow Protests

A COPPER MINE'S WORK is both monstrous and hypnotic. It is monstrous when you are watching from land that belonged to your kin for generations and now belongs to a foreign-backed military-owned conglomerate that has displaced your family, given you inadequate compensation, and likely poisoned your surrounding environment with their mine. This was the case for farmers in Seh-deh Village in Letpataung in central Burma's Sagaing Region. In June 2016, Ko Taw, Soe Aung, and I met them at their protest camp, a minute's walk from the village. We stood and looked far across a road barred by razor wire, watching the mine work. Trucks took dirt down from the scalped top of Letpataung Mountain. Other trucks took copper ore to the processing plant that the villagers call the Acid Factory. Still other trucks moved the opposite direction to dump the refuse dirt on what were once the village's fields. Back and forth and back and forth and back and forth—there was constant movement, but in its inexorable repetition it seemed almost static, like listening to a record skip forever. We stood in silence.

After walking back to the village, Soe Aung led us into Daw Win Yee's house compound, where he was greeted affectionately by the dozen people, mostly women and children, awaiting his arrival. Some lounged on the raised pallet that is common in rural Myanmar homes, others sat on plastic chairs or on benches around a table. Win Yee, a model of the casual host in a ripped blouse whose gaping hole exposed her belly, boisterously berated Soe Aung for being away too long. He spat casually on the gravel ground and explained his absence by relaying that things were bad in Mattaya, the area one hundred miles away in Mandalay Region mentioned in the previous chapter. A temporarily successful plow protest suddenly seemed imperiled: the crony from Great Wall Company had returned from abroad, and the farmers did not know if they would have their lands stolen again. Soon, Soe Aung had stripped off his T-shirt and was scratching his back on the house's support pole like a sweaty cat, still holding forth about developments elsewhere. Soe Aung had not been home to Yangon in three years; he had been going from Letpadaung to Mandalay to Letpadan—the latter a site of the student protest discussed in chapter 2—and back to Mattaya (with two stints in prison along the way). He even told me that when he got the call to join the protest in Letpadaung he was around the corner from his mother's house in Yangon's *hsin-kyay-boun* but did not even return to collect his things. He just went straight to the bus station, never looking back. While this was meant, I took it, to convey the urgency of the struggle, it also perhaps betrayed the difficulty of leaving loved ones behind. Nevertheless, Soe Aung had remained on the move, back and forth, back and forth, mimicking the copper coming from the mine. But unlike the copper, he also seemed at home here in Seh-deh; the following day I would meet a three-year-old who was named after him.

Letpataung—the object of the protest that had ultimately led to the court-compound shirt burning outlined in the introduction—had been a flash point in Myanmar for as long as the country had been in transition and had hence become exemplary of its time of protests. Further, Letpadaung popularized cursing ceremonies (to be examined in the following chapter) that not only circulated to other contemporaneous movements around Burma but informed the anticoup uprising as well. Hence, Letpadaung serves as a point of entry into the types of movements in which peasants across the country defy those in power (state agencies, cronies, even the military), establish protest zones, and occupy lands to which they have no explicit legal "rights." The peasants occasionally succeed, often lose, and more often are left unsure of the outcome, but they continue to mobilize. How do these actions, movements, protests, and events work?

The first half of the chapter examines occupations of space, such as the plow protest (*htun-doun taiq-pwe*), in which the displaced return to plow their own land to materially and symbolically reclaim it. Ethnography of these events and their aftermath illuminates how Burmese peasants understand land ownership, which in turn provides insights into how they conceive of rights in what I will call a reticulate fashion. The latter part of the chapter explores the relationships that activists have with their subaltern clients, probing the ethical challenges they navigate as they endeavor to be exemplary strugglers.

Land over the Ages

Despite dispossession having happened to many of them decades before, farmers were able to mobilize thousands of small-scale land uprisings across Myanmar during the transition period. This speaks to land's cultural importance—not just as a means of subsistence (many farmers told me they wanted their children to exit farming and get better jobs) but also as a material object that enables formation of "quotidian communities" (Simmons 2016). Peasant protesters come back together after dispossession because they as individuals share historical relationships with a specific land plot and because they are motivated to reconnect due to their broader cultural relationship with the land as a provider of life to the broader community (as discussed in the farmer cartoons in chapter 1). Land even mediates the relationship that *non*producers have with the movements, imbuing feelings of empathy in observing publics in Myanmar as they connect with protesters through their own feelings about land. This section discusses the history of land regimes in Burma, outlining the ontologies of land use and possession that ground plow protests while providing more illustration of the general degradation of the political economic conditions introduced in chapter 1.

✳   ✳   ✳

Under Southeast Asian dynastic systems, ecological realities (Rigg 1990, 6–11) meant that land was plentiful but people were dear. Burmese kings attempted to monopolize peasant production of rice paddy, pursuing this monopoly through slave-gathering wars to restock their workforce when individuals fled to the hills or found patrons who could not be fully controlled by kings. Indeed, while kings constantly proclaimed their ownership of "all the water and the lands" (in domains they often imagined as nearly infinite but that waxed and waned in line with regional political exigencies), in extractive terms they were not able to tax many private or monastic-owned lands (Thant Myint-U 2001, 123). As the state could prevent flight to neither open land frontiers nor private patrons, it had interests to "protect" cultivators from debt—although such protections can be interpreted as guarding sovereign assets as much as responding to peasant needs. Further, while lords taxed large landholders and rich merchants, the poor were wholly exempted by law (122). The upshot here is that while peasants never achieved rights to land, they evaded many forms of coercion.

When the British colonized Burma they sought to formally subsume peasants within capitalist circuitry by enclosing common resources and inducting peasants into the cash economy (Scott 1972, 25–26). As John Furnivall, former colonial officer turned scholar, put it, "By the end of the [nineteenth] century [the Burmese] had less money to spend, but there were many things on which they had to spend money" (1956, 114–15). Central to this form of subsumption was the incorporation of land into a private property regime. This process involved a double move in which the *ways* that bodies were sedentarized generated the conditions of possibility for their *subsequent* dispossession: peasants were fixed in place such that they became vulnerable to consequent displacement, a displacement that was channeled into other productive spaces—hence extending the "rice frontier" and turning Burma into Asia's "rice bowl."

To accomplish this objective the British sought to eliminate the earlier legal heterogeneity of space (some private and some state) and of people within it (some taxable and some not).

The first step was to change land regulation, making *all* lands taxable, a move justified by mobilizing the mostly ceremonial and symbolic dynastic declarations about the king owning "all the lands and waters" (Thant Myint-U 2001, 229–30). The British imported a different conception of land ownership, and by extension sovereignty: while the Burmese version permitted an overlapping and heterogeneous admixture of ownership, which consequently restricted alienation, the British imagined ownership as indivisible and land as alienable. Let us consider the numerous ways that land was (and still is, as we will see) embedded in various social relationships.

For an average cultivator, a key sociopolitical concept organizing use of land has long been *dama-ucha*,[1] which is a Burmese phrase literally meaning "the knife's first cut." This phrase is invoked by cultivators to emphasize that *clearing* land confers ownership—although such claims have always been socially attenuated: clearers had claims on the land as long as they cultivated it (and after twelve years it could be considered ancestral land). Another person could freely use the land, however, if the original clearer abandoned it. More centrally, "possession . . . was never absolute against the community; cultivated land could be taken up for house sites, and house sites for a monastery"

(Furnivall 1956, 109–10). Toe Hla finds that while commoners could write mutually binding land contracts, that land could always be appropriated by the king (1987, 55, 231–32).

Conversely, though, tenant protections existed; Furnivall reports that "in practice [ancestral] land could be alienated, but alienation was never final; any member of the family could at any time redeem it" (1956, 110). Such peasant protections were reflected in law as well. Toe Hla found that "moneylenders were . . . forbidden to sue indebted peasant farmers during the growing season . . . suggesting that the kings gave protection to peasant farmers" (1987, 8–9, also 120–21). Moreover, Adas (2011, 28), citing the *Henzada Gazetter*, reports that under Burmese kings, "the vendor had the right to repurchase the land should he decide to do so within ten years of the sale. The buyer could not ordinarily resell the land without the original owner's permission."[2]

Thus, land was not alienable, not considered a possession in an abstracted way but determined by sets of relations between cultivator, nature, and several broader communities (local and translocal). All these relations had to be continually renewed. Indeed, Furnivall stresses that before the British, "land was still for the most part unappropriated, a free gift of nature to the whole community" (1909, 555) but a gift that nonetheless had to be perpetually transformed through labor; land may have been a gift, but it was one that became *valuable* only through the application of the cultivator's knife. And that relationship—and hence the value realized in land—was valorized within a broader set of concentric social relations: with one's neighbors, then with one's village, then with one's regional patron, and perhaps ultimately with the king. When those relationships ceased being tolerable *and* when alternative land was plentiful, it often made sense to move on.

In the eyes of the colonial administrator, such moving on was, effectively, tax evasion. Furnivall outlines a host of "methods by which [British] Government sought to establish a sense of property in land" (1909, 555). Fixing property allowed the British to extract land rent (Furnivall 1939, 101–10), although given such significant mobility and the corresponding recession of cultivated land into jungle, early-era colonial administration land surveys were deemed more expensive than they were even worth (109). Such efforts did, however, facilitate the empire's ambitious transformation of the fecund Ayeyawaddy delta areas into the world's largest rice producer. In the half century from 1855 to 1905, annual exported paddy went from 162,000 tons to 2,000,000 (Adas 2011, 58).

This endeavor was achieved by inducing peasants from upper Burma to leave their natal homes and social networks and go hundreds of miles south to clear land and fight malaria amid never-ending swamps. What made such a miserable venture imaginable, let alone desirable? Adas (2011) focuses on the payoffs, which were vast and thus alluring. Brown, conversely, stresses the push factors ("drought, food shortage, and occasional famine") that made the delta seem an "escape" for "desperate cultivators" from the north; indeed, "the number migrating into the delta at any particular point in these decades reflected the food position in the north" (2013, 36). Although he does not emphasize it, Brown admits that colonial destruction of Burmese society may have pushed cultivators south. For Thant Myint-U, British annexation meant "nothing less than a complete dismantling of existing institutions of political authority and the undermining of many established structures of social organization" (2001, 2–3). He provides evidence in forms both legal (the explosion in land litigation cases waged between peasants in Upper Burma; see page 232) and extralegal (thousands of "bandits" roamed the countryside in the years after British occupation; see page 7). Michael Aung-Thwin defines British rule as "order without meaning" and describes violence against peasant life in the form of British counterinsurgency tactics that involved resettling people in what were, effectively, internment camps (1985, 252). Hence the British, whether intentionally or by benefitting from one of the unintended felicities of imperialism's brutality, deterritorialized bodies to constitute the engine that generated a vast transformation of ecology and economy.

World War II, however, precipitated massive capital destruction, decimating infrastructure, the agrarian sector, and what little industry existed (Brown 2013). The British beat a hasty retreat, leaving an underresourced constitutional state to nationalize all land as the way of effectively transferring it back from moneylenders to cultivators. But as that state immediately faced numerous insurgencies mobilized along ideological and ethnic lines, it struggled to govern beyond its capital or make policies that peasants perceived as relevant or effectual (Badgley 1965; Nash 1965). Burma's military emerged as an ambitious and proficient actor (Callahan 2003), ultimately building a hybrid rentier state (Prasse-Freeman 2012). This means that while fighting off those many insurgencies, the military-state apparatus redeployed rents extracted from natural resource exploitation to develop its own organizational capacity.

As importantly, and consistent with comparative research on such states (Tilly 1985; Bayart 2009), it used those rents to foreclose the ideal-typical citizen-state dialectic in which states rely on citizens for tax revenue, and citizens rely on states for public goods (including security). Because Burma's military state did not depend on subjects for tax revenue, it perceived its nominal citizens as populations to be managed through force and intimidation. Amid its consolidation of power, the military state made a set of bargains with this populace: rural dwellers got to work land but were compelled to give up much of their rice yield to the state; urbanites got cheap rice, but there was no competent industrialization and no growth. Both groups were denied political freedoms. While the military government continued its pro-farmer rhetoric and even enacted directives that appeared to support farmers—such as giving land-use permission to any farmer who worked a plot of land for five years— the military also violated those bargains at will. In the Delta area, for instance, thousands of farmers were dispossessed of their land after not delivering their rice yield quotas (Boutry et al. 2017), resulting in "nearly ten million people largely dependent on laboring wages alone" by 2000 (Brown 2013, 185).

Moreover, various state agencies, including the military, were encouraged to seize land to enhance their own agendas. The military often took land for cantonments or for local commanders to grow crops to support troops or enrich themselves. Often, stolen land merely stood idle as military commanders failed at business endeavors. In other cases, the state pursued massive infrastructure projects that led to the displacement of thousands of villagers (Bosson 2007). Government agencies were meant to establish their own "development" projects, meaning that ill-equipped ministries grabbed land from farmers and attempted to establish industrial projects (such as sugar production), with predictably disastrous results (Woods 2014). After the turn in 1990 to a quasi-free-market model, "crony" businesses were welcomed to implement government-backed extraction schemes or simply grab land as part of a speculation strategy, declaring that land would go to a project (a factory, for instance) but then never taking steps to develop it. As all this occurred, "in order to reach even higher paddy output levels, military commanders encouraged farmers to cultivate on what was termed 'VFV' [vacant fallow and virgin land] as well as on reserve forest land" (Mark 2016, 448).

In the wake of these dislocations, peasants were forced to scramble into new relationships with land and various institutions or patrons. A significant part of my fieldwork was spent looking at these cultivators' documents—land-tax receipts, agricultural loan recording booklets, and complaint letters—that inscribed these maneuvers. The letters weave narratives out of the various documents and the communities' respective histories, describing the unjust processes through which *dama-ucha* (original clearer) cultivators were turned into sharecroppers (*thi-sa*,[3] literally "eaters of the fruit"). Typically, military battalions or state agencies would claim land as their own, dismissing the inhabitants. In their place they would invite poor landless peasants or farmers displaced from *other* areas to work expropriated fields, forcing the original inhabitants to hunt for sharecropping or wage work elsewhere. This especially occurred when wealthy farmers, connected with the state or military but lacking its direct coercive force, dealt with poorer displaced farmers (Boutry et al. 2017, 230).

By contrast, state agents (whether soldiers or government officials) often did not bother physically evicting original owners; less concerned with adverse possession claims, they eschewed searches for outside substitutes and simply invited the just-dispossessed farmers "back" to work their own fields but with a vastly weakened political-economic position. This form of what Marx called "primary accumulation"—in which the ownership of the means of production is stripped from peasants—drastically altered the cultivators' relationships with the land. They still retained an intimate relationship with it in many cases, and they even described themselves as owning it—as we will see—but they had become proletarianized as *thi-sa*.

This set of relationships meant that when the political context evolved— farmers relayed to me how they had heard rumors that President Thein Sein (2011–2015) had declared that they would have lands returned to them, providing discursive cover for their attempts to get land back—farmers were eager to seek redress, a topic to which we now turn.

Plowing Becomes Protest

I have translated *htun-doun daiqpwe*[4] as "plow protests" because this is how the activists described them in English and because the term is alliteratively eloquent. But the actual phrase in Burmese does not include the term for protest at all. Protest is *sanda-pya*[5] (to show one's desire or wish), while *daiqpwe* is "battle" (as in war). Hence, *htun-doun daiqpwe* could more accurately be described as "plow battles" or the less literal "plow struggles."[6] The literal translation directs our attention to these acts as a form of attack—or to use the vocabulary of social movement studies: *direct action*, the essence of which is, as the late anarchist anthropologist David Graeber notes, "the insistence, when faced with structures of unjust authority, on acting *as if one is already free*." In such situations, "one does not solicit the state. One does not even necessarily make a grand gesture of defiance" (2009, 203; emphasis added).

Indeed, plow protests must include plowing but only *might* come to include actions recognizable as protesting (with signs, protest paraphernalia, flags, and chants, for example). If protest is thought of as a performance of resistance (meant in the theatrical sense, as a representation) as well as a performative (an enactment of that claim through the occupation of land and plowing of it), a *htun-doun daiqpwe* may involve only the latter. Because of the material engagements necessary to execute any plowing—involving as it does the pulling of a harrow across a field and then the planting of seeds in the prepared soil—the plowing as a sign can be read as simply denoting plowing itself. Here we can recall the "plausibly deniable" protests introduced in chapter 2, in which cars mysteriously broke down and shoelaces came untied in the middle of the road after the 2021 coup or in which, fourteen years earlier during the Saffron Revolution, those forced to walk to work came to resemble a protest march (Prasse-Freeman 2012).

But of course eliminating the protest signs does not in itself strip the plowing of its indexical content; it can be precisely *because* those protest signs are absent that makes the events potent as acts of resistance. This is because of the mutual joint attention—the "I-know-that-you-know-that-I-know" (Kockelman 2013, 48–50)—to the sedimented cultural-historical meanings created by any plowing: to plow a field is to claim it, to even own it. Plowing without attendant protest metapragmatically calls attention to the ownership relationship that is being asserted: the plowers are consciously *not* performing a symbolic act, such as when holding a protest march, that would act as a disruption, a beckoning to be heard so that negotiations could be commenced. Rather, plowing acts *as if* such other audiences and interlocutors are unratified overhearers (in Goffman's [1981] sense) of an event that marks a relationship between only the farmers and their land. Of course, such a metapragmatic effect (Silverstein 1993) can be *intended even as it is disavowed.*

Indeed, as holding the plowing indexes commitment that intimidates local officials, the latter may look away—as was conveyed in the story from Mattaya from chapter 2 in which the police urged the plowers to finish up quickly. Looking away is only available, made possible, in the first place by the lack of enunciative marking by the peasant plowers; conversely, if they hold a formal rally, complete with paraphernalia and signboards, marching, and speeches, that is also videotaped and uploaded to Burmese Facebook, then security

FIGURE 3.1. Plow protest collage includes (clockwise from top left): Farmers amassed with flags on poles; a local activist exhorts the farmers to action; tax receipts from past years used as documentation to ground claims to land; and Mandalay-based activist stands among the farmers. Source: Ko Taw, 2015.

forces are compelled to respond (fig. 3.1). If, however, the peasants plow land silently, normally, as if the land is theirs, then local officials can themselves employ that logic of plausible deniability and pretend not to see. If such silence forecloses a response on the part of security forces, then those farmers tactically acting "as if" the land was theirs all along (*why would we protest for something that we presuppose is ours?*) and those who truly believe a new democratic day had come and hence were permitted to return to their previous lands (as we will see later in a case from Kantbalu) would never be differentiated in praxis; both would simply plow their lands. A local farmer union leader in Ma-U-Bin (Ayeyawaddy Region) summarized this perfectly, telling me, "MPs [members of parliament] even [declared] that one could plow one's own land. So, what we were doing did not involve thinking yet about doing a plow protest. We didn't attach 'plow protest' to our actions. It was just that the farmers went back and plowed their lands. [But if one] looks at what we did, the name 'plow protest' can be attached to it" [*Bse*].

The following describes groups of farmers who attempted various subversions of the plow protest and how they encountered ambiguous success and dispiriting failures.

> Date: 31-12-2015
> Victory Rally for Those Who Dare to Fight
> Shwegondaing Village Tract, Magwe 100 Village, Sintgu Township
> In 1972–1973 the BSPP [Burma Socialist Program Party] dictatorship government was in existence, and in order to open an agricultural science school they tyrannically and unjustly took the land. Next the BSPP government rented out the area to unconnected farmers, and the owner of Weitha Malaw Company, the crony Great Wall Tin Maung, wanted to put it in his hand. He seized the land tyrannically, and he held it for over 40 years. And so [the farmers] went from having a life where they owned land and paddy to becoming landless slaves. These farmers' families' lives are tattered and torn. Therefore, on the eve of 2016, today we enlist a plow protest, a battle against land theft, a group activity for all. Those with the courage to fight will inevitably be victorious and not miss the mark (we must be victorious in this revolution). (Aye Than's Facebook post)

Ambiguous Success

In late April 2015 I joined CDI activists on a trip to Mattaya, the village tract about an hour north of Mandalay along Route 31 that goes to Sintgu, and other destinations northeast of Mandalay along the Ayeyawaddy River. Farmers in Mattaya had held a plow protest, and many of them were arrested, so CDI comrades based in Mandalay—Aye Than and Lay Gyi—planned to visit them to gauge their progress, answer questions, and provide advice. Ko Taw and Teza wanted to come along as well, so we all sat cross-legged in the back of the

FIGURE 3.2. Signboards, mimicking state signage (white lettering on red), declare the farmers' ownership of the land by *dama-ucha* (land to the clearer) and declare "No Trespassing." Source: Daniel Ginsburg.

flatbed truck—nine people packed in, some of whom I assumed were farmers who had come to help guide us back out. Lay Gyi, who is tiny enough to do this, curled up and slept with his arm draped across my knee, which I took as a good sign given that I thought he never really cared for my presence. (Maybe he still did not, and this meant he considered me useful only as bedding.)

When we got close, we stopped at a roadside cold-drinks shop as the farmers went ahead on motorbikes to round up people for the meeting. Everyone had *yay-keh-thouq*, an ice-and-condensed-milk snack that also involved jelly, peanuts, and pieces of sandwich bread. I demurred. Aye Than talked with some other farmers, and Ko Taw commented that he loves to watch Aye Than interact with farmers; because Aye Than comes from a tiny farming village, he knows how to speak to them—when to cajole, when to scold. Ko Taw remarked, "He can really yell at them. He will even beat them" [*Eng*].

We piled back into the truck, and after a couple more minutes north, we turned east off the main road and parked, walking along a dirt path that divided large fields (see fig. 3.2). Gathered in and around a large open-air shed, two dozen female farmers and a couple of men sat awaiting our arrival. Laid out in front of us was the typical small spread characteristic of Burmese village hospitality—pickled tea-leaf salad, bananas, processed cakes, and bottled water. We sat. The air was impossibly still, and sweat poured down my chest, turning my light-blue shirt dark. Then there was a miraculous breeze, seemingly from nowhere. I turned to see a middle-aged man fanning me with a small hand fan. I did not demur.

Aye Than spoke first, asking them about the situation, in part to explain things to us visitors (Ko Taw, Teza, and myself). The villagers relayed their stories of hardship, versions of which the activists had heard dozens of times: the land was grabbed thirty years before, after which many became either piece workers (referring to amount harvested) or day workers (referring to time worked), on or off farms. Off-farm work included heavy labor for municipal projects (such as building a dam). One of the women described her daughter's death during this time, which she attributed to diseases and that hard life. In 2013, after the transition began, they sent complaint letters to local officials (they handed us copies), but they did not receive any replies.

After the farmers' first meeting with Aye Than and Lay Gyi, they decided to take further action. The crony Maung Tin had been forced to flee abroad because he was charged with running a private hospital without a license. This itself was a curious event that Aye Than interpreted as a fight between cronies—Maung Tin's competitors had used their own connections with officials to wield the law against him. The farmers saw this as their opportunity and plowed the land, after which the police arrived to encourage them to finish up. I was excited to hear this news: the farmers had made it through a whole harvest cycle; victory had been achieved! But my enthusiasm was dampened by the interpretations provided by the farmers and the activists: they shrugged. This was not really a victory, because the crony could always come back tomorrow and destroy the fields. We would wait and see.

Moreover, at this point the farmers suffered a maddening experience with Burmese justice. In some ways their plow protest was successful, in that they "got the land back," at least to the extent that they had been able to work it, and—critically—were able to reap the harvest, which means from the time of plowing and planting to the time of harvesting they were not accosted by any officials or *lu-gyi* (big people) and were thus able to sell their product. But there was also legal action. The villagers showed us the court documents, in which they were charged under articles 447 and 427 (the parts of the criminal code relating to trespassing and damaging property). The woman with the deceased daughter said that she had to hide from the police when they came to look for her. Eventually she gave in, sick of hiding in paddy fields.

Such stories were common. In a similar plow protest in Thabaung Township (Ayeyawaddy), locals relayed that only by getting arrested through conducting a plow protest were they able to initiate a formal legal investigation into their case; this story recalls the discussion of Arendt in chapter 1 in which in Myanmar subjects become legible to the law only by breaking it. The Thabaung peasants' progression to that point had been fairly standard: in 2012 the farmers formed a group and wrote several letters, none of which led to redress. Even after they appealed to farmers' unions and activists, the land was still not given back, and so the farmers proceeded to the plow protest phase. The decision to do so was not taken lightly. A farmer leader named Min Htun relayed how they weighed the process for several months in 2014, considering whether they would have to go to prison and how to mitigate that outcome: "We made a decision to hold the plow protest, saying that the families who don't end up in prison yet will continue to work the land for those who did [get imprisoned]."

The plow protest got their land returned. But again, this was because "only when we held a plow protest did they come to reexamine this issue, and only after they examined it, was land given back" [Bse]—a process instigated after forty farmers were charged with trespassing and destroying crops. But, surprisingly, these forty did not end up in prison. Min Htun and comrades felt this was because of the way the process captured the attention of other actors (police and legal institutions) whom local officials had to that point excluded from involvement. He explained, "Because there were witnesses and evidence and the witnesses were able to show that the owners had full evidence of ownership, [land was returned]" [Bse]. Although it is hardly a representative case, the story describes a victory achieved through collective action, in which protests acted as disruptive events that unsettled the status quo, opening legal and procedural avenues that should have (according to the law) been available all along.

Plow Protests Gone Bad

In Myay Moun Village, Kantbalu, the story was different. Villagers there were displaced in the 1980s and forced to become sharecroppers elsewhere. But the military battalion that grabbed the land merely rented it to others. In June 2012 the villagers sent their first complaint letter, and they sent six letters in total. As there was no response, they held their plow protest in early April 2014, with one hundred people participating. "We had no choice [but] to plow, because we were getting poorer and poorer and cannot live without a change"

[Bse], one villager said, describing their reasoning. The farmers rented oxen and bought seed, and then they plowed and planted. At first, there was only silence. But weeks later, in the interim between planting and harvesting, authorities and sharecroppers destroyed the villagers' crops. The army fired one hundred warning shots above the farmers in the fields and then set up a cordon around the farmers, trapping them inside the village fields for six days. Ultimately the farmers surrendered, and their village was destroyed in retribution. Because they had to borrow money for the plow protest from their relatives, they became destitute. Only twenty-eight of the hundred were charged—apparently the ones that the authorities considered to be leaders (or, villagers said, the ones authorities did not like). Aye Than and Lay Gyi had helped lead this plow protest and then helped them retain a lawyer for the trial. When we sat together, Aye Than reminded them that losing the investment, failing to regain land, and getting arrested were all risks that the activists had stressed. They nodded glumly. But when I spoke to them later without Aye Than and Lay Gyi present and revisited those losses, I received different responses. Did the villagers actually expect to get arrested? "No." What did they expect? "To get our land back" [Bse].

We drove on to another village—Pay Gyi—and sat in a local farming family's front room. There was no electricity, so we used an emergency battery-powered light to read their letters. They brought us spongy processed cake and *Shark*, a Myanmar-brand energy drink. Nine men from the village were in attendance, and there was a great deal of confusion over their story. When they were not disputing the details among one another, they took many photos of us—perhaps to be used for later appeals, to demonstrate that their cause was so worthy that it attracted urban activists and a foreigner.

Their story began with one saying that in 1985 a company stole their land, which Ko Taw gently suggested was unlikely because that was the socialist era when there were no companies.[7] After much debate, it was established that the military took the land with intentions of building a sugar factory. The villagers were compelled to work as sharecroppers elsewhere for nearly three decades. Recently, however, an army man named Min Zaw invited everyone to the factory, telling them, "You will be happy; we will give the land back to you, all the acres." So they applied for a set of bureaucratic forms from the State Land Records Department and the township administrator and started working the land. In their eyes, working the land was emphatically *not* a plow protest, as they had received permission, and from the military, no less. But then things became complicated: the same forms that they had signed and that they were led to believe transferred their land back to them had also been signed by the *other* sharecroppers, the ones who had replaced them during those many years of dispossession. Both groups had reasonable claims to the land: the first under *dama-ucha* (first clearer) logic, the second because of their recent and repeated relationships with the land, thereby implicitly invoking a land-to-the-tiller logic.[8] In the end, a more superior military official annulled the first deal and arrested the farmers for trespassing and destruction of property that was arguably their own. The activists did not really understand all the details, but it had been a long day and we had a long drive back to Mandalay.

The car ride back was quiet. The cases illustrated the misalignment of goals and material realities between some activists and those whom they represent. The activists had repeatedly told the farmers that they would have to prepare for prison and expect that their crops could be destroyed; the farmers, always ready for the worst, nonetheless seemed to see the activists as patrons and protectors who ultimately would prevent such devastating outcomes. Indeed, in my examination of plow protests across the country (from reading NGO reports and speaking with leaders of farmer advocacy organizations), I found that restitution was rare, and even when it did come it was often incomplete or inadequate: some farmers who received verbal or even written orders from officials found that those declarations went unrecognized by officials at different levels of the state; farmers who received compensation for stolen land found it to be incommensurate with what they lost. Sometimes the activists' "brokerage" work crafted a bridge for peasants to participate in contentious politics that merely exposed them to greater violence and more extreme dispossession.

Owning Something You Lack Rights To?

What do these protests tell us about the way Burmese peasants conceive of their relationships with land? I asked a dispossessed farmer from Mandalay Region who was participating in plow protests, in Burmese, "Do you own this land [from which you were displaced]?" He replied, "Yes." When I then asked if he "had a right [*akwint-ayay*] to get the land back," he said, "No. . . . We will try." I heard much the same from other farmers as well.

How can one own something to which they lack rights? It could have been a miscommunication—I meant "right" and perhaps the farmer heard "opportunity" (more on this in chapter 5). But activists and colleagues supplied other possible interpretations as well. Din, a Burmese academic, suggested that "[the farmers] no longer have rights to own land recognized by the government but they still have the right of ownership inherited from and recognized by the community and ancestors." This suggests that rights are highly reticulate in Burma, if the phrase "rights" is appropriate at all. It may be better to say that a person does not simply have *one* single right to land but they have "rights," plural: rights in relation to neighbors; rights in relation to ancestors; and rights in relation the state, the latter relationship being subject to an entirely different set of constraints than the former ones. Indeed, in this situation, in which the state is both strong and capricious, the rights that a farmer can enjoy in that particular relationship become diminished to the point of being extinguished altogether. But the relationship with the land may not cease: that relationship of ownership continues. One can lose rights to land vis-à-vis the state while maintaining them with the community, which (a) remembers and (b) lacks the coercive force of the state to dispossess the claimant. The state has the power to eliminate the right but not the ownership—farmers are still the ones who put their blood and sweat into the soil.

This conversation made me recall an exchange I had with Ko Taw during our first visit with dispossessed farmers in November 2014. He clarified the need for precision when discussing the material affordances and circumscriptions relating to land use: "Don't use *ya-baing-kwint*[9] [entitlement] because the farmers have not learned about it. To give land to your children, you have *ya-baing-kwint*, but if you talk about your land, you don't have it, only *paing-saing-hmu*[10] (ownership)" [*Eng*]. It seems that while one is entitled to confer land to offspring—a relationship in which obligations and responsibilities are clear enough to warrant such an unequivocal assertion—one cannot *generally* describe oneself as being entitled to that land, as such a phrase implies a set of *undefined* and *omnilateral* relations for which "entitlement" may not be the most appropriate descriptor. To wit, when the state owns all the land, as it has officially since 1953, what does it mean to say one is *entitled* to a piece of it? For this reason, Ko Taw recommends using what he perceives as a less assertive descriptive: *paing-saing-hmu* (ownership). This explanation may help provide insight into Ko Taw's assertion that farmers have 'not learned about' the phrase, which I take to mean that farmers have not been acculturated into using rights or entitlements in such a general way, as applying unilaterally to an infinite number of referents.

How to make sense of this comparatively? Christian Lund argues that rights and authority cannot exist without each other. He holds that that "rights do not simply flow from authority but also constitute it" and that in this "dialectic," "rights and political authority are contemporaneous, and the control exercised by institutions over resources and political subjectivities does not represent a pre-existing authority. It produces authority. Conversely, effective rights do not represent pre-existing natural rights. They are political constructions and achievements" (2016, 1202). Lund "therefore understand[s] property as a legitimized claim to something of value sanctioned by some form of political authority" (1204). "Property" is the name given to the relationship of mutual recognition between the owner and political authority vis-à-vis some object (land, for instance).

A question raised by the land struggles and reflections described earlier, however, is whether such models adequately describe the relations that exist in places such as Burma, where the relationship between the governed and the state (or other entity of de facto authority) is based on *mis*recognition. The ruler asserts a form of complete ownership that the governed do not ratify and in fact understand as a sovereign assertion they must vociferously refuse, even if it is one to which they must sometimes accede. The governed in turn engage in forms of use and exchange of land that rulers claim are illegal: Boutry and colleagues (2017, 106–7) found that 36 percent of the households studied in its contemporary survey had engaged in formally illegal land transactions—a general phenomenon that can be adduced across Burmese society. Faxon (2023) finds that farmers intentionally avoid legal formalization; Roberts and Rhoads (2022) demonstrate how urban arrangements often benefit from legal evasion; and Metro (2014) shows how a culture of evasion leads to a general avoidance of writing things. I have found that activists spend more time avoiding the law than seeking it (Prasse-Freeman 2015b).

The consequence of this misrecognition means that multiple reticulate relations persist astride the state. As Din said, farmers may lack rights vis-à-vis the state while retaining them vis-à-vis their neighbors—or their ancestors, as the cursing protests in chapter 4 will suggest. And as Geertz reminds us, this has long been the case in Southeast Asian contexts: "When one considers that not only 'kings,' but also 'gods,' 'villages,' 'families,' and 'individuals' were said to own 'everything'—the same 'everything'—the necessity for a less elementary view of 'possession' becomes apparent" (1980, 127).

These reticulate relations evoke Roberto Esposito's concept of "communitas" (2010). Esposito reads community as a shared gift (*munus*) that the state's social contract contaminates. It does so by *severing* horizontal relations between people and reorienting them as disconnected spokes reattached to the state hub. Property, in this imaginary, is hence not only an icon that reflects the relation with the state but a reification into material form of the emptiness of the community. The Burmese version of rights—as property ownership without rights—suggests an alternative version of property, in which rhizomatic and overlapping claims sediment in the land, thus making community meaningful, a gift that sustains members who constitute it.

Political Economy of Activist Life

These reflections on community direct focus to the relationships between activists and peasants—especially given Aye Than's relatively callous reminder to Myay Moun's ruined peasants that they should have expected failure. The farmers' material destitution brings attention not just to issues pertaining to the differential risk borne by activists and peasants but also to the ethics of the activist political economy.

Becoming Patrons/Becoming Clients

Approximately nine months before the 2015 general election, Ko Taw told me that he and an array of comrades (members of the vague 88 Generation of activists) were being recruited by a new political party called the Farmers' Development Party (FDP) to stand as that party's MPs. Ko Taw assured me that they would not join the party—they were skeptical of the FDP members, as many of them were exiles, and as such their perspectives may not align. Ko Taw had earlier told me that the inside and outside political groups distrusted one another—the insiders thought the exiles were going to nightclubs and eating cheese (emblems of foreign luxury), and using international resources for their own benefit; the exiles, conversely, thought the insiders were radicals and not realistic. "When they met at the airport they hugged and kissed but then didn't really see each other again," Ko Taw explained. Or when they did, the outside groups, still able to mobilize resources from international domains, "try to influence us insiders with money, saying 'we can support you if you do like this, but you should not be radical; you should not support plow protests.' And they want to organize us so that they can go to the government and say that they have this big network, so they can do it for their own glory" [Eng]. Nonetheless, because Ko Taw and other activists were interested in finding out about the party's intentions, they agreed to attend a meeting.

The gathering was on a Sunday evening, and we arrived at a pocket of the *hsin-kyay-boun* that was neither factory nor slum but a complex called Golden

Park, a hotel-spa with understated but luxurious low-slung bungalow-style buildings painted in reds and browns—a complex both wholly out of place in this peri-urban industrial area and yet increasingly present in such spaces. Other cars soon pulled up, and people wearing formal blouses or meticulously ironed white shirts with matching insignia pins over their left breast pockets exited vehicles and stood with rigid posture and smiles, casting a stark contrast against the generally disheveled activists who arrived in twos and threes and milled around the parking lot smoking cigarettes, watching the well-heeled with mild, if respectful, bemusement.

We were ushered into a banquet hall, and the activists were directed to sit on one side, while the FDP officials filled in the other. Snacks were presented and small talk ensued. The seats filled up, but one in the middle was left empty, an absence that seemed tactical: the supporting team greeted the guests while the leader's supreme status was conveyed through his late arrival. He eventually entered the room and called the meeting to order.

Everyone introduced themselves, with those on the FDP side declaring their name and region, and the activists each narrating their own histories (including their organizations, prison time, and activities) in the struggle. The party head then gave his speech, the upshot of which was that he was not trying to recruit the activists to be party members but to ask them to provide the party with advice and insights into how to better serve the people, especially in areas where there are no farmers. It seemed this amounted to trying to recruit them without saying as much. I looked over and saw Ko Taw checking football scores on his phone.

Food arrived; whiskey bottles and beer cans were cracked. Toasts were made to new friendships. While we were eating, a friend from a labor union sitting next to me whispered, "I have been to many hotels, and this is very good food" [Bse]. While we were appreciating the lavish spread, attendants brought out gift bags for each guest, which everyone took without surprise; most placed the bags behind them on their chair, but others opened the bags and read the party's platform contained within. Along with the document was a dress shirt, a collection of 8 x 11 glossy photos of FDP ceremonies (including images of meetings, close-ups of the leaders giving speeches, and garlands being placed on executive members by school children), and an envelope containing 30,000 kyat (USD 25).

After the dinner concluded I caught a ride downtown with some AAPP members. None of them were impressed; one said he would not support them but was happy to eat the dinner and drink the alcohol. He also suspected that they had nefarious intentions—that they were trying to siphon votes from the NLD. The next week I discussed with Ko Taw about the FDP and what had come after that strange meeting. I was particularly interested in the cash: what was the money for? Ko Taw had considered it as well: it was far too much for carfare, but it was too little to be a bribe: "If he had put 1 lakh [100,000 kyat] or 2 lakh in the envelope, it is too obvious; it is a bribe. But this was a *promise* of real bribes to come." Ko Taw mentioned that the Lady—he referred to Suu Kyi by her English nickname—had even once given him pocket money. I inquired about the meaning of such gifts. "So many meanings: One, for [my] organizing; two, for persuading me to be a follower; three, for just helping; four, for bribing . . ." He trailed off. His ellipsis suggested that rather than choosing between altruistic and opportunistic motivations, all were simultaneously in play.

The experience with the FDP introduces the fraught domain of activism's political economy. What are the appropriate ways to pay for activism—what kinds of gifts, payments, and patronage can be accepted by those who spend so much of their time refusing? Who funds the trips—who pays for the B.E. and related lubricants of activist affect—and who decides those trips are necessary? And what about the clients, those poor people who are being served—are they permitted to pay? Alternatively, what about those who *can* pay, can support the activists: given how capital accumulation in Myanmar almost unavoidably requires imbrication in corrupted systems and exploitative arrangements, can patrons be ethically cultivated? Regarding these "farmers" and their party, the fact that the activists took meetings with them spoke not only to their willingness to forge alliances and build networks but to the simple economic imperative to accumulate sufficient funds, which were always fungible, to do their activities and make a living. No relationship with the FDP ever formed—in the next meeting the president implied that activism was less relevant in the new era, to which the activists vehemently objected, and things degenerated from there—but similar relationships were essential for activists to continue their work.

After four months with the group, I finally felt comfortable enough to inquire how CDI funded itself. I was told that it was supported entirely by local people. But while "local people" evokes images of passing the hat around the neighborhood, it became clear that there were two different constituencies embedded in the term—basic supporters and a small group of wealthy donors.

Take Thein Aung Myint, whose prison visit is described in chapter 2. When he was incarcerated for leading, respectively, a protest against the absence of municipal services and one against the military murder of a journalist,[11] CDI members went around the *hsin-kyay-boun* and to contacts in Yangon more broadly and collected 5,000 kyats from here, 10,000 kyats from there, and so on to be given to Thein Aung Myint's family. In situations like these, Teza might donate his truck, used in his ice business, to take the crew up north.

But there were also larger patrons. The economic liberalization after the 1988 uprisings allowed some who were sympathetic to the cause but not politically active to do well in business—these people supported the activists as patrons. For instance, every time we visited Mandalay we slept in the compound of U Gyi, a successful businessman whose house included twelve rooms and a garage the size of an airplane hangar. Despite this wealth, his activist bona fides were solid: he left the NLD in the 1990s when military-state pressure was circumscribing the NLD's ability to carry out grassroots activities but had since worked with local groups around Mandalay and even staged a solo protest that made national news.[12] In addition to lodging, U Gyi provided essentials such as food, beer, cigarettes, and transportation costs for the visiting activists. He also took responsibility for supporting operating costs of activist networks based out of Mandalay, particularly the one working with farmers led by Aye Than and Lay Gyi.

U Gyi's commitment to activism is what permitted him to act as patron. Activists would not cultivate relationships with just anyone. For instance, CDI in Yangon and their comrades in Mandalay worked a great deal on maintaining interreligious peace after the 2012 internecine violence in Rakhine state and associated anti-Muslim pogroms across the country. Because of this, the Organization of Islamic Countries (OIC) tried to give them money for interfaith activities. Ko Taw described how such a narrowing of his platform would constitute a betrayal of the larger cause for which they were working: "OIC tried to give me money to work for all Muslims in Myanmar. But I said that these are not my only people. If people learn that I have taken money from them, no one will trust me anymore."

Finally, the activists also self-funded their work. Ko Taw was credentialed as a "master trainer" with an international educational institution, and he gave trainings to NGOs and foundations for which he earned $100 per day. On good months he worked four or five days, and the revenue allowed him to fund his work, which really meant paying back the people from whom he had borrowed to support his activities and his family. Teza, for his part, subsidized his activities through his family's shop, while Thurein ran the curry stand in the front of his house and eventually rented out his entire top floor (consequently evicting CDI).

These funding sources allowed the activists to develop an ethic in which they could reject contractual, instrumental monetary relations with those they assisted. They looked up or horizontally for support rather than down, which they condemned. This latter form, of soliciting funds from their clients, was called *pyat-sa*,[13] literally "cutting and eating," which evokes the staunching of a flow.[14] In the most egregious version of *pyat-sa*, activists engage with local people, convince them that some wealthy entity nearby is causing them misery, and then become their representative in negotiations with that entity (a form of corruption that the MyoTha businessman tried to create but which Ko Taw rejected, as described in the previous chapter). Keeping both entities separated from one another, the *pyat-sa* activist agrees on a monetary settlement with the elite and then gives to the villagers whatever he believes will placate them. He then pockets the difference.

Pyat-sa became an issue of contention within the activists' larger network when in 2016 farmers from MyoTha relayed to Ko Taw that Aye Than was accepting their money. Aye Than maintained that this was just the farmers' suspicion and that he did not do this. But as Aye Than neither engaged in any alternative income-generating activities nor had English skills that would allow him to participate in the donor economy, and as such was entirely dependent on activism, it was not an unreasonable suspicion. Ko Taw then made inquiries and learned that Aye Than was securing compensation from other communities in Mandalay Region, from which he took a percentage that the farmers and Aye Than deemed fair. When confronted about this, Aye Than defended himself: "Because who would be afraid of the farmers without activists?" [*Bse*]. Aye Than described the payment as reasonable returns for a service. Ko Taw replied, "You are acting like a *pwe-sa*"[15]—meaning "broker," the derogatory term given to the person who sets up social and economic transactions from which he parasitically extracts a percentage. "I don't know if U Gyi knows about this. I will ask him" [*Bse*], Ko Taw muttered to himself, implying he would ensure that the patron knew about the actions of the client.

While Aye Than's actions can be construed as a milder permutation of *pyat-sa* (milder because at least the economy was made transparent to the villagers), Ko Taw still felt it critical to discourage this behavior to protect the reputation of grassroots activists. In fact, two local journalists who often wrote land-grab and protest stories told me that they spoke with such activists at every protest they covered but then wrote them out of their accounts because they did not respect or trust the activists' intentions.[16] Some former political prisoners, whose imprisonment was from direct struggle against the military regime as student activists, were also suspicious of these activists (Prasse-Freeman 2016).

Hence, even the hint of *pyat-sa* sparked contentious interactions. For instance, in late February 2015, during a trip to MyoTha, the driver took us to Pauk-Sein Village even though we were intending to visit Than-Po. Ko Taw became furious, suspecting that as Lay Gyi was close with the leader of Pauk-Sein, he and the headmen were colluding to attempt to use our presence (Yangon-based activists and a foreigner) to demonstrate to the villagers the significant networks and connections the headman retained. "There is no reason to be here, as Pauk Sein is not centrally located. We should be in Than-Po" [*Bse*], Ko Taw declared. Lay Gyi, a serious man and a good organizer, became sullen after this encounter—either because he actually had been falsely accused or because of his shame at having his mild scheme exposed in front of everyone.

More Money, More Problems: Foreigners, Prestige, Masculinity, and Risk

The Pauk-Sein incident leads to a necessary discussion of my presence. Foreigners, especially white foreigners, attracted attention to the group but provided them protection for the same reason. Relatedly, they were both a source of resources and, as a result, a source of more challenges. Foreigners hence both fit into existing paradigms of patronage and were exceptional to them.

When I first met Ko Taw and learned—as conveyed in chapter 2—that he belonged to a force, I had been tagging along on a trip organized by an international NGO to catalogue a series of land grabs in Mandalay and Sagaing Regions. The NGO provided the funding, and Ko Taw was hired as the fixer. He in turn pulled in U Gyi's crew from Mandalay to facilitate access to the specific communities in those regions. My NGO colleague, Ginny, effectively signing the checks and under pressure to meet deadlines, was confused and frustrated by the barrage of activists cramming into the car. At the end of the workday, as we made various stops and completed assorted tasks that seemed outside of the terms of reference for the trip, Ginny stewed in the backseat, complaining about the diversions that appeared to be misappropriations of the trip's resources. As sympathetic as I was to Ginny's deadlines, the political economy in play was clear—and, to be fair, Ginny was also sympathetic to it as well: the daily rate (USD 100) that Ko Taw had secured was significant in relative terms (where average per capita earnings are a tenth of that), and Ko Taw was distributing it by giving work to the rest of those in his network, who were essential for gaining access to the research sites. By disseminating these resources, Ko Taw in turn reinforced his position as a conduit of funds and jobs.

My own personal involvement was more ambiguous—those who interacted with CDI presumed I was a source of funding, even when members assured them that I was not. For instance, my common presence at the office they rented after leaving Thurein's house led the landlord to demand a higher monthly fee. The landlord conveyed that he was already facing pressure from local authorities about CDI's political activities; the higher rent was presented, implicitly, as justification for the risk (or annoyance) the landlord faced. CDI refused and moved its headquarters around the corner.

Another example was Ko Taw's tumultuous relationship with his wife, much of which was centered around money. She never believed that I was not giving CDI loads of cash; that she saw none of it come home made her suspect that he had another wife on the side, or at the very least was squandering it on frivolous living. These misgivings had much to do with the highly gendered nature of activism, a topic that itself warrants discussion.

GENDER AND ACTIVISM

Sometimes on the way back to town from a field visit we would stop off at a river under a bridge to bathe. It went like this: a changing longyi covers the longyi you are wearing, the longyi underneath comes off, the changing longyi becomes the swimming longyi, and then the process is reversed after you exit the water.

A favorite bathing spot was north of Mandalay near Mattaya at a part in a stream where the current is so strong coming through a narrow passageway under a bridge that one can swim into it vigorously and yet not move through the water. Aye Than did backflips off the riverbank. Paing Soe—an activist apprentice—and Teza splashed about. Only Ko Taw could not swim, but the water was not deep enough for concern. Aye Than washed up looking like a demon as his long hair out of its ponytail shrouded his body and his bloodshot eyes contrasted with his face, white from the soap. Teza feigned jumping off the top of the bridge into the water below, but Ko Taw scolded him like a child: "Don't you dare!" Teza smiled and stood down. "I have to raise him more than with my own son," Ko Taw commented to the rest of us. This was funny but also carried a hint of sadness, given that Ko Taw did not get to see his son very often. We dried off and hopped back in the truck.

As the vignette indicates, the members who joined these trips were almost universally boys or men, and the kind of sociality was gendered as highly male. Drinking and cigarette smoking were ubiquitous, both activities that were culturally encoded as masculine and not as available to women. On the trips I joined, sleeping situations were always communal—we would sleep in a row on mats. Even if there was electricity, the lights were never turned out, almost as if there was never a distinction drawn between wake time and sleep time: people slept when they were tired. As there was often no electricity, there was no fan. If there were mosquito nets, there were always holes in them; I was bitten mercilessly and then teased as mercilessly by Teza for not being able to bear it. ("They bite us just as they bite you. But we are tough" [Bse].) That I was able to relatively easily integrate into the homosociality of activist life and that I was able to wield whiteness as a shield to protect myself from bodily harm is a privilege not available to all and demands acknowledgment, as critical activist anthropologists have recently stressed (Berry et al. 2017).

Parents of Burmese women too recognized the masculinity of activist life, considering such situations and practices quite inappropriate for young women. And even if these practices were adjusted (for instance, when CDI allocated money for hotel rooms for female comrades), parents were concerned that their daughters would be in vulnerable positions—or, as importantly, that their community would perceive these situations as inevitably compromising.

The parents' concerns were often borne out: CDI was regularly expelling male members for trying to take advantage of younger female members (and in one case a younger male member) in or around the office. This was one of the corollaries of engaging the *lu-maiq* (thugs) of the ward (such as Koko, described in chapter 2)—sometimes they remained quite *lu-maiq*, even when with CDI.

CDI evolved itself a great deal throughout the years, and by 2020 its female leadership was impressive. Indeed, CDI's leadership continually purged violators, never making exceptions, and so from 2014 CDI's membership trended younger and more educated, with a striking substitution of women for men. That said, a kind of male heroism leeched into the daily life of the activist, inflecting what it meant to be a hero (to recall Ko Taw's words from the introduction).

MONEY: FREEDOM IN THE HUSTLE

Keeping masculine heroism in mind and returning to issues of money, I share a story here about Ko Taw and his wife. When we went to Mandalay for Thein Aung Myint's trial, Ko Taw kept receiving phone calls from his wife, who at that point was living in Karen state and needed money for their son. When Ko Taw told her there was no extra money, she countered that he gets to go to America and other foreign countries for trainings, and so there must be lots of money associated with that. When he relayed this story to the group, many joked that yes, the money is just lying on the pavement in foreign countries waiting to be picked up. But this was unfair to her, and it skirts the real issue at which she gestured, that of *gwin*. *Gwin* is the Burmese slang for all the material that is not salary but is extractable or exploitable from a situation. Figure 3.3 presents a play on words, with the word *kwin* (area) becoming *gwin* (graft) in the mind of the rapacious parliamentarian pupil who is learning how to steal.

But *gwin* is not wholly *illicit*. A colleague told me that in Burma, where formal salaries are so low, *gwin* can be orders of magnitude greater than the wage and hence an essential component of any livelihood arrangement. *Gwin* sustained Myanmar's military regimes' various patronage schemes over decades, as rank-and-file members could resell the resources they received, such as petrol or cooking oil, at higher prices (Kyaw Yin Hlaing 2001).

Nonetheless, Ko Taw expressed his frustration at being as committed to something as he was to the political work and his wife not comprehending it. "She asks me why I do this if I'm not getting something. She doesn't understand why." This also seemed unfair to her. The activist is an enregistered social type of which Ko Taw's wife was aware; I suspected that she was resentful that he had made this choice and that he lived in a country where he felt compelled to make this choice. Such a reading makes her tormented threat to "beat his dead body severely" conveyed after the coup (relayed in the introduction) more comprehensible. Moreover, she likely also resented that he inhabited the social type in a somewhat purist way defined by self-denial even while also engaging in a form of homosociality that he clearly enjoyed. This self-denial was to her a denial of resources to the family, and she seemed to imply that taking more was a way he could compensate himself for the work

FIGURE 3.3.
In the cartoon, the young parliamentarian is incorrectly learning the word "workplace" as "work-graft." Source: Cartoonist Myo Min Myat, 2015.

done for the country and the sacrifices he was making (and the sacrifices *she* had to make as well).[17]

Another way to be fair to Ko Taw's wife: I *did* contribute funding to the organization, in small occasional installments of a few lakh, especially after writing an article for which I was paid and which I would not have been able to write without the access and decoding of complex political situations provided by CDI. My contributions were couched in terms of solidarity and mutual labor (the article was "written" by all of us, with a division of labor), but I was still concerned that it would change our dynamic. Nothing changed, or at least we all pretended that nothing changed.

But near the end of my extended fieldwork period in late 2015, we discussed the future of CDI, and a significant deviation from CDI's existing practices was considered: did they want to get funded by an international organization? This question was precipitated by an impassioned soliloquy given by Ko Taw at the office a couple of days earlier. He railed against the funding system, concluding by saying about international funders that "CDI will never betray the people, the democracy, the national cause. They don't know. All of our people have sacrificed their lives for the country, but they are not interested" [*Eng*]. But "they"—these international funders—*could* be interested, I suggested. I mentioned my acquaintances at international organizations, and we began to discuss the pros and cons. Funding would alleviate the stress and opportunity cost of near-daily hustling for funding. Hours later, in fact, Ko Taw had to call his moneylender.

The potential cons bring us back to Ko Taw's lines in the previous chapter about being a force rather than another *yay-baw-si* (elite) group. Would international funding undermine their role as a force? Would they become captured by logframe logics? Ultimately CDI decided these were only potential cons and they could always pull out if things went wrong.

Thus, I became a sort of *pwe-sa* (broker), linking the funder with CDI. The meeting with the funder's agent was pleasant, and they agreed to fund CDI for two years. Ko Taw would no longer have to work, his deputies would also get salaries, and their project activities would be funded. We wrote a proposal together, in keeping with NGO protocols: we ensured each line item was SMART (Specific, Measurable, Agreed-upon, Realistic, Time-bound); designed a logframe (with inputs, outputs, and outcomes); and mapped out a GANT chart (plotting activities on a two-year calendar). But later, when outside of Myanmar, I received concerned messages from Ko Taw about having to do something called "organizational management planning." After two years of funding, CDI decided not to reapply.

I was a bit shocked. Certainly, it could not have been that bad. When I returned to Burma in June 2017, we talked it out. For forty-five minutes, Thurein, not a loquacious person, expounded on the way the funder, especially its Burmese staff (reminding us of class divides in Myanmar; see Sarkisyanz 1965, 231–33), belittled and underestimated the organization. Deeper than the superiority complex was the misrecognition: the funder could not grasp why CDI conducted the activities the way it did. The funder demanded more structure, less flexibility, more focus, less improvisation, and clear results that could be tracked. "*Let-ma-kan-buu*" (We cannot bear it), Thurein repeated. To outline how CDI's contributions were being unacknowledged by the framework, Ko Taw contributed a particularly stark example: "We will go work with the local people who were victims of murder. If [name of elite NGO head] would go there, they would kill him [the NGO head]" [*Bse*]. The assertion here was that other groups—the darlings of the foreign funders—could not even access the truly distressed people of the violent *hsin-kyay-boun*.

CDI's rejection of the NGO might be interpreted as part of the way rights are refused, as asserted in this book. While the US-based NGO cannot be made perfectly equivalent to rights logics, they both share certain liberal understandings of legibility, rationality, and nonviolence. Conversely, peri-urban life in Burma, as we have seen, is saturated with potential violence, as suggested here in Ko Taw's comments about the murder victims. Ko Taw's words also indexed how many CDI actions were categorically not rightful, a fact they highlighted themselves: "We have to commit crimes to prevent crime," or "We have to teach people about the law, but on the other hand, we have to break the law" [*Bse*]. On one occasion, breaking the law meant severely beating a factory owner who had been sexually assaulting female employees. They threatened his life should the sexual assault continue. Such interventions are difficult to construe as right*ful*—even if they could be seen as right*eous*.

If we return the new political economy of the transition, we can see that the opportunities also put stress on interpersonal relationships, and by late 2017, Thurein and Ko Taw, inseparable for a decade, had ceased working together. I suspected that the funding changed the relationships that governed Thurein's involvement, precipitating his exit. First, as a senior member, Thurein began to draw a salary from the new grant (something made more necessary by the decreasing success of his rice shop). Second, even as this occurred, Ko Taw, pressed by the international funder to delegate more tasks to prevent the organization from being so reliant on him, began to ask more of Thurein. "I told him so many times to write a proposal. He can even write it in Burmese, and I will translate it. But he never did so . . . , and we even support him with a stipend. I cannot bear that" [*Eng*]. The relationships of reciprocity changed: Thurein took more than before and was not able to give back the more that was asked of him. Mutual resentment eventually destroyed their bond—at least until the coup, when the crisis brought Thurein back into the fold.

Sacrifice and the Ah-zah-ni Path

The ever-present sensitivity about money and how broader publics would perceive distributions of resources relates to associated anxiety about sacrifice, an imperative that Gustaaf Houtman marks as central to Burmese politics (1999, 6–7). But while the sacrificial impetus is strong, I repeatedly witnessed activists struggle to find the "true" sacrifice for a given situation. When it came to questions of taking money, joining an NGO, entering a political party, getting a university degree, and so forth, activists were often trying to discern the *correct* sacrifice[18] and, we might add, the best form of refusal— the best mix of engagement with opportunities while maintaining a safe distance, the best combination of presence and absence. Yelling protest slogans was easy compared with managing economies (of resources and affects) that could simultaneously fortify and undermine activism. Anxiety about sacrifice was particularly acute not only because of the ambiguity and uncertainty around the normative standards governing conduct but because one key lodestar for righteous activism—the figure of the *ah-zah-ni*[19]—does not provide easy guidance.

Burmese political history celebrates various key fallen political figures as *ah-zah-ni*, from independence heroes to those who died in the 1988 uprising.[20] Primary textbooks represent the *ah-zah-ni* in an allegorical tale of a leader sacrificing his life for his followers, making his body a literal bridge that allows them to scamper to safety (Cheesman 2002, 215–18). And while death of the *ah-zah-ni* is common, allowing the figure to be glossed as a "martyr," that outcome is less important than the *ah-zah-ni*'s attitude. Indeed, death itself is insufficient; as Phyo Win Latt puts it, the *ah-zah-ni* is "someone who chooses a political path in which he is aware that he will be destroyed in the end without remorse" [*Eng*]. The choice aspect is central: "You are not *ah-zah-ni* if you happen to be killed by a terrorist bomb" (pers. comm., 2015).

But this definition is still incomplete. Houtman (1999), in one of the only academic treatments of *ah-zah-ni* besides Cheesman's, notes that monks "who do not die for a political cause, but merely successfully pass a difficult examination" are *also* designated *ah-zah-ni*. To explain this, Houtman identifies the elements of suffering and struggling associated with *ah-zah-ni* to then go further, describing *ah-zah-ni* as "seeking to encourage the right state of mind for the fight for national independence and freedom" (241). Houtman stresses the element of decision, in which the *ah-zah-ni* is "one who is capable of bold action because of the ability to instantaneously discriminate the proper from the improper" (242).

Regarding the activists, Houtman's point here is key insofar as it emphasizes that it is not enough to sacrifice by simply throwing oneself at the regime, dying for the cause. Indeed, I observed activists constantly disdain such kinds of purity as inefficacious and even selfish. Ko Taw once criticized the austere lifestyle insisted upon by the Burma Communist Party as pious;

the late longtime NLD leader Win Tin has been represented as believing that "taking the saintly route of spiritual detachment could sap the struggle in the hard glare of the here and now" (Schrank 2015, 117). Thurein identified MDCF leader Htin Kyaw as the worst kind of activist: one who *postured* as an *ah-zah-ni*, constantly ending up in prison and not only effectively seeking glory for himself but obscuring the key role that Saya Nyo had played in forming MDC (MDCF's predecessor). CDI leaders knew that returning to prison was always a possibility, but they also "took responsibility" for the organization by limiting their exposure to situations where they might be arrested. Ko Taw and Thurein, for instance, rarely participated in contentious actions together, lest they both get incarcerated at the same time, leaving CDI rudderless.

This ambiguity around the correct way to do sacrifice allows us to return to Ko Taw and his wife. If he did perceive her as misapprehending his vocation, we can also suspect that she stood, to him at least, as a synecdoche of a subset of nonactivists (or of all nonactivists a subset of the time). Activists fear that average Burmese subjects not only suspected the activists of corruption but could not even understand activism as a mode of living—of refusal of status quo conditions—worth committing to (a disjuncture that evokes the separations of populations in chapter 1 and the way political prisoners are "quarantined," described in chapter 2). Indeed, the figures of the political prisoner, the underground organizer, and, of course, Suu Kyi, became *icons* of struggle for Burmese society, inspiring people but also creating a gap between the strugglers and the mere observers—the people. This sentiment was evoked during the 2021 anticoup protests in which an enormous sheet was draped across Yangon's Hledan junction flyover that read, "There is no supreme saviour." It was an attempt to remind people to stop relying on messiahs (especially when one may never arrive). A tension over the hope for transcendent deliverance (whether from Burmese leaders or the international community) crackled across those protests, reflected in the change of colors introduced in the preface: the first days were dominated by the color red—in clothing and paraphernalia, signifying Suu Kyi and her party—to abruptly give way on February 8 to the color black. Youth activists testified that this switch symbolized a need to get beyond the red (Suu Kyi) and green (Min Aung Hlaing) dyads.

This did not mean, of course, that Suu Kyi was symbolically slain; she persisted as that supreme savior even as the social movements (as described earlier) presented alternative models that demanded space for average people to participate in politics. The activists themselves struggled with this distinction—as

Ko Taw mentioned in the introduction, they declared how much they wanted normal people to be their own heroes. But their *habitus*—their body and being—was structured as being an exemplary refuser, marked in their difference from the rest.

Conclusion: Political Brokerage Outside of Political Society

This chapter has ethnographically conveyed the functions and meanings of a ubiquitous protest tactic—the plow protest. By occupying land, protesters' bodies mark an ambiguous defiance: they are returning to—or encroaching on—space, depending on the responses their occupations generate. Plowing hence stands as the hinge point dividing localized from broader domains of engagement: if a plowing becomes a protest, then the relationship is no longer between the plowers and the land itself but also incorporates various other actors—those making counterclaims to the land as well as the various publics being invited to participate (to overhear, assess, endorse, or even ignore or reject the plow protest). Peasants assert a claim that forces the state to either materialize or not. Moreover, by reoccupying and cultivating their former lands, farmers not only perform ownership of land through the material act of tilling but also imply that land should be understood as embedded in an intimate relation with cultivating communities. As with cursing ceremonies, discussed in the following chapter, that call on ancestor spirits to judge the proper owners of land, such rituals suggest that land maintains relations with generations past, reminding everyone that the land's first clearers remain to some degree its owners.

The chapter has also presented the ambiguous outcomes that derive from activists' political brokerage. It has focused on how people who need activists to mobilize them tend to be those who have fallen out of (or who have never been part of) protective patronage orbits and are hence scrambling to find new protectors. The farmers or poor people I observed seemed to deploy a *tactical* acceptance of activist strategies: they described following the activists because that was the only hope they had. Hence, while the activists' main stated goal is to get people to stand for themselves, which does sometimes occur, mostly locals ride on the backs of the activists into the realm of political society and find it difficult to remain in that domain without the continual assistance of their new political patrons.

Ultimately, then, political brokerage stands as an ambiguous tactic for attaining the affordances of political membership: the broker can act as a conduit, ushering the excluded into a new, less precarious space, *and* then help them build the skills and amass the resources to continue to *remain* in that domain. That brokerage could be fleeting, however, either because of inadequate brokerage *or* because it is difficult for activists to inculcate skills and resources in most subjects who have lived their lives excluded; in such situations, those ushered into political society cannot effectively remain there. Finally, brokerage when executed by shortsighted or opportunistic activists actually *holds* the excluded in their positions of exclusion.

In the next chapter, we will observe a contrast in tactics that helps to further illuminate the broader strategy of activist refusal. To wit, plow protests demonstrated the triple move in activist absent presence: first, direct action was masked as no action at all; second, they pivoted instantaneously into protests; and third, they in turn had to be prepared to dissolve away. Chapter 4, by contrast, will focus on a different ambiguity, in which occult cursing ceremonies are shown to be both a more direct and more attenuated form of beckoning the state.

CHAPTER 4

Cartoons, Curses, and the Corpus

CURIOUS SIGHTS WERE COMMON in the first days of the massive protests that inundated Myanmar after the February 1, 2021, coup. Young people dressed as clowns and women wore wedding dresses; gym trainers went shirtless, and women sported bikinis, taunting the senior generals about the source of real power. Boys wore French maid costumes, endorsing BDSM rather than military bondage, while transgender women strutted in stilettos over generals' visages and elderly women rubbed their genitals on photographs of generals' faces.

But even amid this panoply of play, it was impossible to miss one specific subgenre of protest that proliferated across the country; from Bagan to *hsin-kyay-boun* Yangon, from Mandalay to online spaces throughout, Myanmar's masters of the esoteric arts cursed the generals not with vituperative epithets but with dark magic.

Within days of the coup, a document drafted by an organization identifying itself as "The national association representing Nats and Weizzas" declared its intentions to direct cursing ceremonies—*kyeinsa*[1] *daiqpwe*—at the generals. A group of women in Bagan held a collective cursing ceremony against Min Aung Hlaing, and a week later hundreds of people joined them. Funeral processions led by people dressed as *Ma-Hpew-Wa* (cemetery ghosts) hefted coffins meant to carry the senior generals, while *nat-pwes* (spirit festivals) incorporated invocations for nats, those small but devious spirits, to curse the dictators, a practice many online said was innovative. A *kyeinsa daiqpwe* outside of Yangon University declared itself "The People's Cursing Ceremony,"

FIGURE 4.1. Collage of various *kyeinsa daiqpwe* (cursing ceremonies/battles) from the anticoup uprising. Top image: A person dressed as a *ma-hpew-wa* (cemetery ghost) carries a coffin meant to contain senior general Min Aung Hlaing. Middle row (left): A document, circulated by a group identifying its members as experts in the occult, that provides guidance on how to curse Min Aung Hlaing and family members over eighteen years of age; (middle): An arial photo of a *kyeinsa daiqpwe* march through Bagan; (right): *Nat-gadaw* (spirit attendants) curse the dictators. Bottom row (left): Effigies of soldiers with curses written on paper beside them; (right): "The People's Cursing Ceremony," held outside of Yangon University, places cow bones and blood over photos of soldiers and military supporters. Sources unknown.

and observers reported that protesters invited the souls of those murdered by security forces at the same spot during the 1988 uprising to join the current protest.

These protests were potent. We know this because during a time when those holding signboards hurling abusive insults at those in power (many focused on Min Aung Hlaing's anatomical failings, from his short stature to his presumed sexual inadequacy; street performances engaged in call-and-response chants of "Min Aung Hlaing! Motherfucker!") were *not* being arrested, security forces *did* target the cursers. The police went to Yangon's *hsin-kyay-boun* to arrest the astrologer who conceived of The People's Cursing Ceremony. His followers live streamed his arrest and followed him to the police office to demand his release (VOA 2021). Rumors circulated that the curse was successful, causing Min Aung Hlaing a hand injury for which he himself had to seek out his own astrologer to provide countermagic. Social media posts pointed out that Min Aung Hlaing was in fact wearing a bandage on his hand. Later, when it was learned on February 24, 2021, that Min Aung Hlaing's grandchild had been born without a fully functioning heart, protesters made explicit connection to the movement. As one put it, "Although it is very sad for this child . . . , we have to say that MAL [Min Aung Hlaing] has fallen under the People's *Kyeinsa*."

What is at stake in these esoteric improvisations and the response of the security apparatus? Thus far, the book has dealt with activist lives and protest tactics but has not directly engaged the question of why they sometimes win. Why in a highly repressive milieu in which "rights" do not secure actions and sovereign prerogative is both unaccountable and evasive, are their resistance tactics sometimes successful? This is the question addressed here.

Interpellation by Invitation

Louis Althusser (1971) theorized the concept of interpellation to account for the way "state ideological apparatuses" produce consent by the governed to ruling regimes. In his famous illustrative example, the act of a policeman yelling "Hey you!" causes one to turn, to feel hailed, and to hence become formed as a subject under the authority of the policeman and thus the broader state. While the policeman example uses a *dyadic* exchange at a *singular* moment to distill interpellation, Althusser's interlocutors have stressed how collective engagements and longer-term processes better define the concept. James Martel, for instance, argues that for Althusser, "our consciousness is not 'ours,' not private and alone in some realm of ideas, but shaped by countless external forces such as family, society, state, and so forth" (2017, 44).

As such, Althusser's account describes regimes of power as highly integrated, such that a society's various "external forces" would seem to reinforce one another and hence produce totalizing effects. Interpellation, however, not only flows from those standard apparatuses of the school, the family, and mass culture but can emerge from elsewhere as well. As Judith Butler (1997, 141–59) points out in her critique of Pierre Bourdieu's account of symbolic power, if interpellative performatives merely flowed from systems of preordained authority, then we would be incapable of accounting for two key empirical realities: how demands from those in positions of preratified authority occasionally *fail* and how claims made by those previously excluded from positions of authority sometimes *succeed*. Indeed, without considering these key phenomena, endogenously generated social change would be impossible to explain.

Butler hence guides attention to how the practices of interpellation must be separated from the apparatuses of authority from which they are presumed to flow. In other words, the "Hey you!" need not come from the policeman. It can come from various sources. Moreover, the policeman is *also* subject to the "Hey you!" This is because interpellation for Butler is defined by *catachresis*, or *mis*hearing. When the subject hears incorrectly, she comes to recognize herself in a way that is new but also simultaneously the way she "always" was. The upshot here is that, opposed to static conceptions of the subject and society, Butler's version makes them both dynamic and mutable, thereby making social change explicable.

Nevertheless, despite the greater potential revealed through her account, Butler acknowledges that not just anyone at any time can interpellate those in positions of authority. And as James Scott's (1985, 1990) work on everyday resistance makes clear, power-laden situations force significant symbolic work "underground," producing a split in which the marginalized adhere to an "official transcript" aligned with the prerogatives of symbolic power while conveying their relatively more authentic perception of reality only in the safe confines of the "hidden transcript."

Bringing Scott and Butler together, I ask what the rhetoric of the oppressed must sound like to adequately interpellate those in positions of power and authority. What does everyday resistance look like when it is brought out into the open? By this I do not mean the moment in which the erstwhile oppressed break free and "speak truth to power" (Scott 1990, chap. 8). Scott provides accounts of the way subalterns mobilize like wildfire as the hidden transcript is spoken aloud. He does not, however, focus on their failure. Burmese activists, conversely, keep failure always in mind. They know that yelling truths at the generals may feel good but is a form of sovereign challenge that will likely produce their own destruction. They are concerned, instead, with what kind of "Hey you!" could work to make a general turn and think of himself differently.

To understand how such speech acts might function to produce such effects requires a detour through Burmese speech ideology, which can in turn best be grasped through a review of the particularly powerful Burmese text genre, the political cartoon.

Interpellation in Burmese Speech Culture as Vehicle for Social Change

Cartoons hold an outsized position of importance in Myanmar. Although smart phone penetration increased rapidly during the transition years, Burmese people continued to consume a significant amount of printed text; in particular, while other printed text forms (such as comics) appeared to be declining, a surge in new newspapers and journals after the end of military censorship meant an explosion of cartoon publishing (Kyaw Hsu Mon 2016). During the transition era, newspapers and journals published dozens of cartoons per week; cartoons were consumed both in print and online, meaning that they circulated broadly (Brainwave, a Facebook page devoted to daily aggregation of cartoons, had five million "likes" at its peak). Cartoonists (current stars such as Maung Maung Fountain and the late Harn Lay and luminaries of the past such as U Pe Thein and U Ba Gyan) remain today not just celebrities but often committed political actors, taking part in campaigns or meeting with politicians (Tin Htet Paing 2015). (In fact, as I tracked down permissions to feature cartoons for this book—by contacting members of the national cartoonist union that represents Burmese cartoonist interests—I learned that several had become revolutionaries, joining militants in the liberated areas of Kayah state.)

Both causing and deriving from that popularity is the fact that cartoons partake in a broad range of rhetorical genres. While satire still comprises the overwhelming plurality of cartoons, many operate in different registers. Some cartoons are sentimental (presenting the suffering of the downtrodden; commemorating historical moments); others are hortative (containing slogans such as "Power to the people"); still others operate more like op-eds in that they present straightforward critique. Most importantly, many cartoons seem to be primarily informational: a significant number of cartoons do not attempt humor, play, or commentary but exist mostly to re-present (and hence draw attention to) newsworthy events, suggesting that many readers get at least some of their news through this medium. To wit, as a nonnative speaker I often suspected I was missing hidden layers of humor, so I sought readings from Burmese colleagues; they usually concurred that information rather than humor or satire appeared to be the objective of the cartoon in question.

Moreover, cartoons' importance can be measured by the responses that they generate. It is noteworthy that during the transition the military demanded that newspapers deliver official apologies for offensive cartoons (one featured a general firing on clay peace doves for target practice; another had a villager lamenting that the military had already stolen all the country's land). Cartoons also became news when Maung Maung Fountain presented Suu Kyi as an authoritarian in a late 2016 cartoon, something his newspaper reported on (Tin Htet Paing 2016). Newspaper readers responded by flooding Facebook with reports of illicit content, leading to the suspension of his account. Cartoonists rallied to Maung Maung Fountain's defense with—what else?—a cartoon presenting Suu Kyi's party as thin-skinned and needing to become accustomed to such critique.

Cartoons also illustrate important aspects of Burmese speech culture and ideology, in which language is understood not as a neutral vehicle for the conveyance of meaning but as a field of power available for capture.[2] This is best illustrated by a cartoon. In figure 4.2 a cartoon posted by the Rakhine News Group presents a woman who resembles Suu Kyi asking eight pupils seated before her to vote on the orthographic token that she holds up. The two light-skinned characters at the top read the token correctly (as *ei*), while six dark-skinned characters at the bottom read it incorrectly (as the orthographically similar *kyweh*). Their misreading here riffs on a Burmese proverb that uses the same tokens (*ei* and *kyweh*): "Everyone is in agreement that that 'ei' is 'kyweh,'" which implies that truth can be decided by "agreement"—an agreement that is certainly coerced, as those wielding power effect a new truth. In the context of a then formally democratizing Myanmar, the proverb took on new meaning: suddenly the majority, represented by the six dark-skinned figures (icons of the country's beleaguered minority Rohingyas, nonetheless imagined as imminent majorities), can decide what it wants truth to be, suggesting

FIGURE 4.2. Cartoon in which an Aung San Suu Kyi figure asks pupils/MPs to identify the orthographic token *ei*. The light-skinned figures identify it correctly; the dark-skinned figures identify it as *kyweh*. Source: Cartoonist Yein Nweh Ba, July 2016.

that as demographics change (in this case, the accepted truth that Rohingya continue to 'invade' Rakhine state from Bangladesh), truth can change as well.

Figure 4.3 acts as a metapragmatic representation of the process outlined above. Here an editor intervenes to preserve the original spellings—and hence the original meanings—that his typist has altered.[3] While the superior presents the divergences inscribed by the typist as mistakes ("Pay attention to your typing"), and while humor can be found in these malapropisms alone, the humorous effect is intensified by the motivated nature of the "mistakes": the typist is presented as describing the world the way it is; his are not so much mistakes as *corrections*. The cartoon hence stages the recursive semiotic loop in which social actors (a) interpret that actual material conditions diverge from ideal representations of reality, (b) inscribe those divergences

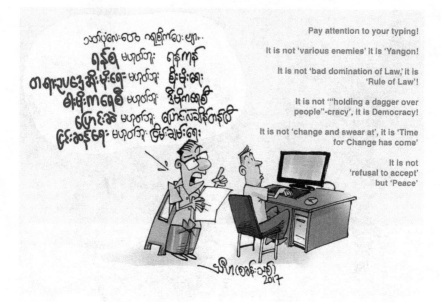

FIGURE 4.3. Cartoon in which a newspaper editor corrects his typist, who has made "mistakes" that arguably reveal deeper truths about Myanmar society. Source: Cartoonist Thiha (Sakan Thit), 2017.

in language, and then (c) circulate them to others—a process that I will show in the next chapter also operates in the Burmese use of *akwint-ayay* (rights).

The above data suggest that the linguistic field is understood as suffused with power relations, rendering collective meanings subject to intervention. While those who wield power arrogate the ability and privilege to decide on truth, others can influence them as well; an essential strategy, then, for achieving goals is to compel those in power to see things your way—a theme that will be developed in the forthcoming data, first in political cartoons and then in cursing protests.

I turn now to a particularly dominant trope within satirical Burmese cartoons, what I will call the staging of catachrestic interpellation. These scenes feature an elite mingling among normal people and overhearing their speech, as can be observed through examination of the tokens collected in figure 4.4. Each image is defined by the central character's look of surprise at speech that he overhears, but the main feature of this type of cartoon is that the elites *mishear* what they overhear (a fact focalized for the reader in some examples of this subgenre by the elite's attendant, who clarifies the actual intended meaning in the overheard speech). When overhearing a conversation between two average people the elite is surprised, scandalized, or ashamed by what he believes is speech directed at him. In each case the elite interprets this speech as *calling him*, as implicating him, as breaking his flow (to wherever he is going but also—consistent with the discussion of processes of subjectivization—to whoever he was *being*).

This mishearing is critical, because the elite's interpellation—the momentary assumption that the villagers are talking to him and not to one another—is

FIGURE 4.4. Plate with tokens of the "catachrestic interpellation" genre of cartoons, clockwise from upper left: "You can't rely on your audience!" (Source: Cartoonist Maung Yay Win, 2016); "He had to meet his lawyer 1,500 times" (Source: Cartoonist Mye Pyin 2016); "The street vendors are just talking about themselves!" (Source: Cartoonist Ko Kit, 2016); "Where do you arrive?" (Source: Cartoonist Chunt Htet, 2016)

presented as emerging from the elite's *own* anxieties. The lower-class characters do not scream castigations at the elite. Rather, the elite himself interprets
the sign as being directed at him: he not only directs the accusation to himself but by so doing admits his shame at being correctly accused and identified.
Here we recall Butler's *catachresis*, which is where a literal mishearing ends up
producing the dissonance in which a new truth is created. Critical to the point
about interpellation and the self-enrolling it elicits is how it feeds off dismissibility—both because of the unthreatening source (typically a child, an average person on the street, and so forth) and because the address is not *meant*
for the recipient. Hence the recipient does not feel accused, is not compelled to
defend himself, to retort; instead he has space to reflect. No one has to come
up directly to him and yell, "You are corrupt!" Because his sovereignty is not
challenged, he is able to entertain that possibility himself. In fact, he can plausibly deny that the (mis)address did anything to him at all, potentially even as
the resubjectivizing work is being done behind his back. Historian Michael
Aung-Thwin has noted the historical roots of this indirect communication tactic, citing its appearance in Burmese chronicles and mentioning its contemporary relevance:

> Advice given by ministers to kings in the past was often meant for contempo-
> raries of the author. This was a method for criticism without fear of punish-
> ment. In present day spoken usage, this particular approach is called *saung
> pyaw*,[4] a sarcastic innuendo referring to disguised criticism or public slander,
> which though directed at (say) your child, is in reality meant for a nearby per-
> son who can also hear one's statement, and for whom the criticism is in fact
> meant. It avoids direct (and in Burmese society, demeaning) confrontation.
> (1982, 97)

Here we can recall in chapter 2 the note of encouragement that Ko Taw
sent to the young activists in the moments before the anticoup uprising commenced. That note focalized the youths' contributions in juxtaposition with
what Ko Taw described as his own decrepit, desiccated generation. One line in
particular stood out for its statement that while young people were mobilizing,
those in Ko Taw's generation were "composing poems." This was a pointed reference to famous 88GS activist Min Ko Naing, who had mostly eschewed politics since the transition, withdrawing into the arts. When I asked Ko Taw if this
was indeed a reference to Min Ko Naing, Ko Taw confirmed that it was, adding, "And Min Ko Naing saw that too. He called me, said, 'Oh, Ko Taw kicks
me to the side!' And so he sent his men to follow with us on the streets today."

Returning to the cartoons, we can ask: should the locals in the cartoons be interpreted as enacting *saung-pyaw* as a form of conscious and intentional metapragmatic attack (Jacquemet 1994) on the elite? It does not appear so. The characters do not seem to indicate (by looking in the direction of the intended but unratified overhearer) to give us (the readers) an indication that they are intending the elite to (mis)hear the address. Rather, it seems it is the cartoonists who are employing *saung-pyaw* with their readers. Instead of calling out the specific example (of corruption, for instance), the cartoonist just gestures in that direction and is able to utilize what Silverstein has called "residual semanticity," which is "the semantico-referential meaning which a speaker can claim after the fact for potentially highly pragmatically charged speech. Thus the characteristic speaker's denial of speech offensive to the hearer takes the form of 'All I said was . . .'" (1976, 48). In a quasi-authoritarian context this is not only instrumentally wise but part of the habitus of many in the speech community; both cartoonists and their bemused readers are attuned to this kind of discourse, a fact that can be adduced from the sheer popularity of this kind of cartoon.

Despite such dismissibility, the real audience for these cartoons—the broader public that reads them—observes the elite being addressed and observes how the elite *should* feel hailed (even if the MP in actual life never gets down to those grass roots). As such it is not just a way of identifying (and critiquing) a class schism that increasingly divided Myanmar into two worlds during the transition but also a way of suturing those worlds back together, if only in the domain of the cartoon (and the imagined community of the reading public). Cartoons beckon certain characters to see themselves in new ways. Contrast this with an editorial, for instance: it announces itself as contentious and wages a form of resistance in which it seeks to meet its opponent head-on. These cartoons, by contrast, are more consistent with refusal—by avoiding direct contestation they invite broader participation. To wit, because the cartoonists try to present the characters as indexical icons of social types, the cartoons (attempt to) compel a secondary interpellation on the part of reading publics: do I identify with the elite and come to see myself as others do? Or do I identify with the person interpellating him and hence see how my fellows see the elite? Such cartoons thus coordinate joint attention.

Moving closer now to the cursing ceremonies, note figure 4.5, in which we see a variation on the catachrestic cartoon: a woman presents at a government office, and rather than get in line, she drops to the floor in prayer. "If there are officials who do not take bribes in these offices, I want to serve and pay

FIGURE 4.5.
Cartoon in which a woman visits a municipal office that performs various services (land records, list inspection, and so on) and prays for service without bribes. Source: Cartoonist Taa Ti Pyay, 2016.

respects to them. Come out for me," she proclaims. A reader may wonder: is this woman really going to give them blessings? Does she actually think that this is a domain where prayers have power? Or is she critiquing or at least teasing the officials by saying in so many words, "I have to promise blessings in order to just get good service"?

The cartoon does not lend any diagetic clues that the character is joking: the woman is on the ground after all; she's not winking at us. Yet friends with whom I read this cartoon insisted that a Burmese reader knows that this is not a contemptuous commentary on how average people are so benighted as to see the need to pursue the realm of esoteric power to get basic government services. Rather, these readers see the woman as strategically switching into a "religious register" of speech in order to comment on purely secular matters, with the cartoon indicating that the distinction blurs in practice. In Burma there is a mutual coconstitution of religious and secular registers that partake in one another.

And yet, commenting *in* a secular matter *on* secular matters would *not* have precisely the same effect. In this regard the prayer is important. The cartoon features a figure behind the divider, likely an official, with anxiety sweat flying off him—presumably that sweat is more intense because of the religious register. He must decide whether the message is "for" him or not and what kinds of consequences—perhaps esoteric ones—attend not taking up the call. This cartoon acts as a useful bridge to the cursing protests examined below. In fact, given the proliferation of cursing protests around Myanmar, it is reasonable to surmise that the cartoon was actually *responding* to such phenomena, or at least operating within a political context that cursing protests have influenced.

Cursing as Catachrestic Interpellation

At the end of March 2014, government forces demolished the protest camp across from Yangon's City Hall in which the Michaungkan protesters mentioned in chapter 2 had been living for over a year. They had been attempting to receive compensation for land they had been dispossessed of two decades earlier.[5] At this point, protesters responded by escalating tactics, holding an occult cursing ceremony to condemn those who continued to thwart their calls for justice. Below an altar were affixed three pictures of ferocious ogres; inscribed on a signboard to the left was what the protesters asked of these monsters—to curse (*kyeinsa*) their enemies:

> The curse is, "The officials who have abused the law, may these aforementioned big people and their following generations meet with violent deaths and with various tragedies and may they live on Michaungkan land as spirit ogres through their successive lives, and may their blood boil till their death in the past, in the future, and in the present on this land. May they live as ghosts and spirit ogres for 505 worlds without being liberated until the end of the earth. May they be led by the earth ogre to violent deaths. May it be so." (DVB 2014 [*Bse*])[6]

Such escalation could also be observed in Letpadaung, site of the aforementioned copper mine implanted on stolen land. In one ritual, protesters dressed as zombies, invoking the dead ancestors meant to judge the present. The *Letpadaung Chronicle* (n.d.), an entire book of dozens of news articles on

FIGURE 4.6. On the left, the photograph features villagers dressed as zombie figures; on the right, hundreds of villagers sit in prayer behind four figures lying in shallow graves, embodying ancestor spirits. Source: *Letpadaung Chronicle*, n.d. Yangon: Spring.

the Letpadaung protests assembled and published during the uprisings, featured a photograph in which participants who had painted their bodies black and eye sockets white stare into the distance. The adjacent photograph shows four figures lying in shallow graves, embodying ancestor spirits, with hundreds of villagers sitting in prayer behind them. The photo's caption reads, "To protect this land, the kin who have died have been called and enrolled" [*Bse*] (fig. 4.6).

In another cursing ceremony, Letpadaung protesters inscribed on their signboards the following: "May military crony U Paing and Wan Bao Company that illegally stole the people's land be cursed." And "'May the military crony U Paing and Wan Bao Company that destroyed the chedi and the ordination hall go to hell.'—The Letpadaung local people" [*Bse*]. In still another ceremony, a *kyeinsa* held at Letpadaung in January 2016, the explicit curse was circulated by activists on Facebook, reading as follows: "The cursing attack has been done. May those people who gave permission for the murder, the land grab, the LPT copper project be known. Daw Khin Win was fired on and killed. The land got grabbed. Acid was deposited into the Chindwin. There is no land for providing food. And 65 farmers will be held with the charge of chapter 18. Today is a kyeinsa from the masses. May those copper project murderers and land stealers go to hell" [*Bse*].

The Hidden Origins of Kyeinsa Daiqpwe

What is going on in these rituals? As described in chapter 3, I visited Letpadaung in 2016 in part hoping to learn more about the village-based esoteric beliefs and practices that grounded these rituals. To arrange the visit, Ko Taw had contacted Soe Aung, who then worked with the Yangon People's Service Network, the activist group that organized the villagers in Letpadaung. When I arrived, I asked Soe Aung, one of three activists who had spent more time in Letpadaung than anyone else in Myanmar, about these rituals. He clarified the mechanics of the *kyeinsa daiqpwe*, pointing out that technically a *kyeinsa* by itself can just mean a casual curse—as in to swear at someone. It only becomes a *kyeinsa daiqpwe* when certain ritualized elements are included.

I then asked Soe Aung about those elements—what kinds of conditions needed to be fulfilled for a *kyeinsa* to become a real *kyeinsa daiqpwe*? And which villager or local monk, I asked, had come up with the rules for the *kyeinsa daiqpwe*—who was responsible for the idea in the first place? But Soe Aung just smiled. Rather than answering, he looked over at the others, who also were grinning. "What?" I asked, wondering where I had gone wrong.

Soe Aung proceeded to reveal that he himself, not the locals, was the *kyeinsa daiqpwe* architect. Soe Aung, who was born and raised in Yangon, explained that his experience years ago working with the volunteer organization Free Funeral Service Society (which they called "FFS" [*Eng*]) gave him deep knowledge of rites and practices associated with the dead. Ko Taw looked at me knowingly, and I recalled our conversations a year before on the importance of these organizations. Free funeral societies, I learned then, not only helped poor people manage the financial burden of caring for the deceased but also helped them learn the esoteric knowledge necessary for dealing with the dead in the correct ways (as many Buddhist monks, I was told, do not engage in such practices, given that the rituals are understood as "non-Buddhist"). Ko Taw had said then, "There are many rites that must be done according to tradition. You must create a shed so that everyone knows there is a death. And then you must burn the slips of paper. And make an invitation letter for the funeral. On the third day hire a car and take the body to get burned. Must break a pot over the body and then break a coconut and without looking throw its shell over your shoulder onto the body. There are so many things" [*Eng*].

This recollection, now recontextualized, ended my search for some imagined organic village culture; rather, the urban activists had access to rare esoteric knowledge, something villagers had reason to value for its political potential. Such knowledge was forged, developed, and cultivated in the context of highly political work. As I mentioned earlier, civil society organizations such as FFS were able during the most intense periods of regime repression (1988–2011) to train and give young activists experience participating in social actions under the cover of ostensibly apolitical service delivery. Involvement in low-stakes social activities (such as volunteer funeral services) then provided—and will likely now provide again, postcoup—not only training in the art of activism but also opportunities for nascent activists to build cultural skills and acumen that they could weaponize.

Soe Aung went on to describe the effects of these *kyeinsa daiqpwe*, noting that holding the ceremonies was a way of unifying the villagers and that as they continued with the cursing ceremonies, people—both villagers and the copper mine company employees—started to observe them producing material effects. Ko Taw later added the following interpretation: "*Kyeinsa* are useful for two [reasons]. One is to be united," and by this he meant locals cohering around a repertoire of collective action. The second was more direct: "To threaten the cronies who took the land." He continued: "Most of the cronies believe in the supernatural. *Kyeinsa* are [meant] to destroy the enemy's life and properties [and so] if something happens—for example, one of the trucks of Wanbao Company crashed down after the *kyeinsa* of Letpadaung people—at that time both sides believed it happened because of *kyeinsa*. The driver is really afraid to drive the car again. He thinks something will bring ill luck to him" [*Eng*]. Ko Taw here describes how the *kyeinsa daiqpwe* asserts a new interpretive framework into a community of overhearers that it simultaneously coheres. This framework coordinates how events in the world are given meaning: accidents cease to be random and become motivated by deeper causes.[7]

But Ko Taw also noted that company owners were able to themselves employ the esoteric realm to attempt to undermine the *kyeinsa daiqpwe*: "The company also asked famous fortunetellers to counteract the *keyinsa* through *yadaya*,"[8] a form of protective magic (Matthews 1998). On one hand, *yadaya*'s efficacy would always remain unclear, mostly because the *kyeinsa*'s causal chains are inscrutable. If death and destruction do not come tomorrow, this does not mean that *yadaya* has neutralized the *kyeinsa*; it could simply mean the *kyeinsa* has not worked yet. As Ko Taw put it, "*Kyeinsa* need time to be effected. Sometimes *kyeinsa* take effect after 10 years or even in the next life" [*Bse*]. On the other hand, the use of *yadaya* did act as a way of attempting to counterbalance the curse.

Ko Taw went on to describe a third way that *kyeinsa* are effective—to embarrass or shame their objects: "The cronies also feel shame about it. They are really angry about it. We heard the news about it through our men and sometimes through authorities and SB. For example, SB told us that the crony boss is really unhappy about *kyeinsa*. He is just a kind man. The farmers misunderstand him and should not do like that" [*Eng*]. Ko Taw describes how the object of the curse—the crony—communicates through proxies about the way he has been affected. It is worth contrasting the *kyeinsa daiqpwe* here with a plain *kyeinsa*—as insult or curse. Rather than dismissing the curse as a desperate or unruly bit of discourse deployed by a group of marginalized farmers and not having any bearing on him, the crony not only feels assaulted by the curse but effectively appeals to the villagers to call it off. Here is the moment of catachrestic interpellation: the crony hears the curse as directed at him. A perfectly illustrative example emerged postcoup on June 17, 2021, in online commentary on a monk funeral that had been transformed by mourners into a *kyeinsa daiqpwe* of Min Aung Hlaing. The Facebook post, shared ten thousand times in the following month, read, "If MAL comes to feel ashamed, he will come to die 10 times" [*Bse*].[9] Here, shame is the key outcome that precipitates literal death, but the use of the conditional "if" distills the importance of self-interpellation: the curse's efficacy is not dependent on the correct enactment of the magic as much as it is by its object coming to feel some kind of way because of it.

This way of coaxing the object to self-interpellate becomes especially apparent when we consider the wording of many of the curses themselves. While they retain a trace of the curse as a violent interjection (as screamed curse word), they are simultaneously less direct, more like the indirect insinuation of the *saung pyaw* described above. Take the January 2016 curse featured earlier: "May those people who gave permission for the murder, the land grab, the LPT copper project be known. . . . May those copper project murderers and land stealers go to hell." Or Michaungkan's publicly circulated curse, which seeks out "the officials who have abused the law." Or a cursing ceremony in Shan state in April 2017 in which a monk declared that "we curse whoever operates this mine. . . . Whoever digs this coal should be struck down with tragedy; and whoever destroys our forest should be struck with poverty" (Sai Aw 2017). Or the late artist and former political prisoner San Zaw Htway, who held a *kyeinsa daiqpwe* as part of an art installation to usher in the new year of 2015. At this *kyeinsa* he posted a curse outside his house that read, "May the government, police, soldiers, and *Swan-ah-Shin*, who gave suffering to the students and people, happen upon all kinds of terrible harm."[10] As with the cartoon featuring the woman praying in the government office (fig. 4.5), all *kyeinsa* here use a public broadcast model of speech, making declarations that outline roles being performed (those who grabbed land, murdered, and stole; those officials who abused the law; and so on), so as to welcome people to identify themselves in the curse. And while some of the curses included more specific objects ("military crony U Paing," which meant the military conglomerate Myanmar Economic Holdings, and "Wan Bao Company," the Chinese mining firm), individuals must decide to what extent they feel interpellated by those categories. If they are members of those companies, or are similar in type and action or even in social class, are *they* then the objects of the curse? We observe here another way of getting the sovereign to become present: by effectively tricking it into revealing itself for critique.

"I Will Follow It Believingly"

Once the object is present, shame is intensified, and perhaps even made possible in the first instance, by the public knowledge of the curse—hence the highly photogenic rituals featured earlier and their strategic stagings and circulations through national newspapers and books. (There are too many citations to list here; the very existence of the aforementioned *Letpadaung Chronicle* or headlines such as "Wan Bao and U Baing Companies Cursed for the 4th Time" [Sa Nay Lin 2014] convey how local media followed the standoff with a running tally of *kyeinsa daiqpwe*.) The enactment of the ritual (and the investment in doing it the right way) and its corresponding mediatization and circulation creates a public who is the audience and indeed the addressee for the cursing ritual: *Everyone hear; we are cursing him (and, you and I know, cursing* might *work)*. What is at stake—what is politically potent—is not only the potential of literal death and destruction raining down on wrongdoers but the shared collective *belief* in that possibility.

Perhaps "belief in that possibility" is still not quite correct, and a more nuanced treatment of "belief" is necessary. By this I mean that protesters may not believe in this form of power, but they may suspect that the objects of it (the generals) *do* believe. Generals themselves may or may not believe *and* may even suspect that protesters do not believe, *but* the generals may be concerned that some overhearers, who we might call broader publics, *do* believe. The generals then may be concerned that these publics are stunned at the audacity of protesters to publicly shame the generals that way. Finally, broader publics may *also* not believe but may believe that generals believe, something they may think is revealed when generals take actions against protesters. And yet generals may take these actions only because they believe that broader publics believe in the power of *kyeinsa*.[11]

What seems at play in *kyeinsa daiqpwe* in Burma, and similar to observations made by others of ontologies that decenter or deemphasize belief and instead foreground material practices (Needham 1972; Ruel 2008), is not only that compelling cultural scripts mobilize people with different levels of belief but that their potency enrolls people into actions difficult to differentiate from the actions of believers, which has secondary effects on interpreters who find themselves pulled into more active participation as well. As a Burmese online commentator put it about an anticoup *kyeinsa daiqpwe*, "I don't believe at all in any of this cursing, *yadaya* . . . , stuff relating to past lives. But if it will hurt the dictators, I will follow it believingly." Regardless of whether the poster tactically acts "as if" he believes or commits to the belief because it will "hurt the dictators," such engagement may produce similar effects.

Thus, what is considered are not just real ogres who will crush the unjust but how and whether an alternative dimension of authority and morality comes to influence the actions of those people otherwise above the law. Ironically, the move beckons the sovereign by refusing the sovereign paradigm: it insists that an alternative domain exists that is impervious to secular realm domination. It says, *You can take the land, grab the reins of the state, but you can never eliminate the curse*, where the curse may at some point lead to some sort of material consequence but more importantly leads *you* (the grabber) to consider it. Hence, the performance works to the extent that it calls the addressee to consider this alternative field and to consider others considering it. It can be used, according to Ko Taw, "when you feel that you are being oppressed and there is no justice for you" [*Eng*]. In this way it is still very much a weapon of the weak, in that its efficacy depends on compelling the addressee to interpellate himself into a new understanding of the situation and himself. But it is also a weapon of the strong, because it operates without the sanction of those in positions of power—it refuses that relationship. It is both.

Curses and the Corpus

But, critically, not just anybody—or rather, any *body*—can enact a *kyeinsa daiqpwe*. Not just any bodily performance can carve out a space for counterinterpellation. The body must be performed in the correct ways, which means that when figuratively and literally "standing in front of the people"—the ubiquitous phrase activists used to describe their actions—activists point to their scars and to their bodily presence in front of certain violence all while narrating their own bodily histories of sacrifice to local state officials and overhearing publics. In so doing, they appeal not to transcendent guarantors (such as the law, which in Burma does not itself secure public assembly or speech) but to their bodies themselves as the only thing that grounds their political performances.

Indeed, while the indirect form of *kyeinsa* partially answers the question, the book has thus far only obliquely addressed why protests have been permitted at all. Why did the state not snuff out the very first actions? The freedom to act derived partly from the new putatively democratic context that had been declared to inhere in Burma during the much-lauded transition. Although activists never invested laws with autonomous power (that is, expected them to work on their own), they could at least point to a constitution that suggested that freedom to assemble existed. But the state often retorted by pointing to the way freedom of assembly is massively circumscribed by law, such as in delimited "protest zones," which were often far away from public spaces. They used activists' violations of those statutes to arrest and repress collective action.

So it was not only law—whether permissive or not—that enabled protests. Indeed, even before the transition, as observed in chapter 2, activists had been on the streets. There they did not encounter the state but rather its agents, men who were susceptible to performances that would not register to the state. This section will address how activists use their bodies to advance such appeals and to carve out space to make them.

The Body's Ambivalence

Butler (2015) explores the signifying effects of the body in political assembly, developing the concept of *chiasmus*: an articulation or hexis of body and speech in which the two together produce multiple signs simultaneously. Rather than thinking of the body as an inert vehicle merely carrying the explicit lexical message (the protest chant or the manifesto), the body is conducting signifying work of its own: "bodies assembled 'say' we are not disposable, even if they stand silently" (18).

Further, the significations that bodies enact are themselves polysemous, constituting sources for multiple sets of bodily significations:

> For when bodies gather as they do to express their indignation and to enact their plural existence in public space, they are also making broader demands:

they are demanding to be recognized, to be valued, they are exercising a right to appear, to exercise freedom, and they are demanding a livable life. . . . The entrance of such populations into the sphere of appearance may well be making a set of claims about the right to be recognized and to be accorded a livable life, but it is also a way of laying claim to the public sphere. (Butler 2015, 25–26, 41)

This is a powerful description, but a powerful description of a *particular kind* of protest outcome, one in which persistence is possible. Ironically, it presupposes presence—the ability to claim and then remain in space. Butler relies on this metaphysics of presence to substantiate her following claims—the rights to appear and to be recognized—thereby presupposing what should be demonstrated. For Butler, any response to that "right to appear" comes *after* that right's existence and exercise, which has been performed into being *already* at the time of bodily appearance: "To attack those bodies is to attack the right itself, since when those bodies appear and act, they are exercising a right outside, against, and in the face of the regime" (2015, 82–83). But while some bodies can persist, there are others that cannot because they never have the chance for any rights to appearance or recognition.

Butler is putatively committed to exploring bodily acts as they perform contentious political assemblages, a project that would seem to necessarily entail a treatment of the range of outcomes imposed by such actions. Indeed, bodily actions generate a semiotic array, as they are only contingently connected to words that could direct their meaning. And yet Butler herself laminates words onto those bodily actions where such words do not exist, casting popular protest and state response in stunningly specific terms: as rights claims.

Let us instead consider actual bodily actions in protest: do their bodies *actually* demand rights—and what would a body demanding rights look like? Would such a body be differently deployed and arranged than one *pleading* with state security forces for mercy, trying to convey a message of "See our suffering"?[12] In the latter case, would hands up, or people crawling on their knees, signify such obeisance? It is difficult here, in the wake of Myanmar's anticoup uprising, not to think of one of the revolution's most indelible images—that of Sister Nu Tawng, a Kachin nun who fell to her knees on a Myitkyina street on March 9, 2021, to beseech police to not murder civilians. The photo is taken from behind her, and captures her with arms outstretched before a group of six Myanmar police. Stunningly, two of them—even though they were apparently Buddhists (Nhkum Lu 2022)—have fallen to their knees as well, hands clasped in prayer. Did her body demand rights? What can we say that her body "said"? How can we decide if we do not ask these people and attend to their actions, study the responses of those to whom protesters present themselves, and then study in turn the responses of the protesters to those responses?

In a gesture in that direction, we can study the body in Burma. It is an ambivalent object, variously interpolated by multiple ideologies that construct it, by state power that inscribes and polices it, and by cultural imperatives that discipline and mold it, often all in opposed ways. The Burmese navigate these forces with their own bodies: adorning, dressing, inscribing, moving, conceiving of, and otherwise performing them in line with perceived normative standards, even as they also absorb and respond to frequently divergent ways of doing the body projected from outside Myanmar. The following discussion will describe some of these forces before transitioning into an exploration of activist bodily practices.

Bodies and Power

Let us return to the song *Yadana* presented in chapter 2. Without straying too far into the psychoanalytic, we should not dismiss the apparent jouissance contained within the song when we imagine it sung by men trapped together in prison. The pain/pleasure felt by prisoners was an existential one: life within the walls nonetheless burst with potential at what could be created in the future through the painful sacrifices of the present. Yet, this pain/pleasure was mediated, and hence accessed, in various ways by bodily experiences. Indeed, *Yadana* points both to the body (to sex and tactility) while also pointing beyond it (to political struggles and life-cycle denials). *Yadana* draws attention to the way the body—through eating, torture, and hygiene—is often the nexus mediating between the state and the political subject. The imprisoned body can be the vehicle through which the "entire person" is broken by the state, but it can also be a weapon (as Aretxaga [1995] and Feldman [1991] demonstrate in the case of the "dirty protest" led by incarcerated Catholic militants in Northern Ireland and as Rudy [2018] shows in his consideration of suicide protesters).

This analysis seems to contrast with that of Houtman (1999, chap. 8), who describes in detail how Burmese political prisoners *withdrew* into their minds through meditation, leaving their bodies irrelevant shells (see also Connelly's 2011 treatment of this in fiction). Houtman (1999) presents this withdrawal as leaving the prisoners *withdrawn*; in other words, the retreats function through evasion or lack of availability to the tormenter. As former political prisoner Ma Thida puts it in her memoir, "I no longer saw myself as in 'this is my body, this is my hand, my leg' but saw my body as something that moved only when my mind told it to do something, and on its own could only decay. . . . There was no longer any 'self'" (2016, 150). Moreover, the *vipassana* meditation elaborated by Houtman's subjects involved conveying *myitta* (loving kindness) to the world (1999, 193), a form of turning away from the prerogatives of power to then refract and transmute them into a different sociopolitical program. This, in one sense, feels a great deal like refusal, in which sovereign logics are inverted. The other side of this turning away, however, is that the body is left denuded of force, the risk being that refusal of this sort approaches quietude, becoming—as mentioned in the introduction—a turning so far away as to no longer trouble that which is being refused.

By contrast, the political prisoners I knew had an ambivalent relationship with the body that seemed inconsistent with the mind-body dualism elaborated by many meditation practitioners. When I asked him about meditation practices in prison, Ko Taw told me, "It was a chaotic place and so meditation wasn't possible" (see also Walton 2017, 124). More importantly, political prisoners talked about torture not as if it happened to *a* body distantiated from themselves (as Ma Thida does in the previous paragraph) but rather as if it happened to *their* body. This was a brutal, inhumane, despicable experience, and it happened to them; it remains a part of them (recall Ko Taw's comments in chapter 2 about his liver disease and how it has poisoned his son in turn). This came home in a bracing and tragic way on the last day of 2017 when San Zaw Htway (whose performance-art cursing ceremony was described earlier) died of liver cancer—a disease attributed to "infections in prison" (Thein-Lemelson 2018).

For their part, many monks perform the same mixed bodily comportment strategy. Wirathu, the infamous racist monk who has advocated ethnic cleansing as the only solution to the "problem" of supposedly high Muslim birthrates, often delivers such statements with a placid look on his pleasant, even cherubic, face. But occasionally, Wirathu performs a (mildly) unrestrained disposition. For instance, at a 2014 rally in Yangon's *hsin-kyay-boun* (not far from the CDI office), Wirathu (2014) used expletives (or approximations) and clicked his tongue (*taut*), an aggressive act often interpreted as conveying the desire to physically fight and having been overtaken by anger.[13]

These examples introduce how an apparent point of tension and departure concerning the body emerges in the soteriological realm. Monastic Burmese Buddhism insists on the body as a decaying integument, a visible manifestation of the impermanence of material things. In temples across the country, murals and sculptures of monks meditating on thoughts of their own putrefying corpses are presented for lay devotee observation (for instance, on Mandalay Hill, a key Buddhist pilgrimage site). Adepts of this version of Burmese Buddhism "seek to deconstruct things, keeping their attention on the process of degradation, impermanence, and destruction (*apyet*) and striving to make themselves conscious of it" (Rozenberg 2015, 174).

By contrast, however, traditional alchemist/tantric Buddhist beliefs take the body as an object for transformation, the final goal of which "is to attain . . . a superhuman body and an eternal youth" (Htin Aung 1962, 42). These superhuman bodies not only perform magical acts (such as flying and being invincible) but also distill power within them such that "jealous rivals wish to eat [the] body, because by eating it, they will come to possess superhuman strength" (44). Here the body is not simply the casing that carries the superhuman power but also material suffused with potency.

Bodies and Gender

The theme of bodily potency invites a discussion of the gendered/sexed dynamics of this conception of power. In Burma, as in other contexts (Chu May Paing 2020, 48), the female has traditionally been construed as a highly ambivalent figure. While traditional Burmese discourses derogate women for their putative inferior intelligence and diminished spiritual power, they do not present women as simply *lacking* what men have (as in a particular Western Freudian/Lacanian understanding of woman as embodied lack). Rather, women in Burma are not relatively impoverished vis-à-vis men but contain the inverse of male power, such that woman's very essence imperils man. As Melford Spiro's book-length exploration of Burmese sexual practices has it, the vagina is construed as "a threat to the very source of a man's strength and power, his *hpoun*" (1977, 236; Tharaphi Than 2011, 541; Chu May Paing 2020, 48). It is considered so destructive that "precautions apply to the woman's skirt, or any other article that is in contact the vagina" (Spiro 1977, 237; see also Irrawaddy 2019), and sexual intercourse is rendered not only dirty but "dangerous" (Spiro 1977, 235) for men. Moreover, traditional beliefs hold that malicious spirits (*ouktazaun*) are likely to disguise themselves as women to entrap men (268), demonstrating woman's equivocal ontological status: somewhere between fully human and divine. Chu May Paing shows how this ideology translates from the intimate realm to the level of the nation, relaying the Burmese proverb "Maphyatma pyipyat"[14] (Only women/femininity can destroy the country; 2020, 50).

Within this understanding, the woman's body, given its poisonous potency, contains significant political potential—especially when used against those who endorse, commit to, or are otherwise interpellated by this discourse. Subaltern myths even highlight this potential, taking exemplary form in upper Myanmar's matron saint of lost causes A-may Gyan,[15] an infamous drunkard, liquor vendor, and creative curser (hence her name, "Mother Insult") who was executed after swearing at an ancient king's troops. After her death she lived on as a *nat* (a minor deity) whose help one can beckon by specifically hailing her vagina to attack one's enemies.[16] Phyo Win Latt, who has been researching A-may Gyan in the context of the current revolution, believes that Suu Kyi herself is seen by subaltern Burmese as evoking elements of A-may Gyan, a connection that emerged dialectically through the junta's own deprecations of her. In other words, the more the junta heaped misogynistic slurs at Suu Kyi (such as *Kalama* Suu Kyi), the more they revealed their gynophobia. Locals, attuned to the discourses that undergirded the junta's fear of women, embraced Suu Kyi as a particularly efficacious weapon against the generals.

Similar weaponization of gynophobia was deployed during the anticoup uprising, as protesters hung women's garments (*htamein*) outside army barracks, forcing soldiers to confront their fears (Khin Thazin 2021). Much was made of these protests' feminism, with analysts presenting the actions as indicting a patriarchy that is particularly concentrated in Myanmar's military but that affects all of Burmese society (Hue 2021). Building on these protests, transnational advocacy campaigns encouraged people to wear such garments on their heads, rejecting the weaponization of the vagina (or perhaps highlighting the wearers' invincibility to it).[17] While these campaigns gained international participants, no English-language medium attention was given to the statements of Pancilo, unequivocally the most influential postcoup online antagonist of the military regime. Her millions of followers reveled in her Facebook posts taunting the *Sit-tat* by taking on the nickname *SaPa Pyan* (Flying Vagina).

Bodies and Protest

With the body so potentially powerful, activists seem aware that they must use their bodies in multiple ways—particularly as passive object and active subject—with attention to the different ways that power flows: to or away from the body. Whereas some practices are designed to *block* flows of power or enhance the ability of the body to deploy power *outward*, others *open* the body, enhancing one's ability to attract others. Ko Taw describes the attractive form of power, *piya*,[18] as pertinent to his own daily actions, declaring that "having strong *piya* means that you can organize the people very easily." He elaborates, saying that such forces are "in your body and by practicing you can enhance it [the body], make it stronger. It involves having a good appearance, a clean body. It means you are polite, not rude. And if I do this, gradually you come to like me. And that way I can persuade and organize you easily. Even if you did not like it, you did not reject it" [*Eng*]. Another set of interlocutors described *piya* as making it such that "no one has a problem with you; everyone laughs with you." Ko Taw also noted that others take shortcuts (what he described as the path of the *akyaun-thama*[19]—an opportunist who wants to get something for nothing) by appealing to the esoteric domain (see also Rozenberg 2015, 42). This involves practices in which a devotee prepares his or her body (you "must take a bath, put oil in your hair," Thu Myat told me) to then have a medium chant spells (*gata*) over objects (a process called *asii-ayin*), the result of which is the endowment of these objects with power that can transfer to the devotee's body through physical contact. For instance, betel once blessed is consumed; a handkerchief is carried with you; blessed water is drunk. Thus the power is transferred to the bearer's body. These are the same *asaung* (talismans) invoked in the *buu* protest (described in the introduction).

By way of illustration, in May 2017 I visited the shrine of Mya Nan Nwe, the guardian spirit of Yangon's Botataung pagoda complex. An attendant greeted me and was pleased that I knew Mya Nan Nwe's name. She asked for one thousand kyats and handed me a leaf wrapped in cloth, and I followed her instruction to hand it to a spirit medium on the inside of the shrine's railing. The medium proceeded to rub it across the Mya Nan Nwe statue while murmuring prayers. When this object—now transformed into an *asaung*—was handed back to me, I was encouraged to pray to Mya Nan Nwe and to her *naga* (serpent) attendant, whose shrine was next to hers (the serpent also received a thousand kyat), and keep the leaf with me from then on.

For his part Ko Taw did not see the esoteric realm as efficacious: "I don't believe that people can get stronger that way. Instead of getting the *asaung* from the medium, we try to find the ways to organize the people." Ultimately, while it is possible that Ko Taw has taken the esoteric practice of *piya* and metaphoricalized it into a disposition and orientation toward attracting followers, I suspect it is actually the opposite: the politicoculturally resonant concept—the need to attract followers through certain practices—results in practitioners of the supernatural pursuing *piya* through esoteric tactics, while activists such as Ko Taw pursue followers through strategies of attraction.

This detour into esoteric power is not meant to make dispositive claims about how Burmese people in general understand these practices.[20] But through this discussion, CDI members ended up giving a name and material (ritual) elaboration to a concept (attractive power) I had observed throughout my participation observation period, and that also manifests in what we seem to know about the history of power in Burma.

Ko Taw also went on to describe how, to him, performance of strong *piya* is an expedient way of attracting followers, but after so doing, the activist should pivot to empowering people so they can lead themselves:

> People have so many things to be afraid of: the government, the military, the disaster. So they find things to worship. And this affects the political situation [such that people] only seek the *heroes*, not the *leaders*. . . . A leader is based on how to organize and educate, [who] will sacrifice for the cause, and people trust him. And [the leader] emphasizes the activities. But people worship heroes; they focus on the way the hero talks and [*Ko Taw gestures toward his body, alluding to bodily comportment*]. Because people are afraid. So, sometimes we activists pretend to be a hero, as it is much easier to organize [the people]. Whenever we are facing troops we tear our shirts [*he mimics tearing his shirt apart to expose his chest*] and say "Aah! Shoot me! I'm ready to die." Once the farmers see that they will follow you. You have to mention your courage and cannot be afraid. When I went to MyoTha, and the many mafia [men] and police came and surrounded me, my appearance is very calm and then we could tell that the farmers were watching. [*He points over at Thurein, who is walking by.*] Thurein is very good at this. He is always calm. [*Thurein looks over and gives a serene nod, acknowledging the compliment and performing the disposition discussed at the same time, adding a cheeky smile as well.*] We yelled at the cronies, at the police, asking how they can do this, showing that we are not afraid. No [farmer] would do that. [*Eng*]

The MyoTha incident was conveyed in chapter 2 (and is resonant with a vignette described in the following chapter in which Ko Taw, also in MyoTha, delivers a speech about standing up to officials who abuse farmers). In the

FIGURE 4.7. CDI activists "stand in front of the people" during a protest in 2013.
Source: Ko Taw.

passage just relayed, Ko Taw comments explicitly on how Burmese activists
foreground their bodies—in front of a law that may technically deny their
claims to space, in front of development projects that erase peasants' claims
to land, in front of cronies who would grab resources. While activists nar-
rate their own histories of struggle, which they weave into the stories of suffering of those they defend, they may make pleas, negotiations, or demands.
But what comes first, or at least simultaneously and in such a way that makes
these speech acts possible, are bodily occupations of space, bodily production
of encounters that say, "We know we have no right to this space, but we will
not go away."

This is much as it is in many comparative situations in which militants
contest systems of oppression (Butler 2015), but the point I seek to draw out
is the iterative and recursive nature of these bodily actions for Burmese activists that builds a bodily disposition that foregrounds political action. In
other words, like many activists around the world, Burmese activists go from
a protest camp, to assisting with an election, to visiting a political prisoner in

prison, to observing a comrade's trial, to standing trial oneself. Then they go to prison, to release, to collecting funds for natural disaster victims, and back to the protest camp. But whereas activists elsewhere can foreground their rights under the law in each of those moments, becoming anonymous wielders of its rules, Burmese activists can rely only on their own body/speech hexis. The activists use their bodies as palimpsests of their own semiotic chains—some of which were literal prison chains—that inscribe their political history; activists figuratively and literally "stand in front of the people," narrating their own stories of abuse and sacrifice to local state officials, the movement participants (farmers), and publics beyond. For instance, at the festive Yangon court compound gathering described in the introduction, a monk among the supporters told me a joke in which he called former dictator Than Shwe a *bilu kway*—an "ogre dog." He then told me that General Khin Nyunt gave him a present, at which point he took out his fake teeth and motioned toward his face with a striking fist, indicating that they were knocked out (either by Khin Nyunt or by his orders, I was meant to surmise).

In a context where transcendent guarantors (such as law) do not themselves secure public assembly or speech, activists use their own bodies as the currency or collateral that makes these actions possible. As mentioned, central to this carving out of space is a mixing of bodily methods; indeed, noteworthy in Ko Taw's description of his own bodily deployment are two seemingly opposite uses of the body: the chest exposed, puffed out, combining with the hortative demand to destroy that body ("Shoot me now!") versus the calm, composed, order-restoring comportment. This finds its analogy in the activists' absent presence: the active, present body "standing in front of the people"[21] versus the body that lurks behind the scenes, the *nauq-gway-ga let-meh-gyi*.[22] This phrase literally means "black hand in the background," but the activists rendered it in English as "black hand behind the curtain" and used it to refer to one another, mocking the label often ascribed to them.

Harn Win Aung, the activist leader of the Letpadaung rebellion and the one who called Soe Aung to action (as relayed in the previous chapter), embodies this tension. He had led the Letpadaung resistance since its beginning, and was described by elite media as "The Person behind Letpadaung Mountain" (*Voice Weekly* 2013), a headline that invokes the "black hand" trope. In 2012, CDI members, organizing a solidarity rally in Yangon for Letpadaung protesters, were surprised to find Harn Win Aung among the marchers, preparing to participate in the demonstration! CDI members were shocked at this

FIGURE 4.8. The artwork/sticker features "Galon Saya Harn," the organizer of the Letpadaung protest, with slogans endorsing his conduct in both English and Burmese. Source: Goh-Sheh-Lay, 2016.

matter out of place. (Harn Win Aung would have been, paradoxically, the protest's subject *and* object—demonstrating solidarity with himself.) They urged him to reconsider. Harn Win Aung, explaining his presence, lamented that "people always say I am *let-meh-gyi*; I am always behind the curtain. I cannot bear that." "You *can* bear that," CDI members insisted. "Without your leadership, Letpadaung will suffer. Do not get arrested."[23] Harn Win Aung relented, retreating behind the curtain once more, although he continued to announce his spectral presence, giving interviews challenging the authorities and reiterating his fidelity to the Letpadaung struggle (Sa Nay Lin 2015).

Figure 4.8 has textual and formal qualities that nicely encapsulate this chapter's themes. First, it identifies Harn Win Aung as *Galon Saya* Harn [*Bse*]. This is a reference to Saya San, the 1930s militant peasant leader who took the "Galon" title, referencing the mythical bird that symbolized divine rule and became "synonymous with the very notion of Burmese resistance" (Maitrii Aung-Thwin 2011, xi). Relevant for our purposes, in his study of Saya San's Rebellion, *Return of the Galon King*, Maitrii Aung-Thwin critiques British colonial (and historiographical) discourses that identified Saya San as merely a premodern seeking to reinstall the past through magic. He observes instead that Saya San largely eschewed divine trappings, organized his movement through "modern" institutions, and focused on material exploitation rather than simply mythical cosmology (174, 6). Hence, religious motivations could have been pursued as ends in themselves but also to mobilize followers. Much as with *kyeinsa* nearly a century later, the religious and the "modern" could "be working simultaneously or by different groups in different areas and in different ways" (182).

Second, figure 4.8 has formal qualities that mirror Harn Win Aung's duality. The words declare, "We will repel the efforts to make Letpadaung a prison," and they identify their leader as "the oppressed farmers' great friend" [*Bse*]. In the image Harn Win Aung is framed by fire on both sides, and his torso is drenched in sweat seemingly because of that heat; his hand is in the air, acting as a challenge to the state and a beacon to those following him. But despite these bodily actions, Harn Win Aung's face is serene, untouched by the flames about him.

If we take these two qualities together, we see again the dialectic of attraction and propulsion that has characterized activist mimesis of the state's slippery sovereign power, in which activists must reach out into the world to then establish themselves as objects that people will gather around. There is hence a dialectic here between *disrupting* and *ordering*. What is more, this dialectic is paralleled in the activists' actions themselves—they perform shattering, order-breaking work that they then attempt to suture into new orders, represented by their discursive construal of that work: that *they* are "taking the responsibility." They act like heroes and then insist that normal people must be their own heroes.

It is worth noting that the tension (between instantiating heroism and insisting that the people embody it themselves) can never be adequately resolved, and perhaps Burmese activists' long history of reterritorializing[24] in authoritarian ways—performed most recently by Suu Kyi—may be at least partially attributable to the foregrounding and privileging of the body. When one "stands in front of the people," one becomes an icon for those people, substituting for them and hence free to act not just *for* them but *as* them.

Efficacy: Circulation and Intensification

We can now return to the curses as part of these activist bodily performances and inquire as to their effects. One noteworthy outcome is that since their improvisation in Letpadaung, cursing rituals have spread across the country. Indeed, while *kyeinsa* were being popularized in Letpadaung and Michaungan protest campaigns, cursing rituals emerged in other parts of the country, from Thaygone (Ye Keh Pyay 2014) to Kayah state[25] to southern Shan (Sai Aw 2017) to Yangon (San Zaw Htway's New Year's *kyeinsa*). *Kyeinsa daiqpwe* orchestrators have been explicit about their objective of using the events to mobilize broader support for their cause. For instance, when I interviewed Michaungkan leaders about their *kyeinsa*, one described the ritual not as a unilateral curse but as a sort of *trial* in which both parties would be judged. If the Michaungkan protesters were unfairly claiming the land then they, rather than the government, would fall victim to the wrath of the ogre, he said. This sort of risk and challenge, in which the protesters put themselves on the line in both legal-juridical as well as moral-cosmological domains, seeks an audience to observe and act as jury.

In another case, protester Thant Zin Htet in Thaygone described his movement's goals: "'May they die with a violent death, may their families break apart,' we cursed. We did it as a performance. Only then will the world know" [*Bse*]. While the protesters called for the painful death of government members and the destruction of their families, Thant Zin Htet also describes the act as a performance (he uses the English loan word *pa-faw-mant*), noting as such that the curse is meant to be directed at the crony but indexes a broader set of publics, extending all the way to the world.

The fact that the state has responded to these cursing rituals demonstrates the way the various activists have achieved interpellation from below. Indeed, Thant Zin Htet of Thaygone gave the above remarks while standing trial for holding the *kyeinsa*. He joined four other protesters charged under the draconian section 505(b), which is a nonbailable offense for inciting unrest. By prosecuting these speech acts, does the state seem to lend credibility to the claims? If they did not feel implicated or interpellated, why respond at all? What cannot be denied is the irony of these punishments, in that—as Thant Zin Htet's interview makes clear—they provide the opportunity for protesters to expand their reach to other audiences.

And while it was difficult in the years spanning 2014 to 2020 to determine dispositively any increase in actual cursing activities or spirit possession, discursive evidence suggests an uptick in discussions of such, helping explain the explosion of *kyeinsa daiqpwe* in the anticoup uprising. During the transition, for instance, political cartoonists portrayed cursings, and religious scholars and laypeople discussed *kyeinsa* on Facebook. Actual spirit possessions also occurred (or were believed to have been): three children thought to be possessed by spirits were murdered by an exorcist in October 2016; in less tragic news, in late September 2016 a number of high-school students in Myaung Mya (Ayeyawaddy) were possessed by spirits, which was attributed to the school being built on stolen cemetery land. *Kyeinsa* discourse 'infects' as it spreads, in that this kind of possession may not be directly related to activism but draws from or is caught up in the cultural script that activism has activated.[26] Seen through the semiotic or pragmatic perspective stressed throughout this book (in which the various chains of responses give an event its meanings), this possession takes on political content. Indeed, an event of possession can happen and be ignored, but if it is taken up, reflected on, circulated, responded to, and so on, then we can say with more confidence that it is reflecting a crucial collective demand. And official state quotations in an article about the Myaung Mya school possession incident index this new context: "When our new government came into power it is not only people who have asked to get their lands back. It is like even the ghosts are asking for their land back" [*Bse*]. In an action that evokes the previous government suing the Thaygone protesters for defamation pursuant to the protestors' *kyeinsa*, a month later the regional parliament voted to evict the ghosts from the school's premises. As senior officials "visited the high school in Shan Yekyaw village . . . , the chief minister read out an order banishing the malevolent spirits from the school's premises while police officers ritualistically fired 18 warning shots into the air" (DVB 2016). This diverges from the Thaygone case in that the state, as it is not the direct object of the curse and hence not directly threatened, might be seen as not needing to insinuate itself into occult affairs; yet it has chosen to do so anyway. The efficacy of spirit possession has produced an audience broad enough that the state must participate and intervene.

Conclusion: "Victory" or Failure?

This chapter has examined two kinds of text genres that appear at first glance radically different. Cartoons seem to be light-hearted commentaries designed to make readers chuckle, while curses seem designed to terrify, threaten, and intimidate through enactments of death and suffering; cartoons are texts that circulate in a particularly public way—in newspapers and on the web pages of news organizations—while curses traffic in the occluded realm of the *auqlan* (the underground where dark magic reigns). Despite these differences, the chapter has argued that cartoons and curses are more similar than expected. Both partake simultaneously in the serious and the playful; both are reliant on calling publics to hear their messages; and both appeal to those in power even as they *also* refuse the precise symbolic terms and terrain on which those in power operate.

In concluding, we may reflect, however, on what is at stake for politics in Myanmar today postcoup by acknowledging the apparent failure of the curses to change conditions in Letpadaung. Indeed, by the time I visited in Letpadaung in May 2016, the protesters' activities had morphed mostly into a standoff. While the protest camp remained "open," it was little more than a 3 m × 3 m raised pallet with a tarpaulin cover and a few tattered flags. While protests and marches were held in May 2016 just before I arrived (Chan Mya Htwe and Khin Su Wai 2016), with one activist conducting a solo walking protest from Mandalay, these were sporadic. Activists continued to live in the Letpadaung villages, but they mostly waited to defend against clearance operations that might come from the police. Throughout the decade-long standoff, the villagers had to continue their lives. In fact, their resistance to displacement became embodied in their refusal to be moved. Or rather, some of them moved far across the country and even beyond so that other household members could refuse to move. Cursings were certainly relevant in creating the conditions for this ongoing refusal, but the villagers did not get their lands back. Whereas cartoons craft a fantasy space in which elites and overhearers encounter the downtrodden, cursings show how difficult those encounters are to materialize: activists not only must carve out real spaces of encounter, in which elites, overhearers, and movement members are all compelled to respond, but also must sustain those encounters.

How then to assess efficacy? Put another way: did the curses ultimately matter? Did the activists "win"? This is a difficult question. When we are assessing the efficacy of a protest, what are the criteria? Was it enough that they lasted for eight years? And if we conclude that Letpadaung's movement ultimately failed, might this be because the military officers and crony businessmen ultimately did not care, *could not feel ashamed*, in front of people so far beneath them? Or could it have been that they did feel ashamed but felt many other things too? Subjectivities are multiply determined, so these cronies may have been bothered by the cursings but ultimately not enough to turn away from the vast increase in wealth and influence the project provided them. This reveals that interpellation is a fairly desperate tactic, and it must be just one of many. We might return here to the mediating figure in the cartoons—the one who explains to the elite that the little people were not really talking to him. This intermediary can either act as the audience of the interpellation, sharpening its effects, or as the one who denudes it of its assault, reassuring the elite that all is well.[27] One interpretation is that during the transition period the NLD played that role. Although earlier it could pose itself as the *audience* witnessing the abuses of the military-state, after coming to control that state—at least formally and symbolically—its role changed. Because it consolidated political and class interests with those other elites (Prasse-Freeman and Phyo Win Latt 2018)—with Suu Kyi going as far as to assure all cronies that they were welcome in the country's future development (Inkyin Naing 2016)—the NLD became the assuaging intermediary.

And hence, the coup is yet again revealed as a potentially revolutionary moment that opens new opportunities for political action. For one thing, it exposed the utter failure of the NLD's attempted class consolidation. For another, while the specific actions in Letpadaung may have failed, the use of *kyeinsa* in the 2021 anticoup protests suggests a different conclusion. Indeed, we might even suggest that the uses of *kyeinsa daiqpwe* traced throughout this chapter influenced the broader propensity to use them and other transgressive resistance tactics during the 2021 uprising, when *kyeinsa* emerged as potent tools in the repertoire of contention. Given the analysis in the chapter, we can now endorse the desire to subsume *kyeinsa* into the same genre of play-based symbolic maneuvers as the ribald chants and transgressive cosplay that were discussed at the chapter's commencement, meaning that rather than dismissing the entire set of tactics, their power becomes clearer. Indeed, while the protest performances diverge in their transgressive, ludic, and threatening aspects, they share a substrate of refusal both of military rule and the generals' desire and need to monopolize the symbolic realm and its meanings (Wedeen 1999, 130). Just as *kyeinsa* appeal to a different value system, the flaunting of bodies, the use of scatological imagery, and the embrace of humor and play convey a double message: "We reject you, and we will tell you how in whatever way we want."

PART III

RIGHTS AS OPPORTUNITIES

CHAPTER 5

Taking Rights, Seriously

THE PREVIOUS CHAPTERS PROVIDED EVIDENCE from everyday life and activist practices that illustrates how average Burmese do not live a relationship with governance institutions that is mediated by what are conventionally understood as "rights." How then to describe the politics of those governed? By inspecting Burmese navigations and negotiations with institutions of power that regulate their lives, this chapter first describes how Burma's versions of rights are lived. It asks: How, in both the traumatic moments of dispossession and abuse and in the banal maneuverings through the challenges of quotidian existence, do subjects survive and object to their daily experiences with sociopolitical power? If contestation and survival strategies are not founded on rights, then what animates them?

To address such questions, the chapter begins by outlining some contemporary linguistic nuances in the Burmese language regarding "rights" (*akwint-ayay* and cognates), illustrating how different social actors interpret those nuances. I then consider historical experiences of governance and domination and their persistence today, sketch a genealogy of *akwint-ayay* across the twentieth century, describe how terms often translated as "rights" are used in the actual Burmese language, and analyze discourse about rights—specifically how social actors use commentary on rights to intervene in politics and direct others to think about rights. Finally, the chapter provides a set of tools for opening up the sign "rights" outside of the Burmese context, encouraging exploration along a number of vectors: How are putative rights claims actually made? How are they founded? How are they possessed?

Two Cultures of Rights

The story told so far in this book, in which Burmese subjects not only avoid rights talk but may refuse rights paradigms, is perhaps an unexpected one to hear told about Burma. This is because the country has been defined internationally as a place where average citizens have long been fighting for their rights. The country's absorption as an object of the global human rights movement-machine has been extensive: The US Congress forged an ever-elusive bipartisan political consensus over the Burma issue, implementing sanctions against Myanmar for decades under a bill called the Burma Human Rights and Democracy Act. Rock stars and celebrities have done their part through cultural-symbolic appropriation of the issue. Most notably, U2 front man Bono penned the song "Walk On" about then imprisoned Suu Kyi and even distributed cutout Suu Kyi masks at concerts for his fans to wear. While much of this advocacy has been in different measures salacious, simplistic, and cynical (Prasse-Freeman 2014, 112), it has also been buttressed by serious organizations both international (such as Human Rights Watch and Amnesty International) and more local (such as Shan Women's Actions Network and Karen Human Rights Group), all of which for decades described the abuses committed by the Burmese regime as *rights* violations. The point here is that there was a robust and sustained field of institutions and actors discussing rights in Burma, mutually reinforcing the fact that "rights" was the appropriate term to use to describe the country's politics.

Moreover, Burmese democratic leaders, many of whom spent decades in prison or in exile in various Thai border towns or global metropoles, have welcomed or capitulated to the discourse to varying degrees. Although Suu Kyi began to disavow human rights in the wake of the Rohingya genocide, she has long defined her country's struggle in its terms. For instance, in 1995 she told the Beijing Women's Conference that "the struggle for democracy and human rights in Burma is a struggle for life and dignity. It is a struggle that encompasses our political, social and economic aspirations." When asked at the beginning of the transition to define her vision of democracy, she declared, "I believe that the Universal Declaration of Human Rights reflects very well what an authentic democracy should consist of" (Sardiña Galache 2011).

The human rights discourse about Burma, conveyed through particular elite Burmese subjects, circulated against the backdrop of a Burmese constitution (2008) that putatively guarantees individual rights (Crouch 2019) and in the worldwide context of what has been called a global "Age of Rights" (Henkin 1990), formed by what has been labeled a broader international "Rights Revolution" (Epp 1998). Scholars describe a rising worldwide rights consciousness as democratic polities have reimagined citizenship as entailing legally inscribed rights. A significant anthropological literature has sprung up around what anthropologists doing fieldwork on human rights call "vernacularization," following the work of Sally Engle Merry (2006), in which a putatively universal concept with immutable values could be transplanted into foreign contexts in ways that would resonate with those local cultures (137).

Nonetheless, despite the global co-optation, I have observed a striking difference in the way that nonelite Burmese communities talk and seem to think about rights. The difference is starkly rendered through a comparison of two communities of practice, conveyed through the outcomes of fieldwork in the pretransition era in two cities—Mae Sot, Thailand, and Yangon, Burma. Mae Sot, a town on Thailand's western border with Myanmar, was then—and is becoming yet again (I visited exiles there in March 2022 and February 2023)—a home base to thousands of exiled Burmese who fled Burma to form groups opposing the military regime. In answers to my inquiries in 2010 about these groups' operations, members repeatedly described themselves as "working for the human rights of all Burmese people" or working to "tell people in Burma that they have human rights" [*Eng*]. While its substantive content seemed irrelevant, the term "human rights" was a central message in their literature; the phrase dominated conversation. Human rights was described as an idea around which entire lives were structured.

In Yangon, by contrast, when I spoke to the same general spectrum of NGO workers and activists, most declared themselves nonpolitical—by which they meant that they neither directly contested the military state nor endorsed the opposition but instead focused on service delivery projects such as education, capacity building, and social development. Why such a difference? Why so much talk of human rights outside of Myanmar and so little in the place where all the abuses were occurring? Was the latter merely tactical evasion, in the sense that those inside Burma, subjected to a state apparatus excessively willing to deploy despotic violence, avoided speaking and strategizing around a concept (human rights) they might have believed in? As James Scott (1985, 1990) has long counseled, dominated populations lack the luxury to publicly enunciate descriptions of the world as they see it. In this reading, border exiles (and a few courageous opponents inside the country) spoke the truth that the others tactically obfuscated.[1]

But rather than the communities retaining the same subjectivities but simply expressing themselves differently, two significantly divided communities of thought and practice seemed to have been developing through their respective lived experiences. It seemed that in those liminal spaces of flight on the border, individuals became re-formed as human rights subjects—that is, as actors who were developing new political identities engendered by their exposure to and engagement with a global discourse of human rights (a phenomenon also experienced by Rohingya refugees and activists decades later, as discussed in chapter 6).[2] Indeed, many Burmese who had fled oppression and violence in Burma described to me then how they found more than refuge on the Thai border; they also "found themselves." These Burmese—regardless of whether they identified as Bamar or as one of Myanmar's many national ethnicities—narrated a progression into humanity itself: they were not yet *full* people until they learned about human rights. Oakkar, reflecting on his experiences with human rights in Mae Sot, described his personal transition as follows: "I got an opportunity to attend the international workshop—[it] helped shape my identity. You have to present your community [and] people; you have to compare your people's [values] and compare yourself with the others. You get a new idea from them, motivating yourself to become a leader; you start to develop your personality. . . . It [takes] more than just one time, but it begins to shape you" [*Eng*].

Some exiles I spoke with also described a thick web of affective connections that centered around human rights language and a global human rights movement instantiated in these peripheral spaces (Prasse-Freeman 2014, 113). These Burmese met activists and volunteers from the West to engage in practices (report writing), rituals (rallies, online campaigns against the military regime), and divisions of labor (Burmese sharing stories of suffering, Westerners recording them and "bringing them to the world") that produced both emotional bonds and rites of passage that allowed these actors to perceive themselves "completely" and "correctly" for the first time.[3]

When these actors arrived at the border and began connecting with others from different ethnic and class backgrounds who nonetheless shared similar experiences regarding their opposition to the military state, human rights became the device cohering this new community. This sense of coherence did not form spontaneously but rather congealed across multiple events and the "dense and multiplex networks"[4] developed through and in between them.[5] These events and the exile space in general were in turn enabled by the political economy of the border, supported as it was by Western aid dollars and the corresponding symbolic power of the transnational human rights regime (South 2008, 91). Under this aegis, life and its opportunities opened up, with human rights acting as the idiom that stood in for and began representing all these dimensions that could not be named, that may not even have been understood, about the intersubjective bonds formed between these actors.

A critical indicator of their commitment to this new identity was how Burmese exiles committed to human rights strategically rather than instrumentally. An instrumental approach would have entailed activists demonstrating tactical fidelity to human rights to mobilize pressure from Western states on the Burmese regime and marshal resources from Western NGOs, only to pivot to more efficacious political language once inside the country. These Burmese human rights activists, however, instead engaged in an ambitious pedagogical project of installing human rights as a new political frame around which future politics would (have to) adhere. "We must teach the Burmese people about their rights," I was often told. And projects often tried to do just that, sneaking translated copies of the Universal Declaration of Human Rights in duffel bags across the border—I myself was asked on one occasion to ferry in copies—to be distributed by U.G. network proselytizers inside. These actors were reprising a phenomenon that, as Mark Goodale has observed, occurs globally: activists seek "to imbricate the Universal Declaration with moral consciousness one person and village at a time, to plant the seeds from which a thousand (arguably liberal) flowers would bloom" (2009, 95).

Given the enormous logistical tasks, the human rights education imagined by these activists ultimately did not reach many Burmese people (Boudreau 2004). The military state stood between those actors and the masses, keeping the former immured underground. The activists did, however, connect with their own partisans (such as the NLD members I met in the safe house, mentioned in chapter 2) likewise toiling in the shadows—a fact that explains the few mentions of human rights heard on the inside. These activists' escape to the border hence can be read through the theorization of refusal described throughout, in which absolute flight displaces a subject so far away as to no longer trouble the object refused. Moreover, by moving out of orbit, so to speak, these activists took up a subjective stance—subjects of human rights—that made them impotent in challenging the state or appealing to other Burmese, for whom such appeals were largely illegible.

Such experiences echoed throughout the transition as well. Consider a Burmese gender activist's description of her journey into new self-understanding as one particularly stark example of the de/reterritorialization cycle through which many human rights subjects are constructed: "I got a scholarship in 2014 that changed my life and my goals. In this social science programme, I learned for the first time that what we are socially conditioned to believe is not the only way to lead our lives. And that, as humans, we are born with rights that nobody—not the government, not even your family—can take away from you. My path to understanding my rights led me to activism" (Nandar 2022, 73). The logical incoherence of this position—this particular activist averring that values are socially constructed while simultaneously reinstalling the particular value of human rights as universal—is explained by the imbrication of knowledge with power outlined just above. Social science courses and border NGO trainings enact a dialectic of critique and remystification: even as Myanmar cultural practices are displaced (as part of social conditioning), human rights are substituted (somehow unindicted by the same logic).

Yet, if these exiles (on the border and inside alike) became subjects of human rights, how did Burmese who did *not* go through such transformations think of politics and imagine their political identities? In an interview in Yangon soon after my 2010 border fieldwork, a Burmese civil society member named Phyu staked a stark contrast to the human rights understandings in Mae Sot:

> If you are invited to go to a training or something, you will use *akwint-ayay*: you will say you "have a *right*" to go to the training! I think in the West you would only say opportunity, no? But this is because this separate Western concept of "right" does not exist in our culture. It has been used a lot in the exile groups, so people have heard it, but people don't have the concept, so average people see "human rights" as a political word; they don't want to really study about it. [*Eng*]

What to make of Phyu's analysis? While her linguistic claims here are suggestive, she may have been revealing only an accident in language, akin to contranyms in English such as "cleave" or "sanction." It may have been that Burmese native speakers knew and easily discerned that *akwint-ayay* used in the context of going to a training meant "opportunity" and when discussed in the context of the law or citizenship meant "rights."

But alternatively, and provocatively, Phyu's argument suggested an inter-mixing of opportunities and rights, implying that it may be impossible for many to ultimately secure claims: that every potential "right" was subject to being revealed as only an "opportunity." And *kwint*'s cognates—which can mean as much as an "entitlement" (*ya-baing-kwint*) and as little as "permis-sion" (*kwint-pyu-chet*) or "chance" (*akwint-alan*)—suggest a broad semantic range in the root. If Phyu was correct, the average Burmese not only had not heard of human rights but did not often think in terms of what "rights" con-ventionally denotes. Consequently, translations of "vernacular" (*akwint-ayay*) into "rights" would involve an unwitting violation of the original conceptual-ization of the relationship between governed subjects and institutions of power.

What's more, it even suggested that this term, so fundamental to concep-tions of political subjectivity in Western liberal democracies, was perhaps misunderstood, misused, and misrecognized by subjects in those polities as well. "Rights" is, of course, a notoriously difficult concept to define (Dembour 2010)—generating multiple and often mutually coexisting meanings, including "aspirations," "moral demands," "just deserts," and "quasi-legal statutes."[6] But the definition that best functionally differentiates rights from other concepts (such as entitlements privileges, hopes, and morals) follows political philoso-pher Raymond Geuss, who identifies rights as a set of entitlements "guaran-teed by some specifiable and more or less effective [enforcement] mechanism" (2001, 143). Rights, as such, are delivered *because they are rights*, not gifts, ex-ceptions, cultural norms, and so on (Geuss 2008, 65), and because they act as *trumps* over other political imperatives (Geuss and Hamilton 2013). And yet, rights are rarely invoked with such specificity. Instead, they are deployed in such varied ways that the concept has ceased to have stable or legible deno-tational content even as, or because, it has become used in increasing num-bers of contexts. That diversity often evades close inspection, making pursuit of Burmese provocations an opportunity to make rights strange and explore how Burma's alternative rights culture is lived in implicit comparison with the ones lived by many in the West.

Adducing Burma's Subaltern Version of Rights Discourse

Many scholars of Myanmar, however, presuppose that rights are a useful way of thinking about politics and power in the country, arguing, for instance, that "the question of citizenship . . . [is] essentially a question of rights" (Cheesman 2015a, 139; see also South and Lall 2018, 10). This is justified in Burma because existing political traditions are assumed to be so corrupted and distorted by sixty consecutive years of military rule—and, after the coup, the possibility of many more—that external models are both necessary and desired (Holliday 2014). But attending closely to the way Burmese people have been governed makes such definitions seem like normative assertions rather than descriptions of reality.

By contrast, that rights are perceived as empty—or at the very least viewed as contingent and dependent on aleatory factors—derives from the longstanding political experience for peasants and poor people in Burma who have never experienced rights as they seem to be understood elsewhere: as a trump against the incursions of power (Dworkin 1977, xi). Indeed, while rights are used in the liberal tradition in various ways—they can mean "just deserts" (one "earns the right" to something through fulfillment of certain labor), "moral aspirations" (claiming a right to X often means that there *should* be a right to that X that does not yet exist), as well as be the modality for enforcing legal-style contracts between governors and the governed—all rely on a particular form of argumentative logic in which they claim to surmount other concerns. As Geuss points out in a critique of Ronald Dworkin, rights are seen as trumps over other political imperatives *even when* they resolutely do *not* trump in practice (Geuss and Hamilton 2013). What allows such logic to persist in the face of manifest evidence to the contrary? Because liberal rights all rely on *transcendent* guarantors; whether from God (natural law tradition), popular sovereignty (Lockean tradition), or metaphysics (normative tradition), rights claims are secured from above by an imagined third party that is external to a sociopolitical situation. God delivers rights to individuals, hence preventing tyranny by governors; popular sovereignty delivers rights to "the people," hence subverting the sovereign's will; and metaphysics delivers rights to people because there *should* be rights, preventing exclusions and exceptions.[7]

Conversely, we have observed throughout this book that in Burma an external guarantor is inaccessible and unimaginable. Consequently, we can surmise that because subaltern Burmese are compelled to attend to the immanent features that inhere in their sociopolitical worlds, emic terms that approximate "rights" would not contain the same linguistic value. To assess this claim let us begin by examining terms in Burmese that most closely resemble "rights" and explore whether they deviate substantively from standard conceptions.[8]

As suggested by Phyu above, the noun-phrase *akwint-ayay* is most commonly translated as "rights" in English. And when *akwint-ayay* suffixes "human" (*lu*), it forms the term "human rights": *lu-akwint-ayay*. When it suffixes "worker" (*a-louq-thama*) it becomes "'worker rights": *a-louq-thama-akwint-ayay*. Yet, *akwint-ayay* also refers to "opportunity." "Golden opportunity" [*shway akwint-ayay*] connects "gold" to *akwint-ayay*. When *akwint-ayay* is affixed to the "doer of something" suffix *thama*, it becomes *opportunist (akwint-ayay-thama)*. Moreover, Burmese translators will use *akwint-ayay* when they must render "opportunity" into Burmese. As one told me, "A few years ago, when I had to translate from English into Burmese and I used *akwint ayay* to mean 'opportunity,' the exile group objected [to] my use of the term and insisted I use *akwint alan*. I was shocked because to me . . . , both are interchangeable. The English word 'opportunist' is *akwint-ayay thama*, so the term *akwint-ayay* is definitely there referring to 'opportunity'" [*Eng*]. These latter examples lead some Burmese, such as Phyu, to go so far as to insist that "opportunity" is the foundational definition and that "rights" is a mistranslation. I also heard this from a legal aid professional based in Pyay, a city in middle Burma, who told me the following when I asked how he differentiated *akwint-ayay* from another cognate, *ya-baing-kwint*:

> "[*Akwint-ayay*] is like 'opportunity'; [*ya-baing-kwint*] is 'entitlement.'"
> "But what about 'right'?" I asked.
> "Our people don't know about that because in their life they never see it.
> No one will give it to them." [*Eng*]

Two important facets of subaltern Burmese conceptions of rights are articulated here: first, rights are presented as illegible as a concept because they do not exist in practice—the lack of knowledge of rights derives from the lack of experience with them; second, rights are presented as something *bestowed* rather than something innate to the subject. As another interlocutor put it, "The basic word *kwint* is ideally subject to permission/approval/consent of the other parties or circumstances" [*Eng*]. The blurring or intertwining of right and opportunity can be perceived through an examination of the root *kwint* and its cognates. In dictionaries, *kwint* contains a broad semantic field, given as "right," "privilege," or "permission,"[9] and combines to form words as assertive and powerful as "authority," as well as those as contingent and weak as "chance" (fig. 5.1 assembles common *kwint* compounds).[10]

Given this array of potential meanings, and building on the language ideology of semantic slipperiness conveyed in chapter 4 in its discussion of cartoons, it is no surprise that the changeable nature of *kwint* has been represented in Burmese popular discourse. In the cartoon in figure 5.2, the cartoonist models how events that demonstrate the manifest failure of human rights change the children's understanding of the sign "Human Rights" itself. The schoolchildren hear one of the many false promises of "human rights" (here, that everyone has a right to security), and because of their experience with actual insecurity (bullets flying over their heads in the second panel),

Table 1: ခွင့် Kwint

ခွင့် *kwint*	(v) 'right to V', 'permission to V' [auxiliary verb]
အခွင့် *akwint*	(n) permission; privilege; chance; opportunity.
အခွင့်အရေး *akwint-ayay*	(n) right / opportunity
အခွင့်အရေးသမား *akwint-ayay-thama*	(n) opportunist [right/opp + person affix]
လူအခွင့်အရေး *lu-akwint-ayay*	(n) human rights ['human' + (possessive marker) + right / opportunity]
အခွင့်အလမ်း *akwint-alan*	(n) opportunity / chance [*kwint* + 'path']
ရပိုင်ခွင့် *ya-baing-kwint*	(n) right / entitlement ['to get' + 'to own' + *kwint*]
လုပ်ပိုင်ခွင့် *louq-baing-kwint*	(n) authority to act; right ['to do/make' + 'to own' + *kwint*]
ခွင့်ပေး *kwint-pe*	(v) to grant permission; allow. [*kwint* + 'to give']
ခံစားခွင့် *kan-sa-kwint*	(n) benefit [enjoy + *kwint*]
အကျိုးခံစားခွင့် *akyokan-sa-kwint*	(n) benefit [benefit + enjoy + *kwint*]
အခွင့်ထူး *akwint-htu*	(n) privilege [*kwint* + special]
ခွင့်တောင်း *kwint-taung*	(v) ask permission [*kwint* + 'to ask']
ခွင့်ပြုချက် *kwint-pyuchet*	(n) permission [*kwint* + 'to establish' + countable-noun forming suffix]
ခွင့်ယူ *kwint-yu*	(v) take leave (of absence) [*kwint* + 'to take']
ကင်းလွတ်ခွင့် *kin-luq-kwint*	(n) exemption; freedom from restriction ['to separate' + 'to be freed' + *kwint*]
ပြောရေးဆိုခွင့် *pyaw-yay-so-kwint*	(n) the authority to speak (on behalf of someone) ['speak' + 'issue' + 'speak + *kwint*]
လွတ်လပ်ခွင့် *luq-laq-kwint*	(n) right to freedom; freedom [freedom + *kwint*]
လွတ်ငြိမ်းချမ်းသာခွင့် *luqnyein-chan-tha kwint*	(n) a pardon ['be freed' + 'peaceful' + *kwint*]
နိုင်ငံခွင့်လက်မှတ် *naingan-kwint-lekhmat*	(n) visa ['country' + 'to enter' + *kwint* + 'form']

Basic uses / common phrases

ခွင့်ပြုပါ *kwint-pyu-oun*	"Give me permission [to leave]"
ခွင့်လွှတ် *kwint-hluq*	"Forgive me" [*kwint* + 'set free'] (polite)

FIGURE 5.1. The table features a collection of *kwint* compounds, compiled by the author and sourced in part from the SEAlang dictionary (http://www.sealang.net /burmese/dictionary.htm).

FIGURE 5.2.
Cartoon featuring
schoolchildren going
through a lesson on
what "human rights"
really means, model-
ing the semiosis of
the learning process.
Source: Cartoonist
Nyan Kyeh Say, 2013.

they reinterpret the passage to mean something different: hit the deck. The use of the tryptic panel models the iterative progression through which signs change as they are affected by lived context (a theme that will be returned to later).

History of Power: Misreading "Rights" through Myanmar's History

What to make of these textual data? At the very least, these linguistic exam-ples serve as provocations, directing attention to how concepts that the po-litical liberal tradition keeps discursively separate (rights and opportunities) have never been differentiated for many in Burma. An examination of histor-ical uses of *akwint-ayay* and cognates will outline the *longue duree* ground-ings of subaltern Burmese rights ontology, one that appears closer to rights as opportunities.

Dynastic Prerogative

It is difficult to know how precolonial Burmese rulers and subjects understood power and its constraints, given that we cannot presume a relationship between contemporaneous textual sources and lived reality. That said, there is a strain of academic discourse that adduces from specific historical texts a protosocial contract in precolonial Burma that could have stabilized into a rights regime if not for British colonialism. While not deemphasizing colonial-era abuses, I would only introduce historical counterdiscourses that cast suspicion on the social contract conclusion.

Burmese jurists and Western academics have asserted that kings had their desires constrained by precolonial law (E Maung 1951; Huxley 1988). Andrew Huxley argues that the existence of *dhammathats*, which fall somewhere between law report and legislation (1988–89, 24), meant that Burmese kings were not wholly sovereign but constrained by law (Huxley 1997a, 15–16). Huxley also highlights how one *dhammathat* "was written specifically to instruct the new king in the rights and duties of kingship" (2001); Huxley and Okudaira (2001) find that the Manugye *dhammathat* provides "a surprisingly detailed account of the economic claims which subjects may make on a king" (254). Elsewhere, Huxley argues that the Manugye *dhammathat*'s message is "that legal wisdom trickling 'top-down' from the capital must be modified in the light of 'bottom-up' tried and trusted rules from the village" (1997b, 21–22).

Michael Aung-Thwin (1982), however, reads a series of historical texts to adduce a divergent theory of sovereign power, one that is "self-justifying." For Aung-Thwin, power articulated itself in Burma's politicolegal system through a logic of natural law borrowing from Buddhist cosmology rather than through the rights of the governed. Using this logic, any action could be, as he observes, retroactively determined through the "Law of Karma," which "states that whatever one sows, one shall reap": "If a usurper were successful, it implied that his past behavior had been so exemplary as to enable him to dispose a person the magnitude of a king, whose status had also been determined by his own past action" (88).

Christian Lammerts concurs that while *dhammathats* claimed that kings were bound to implement the law (2018, 44), they also "were read as incongruous with orthodox conceptions of the proper origin and character of Buddhist legislation, which they regarded as a fundamental prerogative of kings" (2013, 125; see also page 130). Lammerts therefore suggests that the *dhammathats* were interpreted in various ways (2013, 122; 2018, 1), not simply as constraining a ruler. And even in their attempted constraint, we can examine *dhammathat* rhetoric and discern an "epistemic modality" (stressing certain possibilities) rather than a "deontic" one (stressing obligation).[11] To wit, "All kings *should* observe the ten laws [for kings]. . . . The king who carries out these duties bestows great prosperity on the people. . . . The merit made through their meritorious activity will be divided into six shares, and the king will receive one share" (Lammerts 2018, 187; emphasis added).

Moreover, even if kings appeared to capitulate to norms, that does not mean that rulers' *sovereignty* was in any way constrained; abdication of certain tasks could have been done for convenience, a version of control that has long characterized feudal regimes (Mann 1984). Further, as even Huxley acknowledges, *dhammathats* include "ironic or subversive comments on the rules they are intended to illustrate," their fiction "punctur[ing] the pretensions of the normative text" (1997a, 8–9). Summing up, Maung Maung Gyi (1983) argues that "from the historical accounts it will be seen that precept and practices never do tally and it would be folly to interpret the behavior of the king from the ten moral precepts that he was bound morally to follow" (21).[12]

Rights in the Colonial Encounter

It is reasonable to imagine the preceding description of power as at least helping to construct (if not wholly determining) the perspective held by Myanmar's contemporary rulers. This is because while the colonial occupation of Burma was a politically humiliating experience that compelled the Burmese to reassess their position in a global political economy (Turner 2014, 64), there were striking continuities with precolonial structures regarding modalities of rule. For instance, Furnivall describes how the much-vaunted British rule of law became, "in effect, the rule of economic law . . . , [which] naturally expedite[d] the disintegration of the customary social structure" (1956, 295). Jonathan Saha (2013) provides a study of the daily violations of "the rule of law" wrought by members of the colonial administration itself, while Huxley (1998) shows how the British destroyed the civil law that had existed, creating a class of "'barristocrats,' as they were collectively known," who "reject[ed] their Burmese professional heritage and adopt[ed] the robes, discourse and outlook of the Inns of Court" (on comprador Burmese elites, see also Maung Maung 1980, chap. 1).

What is noteworthy, for our purposes, about the anticolonial movement that emerged to contest this despotism, was how it largely did not incorporate rights discourse. Even though Burmese elites were exposed to the ideas of the

colonizer, they made political demands couched in terms of economic liberation and self-determination, which they only occasionally supplemented with
rights commentaries. Khin Yi presents both the English (1988a) and Burmese
(1988b) versions of a number of the texts such as manifestos and songs of the
Dobama Asiayone—the 1930s-era Burmese nationalists who led the independence movement—and related groups. The Dobama anthem, which the radicals used as a "tool to propagate their cause" by teaching "the audience to sing
along with them" (1988a, 9), was a patriotic self-celebration (Min Zin 2016)
that attempted to invert the scales of domination. Moreover, the group's manifestos were focused on racial harmony through political economic emancipa-
tion (Khin Yi 1988a, 5). The Nagani Book Club's song, partially responsible for
the club's enormous popularity (Zöllner 2008, 11), presented economic liberation as key to spiritual and social attainment.

There certainly were examples of rights uses. For instance, the All Burma
Student Unions in 1939 declared that "it is the right of every student to set
up a student union and be a member of one" and that "everyone who insults
the right of a student must be considered as the enemy of every student and
be vanquished" (Zöllner 2008, 19). In a 1937 articulation of its ideology, the
Dobama stated that its members, the Thakins, "were those who strove to attain equal human rights and raise the standard of living." It also "advocated
the dethronement of capitalism and the setting up of a new form of government where equal rights and equal opportunities would be ensured" (Khin Yi
1988a, 43).

It is particularly challenging, however, to assess the minimal rights talk
that did emerge in this period—not only because of the polysemous nature of
akwint but also because much scholarship elides its indeterminacy. Take the
All Burma Youth League's circa 1933 "Undated Manifesto" (Khin Yi 1988a, 16;
1988b, 54). After outlining the importance of independence, the manifesto concludes with a list of declarations, the second of which Khin Yi translates as "to
suppress foreign investments by denying foreigners the *right* to own land and
property," where "right" is *kwint*.[13] She translates the fifth declaration, however, as "to guarantee equal *opportunities* to all Bamars," even though "opportunity" in Burmese is *akwint-ayay*. Translators' decisions can be idiosyncratic,
and perhaps all this demonstrates is that (a) in 1933 political actors were using
akwint-ayay, while (b) at the time of the monograph's publication (1988a, b) a
particular scholar interpreted *akwint-ayay* to mean "opportunity." It is difficult
to know how reading publics interpreted the term at the time of use.

An inspection of a 1929 text featured by Chie Ikeya (2011), however, provides more co-text to allow for a deconstructive reading. Ikeya's example demonstrates not just how the term *kwint* evades easy translation but perhaps also the way that scholars often project their own ontological presuppositions onto texts. Ikeya presents a column that was part of a recurring feature called "Women's Eyes" that ran in the popular magazine *Dagon*; she does not provide the Burmese text but tells us that in "the opening passage" of the column (Khin Swe 1929, 351) the author says the following: "Today, worthy and empowered women are on the rise. . . . They are now being offered rights and opportunities they were previously denied" (Ikeya 2011, 64).

But Ikeya omits the fact that the opening stanza is actually a *lay-gyo* poem roughly titled "Extolling the Women MPs."[14] When consulting the original source, we see that the poem's object is female members of the legislative assembly, and hence the poem is discussing a *specific* swath of upper-class women rather than women in general. This is important, for it necessarily inflects the meaning of *akwint*, which shows up a single time in the nine-line poem.[15] Several points are noteworthy in Ikeya's translation. First, by rendering *akwint* as "right," Ikeya diverges from standard definitions that give *akwint* as "permission/privilege" or "chance/opportunity."[16] More importantly, the co(n)textual data recommend against that translation. Here is where we cannot proceed without an alternative translation of the co-text (the sentence in which *kwint* is embedded), which I generated through discussions with three Burmese interlocutors. One translated the phrase as "So men give chances to women with mercy." Another's version was "Treat women chivalrously and kindly, and give them a soft and smooth time and chance." And a third contributed this translation: "Please be kind to women and give them some privileges." All three emphasized the emotive function (Jakobson 1990) of the three adjectives and adverbs (*hnya*, *atha*, and *kyawq*)[17] and rendered their translations as conveying sentiment. Indeed, because of this co-text, two interlocutors independently interpreted *akwint* here as a *truncated* version of *akha-akwint* (*akha* means "time"), which one reader glossed as "time and chance" and the other as "time of opportunity." In other words, this was not a situation of respecting women's rights but rather a plea to accommodate them with *gifts* of time and space.

Second, these translations also convey the grammatical mood differently: while Ikeya (2011) presents the sentence in the *indicative* mood, the interlocutors' translations are all *imperative* in that they encourage the poem's implicit addressee—presumably men in the legislative assembly—to be kind.[18] This has significant ramifications for how *akwint* can be read: if one is describing a situation in the world (indicative mood), then observing that women are getting more rights is appropriate (if the observation conforms to the situation—the broader societal *context*, which is best indexed by the theme of the poem: the new opportunities provided to female MP candidates); if one is begging, cajoling, or imploring, however, such a mood correlates with opportunity or privilege *gifted* rather than a right achieved.

This leads to the final point, one particularly relevant for this chapter's overarching argument: by presenting women as *holders* of, or at least *candidates* for, rights that "they were *previously denied*," Ikeya implicitly treats rights as inalienable possessions. A central problem here is that no text—in that stanza or in the entire poem—even implicitly construes rights (or anything for that matter) as having been *denied*. Ikeya appears to have projected onto the political actors of that period her own contemporary presuppositions about the way subjects possess rights. In her defense, how she construed women in this passage—whether as having rights or being given opportunities—was not particularly germane to her overall argument (which was that writers at the time were affording women more opportunities and encouraging others to do so as well). What it does suggest, however, is that historiography of Burmese politics has been interpolated (because its authors have been interpellated) by today's liberal presuppositions.

Rights Ascendant? Akwint-ayay in the Constitutional Period

When they did discuss rights, Burma's nationalist leaders often attempted to create hybrid concepts that combined Burmese and Western political theory. The early postcolonial government attempted to instantiate these in government. Matt Walton (2017, 78) shows how Aung San interpreted the *Aganna Sutta*, a canonical Pali text, as only a protosocial contract on which the Burmese could then build; elsewhere Aung San elaborated rights as a concept that originated in Western polities and that was articulated by Rousseau (111). It is noteworthy here that Aung San did not derive rights from Burmese sources such as the *Aganna Sutta* but explicitly cited them as foreign (while worthy of incorporation and eligible for harmonization with local thought).

Myint Zan (2000) highlights a brief moment during the constitutional period (1947–1962) in which judicial independence may have internalized in elites the idea of rights. The 1947 constitution stands as an exemplar. Written in English and then translated into Burmese, the document uses "rights" pro-fusely, which the official translation gives mostly as *akwint-ayay* (as "a right") or *kwint* (as "right to").

While the text seems to diverge from much discourse of the period in its rhetorical strategy, political idioms, and general tone, it is tempting to attri-bute this to a rapidly evolving elite consciousness. But closer inspection of the constitution's drafting process illuminates how the document was more an ex-ample of simple copying from other postcolonial texts. Cindy Ewing reveals that the statements in Burma's constitution about citizen rights were imported wholesale from other sources—either India or Ireland (2020, 193). The sec-tion on fundamental rights copies word for word from the Advisory Commit-tee of the Indian Constituent Assembly. This mimicry was not coincidental. Chan Htoon, the author of Burma's constitution, "developed a friendship with [B. N.] Rau," the author of India's constitution, when visiting New Delhi "to observe [India's] constitutional debates." While there, "Rau reviewed Chan Htoon's draft constitution and assisted in collecting materials for the Burmese constituent assembly. Rau ensured significant areas of commonality between the two constitutions" (Ewing 2020, 193).

Moreover, it is unclear whether Burma's constitution was ever read outside of elite circles and thus whether the concepts in it were vernacularized. Hence, while Cheesman argues that "the rule-of-law idea began to be realized in a wider range of practices, which took the form of a nascent rights-based system after independence" (2012, 21), it appears this system did not operate outside of a narrow urban-elite domain. The transmission of rights was constrained on two planes: they neither spread across the country nor suffused "down" into society from high-court rulings or elite political discussions.

This is in part because soon after independence, various and pullulating rebellions against the state meant that the reach of the administration was immediately constrained: "In many parts of the country, civil administration was practically nonexistent, and courts had ceased functioning" (Cheesman 2015b, 71). The ethnographic village studies conducted during this period pro-vide further evidence of the absence of administration—or rather, evidence of alternative ways of organizing politics (Nash 1965; Badgley 1965). Badgley (1973), presenting a town-based study on intermediaries connecting city and village, in particular outlines the way that flows of elite ideas were interrupted; he cites "the differing and antagonistic visions of 'the political' carried in the minds of government leaders who would build a nation-state, and provincial leaders whose concern is less inclusive, a closed community that preserves their cultural heritage" (4). Cheesman (2002, 62) found that villagers even resisted state-sponsored education, and he acknowledges that "the exercise of rights had its limits," detailing how "rulings on rights in the higher courts did not necessarily correspond to their active protection in subordinate courts— or provoke action against perpetrators of abuses. . . . The government in its early years lacked coercive means to arrest and prosecute its officials, and anyway could not afford to lose more personnel" (2015b, 70). At the national level, Prime Minister Nu attempted to curtail rights by imposing a national religion. Taking the recursive perspective outlined earlier in which signs are given their meaning in context, social actors could not have been guided to interpret *akwint-ayay* as rights through any material delivery of them.

Akwint-ayay *under the Military*

Even if an inchoate rights consciousness had begun to develop, the 1962 military coup preempted its further growth. Cheesman describes this moment as the end of rights; from this point on, "rights all began and ended in the moment of sovereign declaration" (2015b, 107). Research on this period outlines the egregious and systematic state abuse of Burmese subjects across the entire social domain (from political exercise and legal justice to economic opportunity).[19] Cheesman identifies in the military period a form of rule that he calls "sovereign *cetana*," in which rights were *redefined* "in response to policy imperatives" (99).

While Cheesman focuses on the shift in language of those in power, I am also interested in the semiotic process of interpretation. My interlocutor Wai Phyo helped outline the mechanism at work here when emphasizing how "after observing those who do [something] for a long time," observers come to change their perspective on the status of that practice (a phenomenon, we may recall, that was illustrated in the human rights cartoon in fig. 5.2). What is critical is that novel signs need not be developed; *akwint-ayay* and cognates could still be used, but they change their meaning as they are interpreted in the context of new conditions of use.

In such a clearly and unapologetically rightsless environment, consider the 1974 constitution. While Cheesman (2002) avers that the 1974 constitution was not "a rights-based document" (59), it does include dozens of mentions of "rights" and differentiates "opportunity" through its use of *akwint-alan*.[20] In its preamble, for instance, citizens are described as "enjoying the democratic rights and personal rights and freedom bestowed by this Constitution." But it must be mentioned that these rights are only guaranteed to citizens *who fulfill their duties*. Indeed, as Cheesman puts it, "Rights were conditional to state objectives; none could be exercised if contrary to the socialist programme (article 153[b])" (2002, 64–65).

It is true that Aung San Suu Kyi, who emerged as the leader of the democracy movement that erupted in 1988 in response to the BSPP-precipitated economic crisis, often used human rights discourse. She featured it prominently in her speeches, in both Burmese and English, but also arguably attempted to vernacularize the idea by "communicat[ing] her arguments to her majority Buddhist audience through Buddhist concepts" (Doffegnies and Wells 2021, 7) and arguing that "human rights align with Burmese culture and Buddhist teachings and are broadly accepted by Burmese people" (8). But even as this occurred, given the material reality enacted by the military, I suggest that *akwint-ayay* began to be interpreted as moving further away from "right" and much closer to "opportunity" than it ever had before. This argument will be developed in the following section by sharpening the focus on particular ways that *awkint-ayay*/rights are *possessed*.

Fight for *Your* Rights?

The previous sections have presented *akwint-ayay* discourse currently and across history, demonstrating the difficulty in assimilating the term to classic rights conceptions. Indeed, while expressions such as "rights that are denied" and "fight for your rights" have long been invoked by members of the transnational human rights regime to describe the situation in Burma, each is awkward in Burmese syntax. This is because the liberal human rights discourse presupposes that rights are present even in their own absence, that they exist even when denied—something that human rights scholar Jack Donnelly has called the "possession paradox":

> The ability to claim rights, if necessary, distinguishes having a right from simply being the (rights-less) beneficiary of someone else's obligation. Paradoxically, then, "having" a right is of most value precisely when one does not "have" (the object of) the right—that is, when active respect or objective enjoyment is not forthcoming. I call this the "possession paradox": "having" and "not having" a right at the same time—possessing it but not enjoying it—with the "having" being particularly important precisely when one does not "have" it. (2012, 9)

Donnelly's treatment of the grounding of these dispossessed rights is not rigorous—he, like all those effectively adhering to the natural rights tradition, implicitly relies on an external power to grant and guarantee ostensibly ever-present rights.[21] But philosopher Jacques Ranciere (2004) advances a more so-phisticated argument, attempting to collapse the caesura that separates ideal from real by insisting that the ideal acts as a resource that can be invoked or reperformed: "Even though actual situations of rightlessness may give them the lie, they are not only an abstract ideal, situated far from the givens of the situation. They are also part of the configuration of the given. What is given is not only a situation of inequality. It is also an inscription, a form of visibil-ity of equality" (303). While the inscription can act as a resource, the paradox-ical nature remains: to "fight for your rights" is to work to achieve, paradoxi-cally, something one already *possesses*. Even more compellingly, rights claims made by subjects *with no apparent standing to claim them* are often described by rights theorists as claiming rights these subjects somehow already possess. Indeed, Ranciere—as well as Butler and others—have focused on such politi-cal performatives.

It seems incumbent to point out that in the moment of demanding rights—when rights are not realized in practice and hence when they are literally *not* possessed—the speaking of that demand highlights not just the contingent and perilous nature of rights but also the fact that rights require a constel-lation of variables to come together for them to be delivered and that one of those variables is *extrasystemic*. Without the act of *demanding* the right (and the affective intensity therein) and the negotiation that then occurs in the clash between putative rights holder and the object presumed to be responsi-ble for delivering that right, the right does not materialize. And so, if the de-mand succeeds, it does so not on the level of rights fulfilled by contract but on the level of exception.[22] The relationship described as a right conceals (even as it congeals) a process in which a political claim is made and effectively ac-knowledged—this relationship that did *not* exist before it was performed into being. And yet, in linguistic terms, philosophers describe these moves as *re-storative* as much as *creative*.

For instance, note how Butler writes of "undocumented workers . . . claim[ing] *their* rights of assembly . . . without having any legal right to do so" (2015, 78–79; emphasis added). Later, discussing Syrian rebels, she asserts that it is "*their* right to gather" as having been "systematically attacked by the po-lice, the army, hired gangs, or mercenaries" (82–83; emphasis added). Ranciere, for his part, states that "the Rights of Man are the rights of those who *have not* the rights that they *have* and *have* the rights that they *have* not. . . . [They] are the rights of those who make something of that inscription, who decide not only to 'use' *their* rights but also to build such and such a case for the verification of the power of the inscription" (2004, 302–3; emphases added).

How to account for this conception of possessing things before we possess them? Semiotic anthropologist Paul Kockelman (2007a) provides analytical tools useful for considering this phenomenon through his treatment of "inalienable possessions," which, "in the broadest sense . . . are things that are inherently possessed by human beings, such as arms and legs, mothers and fathers, hearts and names" (343). As these are the elements that "a particular speech community discursively presupposes as necessarily belonging to a person" (350), they will vary across cultures. But Kockelman makes a convincing case for cross-cultural commonalities across their various instantiations, suggesting that the things that subjects inalienably possess are central to their respective constructions of personhood.[23] Because these are presupposed qualities, they tend to be observed only when absent—the "cross-linguistic category . . . should be briefly characterized . . . as follows: inalienable possessions are relatively marked (morphosyntactically) when nonpossessed; and this contrasts with alienable possessions, which are relatively marked (morphosyntactically) when possessed" (348). Here recall Donnelly's commentary about the possession paradox in rights—that they are noticed when "they are not in operation"; Kockelman also provides a more general illustration: he explains that after a specific third-party person is introduced as the object of a speech situation between a speaker and an addressee, "the speaker assumes that the addressee assumes that entities belonging to the category of 'person' usually come with bodies, hair, and clothing. Thus, 'there was a woman who had a name/leg/mother' sounds odd, but 'there was a woman whose name/leg/ mother was Anne/broken/dead' sounds fine" (349).

Applying Kockelman's schema, if rights are conceived of as an inalienable possession in the liberal tradition but are not in Burma, we would expect this to be marked in discourse and practice. And indeed, we can use this framework to test the discourse: in America, to say "there was a woman who had rights" sounds a bit odd by itself, but "there was a woman whose rights were denied" sounds fine.[24] By contrast, if in Burma rights are at best *alienable* possessions—things that are not presupposed as attaching themselves to subjects but that must be continually (re)attained—the statement in Burmese, "there was a woman who had rights" would not sound odd at all. It would perhaps be rare, given how few people have rights, but not odd.

Further, Kockelman (2009, 62) provides insight into the processes through which inalienable possessions are formed, arguing for a recursive relationship between the possession's presupposed existence and the frequency with which it is discussed. Put simply, everyone presumes that one *has* a hand, but everyone does not have knowledge as to the *status* of that hand (Does it hurt? Was it wounded recently?), and because hands are important and fundamental not just for navigating through daily life but as part of one's personhood, they get discussed a great deal. Let us again apply this schema to rights: even though they are *presupposed* in American discourse, because they are so important, their *status* is continually being discussed—which in turn reinstalls their importance in the fostering of the social-political subject.

In the Burmese case, conversely, when people do not presuppose *possession* of rights, then they do not *discuss* rights (they are not a common possession or even a potent idiom of resistance), and hence in turn, without their frequent appearance in discourse, they do not become presumed. This is particularly true when the authoritarian state bans discussion of the term (in school textbooks, for instance).[25]

Therefore, while subjects in the West talk about rights as inalienable possessions—like arms or mothers they are still described as *ours* even when lost—rights are typically described as *alienable* possessions for subaltern Burmese. They are not presupposed as attaching themselves to subjects durably and irrefragably but instead are often fleeting and must be continually (re)attained.

For instance, in Myanmar people talk about snatching others' rights, of getting "more" rights than others, a phenomenon illustrated by the cartoon in figure 5.3: the grinning man carrying off a bag labeled *akwint-ayay* tells the stunned man to the left that "I am not the kind of person who takes *everything*. I have left something [a bag labeled *taa-wun* (responsibility/duty)] for you!"[26] Key here is how *akwint-ayay* are alienable—they are discrete nouns that can be physically hefted up and carried to another context. Hence this chapter's title: rather than the "Taking Rights Seriously" insisted upon by Dworkin (1977), we have the serious taking—snatching, stealing, grabbing, and looting—of rights.

Relatedly, a recent report on Burmese citizenship quotes "Bamar respondents who felt that ethnic minorities received *more rights* than them" (Lall et al., n.d., 58; emphasis added). Min Ko Naing, the 88GS leader who is mentioned throughout the book, once made the following observation: "The situation was so bad that we didn't know *how much rights we had*" (Zöllner 2008,

FIGURE 5.3. Cartoon featuring a man running off with a bag labeled "Akwint-ayay." He tells the man left with a bag of *taa-wun* (duties), "I am not the kind of person who takes everything. I left something for you!" Source: Cartoonist Yazathasi, year unknown. The cartoon was blown up onto a six-by-four-foot poster and used as a sign at a farmer's rally in early 2015. Photo by author.

88; emphasis added). Even Suu Kyi, who long spoke about rights in a liberal cadence (especially when she was under house arrest and speaking out to international audiences), spoke about rights in 2015 much as the political cartoonist of figure 5.3 drew about them—as quantifiable possessions that could be stolen: "[When] we will be the government, it is absolutely necessary for us to change from a kind of system that wants to *take akwint-ayay* without wanting to take responsibility."[27] Her party made that quotation into a slogan during its 2015 election campaign.

As with the cartoon of the bag of *akwint-ayay*, rights in these examples are nominalized in a particular way, turned into discrete possessions that can be quantified such that one person could have a greater amount than another. This evinces a different conceptualization of rights than the inalienable rights tradition, in which political-legal rights attach to the general *type* (person) of which specific *tokens* (people) all partake equally. Hence, one person does not have "more" rights than another; both have the *same* rights, but one person has hers *delivered* while the other has his *denied*. This type is defined legibly in law, reaffirmed in political speech and action, and perfectly duplicated in the form of (potentially infinite) tokens that exist in society. The mimesis between token and type is necessary, as the liberal conceit requires formal equality as its point of departure for procedural justice and politics—even if it cannot effect this putative equality in practice. In Burma, however, the subject is not imagined as a generalizable third person; the inequality that suffuses the system preempts such a projection. Any person's rights are outcomes potentially achieved rather than presupposed entitlements.

This helps us understand an additional aspect of rights. In the liberal conception, certain rights (especially political and legal ones) are understood as what the discipline of economics would call "public goods"; this means that they are *nonexcludable* and *nonrival*: no one can be excluded from use of the good, and a single person's use does not impact anyone else's use of it. But in Burma, as my colleague Khine suggested to me, rights are zero sum: "We [Burmese] usually consider that 'if you obtain your rights, I will lose mine . . . , [or] I win and you lose.'"

And sometimes Burmese perceive that rights themselves—or at least the belief that rights will be delivered—can cause them harm. Cartoonist Salai Suanpi (Faxon and Salai Suanpi 2022) penned a series of cartoons critiquing the liberalization of the land law that, ironically, precipitated the dispossession of thousands of Myanmar peasants (Faxon 2023; see chapter 2). In one, an MP (so marked by his distinctive headpiece) sits on the back of a peasant, holding a fishing pole with a sign labeled "awkint-ayay" attached to the end. The peasant runs, carrying the MP along, toward the horizon, on which is marked a flag (signifying a goal). As he runs, the peasant tries to grasp the object of desire: the right. In the ensuing cartoon in the series, the MP, smiling smugly, opens up a present marked "akwint-ayay" for the peasant. A boxing glove springs out, jack-in-the-box style, smashing the farmer in the face and forcing him to drop his hoe. As these works suggest, rights are not unequivocal goods, but they can do violence as well.

The ultimate point in presenting textual representations and data on grammatical usage is not to derive a hermetically sealed ontology based on the proposition that language determines cognition, because, inversely, culture determines language.[28] Grammar instead can be thought of as a set of affordances or pathways that both reflect and help shape the way people understand or inhabit concepts: the fact that Burmese *can*, and many do, speak of rights/*awkint-ayay* as discrete possessions and that this is a grammatical treatment of rights that Americans, say, would likely not entertain provides another piece of evidence that Burmese subalterns live the political world differently. This is perhaps best illustrated ethnographically, as demonstrated in the following subsection.

Akwint-ayay as Counterclaim against Power

In June 2016, as part of an upcountry trip, CDI visited MyoTha to check in with local movement leaders who had been fighting for four years to prevent an industrial zone developer from expropriating their farmland (as discussed in chapter 3). Ko Taw and I sat across from two local leaders at a table in the yard of a small house in Letpagyin Village, while a half dozen or so others lingered or lounged within earshot. The villagers responded to our inquiries about how the standoff between the developer and the villagers had affected livelihoods and daily living, the conversation focusing on debt burden (many people had pawned most of their movable property, such as gold), replacement land prices (up by a factor of ten as speculators bought up land near the new industrial zone), migration (youth had left for the towns), and the role of the new NLD government (they still had hope in it but thus far there were no changes).

After fifteen minutes of conversation, as others drifted in to observe, Ko Taw abruptly switched speech registers. We had been asking short questions—the equivalent of no more than two sentences—and in a casual, conversational style, with cross talk and asides, but at this point he stood up and delivered the following speech, still ostensibly in the form of an interview question but having changed into what we might call "hero speech register." This involved a broadcast form of speech (his projection and tone called anyone within ear's reach to hear) and was attended by hand gestures pointing to imaginary harassers and so on.

> The land problem is a countrywide one. In addition, it relies on the farmers' lack of knowledge and understanding and the problems grow greater. Farmers did not know that their land was taken for some national project! It must be clearly explained. And for those farmers who had their lands taken, the

authority must provide them security. The locals will agree only if security is given! Compensation must be given! And for the families that must move, their daily living that has yet not been taken care of has to be managed! For the elderly especially plans must be made! Human rights means people not being relocated against their wills! But most farmers don't know. Only when their lands come to be affected does it come up to the level of the activists, no? Amongst the peasants, they still have the same desires. Even then, the farmers only heard about rights. The people who actually know about rights are rare. Don't the farmers try to know more about rights? [*Bse*]²⁹

I was bewildered by the sudden shift and looked around to study who was listening and how they were receiving his words. One man, who I had not noticed approach, was not wearing a longyi and a tank top like the others; like the men in Shan state who interdicted me at the NLD office (chapter 2), he stuck out conspicuously in his trousers, sunglasses, and belt-attached cellular phone—a sign that he was Special Branch (SB). He also looked deeply uncomfortable. Critically, Ko Taw never acknowledged him during the speech—this stranger officially remained an unratified bystander (in the sense of Goffman 1981). But he was also made a critical participant in the framework. Indeed, Ko Taw made the villagers the relatively marked addressee of his speech, but the SB man's presence meant that first, the denotational content of the speech was deemphasized relative to the indexical message, and second, that any denotational meaning was influenced and interpolated by the indexical effects.

Just as with the *saung-pyaw* described in the previous chapter, there were many layers to this address. The indexical message of the speech to the villagers was "You don't need to be afraid to speak up to those in power"—a message that somewhat effaced the denotational content of the speech. Further, while delivering this message to the villagers, Ko Taw simultaneously delivered an indexical communication to the SB man: "I am telling these people not to be afraid to speak up to those like you." This can be referred to as a "metapragmatic attack" (Jacquemet 1994), in which a speaker deviates from the unmarked standard (in this case obsequious and deferential speech to or around those occupying positions of power) in order to "produce an awareness of this linguistic selection" as having "consequences for the outcome of the interaction" (392). Finally, this attack conveyed a secondary indexical message to the villagers: "I am insulting him, and you are all witnesses to it."

It is in the context of the metapragmatic attack that the use of rights must be interpreted. Recall the words spoken by Ko Taw that acted as the book's point of departure: "You shouldn't say 'rights,' not the first time. They [the villagers] need someone to protect them." This helps us make sense of his speech in MyoTha, where Ko Taw wielded "rights" as a lexical weapon that a protector dares to speak. Moreover, note how he finally mentions rights only at the end of a long string of political demands that need to be fulfilled: the villagers need to be given information, security, compensation, support in moving, and so on. Ko Taw then says that they might not know about these things as rights, but he, the activist and protector, is inserting himself into the situation to make rights potentially mean something. Given the broader blunt biopolitical context, rights will become meaningful only in the correct situation. Ultimately, rights are weaponized into threats and turned into hortative encouragements rather than denoting anything about rights qua material trumps.

What then is the Burmese subaltern version of a right? As the opportunity to realize the right depends on one's ability to marshal other resources (symbolic, material, and social), one's networks (often patron and client), and one's ability to perform (asserting things to make them real—as in protests), *akwint-ayay* hence does not contain the power of trumps but perhaps is closer to a *counterclaim* against power. And hence, far from having "a right to have rights," as Arendt famously proposed,[30] Burmese people can only possibly claim a "right to demand rights," as Phyo Win Latt put it once, and more likely, as Nway once told me, just "a right to claim." As these counterclaim formulations suggest, I propose we understand Burmese rights in an always tenuous sense, made possible only by the opportunities to realize them.

And so, whereas rights in the political-liberal tradition are carried with the subject from context to context, operating as an imaginary that fosters a sense of subjectivity and even personhood in which the subject abstracts from her own situated experiences to turn herself into a general subject standing in a general relation to authority, the Burmese subaltern is one for whom such abstraction is not possible. Rather, Burmese subjects foster and then draw on multiple moral economies through patterned and repeating interactions with different domains of power.

Ultimately, Burmese uses of rights rarely produce emancipatory outcomes because under the blunt biopolitical regime, the clear lack of legible rights may prove demobilizing or may inhibit people from perceiving an event as wrong, let alone justiciable, as we perceived in chapter 1's examples of personal responsiblization for everyday death. When events do violate political morality, however, actors deploy the vast range of scripts and tactics that can change the conditions of possibility, that can perform new opportunities into being, because they are not bound and demobilized by expecting rights to be delivered, waiting for what may never come.

Conclusion: Rights from the Bottom Up

Burmese subaltern experiences, rendered through language in use and ethnography of activist action, challenges anthropological and sociolegal literature that almost universally takes rights as having universal, if vague, meanings. For instance, in their introduction to the volume *Culture and Rights* (Cowan, Dembour, and Wilson 2001), the editors conceptualize several different conjunctions—rights *versus* culture, a right *to* culture, rights *as* culture, and culture *as analytic to* rights—but never interrogate rights itself. While "culture as analytic to rights" suggests such a possibility, the authors ultimately examine processes around rights, leaving rights reified and static and not inquiring about the ways that those processes substantiate (and hence alter, inflect, and refract) rights themselves.[31] Even when the analytical lens is ostensibly trained directly on rights, rights escapes focus.

This chapter, and the entire book, encourages us to challenge these assumptions. First, it argues that rights should not be presumed to be the way politics *should* be structured. Neither should we presuppose that rights *do* structure political systems—whether in the postcolony or in ostensibly rights-based polities in the Global North.[32] Rather, there are alternative logics and technologies available, perhaps operating beneath our noses. Second, it insists that rights have particularly unstable and incoherent meanings[33] and that a task should be to determine what makes rights so available for co-optation. Consequently, third, it suggests that attenuating rights with other relevant political concepts is helpful but inadequate if "rights" remains fixed.[34] While the sign "rights" can be used to demonstrate the deviation from hegemonic presumptions—such as in James Holston's (2008, 250–67) use of "rights as privilege" and "contributor rights" or Shannon Speed's (2008) brilliant illustration of how Zapatistas co-opt rights and give them new meanings—we can ask whether what has been created is a deviation significant enough to still be categorized under the sign "rights" (see Goodale 2022, 11, 118). When rights are formulated out of local values (Madhok 2015, 2017), or translation processes hybridize new rights registers (Gal, Kowalski, and Moore 2015), we might ask what is gained and lost by still calling them "rights."[35]

Fourth, and most critically, we can observe the importance of close ethnographic attention to how actors themselves view political concepts as their political struggles unfold. Ethnography is particularly suited to demonstrate how something as seemingly fixed as rights can, through the lived experience of those ostensibly bearing those rights, radically change meanings. For instance, do interlocutors alter their approaches to themselves as rights bearers (perceived perhaps through how they approach contentious politics) or their thoughts on rights themselves? To consider rights fully and ethnographically, we need to know how social actors interpret things when sovereign power retaliates: do they still believe they "have rights"? Even if the sovereign does not strike back, does that lack of response buttress and solidify the right? Or do social actors remain uncertain of how to assess their position? Can one ever know? Does it always "depend on the situation"?

Coda: Towards Devernacularization

"It depends on the situation." The continual activist refrain becomes clearer now with this discussion of rights as opportunities. "The situation" is not already there. Rather, the situation in the activists' world is labile and immanent, always becoming.

And yet, such becomings are not always progressive. The following chapter explores what I call Burma's "devernacularization" of human rights during the "transition," exemplified by Suu Kyi's effective repudiation of the concept in the context of her defense of ethnic cleansing against Burma's Rohingya minority.

CHAPTER 6

Rights in Desperation

ON FEBRUARY 27, 2018, in the wake of the *Sit-tat*'s ethnic cleansing of over seven hundred thousand Rohingyas from Rakhine state, a group of Nobel laureates crossed the globe to deliver a message to survivors huddling in squalid camps on the Burma-Bangladesh border. Yemeni journalist Tawakkol Karman stood across a thin barrier of effluent that divided refugees from cosmopolitans and called out, in English: "You are citizens of Myanmar. You will get back your rights. We three Nobel Laureates from Ireland, Iran, and Yemen, have come here to tell you that we are with you on your quest to get your rights back." Irish peace activist Mairead Maguire also had words for the Rohingya. She yelled the following: "We have told your stories to the world and they know about the genocide, rape, murder, and looting that you all have faced. We will take the Myanmar government and their military to the International Criminal Court for their crimes" (Mahmud 2018).[1]

So confident was Maguire in the imminent efficacy of her brokerage role and the power of the tool (rights) she espoused, that despite a genocide and in the midst of spaces that seasoned humanitarians have described as unspeakable (Bennett 2017), she could tell people who had lost family, land, homes, and dignity that nonetheless they had rights—presumably rights to *not* have these atrocities happen—*and* that these rights would be restored to them. If we can presume that the Nobel laureates were not intentionally mocking the miserable with promises they had no means to fulfill, then we might see this incident as a tragicomic distillation of some of the main concerns of the book. Because, from the laureates' side of the stream, the ontological and universal reality of rights is—even as the words leave their mouths—*already* initiating a set of mechanisms that guarantee restitution to the abused. A question is whether speaking makes it so and whether rights work in the same way for everyone.

It is difficult to know what those on the other side of the stream thought about the message (in video of the encounter they intone assent at appropriate moments). The Rohingya have suffered repeated ethnic cleansings over the past six decades, such that those same camps had already been filled with hundreds of thousands after expulsions in 1978 and 1992–1994. Given the repetitive nature of those abuses and the absence of any forthcoming rights to intervene against their eternal recurrence, it is difficult to imagine that the encamped were expecting to see their homes rebuilt or fields returned. Evidence from other subaltern Burmese relayed in earlier chapters would suggest the same.

And yet the Rohingya are in a unique position in postcolonial Myanmar—occupying a space of such intense marginalization (legally, symbolically, and economically) as to stand in a different relation to rights as opportunities than do Burma's other subaltern subjects. As a result of their systematic exclusion from Burmese society, Rohingya elites have embraced rights discourse in a way similar to the exiled Burmese human rights advocates discussed in chapter 5. As blunt biopolitics has extruded them, often literally, from belonging in the polity, it has both constructed them as Rohingya and made them subject to and reliant on a different symbolic field: that of the international human rights regime and its version of "minimalist biopolitics" (Redfield 2013). While this minimalism mostly regulates the Rohingya as mass populations of rightsless victims, it discursively promises them eventually forthcoming rights, as exemplified in the laureates' address.

Sadly, however, an irony of Rohingya elites pursuing rights from the international community is the response it has provoked by much of Myanmar's polity. What we have witnessed is a clash of two versions of rights: when Rohingya claim rights to life, they are presented in Burmese discourse as snatching resources meant for average Burmese people, as cutting in line, as affecting the prosperity of the people—something that can be understood only through the blunt biopolitical paradigm outlined earlier. This has helped spur an unexpected devernacularization of rights, in which the claims made by the Rohingya and by the international human rights regime on their behalf have been used as cudgels to bludgeon away at what little rights-as-trumps ideology may have taken root in the country's symbolic realm.

To outline these dynamics, this chapter will discuss Rohingya collective history, the forms of mass violence they have endured, and the way their elites have used rights as a desperate attempt to utilize external symbolic resources to improve their situation.

Rohingya History: Subjects of a Hybrid Maritime/Paddy State

To adequately describe how Rohingyas relate to the Myanmar state and how in turn they relate both to the broader blunt biopolitical apparatus and to rights, the history of their marginalization must be told.

The ethnic cleansings of the Rohingya derive from interpretations of events that transpired hundreds of years in the past, particularly in the century spanning roughly 1830 to 1930 when the British, colonizers of both Burma and the Indian subcontinent, shifted bodies across their empire, moving hundreds of thousands of laborers from what is now southeastern Bangladesh (Chittagong) into Arakan (now called Rakhine state) to work paddy lands under cultivation. This movement of Chittagonian peoples into what is now Rakhine state is not disputed and is corroborated by census records and reports (Sardiña Galache 2020, chap. 5). What is controversial, however, is that Burmese nationalists and some historians insist that those people who now call themselves Rohingya did not have ancestors who lived in Arakan *before* that time of immigration (and hence merely forged the ethnonym "Rohingya" in the 1950s out of whole cloth to distinguish themselves from their "true" Bengali identity). Others make a slightly more nuanced version of the same argument: that South Asian people lived in Arakan before the British but in such paltry numbers that they became subsumed by the massive flows of Chittagonians into Rakhine during imperial rule.[2] While political belonging can and should be grounded in criteria that leave as irrelevant the immigration date of one's ancestors, in Burma's blunt biopolitical context where citizenship is functionally reliant on being able to prove membership in 1 of the 135 ratified ethnic population groups (Cheesman 2017), these debates are critical.

The problem with nationalist assertions that Rohingyas are late-arriving interlopers is that they defy what is known both about the peopling of the Arakan-Chittagong littoral specifically and about Southeast Asian precolonial state formation generally—particularly regarding those states' reliance on slave gathering for economic production. Regarding the former point, while little is known about the first civilizations of Arakan, archeological evidence demonstrates Indic influence, and Thibaut d'Hubert's research on the seventeenth-century Arakanese court shows that Muslim presence in Arakan was not "a community of foreign merchants only" but rather penetrated "virtually all levels of Arakanese society" (2018, 30). This relates to the second point, on slave gathering. As discussed in chapter 1, given that peasants often fled coercion, human stocks had to be replenished. Consequently, Arakanese kingdoms, led by "Buddhist kings with Muslim names" (Leider 1998), used their vast regional maritime superiority to reach far up the Chittagonian coast to gather slaves. Unlike many maritime powers (Reid 1993) that would resell slaves they accumulated to paddy states who could make ready use of them, the Arakanese kingdoms put them to work in places where other peasants had fled. Michael Charney observes that "Arakanese slave-raiding into Banga [was] for labor inputs at home rather than for sale in maritime markets" (1999, 157), summarizing their use as follows: "For Arakanese ruling elites the most important consideration was maintaining an agricultural cultivator class in the most fertile (and most dangerous) agricultural lands in the Arakan Littoral, in order to draw off the agricultural surplus and other revenues. While the tendency of agriculturalists was to avoid the coastal and rivermouth rim-lands, an important royal project was to keep these areas settled by agriculturalists, often through captive labor inputs (especially by those populations taken from Bengal)" (35). Charney estimates that by 1660, right as Dutch maritime ascension and the 1660 Mughal invasion from western South Asia ended Arakan's superiority, Banga (Bengalis) comprised one-third of Arakan's population. This is consistent with the fact that precolonial kingdoms expanded and contracted like accordions, and Arakan's kingdom for a period controlled much of what is now Chittagong. The ironic upshot is that while Burmese nationalists generally and Rakhine nationalists in particular insist that their "homelands" have been subject to a long-standing "Bengali invasion," those whom they identify as their ancestors are to blame for making proto-Rohingya native to "their" lands.

In response to the second theory—that later import of Chittagonians by British colonizers subsumed the earlier proto-Rohingya community in Arakan—historians advancing it do so without marshaling evidence. Their implicit theory is merely quantitative: that large numbers of migrating people eradicate local culture. An alternative theory, however, is that because slaves were gathered from such a wide geographic domain by Arakan's maritime force, we might expect to observe a different kind of sociodemographic dynamic to emerge than if the people were pulled from a single nearby place.

Consequently, this new mass of people, interacting with the Buddhist community in Arakan over hundreds of years, would generate a community with distinguishing cultural, religious, and physiognomic features, hence developing a fluid but still distinct ethnolinguistic proto-Rohingya community. In this case, Arakan's South Asian population would have generated a relatively discrete identity from those South Asian communities across the River Naf. Later, when the immigration of coreligionists arrived through British importation efforts (after the 1824 colonial occupation of Arakan), those immigrants assimilated and changed that local community into the hybrid that we now know as the Rohingya. The converse—that after 1824 Chittagonians overran the previous proto-Rohingya, creating a population undifferentiable from the one in Bangladesh—is certainly possible but is simply asserted rather than demonstrated by partisans to this debate and is at least challenged by census records, which, their own limitations notwithstanding, suggest that local Muslim communities in Arakan in the early twentieth century saw themselves as distinct from Chittagonians.[3]

Regardless of any plausibility in my historical revisionism here, however, the enduring political understanding, inscribed in Burmese national historiography, is that the Rohingya are inextricably bound to the colonial encounter and are hence perpetual outsiders. Moreover, immediate postcolonial events included intense internecine violence between the Rohingya and Rakhine Buddhists that precipitated a significant rearrangement of populations (Leider 2018), with the Rohingya becoming concentrated in Rakhine state's three northernmost townships along the Bangladesh border, associating them even more fully with foreign lands. While the constitutional government did grant the Rohingya an autonomous zone there, military dictator Ne Win changed tacks after his 1962 coup and instituted a policy of repression and apartheid punctuated by paroxysms of violence.[4]

Rohingya as Object of Blunt Biopolitics' "Making Die"

The episodes of mass violence the Rohingya have endured, particularly when the democratization of the public sphere during the 2011–2021 transition allowed for a profusion of representations of that violence, helped construct the population group Rohingya. For instance, Nursyazwani (in review) finds that many Rohingya fleeing violence "did not know they were Rohingya until they arrived" in Malaysia and were processed as such by the UN refugee agency; they had earlier identified simply as "Arakani Muslims" or "Muslims from

Rakhine." Nursyazwani suggests that "war, conflict . . . , and forced migration" created a crucible that made this change in self-perception possible. I have found (Prasse-Freeman 2023b) that these events created a context for mutual recognition of a shared identity as Rohingya, helping give a name to an identity that was perhaps always there, and spurring, through "Rohingya realization moments" proximate to the violence, deeper commitment to that identity (evidenced by pursuits of further information on what it meant to be Rohingya). It should be added that this was not a universal effect: many attempted to flee the name "Rohingya" because they felt it misdescribed them. Still others fell somewhere in between, standing as and astride Rohingyaness—not in a tactical sense (where to deny being Rohingya would be an instrumental move to reduce insecurity) but in the more fundamental sense of dis/identification. Regardless of these different orientations toward the ethnonym Rohingya, the violence against the various individuals, as elaborated in chapter 1 on the ability of violence to construct populations, created the Rohingya as a recognizable group even as the Myanmar state and polity rejected it.

As the Rohingya became objects of assault, their place in the polity was clarified by the discursive representations of that violence. Indeed, while the scale of the violence endured by the Rohingya during the 2017 expulsion certainly would have alone generated significant global media attention, the callous response by Nobel laureate Aung San Suu Kyi made the story particularly compelling for international audiences. While many of those stories engaged the prurient thrill of an erstwhile savior's betrayal of her putative values, they inadvertently highlighted a key aspect of the violence itself: the symbolic component that helped elucidate its meaning. By deflecting blame leveled at the *Sit-tat* ("I can't imagine why I would have said [that it acted disproportionately]"), slandering Rohingya women's experiences with sexual assault as "fake rape" (Fisher 2017), and inveighing against the partiality of humanitarian workers, Suu Kyi allowed the polity free reign to indulge its hatred of the Rohingya. Further, given that she had long worked to stand as an icon of the people and given that she chose to take these general sentiments to the ICJ to defend her entire country against genocide charges, her actions acted as an emphatic endorsement of violence as necessary in self-defense. She anticipated such a position in statements following an early bout of violence in 2012 that left 140,000 Rohingya displaced: "Global Muslim power is very great and certainly, that is a perception in many parts of the world and in our country as well" (Siddique 2013). Such comments had the effect of ratifying national representations of the conflict in which Indigenous Buddhists fought off invading Muslims,[5] permitting average Burmese to participate in the reproduction—and hence circulation and multiplication—of abhorrence toward the Rohingya.[6] Indeed, within a highly divided polity, Rohingya hatred was perhaps the one unifying issue of the transition. A public sphere long dominated and brutalized by military rule, and hence fractured, found integration through shared animosity against Muslims in general and the Rohingya in particular (Prasse-Freeman 2021);[7] indeed, other marginalized ethnic groups and the majority Bamar Buddhists seemed equally invested in the expulsion of the Rohingya.[8] All of this demonstrates how the Rohingya became Myanmar's definitive constitutive outside.

This social-political exclusion has understandably made Rohingya elites more susceptible to interpellation by external symbolic fields, such as those coming from the human rights regime. Indeed, because they have been rejected by their own society and so cannot even partake in resources of resistance and refusal that derive from the Myanmar context, other versions of justice appear more appealing. Moreover, because they have been rejected by that society, they seek resources—such as rights—that are reliant on transcendent guarantees bestowed from outside the situation. The following vignette helps illustrate this divergence between Burmese subalterns and Rohingya elites, allowing us to continue to develop the ways that rights as opportunities are lived in Myanmar.

Rights as Unattainable Privileges

One Sunday afternoon in June 2016, I attended a meeting called by a high-profile Rohingya activist leader, Tin Aye. Tin Aye was often in New York or Geneva publicizing the plight of the Rohingya but also led an NGO based in Yangon, where the meeting was hosted. Twelve non-Rohingya Muslim civic leaders and activists as well as some observers like me crammed into the office's stuffy conference room.

During the early years of the transition it was not just Rohingya who had been targeted with violence but Muslims across Myanmar who were killed in various pogroms (Schissler, Walton, and Phyu Phyu Thi 2017). Tin Aye thus began the meeting by asserting that the Rohingya and other Muslims shared the same vulnerabilities. As a result, Tin Aye asserted, they should share the same objective: to change Burma's discriminatory and unjust 1982 Citizenship Law. Tin Aye proceeded to outline (in Burmese) ideas for an advocacy action plan.

But it became immediately apparent that Tin Aye had presumed too much. Not everyone was convinced that changing the law was the wisest strategic move. The attendees first highlighted the risk of reform efforts sounding to Burmese publics like a Muslim agenda. "There will be backlash unless everyone is brought in—such as ABSDF [All Burma Students' Democratic Front]—returnees who are *not* ethnic minorities but who struggle with citizenship" [*Bse*], cautioned Kyaw Swa, a Muslim from Yangon.[9] Many concurred that there was no political profit, only risk, for the then democratic government to reform the law. "We have no bargaining power, politically or economically," another added, in English. Still another chimed in that "there is no difference between Suu and the military."

Tin Aye, flailing a bit at this opposition and acknowledging the difficulty in reforming the law, pivoted to the reform's putative benefits: it would grant Muslims a *guarantee* to their place in the country. "You/we want the guarantee [*ah-ma-kan*],[10] no? We haven't been given the guarantee yet" [*Bse*]. By this Tin Aye asserted that citizenship rights would at least provide a bulwark against some of the most egregious potential abuses—perhaps not eliminating daily humiliations or exclusions but preventing destruction of life and livelihoods.

But in riposte, the attendees challenged Tin Aye's interpretation that any law could secure such a guarantee. Some pointed out that legal reform was useless without state acceptance of the simple fact that one could be Muslim and also be a member of one of Myanmar's Indigenous races, something not permitted under the current racialized system of blunt biopolitics. Another suggested that even legal recognition of autochthony would not be enough—that violence would persist; the polity, led by its more bigoted exponents, would remain unchanged. Kyaw Swa spoke slowly at this point, as if to sum things up: "Even if the law is changed, at the level of implementation people will ignore it." He paused. "It will take generations to address these larger problems" [*Bse*]. By "larger problems" Kyaw Swa meant the dual challenges of embedded societal hatred of Muslims and legal institutions impotent to keep that racism contained.

Kyaw Swa pivoted here to a more general political objection to Tin Aye's advocacy plan—not to its specific legal tactics but its overarching presuppositions and orientations toward its objects (the state and public)—characterizing it through metaphor: "If a beggar child demands something, you won't give it. But if he is cowering in the corner, you take pity on him. We are the most discriminated minority in the country—we cannot afford to be so aggressive about demanding things like rights" [*Bse*].[11] The contempt in Kyaw Swa's words indicted the meeting's host, highlighting the way Tin Aye seemed to forget the position of Muslims in Burma. Muslims are not, as they are in Geneva or New York, rights-bearing subjects. They are the beggar in the corner. Demanding rights was an "aggressive" act that only exposed the claimants to more risk.

Tin Aye was befuddled. For those who believe in rights as following ineluctably from one's status as citizen or even as human, demanding them or not seems almost irrelevant. When rights are not forthcoming, to ask for them is to correct a procedural mistake. For Kyaw Swa, however, for Muslims to speak in terms of rights was to place themselves at the same level of those they were entreating, attempting to enact a status they clearly lacked, a lack made obvious by the need to make the claim at all. Kyaw Swa highlighted a sort of logical impossibility of such an action, a performative contradiction within the very act of demanding rights: if one occupied a position in which rights could be demanded, then one would not need to demand them (as the position of rights bearer would allow the subject to enjoy the affordances of the right as a matter of course); but if one lacked the rights and needed them, then one would lack the standing to demand them. The discussion of Butler and Ranciere in chapter 5 is relevant here: while in other political contexts rights not yet attained certainly can be achieved, Kyaw Swa insisted that in Myanmar they would not. They would not presence the sovereign, compelling a response that might perform those rights into existence; they were as likely to generate no response at all.

Or worse still, they might spur a violent response. Indeed, Kyaw Swa's tone suggested a further corollary: that any demand for rights is suffused with risk because for the demand to succeed it must acknowledge the lack of status that it attempts to overcome. Indeed, it must use the recognition of the lack of the desired status as the very material that transcends or transforms that status to its inverse. The risk is that this calling attention to the lack not only confirms that lack, undermining the political appeal for the different outcome (attaining rights), but in its brazenness could produce a vicious rejoinder. Kyaw Swa insisted on the necessity of the opposite tack: acknowledgment of the degraded status as the only way to maneuver. An appeal of that nature contained much less risk. While the question remained whether the beggar child could use his status to potentially transform himself—he could, alternatively, be relegated to begging day after day—for Kyaw Swa perpetual begging seemed better than potential annihilation.

The meeting staggered on from there, but there were no action plans drawn up or next steps agreed on, as the attendees would not devote scarce resources, not to mention take on the risk of angering Burmese nationalists, for such a project.

The altercation typified the unbridgeable chasm between the host and the attendees over belief in the law, and rights as its tool. It suggested that the Rohingya are scorned because they are doing politics the wrong way: claiming *akwint-ayay* is interpreted by Burmese publics as taking unearned *privileges*. For instance, in late 2014 a Burmese colleague, Cho, wrote to me, in English, with the following commentary about the Rohingya: "We can even say the rights of the Rohingya seem to improve now more than before the transition, as the government has been pressured to respect the rights of the Rohingya by the UN and the other countries. I don't think that they are scapegoats." Cho was writing during a time when the material situation was undeniably worse for the Rohingya than it was "before the transition," on every conceivable level—from being free to move, to being able to participate in politics (by voting or forming political parties), to being counted in the census, to being free from assault or slaughter, and so on. I do not think she was aware of these facts. What Cho meant by "rights" seemed to be based only on symbolic recognition, as the Rohingya plight became the subject of international concern and care. They had achieved the rights (opportunities) to be recognized as victims, which—as was clear from the tone of the comment—were privileges *taken* rather than earned.

By way of further elaboration, Maung Maung Fountain, the country's most famous cartoonist (mentioned in chapter 4), in 2016 penned a now-infamous cartoon called "Me First," in which a figure meant to be a Rohingya but merely labeled "Boat People" has jumped a queue of Myanmar's national minorities, identifiable by their specific ethnic clothing (one wearing a shoulder bag marked "Kachin"). The most striking aspect of the cartoon, at least at first glance, is the way it presents the Rohingya as a cultureless figure whose lack of demarcating features is enhanced in juxtaposition to the ornately clad nationals he cuts in front of (see reprint in Prasse-Freeman 2021). This blatant *reduction*—a stripping away of real features as a form of symbolic violence that has indeed occurred against the Rohingya[12]—also *reflects* collective knowledge. Consistent with the effects of blunt biopolitics' absence of knowledge and power, Burmese masses know almost nothing about the Rohingya. More specifically, they know almost nothing not just about the details of Rohingya history, which are admittedly abstruse generally, but also about simply how to identify a Rohingya person in a crowd.

This point was suggested to me by Abdul, a middle-aged Rohingya man who worked for a human rights organization. Abdul testified that he had once led a human rights training of Burmese NGO workers in which he did not reveal his ethnic identity, spoke only in English, and used an interpreter. At the end he asked them if all humans are equal. His pupils responded affirmatively. Then, Abdul reported, he asked if the Rohingya are also equal,

> and they replied, "But they are not human!" Then I asked, "Has anyone seen a Rohingya personally?" Only about half of them said they had. Then I asked, "Do you want to see magic? Close your eyes and I will make a Rohingya appear in front of you." When everyone had closed their eyes I said, "Okay, you can open them." And there I was. I revealed myself as a Rohingya. And because they had learned with me the whole training and we had become very close, some of them were crying, and maybe they changed their minds.

Abdul's point was echoed during the anti-coup protests when, amid the diverse crowd, groups of Rohingya took to the streets of Yangon identifying themselves as Rohingya. Such acts of self-disclosure contrasted typical practice, in which many Rohingya in Yangon have understandably lived undercover. For decades, before and during the transition, they were compelled to merge into the broader Myanmar Muslim community—and as a result many Rohingya never learn their backgrounds.[13] Consequently, many Burmese Buddhists have never seen a Rohingya person—or have not recognized when they have—and so, in a bizarre precipitate of the hate campaigns during the transition, they despised what they could not even identify. Rohingya activists reported to me how striking it was to watch members of the Burmese public observe Rohingyas among them, forced by the context of the coup to see them not as invaders but as allies.

With this broader context clarified, we can return now to the aforementioned cartoon. While it generated opprobrium from abroad,[14] Burmese commentators with whom I read it stressed other meanings: one claimed that it points out that Myanmar is facing problems beyond the Rohingya issue; another averred that such cartoons help portray the complexities of the situation. The cartoonist himself responded in terms particularly germane to our discussion, explaining that "I meant to say that some people want more and more rights and opportunities" (AFP 2017). While the Rohingya are singled out in the broader discourse for their ostensible use of affective appeals to garner international sympathy—a tweet went viral after the coup encouraging the CDM to emulate Rohingya dissimulation to beckon the international (Myo Min 2021)—Maung Maung Fountain's cartoon and his commentary together sharpen the stakes by presenting such moves as akin to cutting a Myanmar-located queue (not an international one).

What is more noteworthy in this cartoon, although it is displaced by the racist imagery, is that there is a queue in the first place. Maung Maung Fountain's comments about rights and opportunities then inflect the meaning of the queue—it is not so much about belonging in the polity per se, as it is often construed, because the term "belonging" is not meaningful outside of the affordances it provides: in this case the rights/opportunities for which they must stand and wait. The cartoonist's phrase "want more rights and opportunities" builds off the point in chapter 5 in which "rights" are not public goods available to all (in which a member becomes included as a part of a set) but finite resources that some can get more of at the expense of others. As Matthew Mullen (2016) relays from an informant, "You cannot talk about human rights in the case of the Rohingyas. If you pity them, they will step on your head and eat your whole country with their generations and religion" (204). This perspective is noteworthy for how, echoing Kyaw Swa and his comments about the beggar child, rights are interpreted as gifts motivated by pity rather than ways of describing equal standing.

Such texts or responses were not idiosyncratic. Take a 2015 article in the popular, often left-leaning, journal *Hot News*, which echoed similar themes. The author gives his name as Myo Chit Maung Buthitaung, which could be translated as "Mr. Buthidaung, Race Lover"[15] (Buthidaung is a township in northern Rakhine state populated largely by Rohingyas). In discussing the putative "Bengali"-Muslim invasion from South Asia, he juxtaposes the national cause—particularly the national *prosperity*—with the vulnerabilities created by human rights:

> if we talk about democracy, human rights for each person, minority rights..., these points are all superseded by the national interest and nationalism only, the most important things. If we do not have a mind to prevent the national/race problem of the Bengalis who are trying to seep in without being prevented, then according to the saying "a race does not disappear by being swallowed by the earth; it will disappear by being swallowed by another race," our race, our religion will come to disappear. (Myo Chit Maung Buthitaung 2015 [*Bse*])

The author quotes the official (if bizarre) slogan of the immigration department, an explicit testament to the xenophobia of the agency (and the state in general). The passage's critical element, however, is the author's focus on mobilization "so that our national prosperity is not destroyed." What becomes apparent is that Rohingya elites effectively subscribe to the version of rights favored by the exiled Burmese elites described in chapter 5, an understanding that diverges from the subaltern perspective. Moreover, this subaltern discourse contains a prominent strain that construes the Rohingyas' rights claims as particularly objectionable, as unjustly claimed and hence destructive of national prosperity.

But how, given their position of intense exclusion and given the oppression they have long endured, can the Rohingya possibly be construed as being in a place to snatch the rightful rights/opportunities of citizens? It is to this question that we now turn.

Rights and Resources

How to make sense of the relationship between rights claims, anxieties over resources, and interethnic conflict in Myanmar? Saskia Sassen (2017) has attempted to articulate a parsimonious explanation, in which the genocidal attacks were motivated *not* by interethnic animus (which she deems epiphenomenal) but by the desire to clear people from land targeted for the site of a gas pipeline and Special Economic Zone (SEZ). But while China's USD 7.3 billion investment in a deep-sea port on the coast of Rakhine, a key link in Beijing's Belt and Road Initiative, is a critical site of a particular form of extractivist economic development, Sassen's analysis faces an empirical spatial problem: land required for the aforementioned infrastructure project was nowhere near the sites of ethnic cleansing, which was occurring at that time hundreds of kilometers south. As Lee Jones (2017) puts it, "One can simply look at a few maps."

Jones points out that the Myanmar government *has*, however, indicated intentions to build a different SEZ directly on the site of land cleansed of Rohingya, which hews more closely to Sassen's argument. Moreover, while many aid organizations, foreign governments, and Suu Kyi herself have proposed economic development as the antidote to the ongoing Rohingya genocide, in November 2017, "development" was revealed to be a massive land grab as the government stated that it would appropriate all fire-damaged land in Rakhine for "redevelopment" purposes, legally dispossessing the genocide victims. As these examples suggest, a more expansive view of natural resource extraction and foreign-state-backed capital investment reveals projects that indeed spur ethnic conflict. A recent report by the Kachin Development Network Group, for instance, well illustrates the connection between displacement and theft of resources: "In 2018, Burmese government troops stepped up their war in Kachin State, further driving out indigenous populations and expanding control over the area's rich natural resources and strategic trading routes. The fiercest offensive was fought in northwest Kachin State's Hugawng Valley, to secure the historic Ledo Road linking India and China, which is part of China's Belt and Road Initiative, and to seize hugely lucrative amber mines" (KDNG 2019, 4). In this offensive it becomes clear how interethnic conflict is exacerbated secondary to the particular ulterior motives of accessing resource extraction opportunities (amber) and securing a key Chinese infrastructural investment project.

As the examples from Rakhine and Kachin states diverge significantly, the cases require synthesis. Particularly, we must ask how to make sense of real interethnic animus against the Rohingya in the broader context of land grabs that often benefit particular population groups over others. As developed in earlier chapters, I believe that as the political economy becomes increasingly focused on the extraction of resources and as Myanmar maneuvers to establish itself as a larger hub in a vast logistical supply chain (vis-à-vis China, India, and Southeast Asia), laborers scramble to avoid becoming populations absolutely surplus to capital (Prasse-Freeman 2022a). As a result, ethnic cleavages become exacerbated along several vectors.

First, ethnicity becomes a way of delineating legitimate membership in the nation, with Muslims in particular being seen as undeserving of the spoils of any development that might be forthcoming. The message conveyed by new minimum wage laws (Noe Noe Aung 2014) and taxation regimes proposed during the transition was that collective resources would be redistributed— something that demanded reconceiving the relationship between a much larger section of the economy and the state. Whereas in the past poor subjects could expect nothing from the state except casual and arbitrary extraction, during the transition they are being *told* that they could expect goods, resources, and opportunities.

Second, and relatedly, because the Myanmar state has never been particularly developmentalist in any material sense—with such paltry percentages of GDP going to health, education, and public goods (McCarthy 2016, 2019)— while people might not expect resources to be automatically forthcoming from this putative revolution in state practice, there was a sense that resources are more available for the taking. In this context, ethnic difference may refract into cleavages over which groups get to access either spoils of extraction or simply labor opportunities.

Hence, pace Sassen, it appears that ethnic conflict (and particularly the Othering of the Rohingya) works through political economic imperatives indirectly rather than directly. Indeed, there are only a few examples of interethnic conflict directly driven through the fact of scarce labor opportunities. In the Hpakant jade mines, "handpicker" teams are often organized by ethnicity (such as Rakhine, Kachin, and Bamar), and these ethnic groups are often backed by their own militias: deaths in mines will generate different compensation prices, depending on the power of those respective militias. Families of deceased Kachin receive the most compensation, then Rakhine, and then Bamar. Such examples notwithstanding, it would be incorrect to describe Myanmar's political economy as devolving along ethnic lines.

Instead, in the context of a highly resource-extractive political economy that is producing massive rents available for potential redistribution, what matters is whether one is a worthy member of the nation, a status accessible only through membership in an ethnic group. Noteworthy here is how in the midst of dispossession and increased precarity, signs of wealth nonetheless exploded—as indexed in glittering shopping malls adorning Yangon's new cityscape, images of which circulate in print and social media around the country. Hence, senses of opportunity and the fear of missing out have generally both intensified. Burmese people are told—sometimes explicitly, and by Suu Kyi no less—that they must suffer now in exchange for spoils at some later moment (Prasse-Freeman and Phyo Win Latt 2018); who is a legitimate claimant to membership in the nation, then, will entail how those spoils are distributed. Rohingya are not seen as legitimate members and as a result are not only physically expelled but also symbolically excluded, as indexed by mobilizations against the Rohingya from being counted in the 2014 census and the enormous backlash over how the Rohingya have distracted attention from the suffering of "real" Myanmar subjects.[16] Meanwhile, the international community presented foreign investment as necessarily fueling democratization (Pauker 2017), even though it seemed to have precisely the opposite effect, especially given the composition of that investment, which was going mostly to extractive industries, the rents of which are captured by elites and channeled into patronage systems based on ethnic belonging, making ethnicity more salient.

But in the context of a blunt biopolitical system it is difficult to *ascribe* identity to specific subjects. This leads to a third point, which is that because Myanmar's different population groups are not particularly legible—one cannot identify members of the group (the Rohingya) who is meant to steal the resources—and the polity knows the state cannot be trusted to contain or constrain them, it is easy for people to imagine the Rohingya as vehicles for immeasurable hordes of Bengalis from densely populated Bangladesh. On this topic of population and ethnicity, Arjun Appadurai (1998) makes a suggestive argument that in situations where there is uncertainty about the numbers of an ethnic Other—especially when that uncertainly affords an imagination of their quantity as being almost infinite—"vivisectionist violence" offers "temporary ways to render these abstractions graspable, to make these large numbers sensuous, to make labels that are potentially overwhelming, for a moment, personal" (919).[17] At the very least, fantasies of boundless invaders have been stoked by Myanmar's blunt biopolitics: Myanmar state representatives have claimed that "the population growth of Rohingya Muslims is 10 times higher than that of the Rakhine (Buddhists)" (Associated Press 2013) but never provided the public with data to secure that claim, providing no circumscriptions on its potential inflation.

These fears were particularly piqued in the context of democratization. Recall here the cartoon from chapter 4 (fig. 4.2) featuring Suu Kyi and the dark-skinned figures wearing parliamentarian costumes (indexed by the telltale *konbaung* headpiece). Although by the time the cartoon was published the Rohingya had already been disenfranchised en masse, the cartoon nonetheless conveys the fear of liberalism by imagining a scenario in which a weak NLD capitulates to international pressure and gives the Rohingya citizenship; this allows the Rohingya representation in politics, the consequences of which are not simply political (in the sense of altering the distribution of resources or promoting specific values) but reality changing. The idea that language itself, the tool for conveying reality, could be changed was an anxiety explicitly conveyed through right-wing/state media (see Tha Sein 2016, for instance).

It is here that we can observe how the trappings of the blunt biopolitical apparatus impel precarious subjects to mobilize as population groups but in evasive ways that mimic the perverse apparatus they interface with. For example, what was striking about Myanmar's 2014 census exercise was how it generated a significant *proleptic* process in which numerous actors attempted to anticipate the forms that the state sought to catalogue. This form of mimesis, in which people acted strategically *with* and *against* the census procedure, sought to distort what actors presumed to be a corrupted process pursued by a state they supposed was acting in bad faith. For instance, the All-Myanmar Islamic Association (AMIA), a Muslim umbrella group, "urged Burmese Muslims to cite themselves as 'Islamic' when it [came] to the census question on religion, as opposed to answering 'Muslim' for the question on ethnic nationality" (Ko Htwe 2014). The AMIA was actively trying to coordinate group identification. While it might have intended to convey the importance of tactical maneuvering at the population level, the AMIA's campaign might have had the effect of altering the meaning of that group identity for its members. This same objective was pursued by a number of different ethnic organizations—the Kachin Baptist Convention instructed Kachin to ignore the subdivisions of their ethnic category and declare themselves "Kachin" (BCUK 2014, 6); the Karen were advocating for a way to ensure that if people record themselves as a Karen subgroup, that is also counted as Karen (EKNPS 2014); the Shan and Mon designed their own censuses in parallel to the state's project;[18] the Rahkine fought to prevent "Rohingya" from being included as a category at all.

These maneuvers reveal, yet again, that such projects do not evince standard forms of governmentality in which the population is known and hence constructed as part of the state's centralizing and simplifying project (à la Scott 1998). Instead, it is a decentralized fictionalization that encourages the groups taken as objects to mobilize in ways that diverge from their subjective (cultural and ethnolinguistic) experiences.

We can now pivot to consider more deeply how those who have perceived the intensification of, simultaneously, exclusion and opportunity have used rights language. In particular, by turning to the concept I will call the "*de-vernacularization*" of rights, I explore how resentful Burmese people object to rights.

Right-Wing Mobilizations and the Devernacularization of Rights

We can return now to Merry's concept of vernacularization, introduced in chapter 5. For Merry (2006), vernacularization is a process that requires "appropriating global human rights frameworks and translating them to fit into particular situations . . . , foster[ing] the gradual emergence of a local rights consciousness among grassroots people and greater awareness of national and local issues among global activists" (134). Merry's concept was eagerly taken up by scholar-activists who had sought to respect local difference (culture) while promoting individual autonomy (through the specific vehicle of rights). Vernacularization appeared to square that circle, allowing "local communities [to] reframe human rights ideas to fit into their system of cultural meanings" (1).

But in reading Merry (2006) closely, it becomes apparent that she was never as sanguine about the ability to satisfy the two imperatives of cultural deference and individual rights as many of her epigones. In fact, by understanding human rights as unalterable, Merry makes vernacularization akin to a colonization project, for better or worse.[19] And although she might not have used that term, Merry is quite forthcoming about this fact, writing that human rights programs "retain their underlying emphasis on individual rights to protection of the body along with autonomy, choice, and equality, ideas embedded in the legal codes of the human rights system. Inside the culturally resonant packaging is a core that radically challenges patriarchy. Despite arguments that human rights must be translated into local webs of meaning based on religion, ethnicity, or place in order for them to appear both legitimate and appealing, such transformations take place only at a relatively superficial level" (137). It is this unyielding aspect of human rights that gives them their power; if they could be harmonized with local culture, they would be denuded of their ability to change that culture. "Resonance is a costly choice since it may limit the possibility of long-term change" (136), as Merry puts it. The reason for belaboring this point is that it focalizes the conflict that attends many vernacularization projects, reminding us that this is to be expected: the objective is not harmony but displacement of what are perceived to be violent or oppressive cultures. Reframed this way, "human rights" must be reassessed as political in the sense of constituting a battle over normative values, in which some win and some lose. Consequently, we can expect vernacularization projects *not* to proceed smoothly, *not* simply inexorably winning over additional hearts and minds to build a human rights culture.

Yet there is often a presumption of gradual realization of rights culture, in which signs of uptake index progressive diffusion. This derives from what I call the "synecdoche problem," which is the way scholars and human rights activists often presume an iconic relation of the *part* of the culture they study or intervene in (say, the social movement that does the translation of human rights) to the *whole* of the place. There is an implicit and often even explicit assertion of an imminent spread of vernacularization across the entire society.

For instance, in an article by Lynette Chua on the vernacularization of human rights in Myanmar, under a section called "Producing Multiplier Effects," we hear, "To date, the movement has established its presence in 16 locations in Myanmar" (2015, 324), which is an empirical statement with indexical content: the sixteen locations can be presumed to be in the process of becoming more.

A problem here is that while it is assumed that the universe to be vernacularized is homogenous and the vernacularization linear, the reality is that the universe is inevitably *plural*. In Burma's case, many Burmese elites have become resubjectivized by the power of human rights ideology, but because these individuals may constitute a minuscule percentage of the entire (plural) universe of Burmese people, the processes of vernacularization may not progressively change all of Burma. Critically, the spreading power of human rights may not just diminish across spatial, subcultural, class, and gender cleavages but may encounter fortified battlelines that oppose it. Further, human rights may inadvertently mobilize reinforcements to the opposite cause, as erstwhile nonpartisans come to realize their view of the world is under threat. And indeed, during Myanmar's transition human rights produced countermovements from social actors who rejected its overtures as corrupting rather than emancipatory. Vernacularization must be considered a semiotic process, one with temporalities that are difficult to presume in advance; the uptake of human rights by part of a social community at an initial moment could give way to a broader *rejection* of human rights by another part of the society in question, leaving ambiguous overall effects on others. I will expand on this hypothesis through several examples that follow.

Devernacularization in Practice

In what constitutes a robust subgenre, Burmese political partisans have used the slipperiness of *akwint-ayay* as a deconstructive tool against the international rights discourses that these commentators perceive as buffeting their country.

In a November 2016 article, "Human *akwint-ayay*, Religious *akwint-ayay*, Myanmar's *akwint-ayay*" [*Bse*], published in the right-wing journal *Thageethway*, author Shwe Saw Thet (Shwebo) repeats the term *akwint-ayay* six times in the first three lines, reiterating the term in different grammatical syntagms and with different authorial voices to throw the term itself into metapragmatic relief.

The first line of the text locates *awkint-ayay* in a global context: "In today's large world, '*akwint-ayay*' words are swarming and teeming like locusts."

Akwint-ayay's meaning here is indeterminate: metalinguistically isolated and framed in the text as the object of the discourse itself, all we know is that *akwint-ayay* is everywhere. What is it doing? How should we think about it?

In the second line, Shwe Saw Thet suffixes *akwint-ayay* to a number of noun phrases: human *akwint-ayay*, worker *akwint-ayay*, farmer *akwint-ayay*, student *akwint-ayay*, and such. The author plays with co-text to highlight how *akwint-ayay* takes different meanings with different affixes: attached to "worker" and "human," it likely reads as "rights." The author then proceeds to say that "in the human world, those who want to get *akwint-ayay* are increasing and spreading significantly."[20] In this final phase of his initial exploration of *akwint-ayay*, however, Shwe Saw Thet pivots, changing authorial voice by invoking the vernacular way of using *akwint-ayay* introduced throughout this book: an opportunity that one should be ashamed of taking or getting. When I read this passage with trusted interlocutors, Phyo Win Latt felt that "opportunity is more suitable here" for *akwint-ayay*, while Wai Phyo went further, saying that the sentence "should simply be translated as 'there are a great number of opportunists in the world.'" Therefore, by putting the *akwint-ayay* tokens in quick succession, Shwe Saw Thet brings attention to the fact that when *akwint-ayay* is used as "rights," it can be infected with opportunism, as if to say: *those calling for human rights are trying to get something they do not deserve.*

But, critically, Shwe Saw Thet does not simply reject *akwint-ayay*. There are two other mentions of it, appearing deep in the body of the article, after Shwe Saw Thet has theorized state formation, the requirements of citizenship, and the foundations of law. Only then, in the broader context of "national race unity, a shared language, shared religious beliefs, a single authorized government, a shared culture, and a loving attitude toward the nation that is shared," does *akwint-ayay* reemerge. He writes, "It is the responsibility of the government to lay down laws to promote our citizens' peacefulness, their education, their economy, their religion, their *akwint-ayay*." I read this as Shwe Saw Thet not rehabilitating the phrase entirely but instead showing how only *if akwint-ayay* is embedded in immanent realities does it shake its opportunist inflection.

Other commentaries echo this point. Thamaga Thein Oo, in an article titled "In Myanmar, Rights Are Not for Buddhism" (2014), critiques the particularity of human rights to then write that "it begs the question of whether the rights that you're talking about have anything to do with Buddhists in Myanmar" [*Bse*]. Even *Pyithu Ayay*, a long-standing middle-class liberal journal, contains articles that introduce ambiguity into the standing of such categories.

For instance, a 2014 editorial, "Only If There Is Truth Will We Get a Certain Victory," asks and then answers a series of rhetorical questions: "Who owns the country's sovereignty? In a country, the people from that country own it, no? Who has the authority to close off and obstruct human rights and the basic democratic rights? Human rights and basic democratic rights are every person's birthright, no?" [Bse]. After establishing textbook definitions, though, the editorial rends them apart: "However . . . , in reality life is another way" (let-dwe t'-myo—using here the same expression featured in chapter 2). The article proceeds to outline all the abuses that Burmese have suffered at the hands of the military regime, grounding the fight of the just in an ethics of moral struggle and perseverance.

Still other texts similarly demonstrate how akwint-ayay takes on meanings only through grounded experiences. Than Htay, then chairperson of the USDP, the military-linked opposition party, in a 2016 speech critiqued "human rights" (as well as "democracy" and "transparency"), as "simply awkward" in Myanmar (Mizzima 2016 [Bse]). Critically, the chairman did not advance a critique of the human rights concept—how it operates (or fails) as a philosophy—but highlighted its mis fit in what he asserted was Burma's particular political system. Human rights' awkwardness derives from the way they are grafted onto real politics: Than Htay identifies them as distracting from the first priorities of protecting race and religion and providing for livelihood concerns,[21] a lack of focus that risks unintended consequences. They are seen as inimical to (at worst) or parallel (at best) rather than facilitative of nationalist and developmentalist goals (a discourse that is of course strong in many parts of Asia—China and Singapore being prime examples).

Maung ThaNoe (2016), writing for a journal sponsored by the right-wing monks' organization MaBaTha, argues that human rights can be used by anyone to justify anything:

> Human Rights is talk that is very noble. However, because this phrase has come to be used not only by good people but by despicable people, it has become an incredibly disappointing and indecent word. . . . For example, in a Western country there is an organization "Men Love Boys" that is for the defense of carnal lust and sexual relations between an adult male and boys five to [ten] years old, and they transparently present their intention to found their organization and call it a human rights organization. [Bse]

Maung ThaNoe effectively argues that the sign "human rights" has no immutable content and hence as a floating signifier is vulnerable to being hijacked by others whose agendas are literally perverted.[22] There is an implicit argument—evoking Perugini and Gordon's (2015) study of the Israeli settler movement's use of human rights to justify occupation—that human rights' lack of grounding makes it susceptible to such appropriation in ways that other ideologies are not. While intellectual reflections persist over which "plurality of values" should be accepted by any reinvented human rights project (Goodale 2022, chap. 6), Maung ThaNoe, as in many of these Burmese-Buddhist commentaries, encourages a foundation in Buddhist values that draw on an unassailable morality.

It should be mentioned here that these Buddhist critiques were so vociferous that Aung Myo Min, a long-term LGBT rights advocate who became the NUG's human rights minister postcoup, felt the need to respond (in English).[23] He introduced an op-ed by acknowledging that "'human rights have caused violent attacks' and 'human rights protect and abet violence' are arguments I have frequently seen on social media" (Aung Myo Min 2017). Unfortunately, Aung Myo Min then attempted to dismiss the attacks with an antipolitical sermon on the ideal standards and legal declarations contained in human rights statutes. Those to whom he was responding may have been incorrect in ascribing violence to human rights during Burma's transition, but their *mode* of thinking—in which speech acts (rights claims) can create outcomes that deviate from their enunciated goals—was at least grounded in the politics of that moment.

How, then, to make sense of this discourse? Doffegnies and Wells (2021) argue that during the transition human rights "vernacularized" in Burma through a splintering of the transnational sign "human rights," such that actors took one of three approaches: *rejection* of human rights, *hybridization* of it with other discourses, or *strategic avoidance* of the term and concept entirely. I would add that this splintering also has had broader effects, in which these different discourses affected one another and impacted the broader discursive field, meaning that nonpartisans to the discourse—members of Burmese publics—also came to reassess human rights during the transition and after the coup. Particularly, Burmese publics who had witnessed Suu Kyi endorse human rights in the past only heard monks slander them during the transition. Suu Kyi hence ceased to be a hybridizer; rather, her unwillingness to speak against a rising tide of anti-human-rights talk (by right-wing Buddhist rejectors) was akin to her rejecting it. Her rejections likely have enabled others to embrace rejection; those who remain committed have shifted to strategic avoidance. The upshot is that rights talk has been silenced. In other words, if vernacularization can occur only through the interactions between rejectors, hybridizers, and strategic avoiders, then when the hybridizers abandon human rights, the elements no longer exist to reproduce vernacularization. The factors combine to produce, instead, devernacularization.

But why was no one—at least before the coup—endorsing human rights anymore? The combination of (1) Rohingya claiming rights the wrong way (appearing to index a desire to take what belongs to others) while (2) dominant groups faced an intensifying precarity and structural violence that evaded recognition in (3) a context in which the field for grasping resources appeared open enough to allow Rohingya claims-making to constitute an apparent threat produced a politics of dangerous resentment that has metastasized and mutated into various expressions of grievance. Even CDI activists were not immune. Keep in mind that they had worked with Muslims around the country and built community watch programs in Yangon and Mandalay *hsin-kyay-boun* areas that intervened in situations of interreligious tension. In more than one case they prevented hired thugs from inciting mobs. But they were not active proponents of the Rohingya cause. This is not to say they were similar to the vast majority of the country's elite political activists, from the 88GS (see Kyaw Kha 2017; and Saw Wai 2018) to Suu Kyi, whose bigotry was undeniable in their repudiation of the Rohingya. Ko Taw instead cited what he saw as the elite nature of the Rohingya activists and their apparent unwillingness to work on behalf of *all* the people as qualities that contrasted to those in the Muslim communities CDI worked with. This demonstrates that even potential allies believe Rohingya to have access to special privileges (rights) that they do not redistribute generously. Again the same paradox emerges in which the Rohingya are excluded from Myanmar society, find solace in transnational domain, and are punished for it—what constitutes a sort "abject cosmopolitanism" (Nyers 2010).

While this resentment is intense, because the blunt biopolitical field is so nebulous, those grievances are themselves generating new identity categories—as will be shown in the following ethnographic example of both human rights rejection and the politicization of the body.

Rejecting Human Rights and Muslims: Politicizing the Body

In June 2015, I sat with activists in a tea shop in Kyaungkoun Township in Myanmar's delta region taking shelter from the monsoon and waiting for a bus that was taking its time. Sipping tea, I observed karaoke videos playing on

FIGURE 6.1. A poster of Thidagu Sayadaw (center) and a poster of a cow and *Zeewita-dana* (left) in Kyaungkoun Teashop. Photo by author.

an elevated television behind me, a middle-aged woman selling mango from a plate balanced on her head, and tea-shop boys scurrying about, taking orders, and bellowing them to the back. It was a familiar scene. And looking to my left, I noticed a familiar face: on a poster behind the cash counter was perched Thidagu Sayadaw, perhaps Myanmar's most influential monk. Thidagu's monastery is in Sagaing, hundreds of miles away in upper Myanmar, but given his peripatetic nature and wide (and ever-widening) sphere of influence, it was not surprising to see him here (fig. 6.1).[24]

Neither were Thidagu's words surprising (fig. 6.2): "Human Rights is not law. There is no country that is controlled by them. If they don't like them, then they can violate the human rights; I call that out. To the extent you like that, may you call that out. All of us must look out for the benefit of all of Myanmar's national races. Therefore, we must adhere to nationalism. Nationalism is not at all evil. We have to do it" [*Bse*]. While Burma's pundits often directed their contestations of human rights discourse toward Western publics, here Thidagu's words were effectively transmitted "down" to the grassroots,[25] conveying how human rights ideology is inimical to national prosperity.

The poster was affixed on the wall next to another that appeared at first glance to describe ways to protect one's cows and buffaloes. But upon looking closer, unexpected messages were discernible, as in the following: "Announcement: So that Kyaungkoun Township donors can be included in the *Zeewita-dana* meritorious royal cow and buffalo life protecting business" [*Bse*]. At the bottom were phone numbers and this message: "To donate, call." In the middle of the poster was the text of a famous colonial-era poem, *Nwa-myitta-sa*, written by Ledi Sayadaw (Walton 2012, 100) and told from the perspective of a cow: "Take my life, eat my flesh, drink my bones / Dry my hide in the sun not leaving my entire body / You act so that your profit remains, oh master! / For you, oh master, whatever did I do wrong to you?"[26] Outside the tea shop on the road there was still another sign publicizing the ceremony (fig. 6.3).

My colleague Thiha, an activist originally from that township, then informed me that the two posters were related. Thidagu travels to the delta and gives sermons that generate millions of kyat (thousands of dollars) in

FIGURE 6.2. Close-up of poster featuring a photo of Thidagu Sayadaw (left) with infamous racist monk Wirathu (right) at his feet. The text of Thidagu's screed against human rights is on the far right. Photo by author.

FIGURE 6.3. *Zeewita-dana* poster along the road outside of the Kyaungkoun Teashop. The poster includes the poem *Nwa-Myitta-Sa*, written from the perspective of the cow. Note the other *Zeewita-dana* sign leaning on the ground to the left. Photo by author.

donations. These donations are then used to "save" the cows. Seeing my confused look, Thiha added that in this township they do not like the Muslims killing the cows. And it seems that villagers believed that the Muslims were violating their slaughtering license in some way. Thiha then looked around nervously and told me that it was better if we discuss this issue later.

When we were in private, Thiha elaborated on the *Zeewita*, this cow-saving organization, and its *dana* (donation) ceremonies:

> For the majority of village peasants, because they are not able to buy machines
> [tractors], it is central for them to use buffaloes and cows. The Muslims buy
> the cow slaughtering license from the government and without respecting the
> rules, kill them. They kill greater than the percentage [that the law allows]. For
> example, if we say that in a day thirty animals can be killed, at night more than
> 100 will be killed. The Muslims send [the beef] out of the country in cars. No

one knows about this. The locals know. And so, the farmers' daily needs were seen and the *Zeewita* was founded. The locals save their money, they buy the cows, and then they free the cows from danger. For this, a subsidy is necessary. And so Thidagu comes to hold a donation event for the money for the *Zeewita*. With this money they buy the cow killing license from the government. [*Bse*]

Thiha described an elaborate economy of Buddhist merit, animal permits, and racioreligious hate—a factor betrayed by MaBaTha's prominent involvement. MaBaTha was the national-scale network of monks and lay supporters devoted to the "protection of [the Buddhist] race and religion" that had congealed out of a national monk-led campaign against Muslim businesses in the early days of the transition. While MaBaTha often appeared to operate in national spheres—holding mass rallies and promoting legislation to protect race and religion—these cow-protection initiatives were led by the organization's local branch offices, demonstrating their effective capture of state function. The campaign's effects ramified across the delta: my own informal survey determined that beef was no longer available in local restaurants; I was able to purchase beef in only one of nine restaurants across five townships in Ayeyawaddy. Many menus had crossed off beef dishes.

These monk-led beef-eating prohibition campaigns are noteworthy for how they provide average Burmese people—here peasants in a far-flung delta township—opportunities to participate in national sociopolitical projects. While Thidagu's arrival was a discrete (and hence fleeting) event, it nested within a broader engagement in which the most fundamental of quotidian actions (eating) was politicized, resignified as a critical contribution to a collective endeavor. Indeed, by participating in *Zeewita-dana* one accomplishes numerous, mutually reinforcing political objectives, including patronizing Buddhism, purifying one's body (through beef abstention), saving the socially esteemed cow (drawing distinction with Muslims who do not),[27] and undermining Muslim businesses (as Muslims own the slaughterhouses).

An additional final goal was only rumored, according to Thiha: that the cows assisted in internal colonization projects, as they were shipped to Rakhine state to help occupy land stolen from ethnically cleansed Rohingya. This sounded so bizarre as to beggar belief, but when I presented on this research months later in Yangon, an investigative journalist confirmed it. She went on to publish her findings (Swe Win 2015c).

Zeewita-dana is one of a number of such mobilizations—joining pork-eating festivals (*wet-sa-pwe*) and snack wars (*moun-daiqpwe*) (events promoting only Burmese snacks)—that I differentiate from other campaigns by how they pack into single signs three particular elements: allowing participants to perform identitarian belonging, publicizing and circulating those performances, and doing so in ways that simultaneously define contours of the in-/out-groups.[28]

We must also highlight how these movements mobilize gender, as they weaponize women's wombs against those from different races (Chu May Paing 2020, 46–47). Women were massively overrepresented at *moun-daiqpwe* and similar events,[29] which stands as one marker of female enrollment into right-wing nationalism (Tharaphi Than 2015, 17–20). Further, lower-class women were enthusiastic supporters of MaBaTha's infamous "four race laws"—those that, inter alia, policed interreligious marriages. As upper-middle-class feminist organizations identified the laws with women's oppression (Chu May Paing 2020, 47) and echoed Suu Kyi's intonations about the so-called rule of law as a guarantor of their rights, MaBaTha braided legal intervention with daily biopolitical labor, encouraging Buddhist women across the country's villages to conduct the reproductive work necessary to reproduce the exclusionary identity. Attending nationalist events, going to monk *haw-pyaw-pwe* (public sermons), and keeping chaste (except with a Buddhist man) were all part of the labor that every woman could provide the cause.

These various movements link their real-life labors with online representations that stage the event for others—and participants themselves—to observe (Prasse-Freeman 2021). Even the general (and much commented on) proliferation of "hate speech" that circulates virulently on Burmese Facebook can be understood in the same general terms—that is, as average citizens applying their labor to construct an infrastructure of nationalism. Particularly in this environment of negligible public faith in standard data sources (Eaint Thiri Thu 2019, 232–35), individuals are interpellated to assemble and reinforce various semiotic ligatures to construct common narratives about the world. By circulating information warning about "radical Islam," users stake their subjective stances while also coproducing knowledge of the potential Muslim threat to the nation. Nationalism is operative at elite and village levels both (Irvine and Gal 2000), such that people do not only consume nationalism but *produce* it. These participatory aspects, and the affects they generate, help explain why epistemological interventions (about truth of information) are impotent to dampen the xenophobia forged online and offline (and in between).

From Rights to (Who Will Take the) Responsibility

Fortunately, in the place of the *akwint-ayay* discourse favored by elites, activists have developed alternative discourses with which to motivate their actions. Instead of talking about rights, activists stress "responsibilities." But this is not, to be clear, the discourse of "Asian values," in which citizens must perform their responsibilities to earn their rights; neither do activists just highlight the ways that those in power do not take responsibility. Instead, they give responsibility a new inflection—such as in those who search for "a guarantee to [their] lives," as displayed in a petition signed by thirty-four grassroots groups in late 2014.[30] This text stressed that "laws must be made so that the workers are able to have a peaceful and secure life and so that workers get salaries that guarantee their lives."

Why is *taa-wun* (responsibility) discourse more efficacious than *akwint-ayay*? First, let us recall the distinction developed in chapter 5 between epistemic and deontic modalities. Where *awkint-ayay* demands resources and tells those in power what they *must* do (deontic modality) by appealing to distantiated and transcendent standards, *taa-wun* is slipperier: it invokes what a good patron, a compassionate ruler, and a truly strong leader *should* do (epistemic modality), inviting those who would like to embody that status to perform those qualities. Much as in the *kyeinsa daiqpwe* of chapter 4, in which the broadcast model of speech beckons those who are curseworthy to feel shame, here the enunciation of *taa-wun* beckons the powerful to interpellate themselves. Hence, as mentioned in chapter 1, *taa-wun* is a way of presencing the sovereign by broadening what they might take responsibility for. A wonderfully emphatic example of this can be found in the title of a 2015 article in *Worker Journal*, a periodical written and edited by laborers in the *hsin-kyay-boun* industrial zones: "Responsible People: Take Responsibility for Resolving Things" (Maung Thitsa).[31] It identifies the addressee by their status and then demands they fulfill it; the reader is invited/compelled to decide whether he or she subscribes—or would be ascribed by others—to the status.

Of course, such invocations mostly fall on deaf ears. But this is not the end of *taa-wun*'s efficacy. By creating a field of joint attention around the object of responsibility, the activists then suggest that because no one was taking responsibility or that no one was guaranteeing lives, it was left to them—the activists—to do so. *We will take responsibility*, they said with a frequency that was nearly comical. This often meant that they would stand in front of the people and bear the consequences for what would happen. This can also be presented as a way of building solidarity: *in a situation where no one takes responsibility, we will do so, but you must do so as well.*

Ultimately, *taa-wun* (responsibility) seems not so much an alternative to *akwint-ayay* as a way to invest the latter with methods of becoming achievable. This works as follows: hearing *akwint-ayay* as opportunities, a Burmese subject reflects on whether that opportunity applies to her or is accessible by her. In the context of a system that before the coup increasingly promised formal rights but provided no opportunities for realizing them, and in a system where those formal procedures allowed those with access to power to neglect the poor or the excluded, the question "Who will take responsibility?" came to mean "Who will insert themselves between the weak on one side and the impersonal operations of the state and market on the other?" When activists respond with "We will take responsibility," this produces a different vision of citizenship, one that suggests that legal and regulatory processes are empty on their own and demands that they must be intervened in. Such responses also claw back at the state's discourse that insist that the citizen's *taa-wun* is to vote and otherwise be silent.

Conclusion: Do Rights Bridge or Divide?

Let us return to the encounter on the refugee camp's stream bank where this final chapter commenced. The conversation there existed in its particular form—with one group of people bellowing promises to another kind across a chasm—because of something associated with that stream. Indeed, ninety seconds into her remarks, Maguire, one of the laureates, apologizes to her addressees: "We cannot cross over to you, as much as we would love to greet you . . . , but our hearts are with you, and we love you." At this point Maguire is being filmed from behind, and so the viewer can see the stream that divides them: the water does not appear deep, and a relatively sturdy-looking bridge runs across it. Access is barred, therefore, not by the terrain but by something else. We are not told what.

On the literal level there is obviously no mystery. "Humanitarian spaces" are aggressively regulated and access to them constrained. Nonetheless, we might linger on the barrier dividing the two groups. Indeed, returning to the laureates' remarks, the presupposition made so blithely on one side of the stream—that the people are Rohingya, that the Rohingya are citizens, that citizenship entails rights, and that rights exist *already* and hence can be called upon for reinstatement—clearly encounters a different reality in the camps.

The divide may not be traversable. In other words, the laureates propose using rights as the tool that would pull the Rohingya out of the "zone of anomie" and *re*-install them into their prefigured humanity—one that had been but momentarily held in abeyance. Yet, the inability of the laureates to conjoin the two zones with rights talk indicates the broader field of power in which they are operating, a field that they do not acknowledge. This field is an ever-widening caesura that cannot be stitched together with rights, at least not rights as they are currently figured.

During the anticoup uprising, however, the Rohingya experienced a transformation of sorts, going from inert objects of calls across great distances to the ones doing the calling. While many Rohingya called out Suu Kyi on social media ("I hope now she can understand the pain of being betrayed"), others took the opportunity to offer solidarity with their would-be countrymen and women. A Rohingya poet, for instance, called on other Burmese to stand with him against the SAC: "My Burmese brothers and sisters, now our country need[s] us. All we need to pay is 'the third struggle.' Last time we did in 1988. We know how to do [it]. Together we can do it again. This time, the struggle should be the last one ever. The last and last one ever." His addressee structure (explicitly to "Burmese brothers and sisters" while broadcast in English to anyone with a Twitter account) here indexically presupposes/asserts a fictive kinship relation and hence publicly inserts Rohingyas into Myanmar's anti-fascist struggles of the past and present. These appeals act as conspicuous maneuvers to claim inclusion in a common struggle with other Burmese subjects ("our country") against a shared enemy. They also convey that their Burmese brethren are more like the hypermarginalized Rohingya than they might want to admit—in the space of the *Sit-tat*'s exception, they are all reduced to enemies, rebels. In this sense, it is tempting to see the Rohingya as politicizing their own bare life status, using it as the common substrate for connection with others experiencing that radical threat for the first time.

But this ignores the connections forged through the protests themselves, ones that seemed to go beyond the instrumentalization of victimhood. It is noteworthy that Burmese social media users barraged members of the NUG who had endorsed the genocide to change their positions, compelling Win Myat Aye to apologize and hounding Khin Ma Ma Myo into removing her Facebook page. Moreover, dozens of non-Rohingya Burmese protesters used their time in the street to publicly apologize to the Rohingya, either for not believing Rohingya suffering or for not speaking out about it because of their own cowardice. While it is impossible to discern "true" motives, it warrants mentioning that there seemed little instrumental advantage to be gained in either of these moves. Rather, it seems that in the struggle against the *Sit-tat*, Rohingya and Burmese went beyond recognition—beyond the stifling dyad in which one person looks at another and observes the differences and the similarities—to become two people joining hands to look out at the horizon at their common enemy and their common future. This is akin to Antoine de Saint-Exupéry's definition of love: it is "not just looking at each other, it's looking in the same direction." It is such a model of political solidarity through shared militancy that might displace the violence of blunt biopolitics (on one hand) and the anemia of rights (on the other).

Conclusion

Rights Erosion and Refusal beyond Burma

RIGHTS REFUSED HAS CONSIDERED how political activists operate in Myanmar's specific authoritarian, neoliberal, blunt biopolitical environment, illuminating not just why these actors choose to refuse extant sociopolitical conditions but how they do so and why they are sometimes successful in those acts of refusal. The book has explored these questions at divergent scales—the micropractices of activists and average people revealing the contours of the macrolevel assemblage of power, and vice versa—by drawing on extended participant observation conducted with peripatetic activists who engaged in various struggles across Burma to defend the land, labor, and livelihoods of Myanmar subjects. In presenting practices as varied as courtroom immolation, occult cursing ceremonies, and land reoccupations, the book has demonstrated how alternative conceptions of politics are lived. Mostly, the book has conveyed the daily life of activists as they mobilize people struggling through their quotidian challenges. In these interactions—in places as diverse as haphazardly assembled protest camps, threadbare political party offices, frigid overnight buses, boisterous beer stalls, sonorous classrooms, rickety lorries, and sterile NGO conference rooms—the book has provided intimate insights into how people navigate political-economic dislocations and evolving practices of state governmentality. Activist stories—about times in prison, in the black-market economy, and in underground movements and aboveground civil society organizations—have revealed a mostly hidden side to Burmese life, one that has built a robust social infrastructure during years of state neglect that enables perduring survival and moments of fierce resistance. In so doing, the book has provided insight into the impressive endurance and creativity on display during the ongoing revolution against Myanmar's generals and their catastrophic coup.

The book has developed three key intellectual interventions. First, it has described Myanmar's novel form of postcolonial governance, defined by a blunt biopolitical apparatus that takes the subject's body, and the masses that bodies form, as its object of governance—one more violated and neglected than promoted or known. Second, the book has used the concept of refusal as the hinge between the governance apparatus and the governed, using this concept as a way of articulating, through activist practices, everyday life for peasants and workers under the regime of blunt biopolitics that impinges on them. Third, *Rights Refused* has described how these conditions have generated conceptions of rights that diverge from conventional understandings. They are not understood as inalienable possessions—rather than belonging irrevocably to each individual, they can be lost or gained, forfeited forever or hoarded greedily. Moreover, when rights presuppose contractual obligations and entitlements disconnected from any material opportunity for their realization, activists and subalterns may refuse rights as well.

A concern here is that, at least implicitly, these descriptions may be interpreted as presenting Burma as sui generis—wholly different from other postcolonial settings, not to mention from the West. I will use this conclusion to suggest otherwise. While Myanmar's own unique features must be taken seriously, they render in stark relief dynamics that exist elsewhere as well. The first section that follows clarifies how refusal acts as a theoretical tool that synthesizes different aspects of resistance theory. The second section outlines similarities to other contexts through a comparison of different forms of biopolitics and how those afford different kinds of refusal that nonetheless share a common substrate of oscillation. The final section turns to rights, asking how rights as opportunities may better describe conditions in the West than might be assumed.

Refusal as Synthesis

By articulating activist refusal as a form of absent presence, the book has theorized contentious politics in a way that addresses resistance theory more broadly, helping to synthesize opposing conceptualizations that have divided resistance studies.

Indeed, over the past several decades, as resistance has become polarized into two separate camps, the general paradigm has become enervated of influence (Prasse-Freeman 2022b, 105–8). On one side, scholars of both Scott-ian (Scott 1985) and Foucaultian (Abu-Lughod 1990) veins critiqued earlier treatments of resistance for their romanticization of direct contestations of power (the face-off with the sovereign as theorized throughout this book). These scholars, conversely, saw resistance in the everyday, suffusing social ex-istence. But these subtle studies of resistance risked, according to the other side of the debate, being altogether too subtle. Marshall Sahlins accused them of "translating the apparently trivial into the fatefully political" (2002, 17), while Michael Brown averred that "the discovery of resistance almost every-where occasionally reach[es] excesses that flirt with self-parody," ultimately degrading true resistance by constituting a false equivalence "that diminishes, rather than intensifies, our sensitivity to injustice" (1996, 730).

Rights Refused's semiotic framework has addressed this debate. Rather than insisting on a choice between muscular contestation and quieter every-day resistance, the book has attended to the way both do or do not create signs—responses that may lead to new futures and trajectories. Such signs are cogenerated through the interpretants they create. This occurs on two princi-pal axes: what we might call a "vertical axis," consisting of the reactions from the sovereign when either directly contested or quietly rejected, and a "hori-zontal axis," in which other subjects are beckoned to attend and assess those actions and how these actors may change their political perspectives or com-mitments as a result.

Thus, pace Brown's dismissal just above, acts such as foot-dragging and evasion should not be derogated as necessarily meaningless. Rather, it is pos-sible that such actions affect the regime being opposed in ways more trou-bling—for example, enacting more costs or compelling more responses—than certain stylized acts of resistance (rallies or protests). In certain contexts, brash and heroic acts of resistance that lead ineluctably and immediately to the resister's annihilation might barely register horizontally: others may never see these acts—eliminated before they had a chance to speak their truth—or they may interpret them, because of their swift snuffing out, as a cautionary example that hence buttresses sovereign power.

Alternatively, however, it is also possible that such quiet actions are so quiet that they signify nothing, creating no long-term substrates that can be drawn on to form collective actions—whether those actions are revolutions directed at the state or movements through which people form alternative ways of liv-ing. As stressed throughout this book, if subjects turn so far away from power that their actions are indiscernible from pacification, then they generate no reactions. As observed repeatedly in the book, evasion only exists if there is an apparatus in pursuit; everyday resistance is not worthy of the name if that which is being resisted does not register or bear any cost to such resistance tactics. Focusing only on the way people retain subjective autonomy—never ceasing to hate the military, not consenting to its rule, and so on—seems a liberal piety when pitted against a regime that is simply not seeking legitimacy, is not trying to persuade. This is only exacerbated if such subjective refusal (as illustrated through the *buu* parable of total denial of sociality that opened this book) rejects intracommunal solidarity as well.

But this focus on outcomes produced goes only part of the way in addressing why resistance has become drained of relevance. Another problem is the way that, along another dimension, resistance paradigms have continued to presuppose legible resisting subjects and coherent resisted objects. Such a rendering, though, seems to misdescribe contemporary power arrangements. On one hand, sovereigns are difficult to identify—as sovereignty becomes diffused into biopolitical apparatuses, blunt or otherwise, it escapes the grasp of those who would oppose it. Rather than being evaded, it does the evading. On the other hand, resistance imagines subjects who share a collective consciousness that emerges deterministically from their "position" in the power structure. But ethnography can highlight that at least in certain situations, consciousness must be built rather than presupposed. *Rights Refused* has highlighted both of these dimensions, focusing on the immense and sustained labor activists must exert to presence the sovereign and interpellate fellow subjects.

Relatedly, the third contribution made to resistance theory involves the book's theorization of resistance/refusal as the oscillation between direct contestation and biopolitical navigation. Incorporating the earlier points—about resisting's necessary semiotic content and the diffuse sovereign—the book has rendered ethnographically the specific ways that activists calibrate their actions, both toward that which they oppose and to those publics whom they are trying to hail. Activists frontally contest sovereign power only rarely—and when they do, mediations abound. In plow protests, the direct-action phase of land reoccupation and plowing effectively ignores the sovereign; in cursing ceremonies, activists invite sovereign power to interpellate itself. But there are also horizontal semiotic effects of these acts of resistance, ones that the activists amplify in their engagement with communities. Indeed, the book has focused its attention on the interactions between activists and peasants and poor people across Myanmar through which activists attempt to gradually weaponize refusal. A key activist objective is to transform stances of mutually rejected recognition—in which state and subject turn away from one another—to encourage people to constitute population groups through which they can create collective projects, either by making demands on the state or by building their own endeavors.

Taken together, these three interventions hope to help reinvigorate studies of resistance (and related descriptors of contentious politics). *Rights Refused* also contributes to the comparative conversation emerging around particular idioms of refusal, pointing out that the contours of any specific resistance/refusal project will take shape in response to the form of the apparatus being engaged. It is here that we turn to another of the book's contributions: the motivation of a comparative biopolitics studies.

Comparative Biopolitics/Comparative Refusal: Bringing It All Back Home

Rights Refused has demonstrated that common assumptions about the so-called postcolony warrant refinement. Tools that have provoked insights—such as biopower and necropolitics—require further tempering, distillation, and synthesis lest they themselves become too obtuse to adequately describe the highly variegated and polymorphous regimes of power that continue to evolve around the globe. By comparing life in Myanmar with Partha Chatterjee's theorization of the postcolony (2004, 2011, 2019), *Rights Refused* has allowed a domain outside Chatterjee's "political society" to come into focus. Blunt biopolitics and the modes of refusal that respond to it, thus refined through comparison, become available for other "lateral" comparisons (between specific cases) rather than simply for the standard "frontal" comparisons with "the West" (Candea 2018, 119–32). Or, put differently, specific Western cases can become invited into the frame as additional opportunities for lateral juxtaposition.

Comparison with the West illuminates the fact that specific deployments of refusal (and cognates: "abolition," "fugitivity," and *petit marronage*) are calibrated to respond to the particular biopolitical elements in the regime being refused. Let us consider late-liberal states such as Canada, France, and the United States. Critically, even as they are inflected by neoliberal withdrawal to differing degrees, the vestiges of a life-promoting (or at least sustaining) biopolitics persist. The Canadian settler-colonial state biopolitics that Simpson (2014) studies seeks to enable a docile, multicultural liberal-Native subject. In the Antillean context studied by Yarimar Bonilla (2015), the French state must recognize the Guadeloupean labor movement's demand for care as wards of the state. The US educational system explored by Damien Sojoyner has a mandate to deploy "liberal, difference-making state projects" (2017, 516). Hence, forms of refusal snap into existence through the specific ways they evade these projects, creating leverage on the part of refusers who thwart those biopolitical imperatives to "care."[1]

But these cases also demonstrate that full evasion is difficult given the extent and proactive reach of the biopolitical apparatus. Subjects are stuck in a maddening dilemma: the biopolitical inducements provide life-sustaining resources but also come with surveillance and symbolic violence in the form of offensive misrecognition. Savannah Shange's ethnography (2019b) of the "willful defiance" enacted by Black youth who identify the canard that is their San Franciscan public school's avowed liberal progress narrative perhaps reveals this biopolitical dimension most clearly. "Abolition," which "encompasses the ways in which Black people and [their] accomplices work *within*, *against*, and *beyond* the state" (10), is available because the biopolitical prerequisite for the state to bestow a modicum of care on the governed still persists (if barely), and those who are invested in justice must work within, and as part of, the racist militarist-capitalist-statist assemblage. In this context, schools are a sieving machine, operating through the mechanism of a Faustian bargain. They offer tantalizing promises of security, care, and symbolic recognition in exchange for respectability, comportment, and self-blame for failure. Those who refuse this capitulation—typically low-class Black students—are extruded to the outside, left to fend for themselves.

There is a moment, late in Shange's monograph, when this impossible situation is rendered most starkly. Aaron, the white principal of the progressive school at the center of the ethnography, attempts to foster a moment of interracial solidarity at a schoolwide meeting. As Shange puts it, "Aaron thanked all the speakers who shared the mic at the Town Hall, and called [two students,] Aura and Bree[,] to the stage to close us out. He beamed proudly and said, 'These young women are going to share part of the Maya tradition with us, that powerful bloodline we all hold!'" Shange zeroes in on this choice of words: "Though Hector [an earlier speaker] had made an argument about Black and Xicanx people sharing Native blood, Aaron here slips his own whiteness into the first person of indigeneity" (2019b, 145).

A counterfactual statement—the one Aaron does not make—is also worth considering here. If he had *not* included himself as white in the Indigenous category he could have been critiqued for avoiding identification, trying to create two versions of humanity in which his white version is implicitly higher: "Aaron refused to allow his whiteness to fraternize with Native and Black blood." There is a similar example in the book when Shange condemns white teachers for not attending a Black-led event (2019b, 141). It would be plausible, however, to criticize teachers for inserting their surveillant white gaze into a Black conversation, a move akin to colonizing Black spaces. Bringing this up does not, of course, embrace the reactionary move that would indict Shange's critiques. There is something in between those poles: presence without dominance, support with condescension, participation without foregrounding white experience.

That said, there might be something analytically compelling in the fact that one action (identification across difference, exemplified by the white principal) and its opposite (anti-identification) are *both* bad politics. One potential solution is the dialectical approach: "We are the same. But we are not completely the same. We can connect across our difference against common enemies and for common goals." This takes more words (something that is not trivial given the earlier problem of white colonization of Black spaces, something done by taking up too much time and space) but seems politically endorsable: a position of identification without consuming and collapsing difference, in which solidarity is understood as a dialectical outcome of the rejection of both hyperidentification and difference.

But another thought is that something about the structural condition of white supremacist late capitalism collapses the possibility of dialectics. My argument is that the form of biopolitics produces a paradoxical mix of anti/identification, in which marginalized subjects are either not seen at all or seen in demeaning ways. And yet because of neoliberal abandonment, biopolitical resources are often necessary for survival. The result is a refusal that oscillates between both positions, of evasion and engagement—a refusal strikingly similar to that of Myanmar activists, who simultaneously presence the state and attempt to avoid capture by it.

Indeed, in today's United States, marginalized subjects must manage an impossible combination of hypervisibility and invisibility, defined by the specific terms of the biopolitical bargain: people can access care and resources from the state-capitalist-carceral assemblage *only* if they submit to discipline and surveillance. Otherwise they are cast off into the realm of invisibility. Shange herself brilliantly identifies this double bind, providing a devastating critique of the enduring liberal narrative that small enclaves of determined antiracists can gradually ameliorate sclerotic and structurally violent conditions. Instead, Shange shows how ostensibly progressive schools do not become bases from which community transformation proceeds; rather, they become infected by the surrounding environment (both by state policies and the general depredations of the capitalist political economy) and survive only by waging war against the Black community and any students marked by excessive Blackness. We observe the school gradually pare and winnow its more "troublesome" students—who are disproportionately lower-class Black—leaving only those who effectively conform to liberal bourgeois values and mimic respectability discourses. With invisibility one is let alone but "let to die"; hypervisibility, by contrast, is a perverse form of recognition, in which poor Black life is seen but in a perverting way that makes it a constitutive outside that is the foundation for the good (non-poor Black) life.

"Refusal," "abolitionist anthropology," and "fugitivity" (espoused by Shange, Sojoyner, Campt, Hartman, and Simpson) all identify how hyperinvisibility is not a stable position in which to exist; the various terms describe ways to *manage* this impossible position. Christina Sharpe explicitly eschews both "representation" and "representational politics" (2016, 123), arguing that when Black stories of pain are finally moved out of the realm of the invisible, they are made hypervisible through a scopic mode that "consists of the traumatizing and retraumatizing of Black children for the education of others" (92). Sharpe instead searches for methods that make "Black life visible, if only momentarily" (123).

Refusal then means a continual movement across the line between hyper and invisible—"a form of strategic entanglement: a way of crafting and enacting autonomy within a system from which one is unable to fully disentangle," as Bonilla (2015, 43) describes *petit marronage*. For some subjects, this movement is literal: they submit to the surveillance and discipline, trying to ride that brittle line toward a modicum of care only to flee that space when the discipline becomes too crushing and demeaning. Tali Ziv (2022) describes how an informant, Wakil, is arrested in downtown Philadelphia for disorderly conduct after he himself had called the police to complain about racial profiling. Wakil becomes deeply perturbed when his affordable housing provider finds out, mere hours after his arraignment, that he had been in court. "How they know I had court?" he repeats, both attempting to identify the surveillant apparatus keeping tabs on him and objecting to its form of control. Wakil identifies the irony of his position: "If I had been in my own little world this wouldn't of happened." Back there, "I know how to make my way, I know the rules, how to maneuver, I never woulda called the cops up there, man, never." Wakil had been enticed out of his safe zone by the promise of affordable housing that he secured by getting a formal sector job (at Walmart). Such resources are offered to Wakil as part of his biopolitical subpopulation, but he can access these resources *only* by submitting to labor discipline (getting the job at Walmart) and then surveillance. All of this is so affecting (his repetition about them knowing he had court bears that out) that he briefly retreats to his old street, refusing the terms of the biopolitical bargain but also refusing its resources. He eventually returns to the job, engaging the bargain again. It seems that Wakil and others are able to persist in the zone of putative care even as/ because they realize that care and opportunities are precarious and ever contingent. Their refusal is a *subjective* one that allows them to persist, proleptically prepared for disaster.

The point, however, as Shange stresses, is not to survive, not even "to win control of the state and its resources," but "to quit playing and raze the stadium of settler-slaver society for good" (2019b, 3). This abolition, she makes clear in the book's final sentences, means "extending Black life through any means at hand, including nickel-and-quarter progressive reforms" (159) but only by taking a subjective stance of disengagement, to avoid capture by faux-emancipatory rhetoric and pacifying systems. The question we turn to now is whether this is possible under the current rights-based framework and whether refusing rights may assist in this kind of broader project of refusal.

Can Rights Be Quit?

Rights Refused has built from the insight that many human communities not only lack a conception of liberal rights but that attempts to translate rights across cultures encounter what Mark Goodale calls "elemental incommensurabilities" (2022, 112; see also Holcombe 2018). But rather than merely critiquing "rights" as inappropriate for Myanmar, this book has attempted to explore what is produced in mistranslation, what is generated in the divide between incommensurable zones. Through comparison, it has demonstrated the specific ways in which alternative understandings of rights (rights as opportunities) are close enough to the standard liberal version to trouble it. The book has therefore challenged certain presumptions regarding how "rights" actually function. It has sought to "provincialize" the discursively hegemonic concept (Chakrabarty 2007b), reducing it to one technology among many that may organize the relationships between the governed and apparatuses of power. This has allowed us to see how rights might be refused by those denied them—by those standing on the outside looking in (outside both the enjoyment of actual rights and the hegemonic field that insists that everyone always-already "has" them).

One theme that has continually reemerged throughout the book is that activists are acutely aware that the efficacy of their actions cannot be secured by classic performatives—the verbal claiming of rights, the occupation of space, and so forth. When Judith Butler writes that those gathering in protest "are exercising a right to appear" (2015, 26), such claims appear premature from the subaltern Burmese perspective. Such acts may eventually stabilize into a right, but they may not. If a protest gathering is put down and its leaders imprisoned or murdered, any right to appear would seem to dissolve as well.

How relevant, though, are these Burmese experiences to other political contexts, ones that explicitly endorse a biopolitics devoted to life's promotion and that proclaim a staunch commitment to rights and the so-called rule of law? While the Burmese experience was presented as divergent from the Western orthodoxy to compel a reconsideration of *doxa*, the actual functional differences between biopolitics and rights in, say, the United States and in Myanmar today have not been established through this inquiry. Rather, the question remains open for reflection.

So, put more plainly, do those in the West have the rights they think they have? Should we see rights there more as opportunities? Do underclass or nonwhite subjects have them at all? Is it racial and class privileges, rather than rights, that white elites enjoy? And what of poor whites, the object of much reflection in the wake of their support for faux-populist demagogues such as Donald Trump? Do they still have the rights that enabled so-called social contracts to deliver stable lives to their progenitors?

The Dispossession Paradox

As has been discussed throughout the book, the hegemonic version of rights insists on a static and linear logic: once a right comes to exist it cannot be eliminated—it can only be *denied* to a subject who has become always-already a rights holder. As Costas Douzinas notes, this has led to an "inflation of rights-talk" (2007, 36). What allows this to occur? One striking aspect regarding Western conceptions of rights is how they seem to ignore the difference between a rights *claim* and its material *realization*. Rights are asserted in their claims as already achieved: in their contractual versions, they are asserted because of that contract (even if the contract does not function to deliver the rights claimed); in their moral versions, they exist because they are asserted as moral (even when that morality is asserted by the speaker and not mutually recognized and collectively ratified). Even in their Lockean strain, labor is presented as generating the right itself rather than generating merely a *claim* to a right. In all these senses, rights claims seem, following Wendy Brown (1995), to be nondialogical: "Rights have no inherent political semiotic, no innate capacity either to advance or impede radical democratic ideals. Yet rights necessarily operate in and as an ahistorical, acultural, acontextual idiom: they claim distance from specific political contexts and historical vicissitudes, and they necessarily participate in a discourse of enduring universality rather than provisionality or partiality" (97).

As Butler (2015) and Ranciere (2004) note, respectively, this expansionary aspect is politically hopeful, as it may allow the excluded to attain access to dignity and equality. Moreover, as developed in chapter 5, because of the recursive, iterative, and mutually reinforcing relationship linking discursive practice (rights talk as saturating political imaginations in the West) and linguistic encoding (rights as inalienable possessions), rights become inextricably linked with subject formation.

But there is also an underappreciated risk here. While Butler and Ranciere highlight the transformative potential in the performative body/speech act, they stress only one direction of transformation: from being dispossessed of to then (re)possessing rights. In contrast, however, infelicitous rights performatives can draw attention to what is absent, only confirming the failed status. Indeed, often the protester is beaten, the activist is disappeared; the putative rights are neglected. Given these realities, we should ask: what happens to those performatives that fail?[2] Such a focus on failure leads to a reconceptualization of the processural nature in which rights are not only gained but also lost. Even those who are *not* explicitly excluded (those who *are* citizens, for instance) are denied "their" rights, unable to have (in practice) the rights they already have (by right): sexual minorities witness "their rights" bandied about as fodder in broader culture wars (Gamble 1997; *New York Times* 2016); conservative and liberal pundits alike insist that Muslim Americans have to *earn* "their rights" by participating in surveillance of their coreligionists (Tomasky 2015); a half-century-long "right" to reproductive freedom evaporated for American women with the 2022 *Dobbs* Supreme Court decision, in part because the undemocratic nature of America's democracy led to the stacking of the court by Republican presidents who did not win the plurality of votes. "Even" poor whites find that America's long commitment to white supremacy no longer secures their well-being, either symbolically or materially (Bhandar 2018).

Indeed, while Donald Trump in his 2018 State of the Union declared that all Americans have "the right to the American Dream" (*Time* 2018), deindustrialization and stratifying wealth distribution together have eliminated the opportunities for most people to access that putative right. With the transition from Fordism and welfarism (for white men) of the 1950s to flexible regimes of accumulation that define today (Harvey 1990), fewer people can meaningfully participate in the market and perform their belonging. While America's brand of neoliberalism diverges from Burma's, the former's is, as mentioned earlier, increasingly defined by biopolitical abandonment, such that nonproducers are symbolically and socially devalorized (Foucault 2008; Ferguson 2015). This logic leaches into and infects the domain of the inalienable right, stripping the latter of the guarantees that make that right real.

Taking these two thrusts together—biopolitical abdication and rights inflation—we are left with a machine of symbolic inclusion and material extrusion. And yet, even as rights old and new erode—meaning that they do not secure standards of conduct for their putative bearers—this fact seems to go mostly unremarked on or does not redound on the rights logic itself. I submit that the chasm persists because rights as possessions are intimately tied to the construction of political personhood, an idea that expands from observations of "possessive individualism" (MacPherson 1962) long made about personhood in the West. To lose rights would be to dissolve the person. Hence, failures to realize rights in practice results in a splitting of the person into two—the ideal rights-bearing self and the degraded one trying or waiting to be restored to the former.

Here recall Douzinas's comments on "rights inflation." Such inflation leads to an engorged concept of the person, a phenomenon that Roberto Esposito (2012) puts at the center of one of his philosophical projects. Esposito, drawing a distinction with the contemporary period, reminds us that the category of person was not always presumed. In Roman social life, the movement from slave to person, from child to adult, made this distinction clear. In contrast, the post–World War II era, in response to European anthropology's biopolitical reduction of human to animal (which the Nazis took to its horrifying thanatopolitical conclusion), enlarged the category and insisted that all humans fit inside of it (despite manifest evidence that the basic "right to life" is the one most denied in the world today).[3] Yet, Esposito argues that even though personhood has now been universalized, bestowed upon everyone, this act has not eliminated biopolitical realities but instead called attention to them: the category of person "revealed itself to be different and superimposed on the natural substrate it was implanted in" (82). Whereas the split, introduced by the French Revolution and much commented on by Hannah Arendt (1973, chap. 9), was once between citizen and human-as-bare-life, the split has now been internalized within that figure of the citizen: "The very logic of citizenship, with the exclusion it establishes toward those who lack it, can be considered an internal structure of the ancient and very effective mechanism of splitting, or doubling, which finds its primary expression in the idea of person" (Esposito 2012, 73–74).

It is important to note that this splitting is itself doubled—or it exists on two planes simultaneously: within the citizenry and within the subject. Regarding the citizenry, the category contains subjects (nonwhite minorities, economically precaritized whites, and so on) who are incapable of performing the same kinds of personhood (the normative personhood roles) and hence are internally differentiated under the sign of equality. The second splitting is defined by the individual's own internal bifurcation between the idealized citizen-person guaranteed by the discursive rights regime and the actually existing subject who struggles to (re)achieve those rights.

This splitting has serious ramifications. First, while those denied "their rights" can be mobilized by their own righteous anger, they can also be demobilized as they become oriented toward administrative and procedural restoration projects rather than political action and because if they do mobilize, they are left with few other recourses than to ask for their rights again and again. Second, subjects who "have" discursively what they are denied substantively may experience a particular kind of alienation. As Maurice Godelier contends about the sacred, it is that which "cannot be alienated," and it gives people "an identity and root[s] this identity in the Beginning" (1999, 120–21). In the secular age, rights as inalienable possessions—that which "cannot be alienated"—fulfill the definition of the sacred, thereby forming identity. Thus, when rights are tied inextricably to the subject and this subject is presumed to carry them regardless of the context, the subject is split from herself when those contexts lead to the denigration of the subject—to the effective and material denial of rights: on one hand she is the living, breathing, and often abused body who has not the rights she has, and on the other hand she remains the idealized rights-possessing self. The former waits or works to be *restored* to the latter[4] and until that point exists in a state of self-dispossession.[5] While such failures can implicate the right itself—and it might be liberatory if they did—the power of the ideology of rights leaves people trapped in between: wanting what they cannot have and having a want they cannot not want (Spivak 1996, 28) but cannot be satisfied with.

Refracting Rights

Part of refiguring rights would seem to require contesting them as subject-bound possessions. Rights can be rearticulated as relations, in which rights can go from being possessed by all (which really means possessed by some while excluding most) to being a shared demand that insists on degrees of mutual consubstantiation. The late Werner Hamacher gestures in this direction, toward a conception of rights that are worth having only to the extent that we do *not* have them: "The sole human 'right' exists only if there are those who care for it and take care of it, who transfer it over to others and thereby maintain it in the movement of giving. Unable to be a right in any conventional sense, the only human right there is is a *praxis*—perhaps the one and only praxis. . . . The one and only human right there is can only be given as something that nobody ever has" (2017, 960).

Let us return to the Burmese social movement practices and their experiences with indeterminacy and rightslessness. Central to their actions is the fact that it is impossible to know how things will end, and given that in every iterative stage apparent victories might end up suddenly sundered, it becomes clear that rather than focusing on whether rights are realized, we should look at the actions (and the activist lives that enable them) as powerful constellations exploding with potential future trajectories. To recall San San from this book's introduction, when she claims "victory had been achieved" in a situation that was difficult to construe as such, she invited many interpretations. She could be dismissed as insane, or sanguine, or cynical. But she could instead be seen as initiating a political trajectory alternate to the apparent one. She does not, of course, immediately enact a new and inevitable future; instead, her body and words initiate only a potential trajectory, one that haunts the existing one and that threatens to return later as a revenant.

Activists are hence guides to alternative futures, laying down different pathways that people could potentially take—something rendered in stark terms in the 2021 anticoup uprising. It seems apt to reveal here that Ko Taw, Thu Myat, Mya, and most of their crew never left Yangon for the jungle camp—they continued to participate in the uprising, moving from hide house to hide house every few weeks, distributing funds, and doing much else that should not be mentioned here. Their actions in the revolution, and the actions that activists featured in this book were taking in 2014 and 2015 and much earlier, were not always successful. But the earlier actions seeded the ground of the repertoire of contention that enabled anticoup movements to sprout up without any central organization and play on ludic and transgressive tropes, drawing from the symbolic cultural material. This does not guarantee that the revolution will be realized, of course. There is undoubtedly a *right* neither to victory nor to escaping death. But activists insist that a trajectory exists that gets everyone to victory, and that if everyone has the courage to go together, it can be achieved.

Notes

Preface

1. "Burma" (ဗမာ) and "Myanmar" (မြန်မာ) have always *both* been used by those native to the space, the former traditionally describing the spoken language (and vernacular register) and the latter the written language (and formal register). The book will follow vernacular use, where both are used interchangeably.

2. A Rohingya colleague summed up the damage done: "What is different between the previous crisis such as [the] 1988 uprising, [2007's] Saffron Revolution and NOW? There is a huge division between the Bamar ethnic group and other ethnic groups. This division is an outcome of a decade-long quasi-civilian government leadership[']s ill-treatment toward [its] ethnic, minority populations and the version of 'democracy' sponsored by the international community. Until now, no leadership from mainland Myanmar is seen to unite this enormous division."

3. Featured in Scott (1976, vii).

Introduction

1. The indispensable Assistance Association for Political Prisoners keeps a macabre running tally at https://aappb.org/coup. At the time this book went to print, the number was 3,171.

2. The group has had a number of names, and its activists have typically participated in multiple groups and networks. "CDI" will act as the proxy for these various names. All activist names are pseudonyms.

3. အရေးတော်ပုံ အောင်ရမည်

4. While Myanmar's military refers to itself as the *Tatmadaw* (တပ်မတော်) using a royal register (*daw*, တော်), Burmese people largely eschew the term, especially given the honorific. They refer to it instead as the *Sit-tat* (စစ်တပ်)—a simple descriptor of an organization of violence, a military. This use also contains a "metapragmatic attack"

(Jacquemet 1994) on the military by denying them the respected name they desire. The book will follow this vernacular usage.

5. ဆင်ခြေဖုံး

6. For a longer discussion of these dynamics, see Prasse-Freeman (2023a).

7. ဘူးတစ်လုံးဆောင် အိုတော်မဆင်းရဲ။

8. For citations, see Prasse-Freeman (2022).

9. For John Austin (1975), a performative describes how the enunciation of specific words, provided specific "felicity conditions" are met, will directly and ineluctably enact specific ends. See also Kockelman (2007c); and Bauman and Briggs (1990, 66).

10. I use "subjects" for two reasons. The first is empirical: many Burmese—those who have been born and raised in the country, speak Burmese and/or one of the many ethnic nationality languages, and so on—may de jure lack citizenship documentation. Many more lack the effective affordances often associated with citizenship. Second, "subject" captures their position vis-à-vis power more accurately through its double meaning in the theoretical sense: subject as agent conducting action—as in "the subject of the sentence"—as well as subject as *subjected to power*. These simultaneous senses together highlight the mutual imbrication of agency and structure necessary to comprehend social action.

11. This can be observed in the dynastic paradigm, such as in the example made famous by Michel Foucault (1976, 23) in which the king was contested by an attempted regicide, whose execution beckoned an audience and even put the sovereign's authority on trial. In the contemporary liberal paradigm, a subject identifies herself as a rights holder under the law and identifies the sovereign as the duty bearer, and she enacts a contest in the public sphere that is imagined as adjudicating the claim, and hence the identity, of both. In the militant paradigm, revolution against the state identifies each as contestants for control of that position.

12. See Mitchell's (1990) and Ortner's (1995) respective critiques of Scott's presumptions about subalterns evading hegemonic effects of dominant ruling regimes.

13. I am inspired by theories of the state (Taussig 1997; Mbembe 2001) that in turn develop debates on the power of the exception (Benjamin 1978; Schmitt 1976; and see Agamben 2005 for interpretations) to stress the ephemeral but dangerous potentiality of sovereign power.

14. A recent edited volume (Kyed 2020) puts "state evasion" in its title.

15. In a recent article on state evasion (Harrisson 2021), a member of the resettled squatter settlement in peri-urban Burma encounters the state in only one of the four ethnographic vignettes—and this appears quite an exceptional case. In the other three, actors choose to remain disengaged from the state.

16. For decades, scholars have suggested that the term "the state" should be used with caution. Phillip Abrams's highly influential 1977 article observed that although the state is referred to in common parlance as a coherent unit, as a functional entity it lacks "cohesion, purpose, independence, common interest and morality" ([1977] 2006, 117). While Abrams acknowledged the persistence of the discursive reality of the state—that is, it continues to be thought about and discussed as "a 'real-concrete'

agent with will, power and activity of its own"—in reality it is a congeries of institutions and effects that do not form an undivided whole. The state "is a unified symbol of an actual disunity" (118).

If this is true, how have so many been so mystified? Scholars of "the state" have emphasized the mutually constitutive relationship between governance apparatuses and subjects, in which institutions, processes, and effects come to all be seen as the state through the way they operate on—and hence make—subjects (Gupta 2005, 17). Not only does the state represent citizens (in school textbooks or in leaders' speeches), but local officials pedagogically instruct subjects how to act (Das and Poole 2004). In turn, simultaneously "the daily practices of ordinary people construct the state" (Auyero 2012, 6) through their engagements with various actors (e.g., police, administrators, and social welfare officials) that these ordinary people take as representatives of the state. The mystification is made, then, in these iterative interactions.

But how do the quotidian actions of these agents come to be understood as similar to, representative of, or intercalated with operations that average people construe as standing "above" (Ferguson and Gupta 2002; Gupta 2012, 70) these local interactions? As Timothy Mitchell (2018) asks, how can the state be seen simultaneously as "individuals and their activities" in daily bureaucratic interactions and as "an inert 'structure' that somehow stands apart from individuals, precedes them, and contains and gives a framework to their lives" (89)? He answers by applying Foucault's disciplinary power to the state form, showing how it "consolidate[s] into the territorially based, institutionally structured order of the modern state" (87). Mitchell argues that "the organized partitioning of space, the regular distribution of bodies, exact timing, the coordination of movement, the combining of elements, and endless repetition" make the bureaucrat appear to share the will of her bureaucrat colleague, who both in turn share the single will of the state. Discipline hence articulates "the modern state" with "the modern individual" (89).

But are all modern states disciplinary? Are all modern individuals disciplined? Scholarship on Myanmar has proceeded as if the answer to both questions is yes, employing an implicit syllogism: modern states regulate in specific ways; Myanmar is modern; therefore, Myanmar regulates similarly. To take one example, Annika Harrisson distinguishes what she calls contemporary "state evasion" techniques from the precolonial era ones highlighted by James C. Scott (2009). She writes that the "modern state cannot be evaded, because the state is already omnipresent in that very decision that makes people turn away" (Harrisson 2021, 256). This book, by contrast, presumes no such state presence in Myanmar and hence no necessary discipline.

17. For another meditation on interpellating from positions of marginalization in Myanmar, see Edwards (2022, forthcoming)

18. Derrida (2006) describes specters as so divided, simultaneously more than many ("a crowd, if not masses, the horde, or society") but also "less than one of pure and simple dispersion" (2). Contrast with Bayat (2013), whose work on "nonmovements" in the Middle East only emphasizes citizens' "art of presence" while presupposing that states seek to maximize their presence.

19. For "rhizomatic," see Deleuze and Guattari (1987); I acknowledge Sayres Rudy for suggesting the phrasing "rhizomatic pursuit of asymmetry." On related themes, see Rudy (2010).

20. I draw on Kockelman's semiotic interpretation (2007c, 379) of Bourdieu's famous concept (1977).

21. DVBTV, "Anger at Suu Kyi," video uploaded March 14, 2013. For an analysis of Suu Kyi's encounter with Letpadaung villagers, see Prasse-Freeman (2016).

22. အောင်ပြို

23. For video (taken by author), see https://www.facebook.com/100007577414909/videos/1833840246878538/.

24. These informants argued that San San donned such dress likely as a way of both evoking the supramundane register and counteracting potential accusations that she was using black magic (as yogis do not dabble in dark arts).

25. See RFA (2015a) for a video on the protest and the early stages of the trial. While the video is in Burmese, nonspeakers can still note the near-festive atmosphere as supporters crowd the court compound and cheer the defendants.

26. ကိုယ့်အခွင့်အရေးကို ကာကွယ်ရမယ်။

27. "We must strive and work, all of us, until we become heroes all, so that we can ultimately dispense with any leader or leadership. For only then we can have freedom in a real and absolute sense" (Aung San 1946).

28. See also Prasse-Freeman and Ong (2021); Whitehead (2004); and Fujii (2021).

29. This theorization is inspired, inter alia, by Michael Taussig's tracing of such states' oscillation between ludic disregard of rules and priorities and "back-stiffening rites of recognition of founding fictions" (1997, 94).

30. Prasse-Freeman (2023b).

31. Indeed, if a coin is flipped (and one is told it is a fair coin) fifty times and every time the coin turns up heads, according to probabilistic reasoning the next time one should still expect a fifty-fifty chance of tails. But to retain belief in the probability of fifty-fifty, one must accept the presuppositions of probabilistic reasoning. At what point, however, does one start to assess the *outcomes* of the game as implicating the *rules* of the game itself? When does one start to ask: "Is the coin actually fair? Is the coin flipper cheating? Is the table on which the coin lands uneven? Is this just not my day?" (I thank Matt Schissler for helping articulate this point.)

32. So sings Ani DiFranco in her song *My IQ* (1993).

33. This is akin to Bonilla's use of the term *petit marronage* (2015) or Deleuze and Guattari's concept of the molecular space that fosters war machines (1987), as each affords subjects the opportunity to move slightly away from sovereign capture.

34. အခြေအနေ အရ မှုတည်တယ်။ For a similar description of maddeningly evasive truth, see Tahir (2017, 11).

35. In describing such acts, I am indebted, inter alia, to Austin's (1975) conception of the perlocutionary; Tomasello's (2010) study of initiatory gestures in human communication, Peirce's (2012) concept of indexicality; and Kockelman's (2007b) treatment of epistemic modality.

36. Levi-Strauss (1982) has described this process similarly.

37. Comparatively, see Feldman (1991).

38. See, among others, Thawnghmung (2004) for agrarian relations amid authoritarian rule; Cheesman (2015b) on the "rule of law" under despotism; Aung (2018), and Campbell (2022) on refractions of postcolonial capitalism; MacLean (2010) on mutations of the state amid violence; Ong (2023) on diffracted subsovereignty; Sadan (2013) on ethnogenesis across history; and Leehey (2010) for alternative understandings of propaganda.

39. See Prasse-Freeman (2023c).

40. အခွင့်အရေး

41. I considered *Thuirya Nay-Wun* and *Hot News* to be right-wing and left-wing populist, respectively (both are equally nationalistic when it comes to Rohingya issues, for instance); *Pyithu Ayay* (formerly *Phyithu Kit*) represented the mainstream liberal positions associated with Aung San Suu Kyi's National League for Democracy (NLD) party; *Eleven* was the journal of the upwardly mobile, free-market liberal; and *Irrawaddy* was the journal of antigovernment human rights adherents.

42. I thank Kevin Woods for stressing this point several times over the years.

Chapter 1

1. See Fujii (2021, 3) for the inverse phenomenon, in which a military first disappears bodies to later reappear them for public display.

2. The Free Funeral Society (FFS) was a key fixture of civil society's politics of plausible deniability (Prasse-Freeman 2012); see Hsu (2019) for a thorough exploration of the organization.

3. *Pyithuludu-shay-hmha yaq-tee deh* [ပြည်သူလူတု့ ရှေ့မှာ ရပ်တည် တယ်]

4. In a government system that grossly underpays teachers, remunerating them at the equivalent of USD 25 per month, teachers regularly withhold content, compelling students to hire them after hours, thereby privatizing a public good.

5. Comparative social movement studies would identify this as consistent with "resource mobilization theory," in which barriers to entry for participants can be reduced only by gradually exposing them to risky activities. See McCarthy and Zald (2001, 542–44).

6. ကျေးဇူးရှင်

7. On the *kyay-zu-shin* as generating infinite indebtedness, see Watanabe (2015); and Carstens (2020).

8. I thank Izzy Rhoads for this insight (pers. comm., November 2014).

9. See Prasse-Freeman (2019).

10. တာဝန်

11. လက်ပတ်နီ

12. စွမ်းအားရှင်

13. The meme reads: "Before election: 'ပြည်သူတွေက ကျွမတို့ ပါတီကိုသာ မဲ ပေးလိုက်ပါ။ ကျွန်တာ ကျွမတို့ တာဝန်ယူတယ်' After election won and became government: 'အစိုးရချည်း အားကိုးမနေနဲ့၊ အစိုးရချည်း အားကိုးနေရင် ဘာလို့ ဒီမိုကရေစီ

တောင်းနေလဲ၊ အာကာရှင် အစိုးရ လက်အောက်မှာနေပါလား၊ အာကာရှင်က အကုန် လုပ်ပေးတယ်." See Callahan (2017b) for similar comments by Suu Kyi.

14. The use of fire legally resulted in the de-gazetting of that land, returning it to state ownership, meaning that the *Sit-tat* did not simply drive out the Rohingya but "legally" appropriated their homeland. Arson here appears as a tool aiding land acquisition, with the added wrinkle that it was done quasi-legally rather than as the exception.

15. For discussion, see Prasse-Freeman (2023b).

16. For more on these brutal mining zones, see Prasse-Freeman (2022a).

17. Sarkisyanz (1965) traces the long history of this welfare state ideal, from Ashokan influences, through eleventh-century Kyanzittha's proclamations that "all the people . . . shall eat plenty of food, . . . shall enjoy happiness" (50) to nineteenth-century Mindon, who "refused to arm his forces with modern weapons in order not to be responsible for the destruction of life" (97). This lineage culminates, in Sarkisyanz's narrative, with the syncretic Marxist nationalist leaders of the 1940s but even more so in U Nu, prime minister in the independence era (1948–1962), who eliminated the death penalty (221) and was seen by monks interviewed by Sarkisyanz in 1959 as the "closest approximation to the ideal of the perfect Buddhist ruler in the Ashokan tradition" (226). Ultimately, Sarkisyanz attempts to adduce in this tradition an "aspiration to base the state on an ethical maximum" (236), although he does at least admit that the Ashokan ideal must contend with other models of kingship: "Against the background of ruthless power practices of numerous historic monarchs, the Bodhisattva ideal of kingship proved only a partial ideational foundation for the royal charisma" (80). Indeed, as a BSPP ideologue gloated after the 1962 coup, "U Nu's government did not know 'what it means to care *for* the people, far less capable of carrying out what little it knew.' It was elected by a majority of the people. But: 'Sometimes what a man desires to have is not what he actually needs. . . . It happens that what a man desires is actually dangerous for him and for society. So also with nations.'" (234). The BSPP and the SPDC after it would endorse a form of "tough love" that would recenter the ruthless imperatives of rule.

18. ကိုတော

19. လူမျိုး

20. See Prasse-Freeman (2023c) for an elaboration of this thesis.

21. လက်တွေ့ တစ်မျိုး

22. Callahan also found a lack of standardization in how the 2014 census recorded "Myanmar" (2017a, 466), suggesting that categorical blurriness is not even being corrected by state standardization. Lall (n.d.,153) finds that self-identified Rakhine respondents present "Myanmar" both as the ethnonym for a distinct alter group *and* as the set of which they are a part.

23. For elaboration, see Campbell and Prasse-Freeman (2022).

24. Scholar Michael Aung-Thwin (2013), echoing regime propaganda, referred to politically active monks as "bogus monks."

25. သူပုန် လူမျိုး

26. I thank Izzy Rhoads for this insight (pers. comm., September 2021).

27. See essays in Gudavarthy (2012).

28. In a highly influential Facebook post, a female Burmese writer discussed how class mattered more than ethnicity. She has taken that post down, but she told me, "Class . . . need[s] to be intersected with other things (ethnicity, gender, and center-periphery concept)" (April 4, 2022).

29. I took my lead from Thinzar Shunlei Yi, who suggested in one of our many conversations that certain images might end up putting their authors at risk. For a full treatment of these images, see Prasse-Freeman (2023a).

Chapter 2

1. Ko Ko Thett (2022, 187) clarifies the etymology: "B.E." derives from "Burma Economic Development Corporation," not Burmese Engineering.

2. The military junta that proceeded Ne Win's BSPP first called itself the State Law and Order Restoration Council, or SLORC; SPDC was mellifluous by comparison but was merely a cosmetic change.

3. For a full description of the Michaungkan movement, see Prasse-Freeman (2016).

4. For the distinctions between sovereign and governmental power, see Foucault (2007, 4–8).

5. President Thein Sein declared on November 21, 2011, that "we punished them because they violated the law. There are a lot of people in prison for breaking the law, so if we apply the term ['prisoner of conscience'] to just one group, then it will be unfair on the others." This quotation appears in Nay Thwin (2011). See also Cheesman (2009/2010, 607).

6. Given that economic conditions are so predictive of criminality in Burma, I reject the implicit normative split that asserts that the political prisoners are of a superior quality than the other prisoners. The point remains that activists had reason to believe that political prisoners are qualitatively of a different type, a claim then rejected by the military.

7. While rape in prison has not been the subject of any literature in Myanmar that I have found, rape by the military has received significant treatment, with a Women's Refugee Commission report (2018) focusing on sexual abuse of men.

8. The classification of prisoners into levels existed during colonial times, with those classified as A and B receiving superior food and treatment compared with C, or regular, prisoners (Ei Ei Toe Lwin 2014). Although the military eliminated the divisions, it is possible that political prisoner mobilization for better treatment evoked those classifications. Thanks to Nick Cheesman for pointing this out.

9. AAPP tracked the imprisoned and killed at https://aappb.org/, for which it was awarded the International Peace Bureau's 2021 MacBride Peace Prize, given annually to "a person or organization that has done outstanding work for peace, disarmament and/or human rights."

10. See also Rajagopalan (2012), who juxtaposed two prisons: "At Taunggyi, Zaw Thet Htwe said he had more freedom than during his previous stint at more restrictive Insein."

11. U Win Tin's (2012) prison memoir was entitled *What Is That? Man-Made Hell*, indicating misery, but the text also described camaraderie, organizing, intellectual production, mutual learning, and so on.

12. For a similar relationship, see Jefferson and Martin (2020, 115–16).

13. Schrank identifies the same anxiety present in activists she studied (2015, 160).

14. When Khin Nyunt was deposed in 2004, his Military Intelligence was replaced by the Special Branch; see Selth (2019).

15. Cheesman suspects (pers. comm., March 2022) that because these are not forms that are duplicated through bureaucratic process there may be various iterations, hence this one should not be seen as definitive of all.

16. And it has proven to be more than an idle threat. Cheesman (2015b) has found that this "gift of conditional freedom" (213) can be retracted: he relays how a police officer bringing a case against comedian Zaganar for actions in 2008 effected the reactivation of charges from 2007 pursuant to Zaganar's violation of his pledge.

17. Schrank (2015, 278–79) finds the same general phenomenon.

18. This helps explain the numerous Burmese who asked me in 2004 and 2005, "When is George Bush going to come bomb Myanmar?"; see Prasse-Freeman (2014).

19. For a discussion of the ways the NLD eschewed socioeconomic politics, see Prasse-Freeman (2012, 390–95).

20. He describes here a *sit-kyaw-yay sa-kan*.

21. It is also misnamed because Burmese monks do not wear saffron-colored robes but burgundy ones.

22. အင်အားစု

23. ရေပေါ်ဆီ

24. I thank Kirt Mausert for highlighting the point about mixing.

25. For instance, a Mandalay farmers' group that is part of the activist's network was called FNI, which at one point stood for Facilitator's Network with ILO, but after they stopped working with ILO it became Facilitator's Network with Farmers and Laborers (FNIFL). And yet, everyone still calls them FNI. A signboard of theirs that contains their name in English ("FNI [Upper Myanmar]") and then in Burmese has "alouq-thama leh-thama thamaga cheiq-set hsaung-ywet thu-mya apwe," which would be "Association of Facilitators connecting worker and farmer unions."

26. For an insightful ethnography of broker life, see Brac de la Perrière (2014).

27. *U-ba-day neh-pet-thet-bi Sa-ywet-paw-hma-beh . . . let-tway t'-myo.* (ဥပဒေ နဲ့ပတ်သက်ပြီး စာရွက် ပေါ်မှာပဲ လက်တွေ့တစ်မျိုး)

28. For other reasons, see Brett (2021); for identification documents and the byzantine nature of Myanmar law, see Rhoads (2023).

29. The Critical Legal Studies (CLS) tradition understands law similarly (see Kennedy 2002 for a seminal CLS critique of rights). Burmese subalterns could be said to be CLS-ers *sin la lettre*.

30. See Prasse-Freeman (2016).

31. ဦးအရေး ။ အလိုမရှိ ။ ချက်ချင်းပေး

32. See Prasse-Freeman (2016).

Chapter 3

1. စားမ ဦးချ

2. It should be added that exceptions also mitigated these protections: Toe Hla finds that "in spite of the fact that . . . kings issued edicts for the protection of debtors from exceedingly high interest rates and from any form of torment, some people were arrested and put into confinement for unpaid debts" (1987, 232). When this happened "they lost their lands to the money-lenders," (239) and, we learn, "lands . . . once mortgaged or sold were seldom redeemed" (237).

3. သီးစား

4. ထွန်တုံး တိုက်ပွဲ

5. ဆန္ဒပြ

6. I thank Stephen Campbell for encouraging this line of thought.

7. In defense of the villagers, Fenichel and Khan found that even during the BSPP period, "small-scale industry ha[d] remained predominantly private" (1981, 816).

8. I encountered multiple similar cases in Ayeyawaddy during a 2015 visit there.

9. ရပိုင်ခွင့်

10. ပိုင်ဆိုင်မှု

11. See Prasse-Freeman (2019) for a full account.

12. This protest even made national media, but to protect anonymity, I will not provide a link.

13. ဖြတ်စား

14. Rohingya Blogger writes, "The responsible people of Payounkyaung Pyaing Taung cut and ate the donated water disaster help items," using *pyat-sa* and translating it as "cut and ate." See http://burmese.rohingyablogger.com/2015/08/blog-post_80 .html.

15. ပွဲစား

16. Interview with two writers from a weekly newspaper, January 8, 2015, Yangon.

17. Schrank (2015, 43) outlines many of the consequences for activists' families.

18. Schrank (2015, 197–98) likewise describes an activist struggling to discern the correct path.

19. အာဇာနည်

20. Aung Kyaw, a student protester killed by the British in 1938, and U Wizara, a monk who in 1929 died in prison after an extended hunger strike (Houtman 1999, 34), both had the appellation *ah-zah-ni* added to their names after being killed in struggle; the seventeen Mandalay students killed by the British became "the seventeen martyrs"; and *ah-zah-ni* was immediately applied to Aung San and the seven cabinet members who were assassinated in 1947 in Yangon's Secretariat building. *Ah-zah-ni* Day is held annually in their honor, and in 1989 Aung San Suu Kyi's desire to honor her father by walking to his mausoleum on *Ah-zah-ni* Day had such a symbolic effect that the military responded by imprisoning her for the first time. The anthem *Kaba ma' chay bu:* (The world is not fulfilled), written by Naing Myanmar after the 1988 antigovernment uprising, contains the line *ah-zah-ni dway nay de' dain: pyi*, "The country where the martyrs live"; see Min Zin (2016, 225–26) for a discussion of the song.

Chapter 4

1. ကျိန်စာ

2. If what Whorf (1956, 138) calls "Standard Average European languages" privilege language's denotational content, and Ilongot—to give another example—understands language "first in terms of directives, as a means of getting people to do things," Burma's is closer to how Webb Keane describes the Anakalangese, in which language works "to make things happen" (Keane 1997, 98).

3. The form of these corrections mimics pedagogic texts on correct and incorrect spelling and pronunciation.

4. *Saung-pyaw* [စောင်းပြော] can be decomposed into "askance" and "speak." Taken together the term can be described as "insinuation." I thank Aung Soe Min for insights concerning this term.

5. For an extended treatment of the Michaungan protest, see Prasse-Freeman (2016).

6. Author's translation from Sa Nay Lin (2014) here and in the following passages.

7. This idea of obscured causality recalls Evans-Pritchard's (1937) foundational description of Azande magic.

8. ယတြာ

9. မအာလ ရှက်တတ်ရင် ရှေ့ကျမ်း နောက်ကျမ်း ဆယ်ခါပြန်ပစ်ပြီး သေလို့ရတယ်။ https://www.facebook.com/permalink.php?story_fbid=124171356507289&id=1000674 32752892, accessed September 21, 2021.

10. Recall from chapter 1 the discussion of *Swan-ah-Shin* as unaccountable violent laborers.

11. Spivak (1988) answered her famous question, "Can the subaltern speak?," in the negative: subalterns cannot make themselves legible to higher classes, as both groups are subject to different semiotic logics and interpellative fields. This same dynamic, however, does not apply to the relationship between Burmese subalterns and generals. Rumor and academic literature alike (Matthews 1998) suggest that military leaders are arguably the most committed to esoteric power. As suggested in the introduction, the definition of subaltern employed here is a reticulate one, and hence peasants and military elites may share more in common vis-à-vis ontologies of power than both do with democratic elites, who are interpellated by Western rights discourses.

12. See Zuckerman and Matthias (2022) for Indian protesters performing suffering to "act . . . like 'the people'" (7).

13. "I oppose those who have not given any kind of help resolving things. [*Taut!*] They don't fucking care, do they?" The *taut* (တော့တ်) is a nonlexemic interjection taking the form of a click of the tongue. Unlike the click of the tongue in some English-speaking speech communities, where it marks disapproval (and is defined in dictionaries as *tsking*: http://www.yourdictionary.com/tsking), the tongue click in Burmese can be an *aggressive* action, akin to saying, "I will now fight you," and hence a literal fighting word that exists somewhere between indexing the attack and being the attack itself. By using it here, Wirathu communicates that he's overtaken by anger. Of

course, without context showing the bodily dispositions of Wirathu while speaking the *taut*, we can only speculate on how it was interpreted by the audience or how Wirathu wanted to be interpreted.

14. မ ဖျက်မှ ပြည်ပျက်. The Wikipedia version gives a slightly different translation, but the meaning is the same: https://my.wikipedia.org/wiki/%E1%80%99%E1%80%AD%E1%80%94%E1%80%BA%E1%80%B8%E1%80%99%E1%80%96%E1%80%BB%E1%80%80%E1%80%BA_%E1%80%95%E1%80%BC%E1%80%8A%E1%80%BA%E1%80%95%E1%80%BB%E1%80%80%E1%80%BA?fbclid=IwAR1pZXuqUsdZzLDjGR-A8gRkF5XCSaonxqr4G_BqGPwzEB1n-qGXsXmY9nE.

15. အမေဂျမ်း

16. There is little research on A-May Gyan, but see https://wikihmong.com/en/Amay_Gyan and the 2001 documentary film *Friends in High Places* (directed by Lindsey Merrison) that features an A-May Gyan spirit medium berating a villager: "So you fucked the general? You fucked General Than Shwe? You stupid cunt. You're world famous."

17. This campaign was co-led by middle-class Burmese-Americans in the diaspora and was promoted by other international groups, such as one named SEAD. https://www.facebook.com/theseadproject/posts/today-on-internationalwomensday-our-friends-in-myanmar-are-asking-for-internatio/3921284754626478/.

18. ဝိယ

19. အချောင်သမား

20. For ethnographies of communities of practice organized around esoteric rites, see Patton (2016, 2018); Rozenberg (2015); and contributions to Brac de Perrière, Rozenberg, and Turner (2014).

21. See chapter 1, note 34.

22. နောက်ကွယ်က လက်မည်းကြီး

23. This story was relayed to me by Teza and Ko Taw, as it occurred before I met them.

24. In the sense described by Deleuze and Guatarri (1987).

25. This *kyeinsa* came to my attention on Burmese Facebook and featured photos from the ritual itself. It identified itself as follows: "Moebyeh Camp KaMaYa 422, because out of the land that the battalion stole was cemetery land, the dead and the spirits were called in a protest" [Bse].

26. Guillaume Rozenberg argues that possession in Burma "is the means of expression for collective speech. The medium's assumed vacuity and absence of responsibility make the mechanism's effect unopposable" (2015, 175). While Rozenberg's Durkheimian functionalism need not be taken in full (meaning that any single action of possession is not necessarily channeling collective values), it is indeed likely that, whether consciously or not, those who are possessed are attempting to channel collective values.

27. I thank Andrew Ong for this insightful addition.

Chapter 5

1. See Madson (2022, 512) for an example, in another context, of human rights advocates strategically avoiding human rights talk when communicating with a hostile local population. Further, the inverse scenario—that Burmese activist communities shared the opposite subjectivity (*not* believing in the efficacy of rights) but diverged in how they *expressed* it (with the border groups appealing to human rights as an instrumental tactic while the internal groups did not) – seemed less likely. After all, the foreigner (me) remained constant across environments, and hence the difference would have to be explained *entirely* by the border groups being more sophisticated in their foreigner engagement tactics. While this is plausible, the interpretation is mitigated by the attendant ethnographic content.

2. For a comprehensive account of resubjectivation processes that can occur in spaces of exile, albeit in a different setting, see Malkki (1995). For the power of rights to produce new subjectivities, see Merry (2006, chap. 6).

3. For a thorough treatment of the practices of such transnational networks, albeit in the Fijian context, see Riles (2001).

4. A network is dense and multiplex according to Milroy and Milroy (1999) if all members know one another (dense) and a person knows another in multiple ways—for example, as colleague, neighbor, and cousin (multiplex).

5. On the dynamics of resubjectivation, see Wortham (2005).

6. We should also mention the way the noun "rights" borrows, in English at least, from nonnominative meanings, becoming infected from its adjectival version, "it is right," meaning correct, morally or otherwise (Donnelly 2012, 7). For a discussion of this same indexical relationship in the Arabic and South Asian term for rights (*haq*), see Madhok (2017, 487). This association is not available in languages such as Burmese, however.

7. Rights rely on a kind of political theodicy, in which their manifest failures never indict their potential.

8. In exploring *awkint-ayay* I follow Carruthers (2023) both in his critique of static "key-word" studies and in his elaboration of, instead, a focus on the "configurative rapport" developed within a sociolinguistic system between various signs and their conditions of use.

9. In the authoritative SEAlang dictionary (http://www.sealang.net/Burmese /dictionary.htm), *kwint* is given as "(1) n. permission; leave (of absence) and (2) n. rights and privileges."

10. Ma Thida (2021) has intervened in a similar way, trying to coin a new phrase, *lu-ya-baing-kwint* ("human entitlement"), for "human right" as a way of completely circumventing the problem with using *akwint-ayay* while also linking "human rights" with a sign, *ya-baing-kwint*, that conveys the solidity of an entitlement.

11. For epistemic versus deontic, see Kockelman (2007b, 152–58).

12. Evidence seems to refute Thaung, who writes that "the 'conditional' aspect of Burmese kingship was . . . emphasized during the coronation ceremonies of the

Konbaung period - the contract theory epitomizing in the coronation oaths of the Konbaung kings" (1959, 177). Thaung stands as an exemplar of those who attempt to adduce a "social contract" from Buddhist texts such as the *Aganna Sutta*. But even Huxley, who is sympathetic to the normative project (1997a, 14–15), finds in his analysis of the *Aganna Sutta* (1996) that "if we call it a social contract, even a 'weak social contract,' our attention will be misdirected. The contract metaphor portrays the bond between subject and state as legalistic, as absolute and unbreakable . . . , while a popular consent theory portrays it as mutable and contingent" (409). Rather than a "social contract," in which two parties (ruler and ruled) are bound by legible standards inscribed in (something like) law or norm, Burmese kings were unbound by claims from below.

13. Emphasis added.

14. *Lay-gyo*, meaning "four folds," is a type of poem that organizes its rhyming pattern in stanzas of fours.

15. In the phrase *meinma ko hnya-ta pay-pa-loq atha-ga-lay kyawq-sha deh akwint-pay-paw*.

16. See figure 5.1 or the SEAlang dictionary.

17. The SEAlang dictionary (http://www.sealang.net/Burmese/dictionary.htm) defines the words as follows: "*Ahnya*: v. be considerate; show concern for someone; be lenient; *atha*: adv. tenderly; gently; softly. *kyawq*: v. coax; persuade; soothe; pacify."

18. Jakobson (1990) would describe these as the referential and the conative functions.

19. Myint Zan (2008) relays how the bar was deprofessionalized as the importance of actual legal knowledge was obviated within the context of an increasingly politicized system. Andrew Selth (2015) demonstrates the Burma's police force's subsumption under the military, becoming the latter's frontline coercive apparatus.

20. Article 174: "(c) All citizens who have the right to vote shall enjoy equal voting rights."

21. While Donnelly (2012) claims to rely on social construction, his own discussion does not engage the consequences of that theorization. For instance, he insists that rights do not need an enforcement mechanism to make them real, but he also admits that they are socially constructed (rather than eternal), and so if there is no enforcement and hence they are continually shown in praxis to not be real, then the appeal to the external standard (the text of the UDHR, for instance) might be seen by actual social actors as a dead letter. One cannot have it that rights are socially constructed while not admitting that such a social construction (qua construction) is subject to constant reconceptualization as people realize or admit that those ostensible duty bearers seem to reject or abrogate their role.

22. Bataille's (1993) definition of sovereignty as the excessive *gift* is suggestive here: the gap, that saving lie that allows this reality of power to remain somewhat perceived but unacknowledged, is maintained.

23. See Ball (2011) for an application.

24. And indeed, as the Beastie Boys have exhorted us since 1986 (on *License to Ill*), "(You gotta) fight, for *your* right (to party)" (emphasis added).

25. Cheesman (2002) finds that "commentary on 'rights' is altogether absent from the Myanmar schoolbooks. One's rights are expressed merely as the duties of others. An explicit reference to 'rights' is made only fleetingly in [the] fourth standard, with regard to how 'the law protects people's rights' (4.14)" (141). See also Treadwell (2013, 177) for a similar observation.

26. The cartoon was affixed as a decoration/art installation to FNI's (the Mandalay-based CBO mentioned in previous chapters) celebration of 1930s-era peasant rebel leader Saya San; photo taken February 2, 2015.

27. Emphasis added.

28. For a critique of this "strong" version of the linguistic relativity hypothesis (LRH), see Whorf (1956). Indeed, my argument instead deploys a weak version of the LRH to show how culture/political experience in Myanmar has inflected the understanding of a term ("rights") there, such that there are meaningful differences and opportunities for comparison with how "rights" is understood in liberal-democratic societies. A final point about grammatical renderings: while subaltern Burmese do not always speak about rights in these ways, we can attend to *reactions* to such cases—that is, when speech acts are made that do not conform to expectations. For instance, in an impromptu speech delivered at his trial, activist Thein Aung Myint declared, "We must demand our citizen *akwint-ayay*." Three Burmese interlocutors with whom I read this passage found it unproblematic, at least grammatically. Two others, however, objected to it. Ko Taw described Thein Aung Myint as speaking "wrongly in Burmese," adding that he "is not clever in Burmese words." Phyo Win Latt noted something not quite right about the wording, leading him to interpret Thein Aung Myint as saying it is "more like they have rights to demand their rights. This is considered a first step."

29. I tape-recorded this conversation and translated it later.

30. See Rudy (2021) for a critique of Arendt's concept.

31. One of the editors, in a follow-up article a half decade later entitled "Culture and Rights after Culture and Rights" (Cowan 2006) again ignores rights, even while directly quoting a review of the initial volume by moral philosopher Will Kymlicka that pointed out this fact: "[In Culture and Rights] there is no sustained discussion of the concept of 'rights' and how it differs from other legal concepts, such as 'duties'" (quoted in Cowan 2006, 13).

32. Even as Goodale (2009, 15, 111) explicitly recognizes rights as a *specific* political modality—one of an array of political expressions—through which the principles of common humanity could be instantiated or codified, his book does not examine what constellation of knowledge and power has compelled this choice rather than alternatives (why rights?); neither does it consider the ramifications of this form of regulation on the kind of human hence constructed (what human?). Rights are presumed to be the only possible operative logic.

33. Merry, whose work on the vernacularization of rights is central to the field, treats human rights as immutable even when they are introduced into different

systems: "Human rights retain their fundamental meanings even as they become resources in local struggles" (2006, 137). While Merry may have found in her *own* work
that "fundamental meanings" did not change, the concern is that she makes a claim
here about *all* potential situations—a claim that stood as methodologically unsound
even before historical (Moyn 2010) and empirical research (Perugini and Gordon 2015)
exposed it as false.

34. Englund (2006) objects to human rights being translated into the Malawian
Chichewa language as "freedoms" instead of "entitlements," not exploring that the
choice to use "freedoms" could also have reflected a Malawian political ontology
highly contingent on specific interactions, one that hence cannot be pinned down in
such a concrete way as entitlements implies. Such a lack of specificity, or rather, a presumed fixity, of the sign "rights" can be observed in the predominance of rights ethnographies (Tate 2007).

35. I read Reddy (2022, 1009) as arguing that most contexts make rights translation impossible.

Chapter 6

1. See here for video: https://youtu.be/N8hRVOEnzrA.

2. See Prasse-Freeman and Mausert (2020, 266–77) for a summary of these debates and responses.

3. See Prasse-Freeman and Mausert (2020).

4. The military government has used both legal (Rhoads 2023) and extralegal
(Cheesman 2017) mechanisms to denaturalize the Rohingya.

5. For a full elaboration of this argument, see Prasse-Freeman and Ong (2021).

6. For an expansion of this argument, see Prasse-Freeman (2021).

7. An additional observation about the cartoons discussed in chapter 4 helps illustrate the point about a divided public sphere: quite often the humor or point of a given
cartoon was not clear to my interlocutors or was read in vastly different ways, suggesting the existence of conversations or events (perhaps) legible to only certain subcom-
munities in Myanmar but not to my colleagues. I suspect that Burmese cartoons are
complicated because they cannot presuppose a general reader; rather than being para-
lyzed by this fact, Burmese cartoonists seem to accept it, and even revel in it.

8. See Chambers (2019, 208–26) for Karen Buddhists' demonization of the Rohingya; Nyi Nyi Kyaw (2018) describes how the Kaman, the only majority-Muslim
ethnicity recognized by Myanmar as *taingyintha*, have strategically avoided association with the Rohingya.

9. Schrank (2015, 108–9) describes how Win Tin, one of the country's most famous political prisoners before his death in 2014, had his citizenship number revoked
when he was imprisoned in 1989 and sought with great difficulty to reattain it after his
2008 release.

10. အာမခံ

11. I was assisted in translating this speech by a colleague.

12. See discussion in Prasse-Freeman (2013).

13. See Prasse-Freeman (2023b)

14. See discussion and summary in Prasse-Freeman (2021).

15. *Myo*, as discussed, means "kind" generally, or "race." *Chit* is "love." A classic translation would be "patriot," but given the author's inflammatory language about Bengali invasion, "race lover" seems appropriate.

16. This observation draws from Prasse-Freeman and Ong (2021).

17. While Appadurai's argument is suggestive, it does not appear robust in the sense of being a sufficient condition that would explain mass violence in multiple cases or the absence of violence in cases in which uncertainty nonetheless inheres.

18. Win Myint of the Committee to Verify the Accurate Number of Ethnic Nationalities in Shan State put the objective as follows: "We aim to determine the exact populations of different ethnic groups under our own terms—but there is no plan to submit the findings to the government" (Nang Mya Nadi 2014).

19. See also Gal, Kowalski, and Moore (2015, 614) for a similar critique.

20. ယနေ့ကမ္ဘာကြီး၌ အခွင့်အရေးဆိုသည့်စကားများ ပလူပျံဝေစည်နေကြပါ၏။ လူ့အ ခွင့်အရေး ၊ အလုပ်သမားအခွင့်အရေး၊ လယ်သမားအခွင့်အရေး၊ ကျောင်းသားအခွင့်အရေး ဆိုသည်များ၊ လူ့ဘဝတွင် အခွင့်အရေးရလိုသူများ များပြားလှပါ၏။

21. "Security and mass welfare is given priority over human rights. That is our party's issue that we will give second priority" [Bse].

22. The author appears to be referring to the North American Man/Boy Love Association (or NAMBLA); https://en.wikipedia.org/wiki/North_American_Man/Boy _Love_Association.

23. There does not appear to be a Burmese version of his article.

24. While interlocutors often stressed that he was nationally popular long before 2008, Thidagu became better known to foreigners after he mobilized hundreds of thousands of dollars in aid from Myanmar communities to assist victims of 2008's massively destructive Cyclone Nargis. But Thidagu went from being internationally lauded to condemned after delivering, just after the Rohingya genocide, a sermon to Burma's military in which he justified slaughter of the nonfaithful if the bloodshed was in the defense of Buddhism. His comments were impossible to dismiss as idle rumination on theology given that his audience was the National Defense Services, part of the institution responsible for genocide (see Fuller 2017 for a review of the sermon and for a photo of Thidagu with Barack Obama, then the US president).

25. For another example of a Thidagu sermon condemning human rights, see Cheesman (2015a, 146–47).

26. Ledi encouraged abstinence from beef eating as a form of moral purification that would assist the Burmese in resisting colonialism.

27. For reporting on the revival of this sentiment, see Swe Win (2015b).

28. Other emergent civil-society activities do not qualify—Sunday Schools allow children to perform piety but do not publicize or exclude. Charitable foundations allow performance and publication of civic ethics but do not explicitly exclude.

29. I could not attend these events myself, given security concerns, but Burmese research collaborators attended several of them in 2018, conducting participant

observation and basic demographic tabulations. All four events were attended by a disproportionate number of middle-aged women.

30. Signatories included MCDF and Harn Win Aung's People's Service Network (copy in author's possession).

31. တာဝန်ရှိသူတွေ တာဝန်ယူဖြေရှင်းပေးကြပါ

Conclusion

1. The enigmatic Bartleby, the office scribe in Melville's famous story (1853) who refuses to conduct the work he is paid to do—a refusal that extends all the way to his own death—has long posed puzzles that various philosophers have tried to decipher. Agamben (1999) takes Bartleby as pure potentiality, while Deleuze (1997) identifies Bartleby as scrambling the codes of the extant order through his agrammaticality. I appreciate such readings but would suggest shifting the focus from Bartleby as speaking subject to the overarching interactional context in which his speech can be heard and conjure interpretants. Indeed, it is critical that Bartleby has the capacity to hystericize the Wall Street attorney (who I take as metonym not only of "the Law" as Agamben has it but of the entire liberal capitalist biopolitical order). He is interpellated by Bartleby's "I would prefer not" and hence pursues, coaxes, begs, and cajoles Bartleby to affirm the narrator's commands; the attorney is flummoxed, undone by Bartleby's refusal, and ultimately laments (however mildly) Bartleby's refusal unto death (Deleuze 1997, 74–75). But we might imagine the narrator reacting otherwise. It is possible that Bartleby's first enunciation of "I would prefer not" precipitates an ejection onto the street, with Bartleby left to die alone, without trace or signification. And indeed, Bartleby's "prefer not" would remain unheard and unconsidered in blunt biopolitical contexts of indifference to individual life. A question is which scenario is more likely today.

2. As Martha Nussbaum (1999) put it in a critique of Butler, "Subversion is subversion, and it can in principle go in any direction."

3. Esposito 2012, 73–74.

4. Note that this holds both for versions of rights insured by explicit contract (such as a legal constitution) and those provided by norms (such as natural rights or so-called human rights).

5. The language of "dispossession" evokes Butler and Athanasiou in their eponymous book (2013). There Butler appears to embrace a certain form of self-dispossession, but in the discussion that follows I will argue that her insistence on rights reinstalls the "sovereign" subject as the goal, hence betraying the radical promise of dispossession. It is much the same with subjects under the rights regime—the potential to reorient their stances to embrace a politics of self-dispossession is interrupted by the interpellating force of rights as inalienable possessions that all must seek to restore and retain.

References

Abrams, Philip. (1977) 2006. "Notes on the Difficulty of Studying the State." In *The Anthropology of the State*, edited by Aradhana Sharma and Akhil Gupta, 112–30. Oxford, UK: Blackwell.

Abu-Lughod, Lila. 1990. "The Romance of Resistance: Tracing Transformations of Power through Bedouin Women." *American Ethnologist* 17, no. 1: 41–55.

Adas, Michael. 2011. *The Burma Delta: Economic Development and Social Change on an Asian Rice Frontier, 1852–1941*. Madison: University of Wisconsin Press.

AFP. 2017. "Myanmar Cartoonists Lead Media-Jeering as Rohingya Flee." Agence France-Presse, September 24, 2017.

Agamben, Giorgio. 1999. "Bartleby, or On Contingency." In *Potentialities: Collected Essays in Philosophy*, translated by Daniel Heller-Roazen, 243–71. Redwood City, CA: Stanford University Press.

———. 2000. *Means without End: Notes on Politics*. Minneapolis: University of Minnesota Press.

———. 2005. *State of Exception*. Translated by Kevin Attell. Chicago: University of Chicago Press.

Ahmann, Chloe. 2018. "'It's Exhausting to Create an Event Out of Nothing': Slow Violence and the Manipulation of Time." *Cultural Anthropology* 33, no. 1: 142–71.

Al Jazeera. 2021. "Outcry in Myanmar as Military Airs Images of 'Tortured' Detainees." April 19, 2021. https://www.aljazeera.com/news/2021/4/19/outcry-in-myanmar-as-military-airs-images-of-tortured-detainees.

Althusser, Louis. 1971. "Ideology and Ideological State Apparatuses." In *Lenin and Philosophy and Other Essays*. New York: Monthly Review Press.

Appadurai, Arjun. 1998. "Dead Certainty: Ethnic Violence in the Era of Globalization." *Development and Change* 29, no. 4: 905–25.

Arendt, Hannah. 1970. *On Violence*. New York: Houghton Mifflin Harcourt.

———. 1973. *The Origins of Totalitarianism*. New York: Houghton Mifflin Harcourt.

Aretxaga, Begona. 1995. "Dirty Protest: Symbolic Overdetermination and Gender in Northern Ireland Ethnic Violence." *Ethos* 23, no. 2: 123–48.

Arnold, Matthew B. 2019. "Why GAD Reform Matters to Myanmar." *East Asia Forum*, August 24, 2019.

Arraiza, José-María, Phyu Zin Aye, and Marina Arraiza Shakirova. 2020. "Fighting Imagined Invasions with Administrative Violence: Racism, Xenophobia and Nativism as a Cause of Statelessness in Myanmar, the Dominican Republic and Assam (India)." *Statelessness & Citizenship Review* 2, no. 2: 195–221.

Associated Press. 2013. "Burmese Muslims Given Two-Child Limit." *Guardian*, May 25, 2013. https://www.theguardian.com/world/2013/may/25/burma-muslims-two-child-limit.

Aung, Geoffrey. 2018. "Postcolonial Capitalism and the Politics of Dispossession: Political Trajectories in Southern Myanmar." *European Journal of East Asian Studies* 17, no. 2: 193–227.

———. 2021. "Dead Generations." *N+1*. April 8, 2021.

Aung Myo Min. 2017. "Toward National Security Based on Human Rights." *Irrawaddy*, September 6, 2017.

Aung Naing Soe. 2016. "One Day after Teen Electrocuted on Yangon Street, Site Not Blocked Off or Secured." *Coconuts Yangon*, May 25, 2016.

Aung San. 1946. "Problems for Burma's Independence." http://www.aungsan.com/Prob_Burma.htm.

Aung Shin. 2014. "Myanmar's Power Struggle." *Myanmar Times*, May 12, 2014.

Aung Thu. 2014. "Lepadaung Mountain Locals Appeal to the Mountain Father Guardian Spirit to Curse U Baing and Wan Baung Company." [In Burmese.] *Eleven*, May 24, 2014.

Aung-Thwin, Maitrii. 2011. *The Return of the Galon King*. Singapore: NUS Press.

Aung-Thwin, Michael. 1982. "Prophecies, Omens, and Dialogue: Tools of the Trade in Burmese Historiography." In *Moral Order and the Question of Change: Essays on Southeast Asian Thought*, edited by David Wyatt, Alexander Woodside, and Michael Aung-Thwin, 78–103. Yale University, Southeast Asia Studies.

———. 1985. "The British 'Pacification' of Burma: Order without Meaning." *Journal of Southeast Asian Studies* 16, no. 2: 245–61.

———. 2013. "Those Men in Saffron Robes." *Journal of Burma Studies* 17, no. 2: 243–334.

Austin, John. 1975. *How to Do Things with Words*. New York: Oxford University Press.

Auyero, Javier. 2012. *Patients of the State*. Durham, NC: Duke University Press.

Badgley, John. 1965. "The Theravada Polity of Burma." *Zonam Aija Kenkyu* II: 52–75.

———. 1973. *Politics among Bamars*. Athens: Ohio University Center for International Studies.

Balibar, Étienne. 2016. *Violence and Civility*. New York: Columbia University Press.

Ball, Christopher. 2011. "Inalienability in Social Relations: Language, Possession, and Exchange in Amazonia." *Language in Society* 40, no. 3: 307–41.

Bataille, Georges. 1993. *The Accursed Share*. Vols. 2 and 3. New York: Zone.

Bauman, Richard, and Charles Briggs. 1990. "Poetics and Performance as Critical Perspectives on Language and Social Life." *Annual Review of Anthropology* 19: 59–88.

Bayart, Jean-François. 2009. *The State in Africa: The Politics of the Belly.* Cambridge, UK: Polity.

Bayat, Asef. 2013. *Life as Politics: How Ordinary People Change the Middle East.* Redwood City, CA: Stanford University Press.

BBC. 2021. "Myanmar Coup: Six-Year-Old Shot 'as She Ran into Father's Arms.'" BBC News, April 1, 2021. https://www.bbc.com/news/world-asia-56501871.

BCUK (Burma Campaign UK). 2014. "Burma's Census – Not Worth Dying For." *Burma Briefing*, no. 31 (February 2014).

Beemer, Bryce. 2009. "Southeast Asian Slavery and Slave-Gathering Warfare as a Vector for Cultural Transmission: The Case of Burma and Thailand." *Historian* 71, no. 3: 481–506.

Bell, Thomas. 2008. "Burma Cyclone: Junta Tells Victims to Eat Frogs." *Telegraph*, May 30, 2008.

Benjamin, Walter. 1978. "Critique of Violence." In *Reflections: Essays, Aphorisms, Autobiographical Writings*, edited by Peter Demetz, 277–300. New York: Shocken Books.

Bennett, James. 2017. "Rohingya Refugees: 'No Words' to Describe Bangladesh Camps, Red Cross Says." Australian Broadcast Corporation, September 16, 2017.

Berry, Maya, Claudia Chávez Argüelles, Shanya Cordis, Sarah Ihmoud, and Elizabeth Velásquez Estrada. 2017. "Toward a Fugitive Anthropology: Gender, Race, and Violence in the Field." *Cultural Anthropology* 32, no. 4: 537–65.

Beyer, Judith. 2015. "Finding the Law in Myanmar." *Anthropology Today* 31, no. 4: 3–7.

Bhandar, Brenna. 2018. "Possessive Nationalism: Race, Class and the Lifeworlds of Property." *Viewpoint Magazine*, February 1, 2018.

Bhungalia, Lisa. 2020. "Laughing at Power: Humor, Transgression, and the Politics of Refusal in Palestine." *Environment and Planning C: Politics and Space* 38, no. 3: 387–404.

Bo Bo Nge. 2020. "Urban Real Estate and the Financial System in Myanmar." In *Unraveling Myanmar's Transition*, edited by Pavin Chachavalpongpun, Elliott Prasse-Freeman, and Patrick Strefford, 111–35. Singapore: NUS Press.

Bonilla, Yarimar. 2015. *Non-sovereign Futures.* Chicago: University of Chicago Press.

Bosson, Andrew. 2007. *Forced Migration / Internal Displacement in Burma with an Emphasis on Government Controlled Areas.* Geneva, CH: Internal Displacement Monitoring Center.

Boudreau, Vince. 2004. *Resisting Dictatorship: Repression and Protest in Southeast Asia.* Cambridge, UK: Cambridge University Press.

Bourdieu, Pierre. 1977. *Outline of a Theory of Practice.* Cambridge, UK: Cambridge University Press.

Boutry, Maxime. 2016. "Bamar Territories and Borders in the Making of a Myanmar Nation State." In *Myanmar's Mountain and Maritime Borderscapes*, edited by Su-Ann Oh, 99–120. Singapore: ISEAS.

———. 2021. "Yangon Peri-Urban Areas as Significant Places of Resistance?" Paper presented at the Burma Studies Conference, online, September 17, 2021.

Boutry, Maxime, Celine Allaverdian, M. Mellac, Stephen Huard, San Thein, Tin Myo Win, and Khin Pyae Sone. 2017. *Land Tenure in Rural Lowland Myanmar: From Historical Perspectives to Contemporary Realities in the Dry Zone and the Delta*. Of Lives of Land Myanmar Research Series. Yangon: Gret.

Boutry, Maxime, A. B. Htike, and Y. Wunna. 2014. "Urban Poverty in Yangon Greater City: A Qualitative Study of Urban Poverty, Its Causes and Consequences." Unpublished report for the World Food Program, Yangon.

Brac de la Perrière, Bénédicte. 2012. "From Weikzahood to Mediumship: How to Master the World in Contemporary Burma." *Religion Compass* 6, no. 2: 103–12.

———. 2014. "A Woman of Mediation." In *Burmese Lives*, edited by Wen-Chin Chang and Eric Tagliacozzo, 71–82. Oxford, UK: Oxford University Press.

Brac de Perrière, Bénédicte, Guillaume Rozenberg, and Alicia Turner, eds. 2014. *Champions of Buddhism: Weikza Cults in Contemporary Burma*. Singapore: NUS Press.

Brenner, David, and Martina Tazzioli. 2022. "Defending Society, Building the Nation: Rebel Governance as Competing Biopolitics." *International Studies Quarterly* 66, no. 2: sqac007.

Brett, Peggy. 2021. "The Ambiguities of Citizenship Status in Myanmar." In *Living with Myanmar*, edited by Justine Chambers and Charlotte Galloway, 336–52. Singapore: ISEAS.

Brown, Ian. 2013. *Burma's Economy in the Twentieth Century*. New York: Cambridge University Press.

Brown, Michael. 1996. "On Resisting Resistance." *American Anthropologist* 98, no. 4: 729–49.

Brown, Wendy. 1995. *States of Injury*. Princeton, NJ: Princeton University Press.

Bünte, Marco. 2022. "Ruling but Not Governing: Tutelary Regimes and the Case of Myanmar." *Government and Opposition* 57, no. 2: 336–52.

Buscemi, Francesco. 2022. "'Blunt' Biopolitical Rebel Rule: On Weapons and Political Geography at the Edge of the State." *Small Wars and Insurgencies* 34, no. 1: 81–112.

Butler, Judith. 1997. *Excitable Speech*. New York: Abingdon, UK: Routledge.

———. 2006. "Indefinite Detention." In *Precarious Life: The Powers of Mourning and Violence*. New York: Verso.

———. 2015. *Notes toward a Performative Theory of Assembly*. Cambridge, MA: Harvard University Press.

Butler, Judith, and Athena Athanasiou. 2013. *Dispossession: The Performative in the Political*. Malden, MA: Polity.

Callahan, Mary. 2003. *Making Enemies: War and State Building in Burma*. Singapore: NUS Press.

———. 2004. "Making Myanmars: Language, Territory, and Belonging in Post-Socialist Burma." In *Boundaries and Belonging: States and Societies in the Struggle to Shape Identities and Local Practices*, edited by Joel S. Migdal, 99–120. Cambridge, UK: Cambridge University Press.

———. 2017a. "Distorted, Dangerous Data? *Lu-myo* in the 2014 Myanmar Population and Housing Census." *Sojourn: Journal of Social Issues in Southeast Asia* 32, no. 2: 452–78.

———. 2017b. "Aung San Suu Kyi's Quiet, Puritanical Vision for Myanmar." *Nikkei Asia*, March 29, 2017.

Campbell, Stephen. 2020. "Debt Collection as Labour Discipline: The Work of Finance in a Myanmar Squatter Settlement." *Social Anthropology* 28, no. 3: 729–42.

———. 2022. *Along the Integral Margin*. Ithaca, NY: Cornell University Press.

Campbell, Stephen, and Elliott Prasse-Freeman. 2022. "Revisiting the Wages of Bamar-ness: Contradictions of Privilege in Myanmar." *Journal of Contemporary Asia* 52, no. 2: 175–99.

Campt, Tina. 2019. "The Visual Frequency of Black Life: Love, Labor, and the Practice of Refusal." *Social Text* 37 (3): 25–46.

Candea, Matei. 2018. *Comparison in Anthropology*. Cambridge, UK: Cambridge University Press.

Carruthers, Andrew. 2023. "In Lieu of 'Keywords': Toward an Anthropology of Rapport." *American Anthropologist* 125, no. 3.

Carstens, Charles. 2018. "Religion." In *The Routledge Encyclopedia of Contemporary Myanmar*, edited by Ian Holliday, Nicholas Farrelly, and Adam Simpson, 126–35. Abingdon, UK: Routledge.

———. 2020. "Gift Narration: Dynamic Themes of Reciprocity, Debt, and Social Relations in Theravāda Buddhist Myanmar." *Journal of contemporary religion* 35, no. 1: 31–51.

Chakrabarty, Dipesh. 2007a. "'In the Name of Politics': Democracy and the Power of the Multitude in India." *Public Culture* 19, no. 1: 35–57.

———. 2007b. *Provincializing Europe*. Princeton, NJ: Princeton University Press.

Chambers, Justine. 2019. "In Pursuit of Morality: Moral Agency and Everyday Ethics of Plong Karen Buddhists in Southeastern Myanmar." PhD thesis, Australian National University.

Chan Mya Htwe and Khin Su Wai. 2016. "Wanbao Requests Talks with Letpadaung Protesters." *Myanmar Times*, May 12, 2016.

Charney, Michael. 1999. "Where Jambudipa and Islamdom Converged: Religious Change and the Emergence of Buddhist Communalism in Early Modern Arakan (Fifteenth to Nineteenth Centuries)." PhD diss., University of Michigan.

Chatterjee, Partha. 2004. *Politics of the Governed*. New York: Columbia University Press.

———. 2011. *Lineages of Political Society*. New York: Columbia University Press.

———. 2019. *I Am the People*. New York: Columbia University Press.

Cheesman, Nick. 2002. "Legitimising the Union of Myanmar through Primary School Textbooks." Master's diss., University of Western Australia, 2002.

———. 2009/2010. "Thin Rule of Law or Un-Rule of Law in Myanmar?" *Pacific Affairs* 82, no. 4 (Winter): 597–613.

———. 2012. "The Politics of Law and Order in Myanmar." PhD thesis, Australian National University.

———. 2015a. "The Right to Have Rights." In *Communal Violence in Myanmar*. Yangon: Myanmar Knowledge Society and Australia National University.

———. 2015b. *Opposing the Rule of Law*. Cambridge, UK: Cambridge University Press.

———. 2017. "How in Myanmar 'National Races' Came to Surpass Citizenship and Exclude Rohingya." *Journal of Contemporary Asia* 7, no. 3: 461–83.

———. 2019. "Routine Impunity as Practice (in Myanmar)." *Human Rights Quarterly* 41, 873–92.

———. 2021. "Myanmar's Theatre of Violence: The Act of Killing—Online." ABC Religion & Ethics, June 14, 2021. https://www.abc.net.au/religion/myanmar%e2%80%99s-theatre-of-violence-the-act-of-killing-online/13387100.

Chowdhury, Nusrat. 2019. *Paradoxes of the Popular: Crowd Politics in Bangladesh*. Redwood City, CA: Stanford University Press.

Chua, Lynette. 2015. "The Vernacular Mobilization of Human Rights in Myanmar's Sexual Orientation and Gender Identity Movement." *Law and Society Review* 49, no. 2: 299–332.

———. 2019. *The Politics of Love in Myanmar*. Redwood City, CA: Stanford University Press.

Chu May Paing. 2020. "In Need of Daughters of Good Lineage: Placing Gender in Myanmar's Buddhist Nationalist Discourse." *Journal of Southeast Asian Linguistics Society* 13, no. 4: 42–52.

Clarke, Kamari. 2009. *Fictions of Justice: The International Criminal Court and the Challenge of Legal Pluralism in Sub-Saharan Africa*. Cambridge, UK: Cambridge University Press.

Clifford, James, and George E. Marcus, eds. 1986. *Writing Culture: The Poetics and Politics of Ethnography: A School of American Research Advanced Seminar*. Berkeley: University of California Press.

Coconuts Yangon. 2016. "9 Photos That Show the Weird, Wondrous Side of Myanmar Life." October 20, 2016. https://coconuts.co/yangon/news/7-photos-show-weird-wondrous-side-myanmar-life/.

———. 2021. "Yangon Youths Joined Hands before Fatal Leap to Escape Soldiers: Witnesses." August 11, 2021. https://coconuts.co/yangon/news/yangon-youths-joined-hands-before-fatal-leap-to-escape-soldiers-witnesses/.

Collier, Stephen. 2009. "Topologies of Power: Foucault's Analysis of Political Government beyond 'Governmentality.'" *Theory, Culture and Society* 26, no. 6: 78–108.

Connelly, Karen. 2011. *The Lizard Cage*. New York: Spiegel and Grau.

Cowan, Jane. 2006. "Culture and Rights after Culture and Rights." *American Anthropologist* 108, no. 1: 9–24.

Cowan, Jane, Marie-Bénédicte Dembour, and Richard Wilson, eds. 2001. Introduction to *Culture and Rights: Anthropological Perspectives*. Cambridge, UK: Cambridge University Press.

Crehan, Kate. 2002. *Gramsci, Culture and Anthropology*. Berkeley: University of California Press.

Crouch, Melissa. 2019. *The Constitution of Myanmar: A Contextual Analysis*. London: Hart.

Daniel, E. Valentine. 1996. *Charred Lullabies*. Princeton, NJ: Princeton University Press.

Das, Veena, and Deborah Poole. 2004. "State and Its Margins: Comparative Ethnographies." In *Anthropology in the Margins of the State*, edited by Veena Das and Deborah Poole, 3–33. Santa Fe: School of American Research Seminar.

Dave, Naisargi. 2012. *Queer Activism in India: A Story in the Anthropology of Ethics*. Durham, NC: Duke University Press.

Deleuze, Gilles. 1997. *Essays Critical and Clinical*. Translated by Daniel Smith and Michael Greco. Minneapolis: University of Minnesota Press.

Deleuze, Gilles, and Felix Guattari. 1987. *A Thousand Plateaus: Capitalism and Schizophrenia*. Vol. 2. Translated by Brian Massumi. Minneapolis: University of Minnesota Press.

Dembour, Marie-Bénédicte. 2010. "What Are Human Rights? Four Schools of Thought." *Human Rights Quarterly* 32, no. 1: 1–20.

Derrida, Jacques. 1988. "Signature Event Context." In *Limited Inc*. Evanston, IL: Northwestern University Press.

———. 2006. *Specters of Marx*. Abingdon, UK: Routledge.

Development Ko Ko Lay. 2013. In *A Taste of Prison*, 17–39. [In Burmese.] Yangon: Myanmar's Age.

d'Hubert, Thibaut. 2018. *In the Shade of the Golden Palace*. Oxford, UK: Oxford University Press.

Doffegnies, Amy, and Tamas Wells. 2021. "The Vernacularization of Human Rights Discourse in Myanmar: Rejection, Hybridization and Strategic Avoidance." *Journal of Contemporary Asia* 2021: 1–20.

Donnelly, Jack. 2012. *Universal Human Rights in Theory and Practice*. 3rd ed. Ithaca, NY: Cornell University Press.

Douzinas, Costas. 2007. *Human Rights and Empire*. Abingdon, UK: Routledge.

DVB (Democratic Voice of Burma). 2014. "Michaungkan Protesting Camp's Land Ogre Spirit Curse (News Photographs)." [In Burmese.] April 28, 2014.

———. 2016. "Vengeful Ghosts Evicted from Delta High School." October 26, 2016.

Dworkin, Ronald. 1977. *Taking Rights Seriously*. Cambridge, MA: Harvard University Press.

Eaint Thiri Thu. 2019. "Covering Rakhine: Journalism, Conflict and Identity." In *Myanmar Media in Transition: Legacies, Challenges, and Change*, edited by Lisa Brooten, Jane Madlyn McElhone, and Gayathry Venkiteswaran, 229–38. Singapore: ISEAS.

Edwards, Michael. 2022. "Circulating in Difference: Performances of Publicity on and beyond a Yangon Train." *Journal of the Royal Anthropological Institute* 28, no. 2: 451–76.

———. Forthcoming. *Real Change: Myanmar and the Dissonance of Salvation*. Berkeley: University of California Press.

Ei Ei Toe Lwin. 2014. "Activists Say Political Prisoners Remain in Jail." *Myanmar Times*, January 6, 2014.

EKNPS. 2014. "Ethnic Karen National's Position Statement on 2014-Population Census Enumeration in Burma/Myanmar." Copy with author, January 10, 2014.

Elgee, Alex. 2010. "Silencing the Sangha." *Irrawaddy* 18, no. 11, November 2010.

E Maung. 1951. *The Expansion of Burmese Law.* Rangoon: Royal Printing Works.

EMReF (Enlightened Myanmar Research Foundation). 2019. *Youth Perceptions of Pluralism and Diversity in Yangon, Myanmar.* Paris: UNESCO.

Englund, Harri. 2006. *Prisoners of Freedom.* Berkeley: University of California Press.

Epp, Charles. 1998. *The Rights Revolution.* Chicago: University of Chicago Press.

Esposito, Roberto. 2008. *Bios.* Minneapolis: University of Minnesota Press.

———. 2010. *Communitas.* Translated by Timothy Campbell. Redwood City, CA: Stanford University Press.

———. 2012. *Third Person.* Translated by Zakiya Hanafi. Cambridge, UK: Polity.

Evans-Pritchard, Edward. 1937. *Witchcraft, Oracles and Magic among the Azande.* London: Oxford University Press.

Ewing, Cindy. 2018. "The Asian Unity Project." PhD diss., Yale University.

———. 2020. "Codifying Minority Rights: Postcolonial Constitutionalism in Burma, Ceylon, and India." In *Decolonization, Self-Determination, and the Rise of Global Human Rights Politics*, edited by Roland Burke, Marco Duranti, and A. Dirk Moses, 179–206. Cambridge, UK: Cambridge University Press.

Farzana, Kazi Fahmida. 2017. *Memories of Burmese Rohingya Refugees: Contested Identity and Belonging.* New York: Springer.

Faxon, Hilary. 2023. "After the Rice Frontier: Producing State and Ethnic Territory in Northwest Myanmar." *Geopolitics* 28, no. 1: 47–71.

Faxon, Hilary, and Salai Suanpi. 2022. "Engaged Anthropology Grant: Hilary Faxon." Wenner-Gren Foundation, December 14, 2022. https://wennergren.org/article/engaged-anthropology-grant-hilary-faxon/.

Feldman, Allen. 1991. *Formations of Violence.* Chicago: University of Chicago Press.

Fenichel, Allen, and Azfar Khan. 1981. "The Burmese Way to 'Socialism.'" *World Development* 9, nos. 9–10: 813–24.

Ferguson, James. 2015. *Give a Man a Fish.* Durham, NC: Duke University Press.

Ferguson, James, and Akhil Gupta. 2002. "Spatializing States: Toward an Ethnography of Neoliberal Governmentality." *American Ethnologist* 29, no. 4: 981–1002.

Ferguson, Jane. 2015. "Who's Counting? Ethnicity, Belonging, and the National Census in Burma/Myanmar." *Bijdragen tot de Taal-, Land- en Volkenkunde* 171 (2015): 1–28.

Ferme, Mariane. 2004. "Deterritorialized Citizenship and the Resonances of the Sierra Leonean State." In *Anthropology in the Margins of State*, edited by Veena Das and Deborah Poole, 81–116. Santa Fe: School of American Research Press.

FIDH. 2017. *Land of Sorrow: Human Rights Violations at Myanmar's Myotha Industrial Park.* Report no. 702a. Paris: International Federation for the Defense of Human Rights.

Fink, Christina. 2009. *Living Silence*. London: Zed Books.

Fisher, Jonah. 2017. "Hounded and Ridiculed for Complaining of Rape." BBC News, March 11, 2017.

Foucault, Michel. 1976. *Discipline and Punish*. New York: Vintage.

———. 1984. "Of Other Spaces, Heterotopias." Translated by Jay Miskowiec. *Architecture, Mouvement, Continuité*, no. 5 (October): 46–49, http://foucault.info/documents/heteroTopia/foucault.heteroTopia.en.html.

———. 1997. *Ethics: Subjectivity and Truth*. New York: New Press.

———. 2003. *Society Must Be Defended: Lectures at the College de France, 1975–76*. Translated by David Macey. New York: Picador.

———. 2007. *Security Territory Population: Lectures at the College de France, 1977–78*. Edited by Michel Senellart. New York: Picador.

———. 2008. *Birth of Biopolitics: Lectures at the College de France, 1978–79*. Translated by Graham Burchell. New York: Palgrave MacMillan.

Frankfurt, Harry. 1958. "Peirce's Notion of Abduction." *Journal of Philosophy* 55, no. 14: 593–97.

Frontier. 2021. "A Day of Tragedy and Terror in Hlaing Tharyar." *Frontier Myanmar*, March 17, 2021.

Frydenlund, Shae. 2020. "Motherhood, Home, and the Political Economy of Rohingya Women's Labor." In *Unraveling Myanmar's Transition*, edited by Pavin Chachavalpongpun, Elliott Prasse-Freeman, and Patrick Strefford. Singapore: NUS Press.

Fujii, Lee Ann. 2009. *Killing Neighbors*. Ithaca, NY: Cornell University Press.

———. 2021. *Show Time*. Ithaca, NY: Cornell University Press.

Fuller, Paul. 2017. "Sitagu Sayadaw and Justifiable Evils in Buddhism." *New Mandala*, November 13, 2017.

Furnivall, John. 1909. "Land as a Free Gift of Nature." *Economic Journal* 19, no. 76: 552–62.

———. 1939. "The Fashioning of Leviathan: The Beginnings of British Rule in Burma." *Journal of Burma Research Society* 29, no. 1: 3–137.

———. 1956. *Colonial Policy and Practice*. New York: New York University Press.

Gal, Susan, Julia Kowalski, and Erin Moore. 2015. "Rethinking Translation in Feminist NGOs: Rights and Empowerment across Borders." *Social Politics: International Studies in Gender, State and Society* 22, no. 4: 610–35.

Gamanii. 2012. "135: Counting Races in Burma." *Shan Herald*, September 25, 2012.

Gamble, Barbara. 1997. "Putting Civil Rights to a Popular Vote." *American Journal of Political Science* 41, no. 1: 245–69.

Geertz, Clifford. 1980. *Negara*. Princeton, NJ: Princeton University Press.

Geuss, Raymond. 2001. *History and Illusion in Politics*. Cambridge, UK: Cambridge University Press.

———. 2008. *Philosophy and Real Politics*. Princeton, NJ: Princeton University Press.

Geuss, Raymond, and Lawrence Hamilton. 2013. "Human Rights: A Very Bad Idea." *Theoria: A Journal of Social and Political Theory* 60, no. 135: 83–103.

Glissant, Édouard. 1997. *Poetics of Relation*. University of Michigan Press.

Global Witness. 2015. *Jade: Myanmar's Big State Secret.* https://www.globalwitness.org/en/campaigns/oil-gas-and-mining/myanmarjade/.

Godelier, Maurice. 1999. *The Enigma of the Gift.* Chicago: University of Chicago Press.

Goffman, Erving. 1981. "Footing." In *Forms of Talk*, 124–57. Philadelphia: University of Pennsylvania Press.

Goodale, Mark. 2009. *Surrendering to Utopia.* Redwood City, CA: Stanford University Press.

———. 2022. *Reinventing Human Rights.* Redwood City, CA: Stanford University Press.

Graeber, David. 2009. *Direct Action: An Ethnography.* Chico, CA: AK Press.

———. 2015. "Radical Alterity Is Just Another Way of Saying 'Reality': A Reply to Eduardo Viveiros de Castro." *HAU: Journal of Ethnographic Theory* 5, no. 2: 1–41.

Gramsci, Antonio. 1971. *Prison Notebooks.* New York: International.

Gravers, Mikael. 2021. "The Making of a Fixed National Hierarchy of Ethnicity and Religion in Myanmar." In *Ethnic and Religious Diversity in Myanmar*, edited by Perry Schmidt-Leukel, Hans-Peter Grooshans, and Madlen Kreuger. London: Bloomsbury.

Griffiths, Michael. 2020. *Community Welfare Organisations in Rural Myanmar: Precarity and Parahita.* Abingdon, UK: Routledge.

Gudavarthy, Ajay, ed. 2012. *Reframing Democracy and Agency in India.* London: Anthem Press.

Guha, Ranajit. 1997. *Dominance without Hegemony: History and Power in Colonial India.* Cambridge, MA: Harvard University Press.

Gupta, Akhil. 2005. "Narratives of Corruption: Anthropological and Fictional Accounts of the Indian State." *Ethnography* 6, no. 1: 5–34.

———. 2012. *Red Tape.* Durham, NC: Duke University Press.

Hamacher, Werner. 2017. "The One Right No One Ever Has." *Philosophy Today* 61, no. 4: 947–62.

Harms, Erik. 2011. *Saigon's Edge.* Minneapolis: University of Minnesota Press.

Harrisson, Annika. 2021. "Everyday Trepidation: State Affects and Mental Absconding in a Marginal Neighbourhood in Mawlamyine." In *Everyday Justice in Myanmar*, edited by Helene Kyed, 230–56. Copenhagen: NIAS Press.

Hartman, Saidiya. 2018. "The Anarchy of Colored Girls Assembled in a Riotous Manner." *South Atlantic Quarterly* 117, no. 3: 465–90.

Hartman, Saidiya, and Fred Moten. 2018. "To Refuse That Which Has Been Refused to You." *Chimurenga: Who No Know Go Know*, October 19, 2018.

Harvey, David. 1990. *The Condition of Postmodernity.* Hoboken, NJ: Blackwell.

Henkin, Louis. 1990. *The Age of Rights.* New York: Columbia University Press.

Herbert, Zunetta. 2020. "The NLD Needs to Rethink Its Assumptions about Land." *Frontier*, October 25, 2020.

Herzfeld, Michael. 2016. *Siege of the Spirits.* Chicago: University of Chicago Press.

Holcombe, Sarah. 2018. *Remote Freedoms: Politics, Personhood and Human Rights in Aboriginal Central Australia.* Redwood City, CA: Stanford University Press.

Holliday, Ian. 2014. "Addressing Myanmar's Citizenship Crisis." *Journal of Contemporary Asia* 44, no. 3: 404–21.

Holquist, Michael. 1990. *Dialogism: Bakhtin and His World*. New York: Routledge.

Holston, James. 2008. *Insurgent Citizenship*. Princeton, NJ: Princeton University Press.

Honig, Bonnie. 2021. *A Feminist Theory of Refusal*. Cambridge, MA: Harvard University Press.

Houtman, Gustaaf. 1999. *Mental Culture in Burmese Crisis Politics: Aung San Suu Kyi and the National League for Democracy*. Monograph Series, no. 33. Tokyo: Tokyo University of Foreign Studies, Institute for the Study of Languages and Cultures of Asia and Africa.

Hsu, Mu-Lung. 2019. "Making Merit, Making Civil Society: Free Funeral Service Societies and Merit-Making in Contemporary Myanmar." *Journal of Burma Studies* 23, no. 1: 1–36.

Htin Aung. 1962. *Folk Elements in Burmese Buddhism*. Oxford, UK: Oxford University Press

Hue, Emily. 2021. "On Transnational Abolitionist Relationalities: From Mandalay to Minneapolis." *Society + Space*, May 10, 2021.

Hull, Matthew S. 2012. *Government of Paper: Materiality of Bureaucracy in Pakistan*. Berkeley: University of California Press.

Huxley, Andrew. 1988–89. "Burma: It Works, but Is It Law?" *Journal of Family Law* 27, 23–34.

———. 1996. "The Buddha and the Social Contract." *Journal of Indian Philosophy* 24, no. 4: 407–20.

———. 1997a. "The Importance of the Dhammathats in Burmese Law and Culture." *Journal of Burma Studies* 1, 1–17.

———. 1997b. "The Village Knows Best: Social Organisation in an 18th Century Burmese Law Text." *South East Asia Research* 5, no. 1: 21–39.

———. 1998. "The Last Fifty Years of Burmese Law: E Maung and Maung Maung." *Lawasia: Journal of the Law Association of East Asia and the West Pacific*, 9–20.

———. 2001. "Pre-colonial Burmese Law: Conical Hat and Shoulder Bag." International Institute for Asian Studies newsletter, no. 25.

Huxley, Andrew, and Ryuji Okudaira, 2001. "A Burmese Tract on Kingship: Political Theory in the 1782 Manuscript of Manugye." *Bulletin of the School of Oriental and African Studies* 64, no. 2: 248–59.

Ikeya, Chie. 2011. *Refiguring Women, Colonialism, and Modernity in Burma*. Honolulu: University of Hawai'i Press.

Inkyin Naing. 2016. "Daw Su Gives Warning to Cronies to Not Act with Intentions Like Before." [In Burmese.] *Voice of America*, October 23, 2016.

Irrawaddy. 2011. "Nay Myo Zin Sentenced to 10 Years." August 26, 2011.

———. 2019. "Art Exhibition Questions a Gender Discriminatory Status Quo." May 9, 2019.

———. 2021. "Myanmar Reacts as Resistance Fighters Make Deadly Jump to Avoid Raiding Troops." August 11, 2021.

———. 2022. "NUG: Over 3,000 Civilians Killed by Myanmar Regime Since Last September," September 13, 2022.

Irvine, Judith, and Susan Gal. 2000. "Language Ideology and Linguistic Differentiation." In *Regimes of language*, edited by Paul Kroskrity, 35-83. Woodbridge, UK: James Currey.

Jacquemet, Marco. 1994. "T-offenses and Metapragmatic Attacks: Strategies of Interactional Dominance." *Discourse and Society* 5, no. 3: 297–319.

Jakobson, Roman. 1990. "The Speech Event and the Functions of Language." In *On Language*, edited by Linda R. Waugh and Monique Monville-Burston, 69–79. Cambridge, MA: Harvard University Press.

Jap, Jangai. 2021. "Winning Hearts and Minds: Street-Level Bureaucracy and Attachment to the State in Myanmar." PhD diss., George Washington University.

Jasper, James, and Jeff Goodwin, eds., 2004. *Rethinking Social Movements: Structure, Meaning, and Emotion.* Lanham, MD: Rowman and Littlefield.

Jefferson, Andrew, and Tomas Martin. 2020. "Connecting and Disconnecting: Exploring Prisoners' Relations with the Outside World in Myanmar." *Cambridge Journal of Anthropology* 38, no. 1: 105–22.

Jones, Lee. 2017. "A Better Political Economy of the Rohingya Crisis." *New Mandala.* September 26, 2017.

———. 2018. "Myanmar's Political Economy." In *Handbook of Contemporary Myanmar*, edited by Ian Holliday, Adam Simpson, and Nicholas Farrelly. Abingdon, UK: Routledge.

Jordt, Ingrid. 2007. *Burma's Mass Lay Meditation Movement: Buddhism and the Cultural Construction of Power.* Athens: Ohio University Press.

JPaing. 2014. "Letpadaung Protesters Burn Coffins, Curse Mining Companies." *Irrawaddy*, May 29, 2014.

Kaba, Mariame. 2021. *We Do This' til We Free Us: Abolitionist Organizing and Transforming Justice.* Chicago: Haymarket Books.

KDNG (Kachin Development Network Group). 2019. *Blood Amber.* Myitkhina: Kachin Development Network Group. https://kdng.org/2019/08/19/blood-amber/.

Keane, Webb. 1997. *Signs of Recognition.* Berkeley: University of California Press.

Keeler, Ward. 2009. "What's Burmese about Burmese Rap?," *American Ethnologist* 36, no. 1: 2–19.

———. 2017. *The Traffic in Hierarchy.* Honolulu: University of Hawai'i Press.

Kennedy, Duncan. 2002. "Critique of Rights in CLS." In *Left Legalism/Left Critique*, edited by Wendy Brown and Janet Halley. Durham, NC: Duke University Press.

Khin Swe. 1929. "Yuvati Cakkhu." *Dagon*, September 1929, 351–61.

Khin Thazin. 2021. "Keeping the Streets: Myanmar's Civil Disobedience Movement as Public Pedagogy." *PRATA* 1, no. 1: 1–33.

Khin Yi. 1988a. *The DoBama Movement in Burma (1930–1938).* Ithaca, NY: Cornell University Press.

———. 1988b. *The DoBama Movement in Burma: Appendix.* Ithaca, NY: Cornell University Press.

Kockelman, Paul. 2007a. "Inalienable Possessions and Personhood." *Language in Society* 36, no. 3: 343–69.

———. 2007b. "From Status to Contract Revisited: Value, Temporality, Circulation and Subjectivity." *Anthropological Theory* 7, no. 2: 151–76.

———. 2007c. "Agency: The Relation between Meaning, Power, and Knowledge." *Current Anthropology* 48, no. 3.

———. 2009. "Inalienable Possession as Grammatical Category and Discourse Pattern." *Studies in Language* 33, no. 1: 25–68.

———. 2010. "Enemies, Parasites, and Noise: How to Take Up Residence in a System without Becoming a Term in It." *Journal of Linguistic Anthropology* 20, no. 2: 406–21.

———. 2013. "The Anthropology of an Equation: Sieves, Spam Filters, Agentive Algorithms, and Ontologies of Transformation." *HAU: Journal of Ethnographic Theory* 3, no. 3: 33–61.

Ko Htwe. 2014. "Burmese Islamic Group Issues Census Directives." *Democratic Voice of Burma*, March 19, 2014.

Ko Ko Thett. 2022. "Remembering Lynn Moe Swe (1976–2017)." In *Picking Off New Shoots Will Not Stop the Spring*, edited by Ko Ko Thett and Brian Haman, 187–90. Singapore: Ethos.

Ko Thet. 2012. "Ministry of Finance Unveils New Tax System." *Democratic Voice of Burma*, April 5, 2012.

Kramer, Marshall. Forthcoming. "Working with the Drugs: Barefoot Medicine and the Reproduction of Migrant Labour on an Inter-Asian Frontier."

Kyaw Hsu Mon. 2014. "Rangoon Power Board to Seek Private Sector Involvement from 2015." *Irrawaddy*, November 26, 2014.

———. 2015. "Power Chief Pledges End to Rangoon Outages." *Irrawaddy*, April 8, 2015.

———. 2016. "Artist APK: 'Cartoons in State-Run Newspapers Aren't Real Cartoons.'" *Irrawaddy*, January 16, 2016.

Kyaw Kha. 2017. "88 Generation Peace and Open Society Stand by Government on Rakhine." *Irrawaddy*, September 13, 2017.

Kyaw Yin Hlaing. 2001. "The Politics of State-Business Relations in Postcolonial Burma." PhD diss., Cornell University.

Kyed, Helene. 2020. *Everyday Justice in Myanmar: Informal Resolutions and State Evasion in a Time of Contested Transition*. Copenhagen: NIAS Press.

———, ed. 2021. "Hopes for a New Democracy in Myanmar: Multiethnic Unity against Military Power." *Tea Circle* (blog), March 19, 2021. https://teacircleoxford.com/policy-briefs-research-reports/hopes-for-a-new-democracy-in-myanmar-multiethnic-unity-against-military-power/.

Lall, Marie, Thei Su San, Nwe Nwe San, Yeh Tut Naing, Thein Thein Myat, Lwin Thet Thet Khaing, Swann Lynn Htet, and Yin Nyein Aye. n.d. *Citizenship in Myanmar, Contemporary Debates and Challenges in Light of the Reform Process*. Yangon: Myanmar Egress.

Lammerts, Christian. 2013. "Narratives of Buddhist Legislation: Textual Authority and Legal Heterodoxy in Seventeenth through Nineteenth-Century Burma." *Journal of Southeast Asian Studies* 44, no. 1: 118–44.

———. 2018. *Buddhist Law in Burma: A History of Dhammasattha Texts and Jurisprudence, 1250–1850.* Honolulu: University of Hawai'i Press.

Leach, E. R. 1959. *Political Systems of Highland Burma.* Oxford, UK: Berg.

Leehey, Jennifer. 2010. "Open Secrets, Hidden Meanings: Censorship, Esoteric Power, and Contested Authority in Urban Burma in the 1990s." PhD diss., University of Washington.

———. 2016. *Community-Based Social Protection in the Dry Zone.* Yangon: HelpAge International.

Leider, Jacques. 1998. "Those Buddhist Kings with Muslim Names." *Etudes birmanes en hommage à Denise Bernot,* EFEO: 189–215.

———. 2018. "Conflict and Mass Violence in Arakan (Rakhine State): The 1942 Events and Political Identity Formation." In *Citizenship in Myanmar,* edited by Ashley South and Marie Lall. Singapore: ISEAS-Yusof Ishak Institute.

Letpadaung Chronicle. n.d. Yangon: Spring.

Levien, Michael. 2013. "Regimes of Dispossession: From Steel Towns to Special Economic Zones." *Development and Change* 44, no. 2: 381–407.

Levi-Strauss, Claude. 1982. "The Sorcerer and His Magic." In *Structural Anthropology.* New York: Basic.

Lieberman, Victor. 1984. *Burmese Administrative Cycles.* Princeton, NJ: Princeton University Press.

———. 2010. "A Zone of Refuge in Southeast Asia? Reconceptualizing Interior Spaces." *Journal of Global History* 5, no. 2: 333–46.

Lin, Minzarni. 2019. *Artisanal Jade Mining in Myanmar.* Report F-53424-MYA-1. London: International Growth Center.

Lund, Christian. 2016. "Rule and Rupture: State Formation through Production of Property and Citizenship." *Development and Change* 47, no. 6: 1199–1228.

MacLean, Ken. 2010. "The Rise of Private Indirect Government in Burma." In *Finding Dollars, Sense and Legitimacy in Burma,* 40–52. Washington, DC: Wilson Center.

———. 2018. *Famine Crimes: Military Operations, Forced Migration, and Chronic Hunger in Eastern Burma/Myanmar (2006–2008).* IDCE Occasional Research Paper Series. Worcester, MA: Clark University, International Development, Community, and Environment.

———. 2022. *Crimes in Archival Form.* Berkeley: University of California Press.

MacPherson, C. B. 1962. *The Political Theory of Possessive Individualism.* Oxford, UK: Clarendon Press.

Madhok, Sumi. 2015. "Developmentalism, Human Rights, and Gender Politics: From a Politics of Origins to a Politics of Meanings." In *Human Rights: India and the West,* edited by Ashwani Peetush, and Jay Drydyk, 95–122. New Delhi: Oxford University Press.

———. 2017. "On Vernacular Rights Cultures and the Political Imaginaries of Haq." *Humanity* 8, no. 3: 485–509.

Madson, Nathan. 2022. "I Am an Ordinary Citizen: Human Rights Discourse and the Limits of Human Rights Law." *American Anthropologist* 124, no. 3: 504–14.

Mahmud, Tarek. 2018. "Visiting Nobel Laureates: Don't Hesitate to Call Yourselves Rohingya." *Dhaka Tribune*, February 28, 2018.

Malkki, Liisa. 1995. *Purity and Exile*. Chicago: University of Chicago Press.

Mann, Michael. 1984. "Autonomous Power of the State: Its Origins, Mechanisms, and Results." *European Journal of Sociology* 25.

Mark, SiuSue. 2016. "Are the Odds of Justice 'Stacked' Against Them? Challenges and Opportunities for Securing Land Claims by Smallholder Farmers in Myanmar." *Critical Asian Studies* 48, no. 3: 443–60.

Martel, James. 2017. *The Misinterpellated Subject*. Durham, NC: Duke University Press.

Ma Thida. 2016. *Prisoner of Conscience: My Steps Through Insein*. Chiang Mai: Silkworm.

———. 2021. "Only When Basic Entitlements Are Guaranteed, Can Inclusivity Happen in Burmese Culture and Religious Circles." [In Burmese.] *Independent Journal of Burma Scholarship* 1, no. 1: 338–65.

———. 2022. "Picking Off New Shoots Will Not Stop the Spring." In *Picking Off New Shoots Will Not Stop the Spring*, edited by Ko Ko Thett and Brian Haman, 28–34. Singapore: Ethos.

Matthews, Bruce. 1998. "The Present Fortune of Tradition-Bound Authoritarianism in Myanmar." *Pacific Affairs* (1998): 7–23.

Maung Maung. 1980. *From Sangha to Laity*. New Delhi: Manohar.

Maung Maung Gyi. 1983. *Burmese Political Values*. New York: Praeger.

Maung ThaNoe. "Every Cry for Human Rights Is Not Good." [In Burmese.] MaBaTha Facebook post, June 27, 2016.

Maung Thitsa. 2015. "Responsible People: Take Responsibility for Resolving Things." [In Burmese.] *Worker Journal*, no. 6.

Mbembe, Achille. 2001. *On the Postcolony*. Berkeley: University of California Press.

———. 2019. *Necropolitics*. Durham, NC: Duke University Press.

McAuliffe, Erin. 2017. "Caste and the Quest for Racial Hierarchy in British Burma: An Analysis of Census Classifications from 1872–1931." Master's thesis, University of Washington.

McCarthy, Gerard. 2016. "Buddhist Welfare and the Limits of Big 'P' Politics in Provincial Myanmar." In *Conflict in Myanmar*, edited by Nick Cheesman and Nicholas Farrelly, 313–32. Singapore: ISEAS.

———. 2019. "Democratic Deservingness and Self-Reliance in Contemporary Myanmar." *Sojourn* 34, no. 2: 327–65.

———. 2020. "Class Dismissed? Explaining the Absence of Economic Injustice in the NLD's Governing Agenda." *Journal of Current Southeast Asian Affairs* 38, no. 3: 358–80.

McCarthy, John, and Mayer Zald. 2001. "Resource Mobilization Theory: Vigorous or Outmoded?" In *Handbook of Sociological Theory*, edited by Jonathan H. Turner, 533–66. New York: Springer.

McDowell, Robin, and Margie Mason. 2021. "Myanmar's Junta Using Bodies to Terrorize." Associated Press, May 26, 2021.

McGranahan, Carole. 2018. "Refusal as Political Practice: Citizenship, Sovereignty, and Tibetan Refugee Status." *American Ethnologist* 45, no. 3: 367–79.

Meari, Lena. 2014. "Sumud: A Palestinian Philosophy of Confrontation in Colonial Prisons." *South Atlantic Quarterly* 113, no. 3: 547–78.

Melville, Herman. 1853. *Bartleby, the Scrivener: A Story of Wall-Street.* https://www.bartleby.com/129/.

Merry, Sally Engle. 2006. *Human Rights and Gender Violence.* Chicago: University of Chicago Press.

Metro, Rosalie. 2014. "From the Form to the Face to Face: IRBs, Ethnographic Researchers, and Human Subjects Translate Consent." *Anthropology & Education Quarterly* 45, no. 2: 167–84.

Milko, Victoria, and Kristen Gelineau. 2021. "Myanmar's Military Disappearing Young Men to Crush Uprising." AP News, May 5, 2021. https://apnews.com/article/united-nations-myanmar-technology-e5c0036949f7e7fb8ce1da5884f250a4.

Milroy, James, and Lesley Milroy. 1999. *Authority in Language.* 3rd ed. New York: Routledge.

Min Zin. 2016. "'Kabar Ma Kyei': Imagining the Nation through Songs." *Myanmar Affairs*, October 1, 2016.

Mitchell, Timothy. 1990. "Everyday Metaphors of Power." *Theory and Society* 19, no. 5: 545–77.

———. 2018. "Society, Economy, and the State Effect." In *State/Culture: State-Formation after the Cultural Turn*, edited by George Steinmetz. Ithaca, NY: Cornell University Press.

Mizzima. "'Democracy' and 'Human Rights' in Reality Are 'Simply Awkward' Criticizes USDP Chairman." [In Burmese.] October 30, 2016.

MMID (Mandalay MyoTha Industrial Development Public Company, Limited). 2013. "Prospectus," copy with author.

Morreira, Shannon. 2016. *Rights after Wrongs: Local Knowledge and Human Rights in Zimbabwe.* Redwood City, CA: Stanford University Press.

Moyn, Samuel. 2010. *The Last Utopia.* Cambridge, MA: Harvard University Press.

Mullen, Matthew. 2016. *Pathways That Changed Myanmar.* New York: Bloomsbury.

Myanmar Census. 2015. *The 2014 Myanmar Population and Housing Census: The Union Report, Volume 2.* Department of Population, Ministry of Immigration and Population. https://unstats.un.org/unsd/demographic-social/census/documents/Myanmar/MMR-2015-05.pdf.

Myanmar Now. 2021a. "Aspiring Engineer Maimed in Sadistic Attack Becomes an Emblem of His Generation." April 9, 2021. https://myanmar-now.org/en/news/aspiring-engineer-maimed-in-sadistic-attack-becomes-an-emblem-of-his-generation.

———. 2021b. "At Least 18 Locals, Including Unarmed Civilians, Killed in Magway Region." September 12, 2021. https://myanmar-now.org/en/news/at-least-18-locals-including-unarmed-civilians-killed-in-magway-region.

———. 2021c. "Soldiers Use Arson and Bombings as Collective Punishment after Meeting with Armed Resistance." July 20, 2021. https://www.myanmar-now.org/en/news/soldiers-use-arson-and-bombings-as-collective-punishment-after-meeting-with-armed-resistance?page=1.

Myint Zan. 2000. "Judicial Independence in Burma: No March Backwards Towards the Past." *Asian-Pacific Law and Policy Journal* 5.

———. 2008. "Legal Education in Burma Since the 1960s." *Journal of Burma Studies* 12, no. 1: 63–107.

Myo Chit Maung Buthitaung. 2015. "With the Bengali Issues Our Blood Should Not Be Calm." [In Burmese.] *Hot News*, 5, no. 244: May 29–June 4, 2015.

Myo Min. 2021. "Equality or Animosity: Where Will the Democratic Uprising Take the Rohingya?" *Tea Circle Oxford*, March 25, 2021.

Nadi Hlaing, and Michael Haack. 2021. "Amid Myanmar's Post-coup Violence, There Is One Township in Yangon That 'Scares the Military.'" *South China Morning Post*, April 4, 2021.

Nandar. 2022. "A Nightmare You Can't Wake Up From." In *Picking Off New Shoots Will Not Stop the Spring*, edited by Ko Ko Thett and Brian Haman, 73–76. Singapore: Ethos.

Nang Mya Nadi. 2014. "Shans Plan Their Own Census." *Democratic Voice of Burma*, March 13, 2014.

Nash, Manning. 1965. *The Golden Road to Modernity*. New York: John Wiley and Sons.

Naw, Theresa. 2022. "Prophecies, Rituals, and Resistance in Myanmar." *Diplomat*, April 19, 2022.

Nay Thwin. 2011. "Thein Sein Says No Political Prisoners." *Democratic Voice of Burma*, November 21, 2011.

Needham, Rodney. 1972. *Belief, Language, and Experience*. Oxford, UK: Basil Blackwell.

New York Times. 2016. "More Attacks on Transgender Rights." August 24, 2016.

Nhkum Lu. 2022. "Siser Nu Tawng: Extraordinary Courage Out of Everyday Kindness." In *Picking Off New Shoots Will Not Stop the Spring*, edited by Ko Ko Thett and Brian Haman, 49–54. Singapore: Ethos.

Noe Noe Aung. 2014. "Can a Minimum Wage Law Work?" *Myanmar Times*, February 2, 2014.

Nursyazwani. In review. "Re/producing Rohingyaness: Becoming Legible Rohingya in Malaysia."

Nussbaum, Martha. 1999. "The Professor of Parody." *New Republic*, https://newrepublic.com/article/150687/professor-parody.

Nyers, Peter. 2010. "Abject Cosmopolitanism." In *The Deportation Regime*, edited by Nicholas De Genova and Nathalie Peutz, 413–42. Durham, NC: Duke University Press.

Nyi Nyi Kyaw. 2018. "Myanmar's Other Muslims: The Case of the Kaman." In *Citizenship in Myanmar: Ways of Being In and From Burma*, edited by Ashley South and Marie Lall, 279–300. Singapore: ISEAS.

Nyunt Nyunt Win. 2021. "Tolerant Tea Shops: The Social Construction of Forbearance of Child Labour." Paper presented at the 3rd International Conference on Burma/ Myanmar Studies, Chiangmai, Thailand, March 5–7, 2021.

O'Brien, Kevin, and Lianjiang Li. 2006. *Rightful Resistance in Rural China*. Cambridge, UK: Cambridge University Press.

Ong, Andrew. 2020. "Tactical Dissonance: Insurgent Autonomy on the Myanmar-China Border." *American Ethnologist* 47, no. 4: 369–86.

———. 2023. *Stalemate*. Ithaca, NY: Cornell University Press.

Ortner, Sherry. 1995. "Resistance and the Problem of Ethnographic Refusal." *Comparative Studies in Society and History* 37, no. 1: 173–93.

Paddock, Richard. "In Myanmar, Health Care's Collapse Takes Its Own Toll." *New York Times*, June 12, 2021.

Patton, Thomas. 2016. "The Wizard King's Granddaughters: Burmese Buddhist Female Mediums, Healers, and Dreamers." *Journal of the American Academy of Religion* 84, no. 2: 430–65.

———. 2018. *The Buddha's Wizards*. New York: Columbia University Press.

Pauker, Ben. 2017. "Can Anyone Stop the Tragedy in Myanmar—Before It's Too Late?" In *Foreign Policy*. Podcast with Derek Michell, former US ambassador to Burma, November 3, 2017.

Peirce, Charles. 2012. "Logic as Semiotic: The Theory of Signs." In *Philosophical Writings of Peirce*, edited by Justus Buchler, 98–119. Chelmsford, MA: Courier.

Perugini, Nicola, and Neve Gordon. 2015. *The Human Right to Dominate*. Oxford, UK: Oxford University Press.

Prasse-Freeman, Elliott. 2012. "Power, Civil Society, and an Inchoate Politics of the Daily in Burma/Myanmar." *Journal of Asian Studies* 71, no. 2: 371–97.

———. 2013. "Scapegoating in Burma." *Anthropology Today* 29, no. 4: 2–3.

———. 2014. "Fostering an Objectionable Burma Discourse." *Journal of Burma Studies* 18, no. 1: 97–122.

———. 2015a. "Myanmar Conceptions of Justice and the Rule of Law." In *Myanmar: Dynamics, of an Evolving Polity*, edited by David Steinberg, 89–114. Boulder, CO: Lynne Rienner.

———. 2015b. "Seeking and Avoiding the Law in Burma." *Anthropology Today* 31, no. 6: 29–30.

———. 2016. "Grassroots Protest Movements and Mutating Conceptions of 'the Political' in an Evolving Burma." In *Metamorphosis: Studies in Social and Political Change in Myanmar*, edited by Renaud Egreteau and Francois Robinne, 69–100. Singapore: NUS Press.

———. 2019. "Of Punishment, Protest, and Press Conferences: Contentious Politics amidst Despotic Decision in Contemporary Burmese Courtrooms." In *Criminal Legalities in the Global South*, edited by George Radics and Pablo Ciocchini, 124–42. Abingdon, UK: Routledge.

———. 2021. "Hate Bait, Micro-publics, and National(ist) Conversations on Burmese Facebook." *Independent Journal of Burmese Scholarship* 1, 144–204.

———. 2022a. "Necroeconomics: Dispossession, Extraction, and Indispensable/Surplus Populations in Contemporary Myanmar." *Journal of Peasant Studies* 49, no. 7: 1466–96.

———. 2022b. "Resistance/Refusal: Politics of Manoeuvre under Diffuse Regimes of Governmentality." *Anthropological Theory* 22, no. 1: 102–27.

———. 2023a. "Bullets and Boomerangs: Proleptic Uses of Failure in Myanmar's Anti-coup Uprising." *Public Culture* 35, no. 1: 73–112.

———. 2023b. "Refusing Rohingya: Reformulating Ethnicity amidst Blunt Biopolitics." *Current Anthropology* 64, no. 2.

———. 2023c. "Reassessing Reification: Ethnicity amidst 'Failed' Governmentality in Burma and India." *Comparative Studies in Society and History* 65, no. 3.

Prasse-Freeman, Elliott, and Kirt Mausert. 2020. "Two Sides of the Same Arakanese Coin: 'Rakhine,' 'Rohingya,' and Ethnogenesis as Schismogenesis." In *Unraveling Myanmar's Transition*, edited by Pavin Chachavalpongpun, Elliott Prasse-Freeman, and Patrick Strefford, 261–89. Singapore: NUS Press.

Prasse-Freeman, Elliott, and Andrew Ong. 2021. "Expulsion / Incorporation: Valences of Mass Violence in Myanmar." In *Political Violence in Southeast Asia since 1945*, edited by Eve Zucker and Ben Kiernan, 41–55. Abingdon, UK: Routledge.

Prasse-Freeman, Elliott, and Phyo Win Latt, 2018. "Class and Inequality in Contemporary Myanmar." In *The Routledge Handbook of Contemporary Myanmar*, edited by Ian Holliday, Nicholas Farrelly, and Adam Simpson, 404–18. Abingdon, UK: Routledge.

Pyithu Ayay. 2014. "Only If There Is Truth Will We Get a Certain Victory." [In Burmese.] Editorial. October 14, 2014.

Radio Free Asia. 2015a. "Nay Myo Zin and Naw Ohn Hla Brought to Trial over Chinese Embassy Protest." January 15, 2015. https://www.youtube.com/watch?v=Bw N4hhLxx7Q.

———. 2015b. "Aung San Suu Kyi Urges Support For NLD Amid Myanmar Candidate Row." August 10, 2015. https://www.rfa.org/english/news/myanmar/support -08102015151253.html.

———. 2020a. "Jade Scavengers Keep Working in Myanmar's Hpakant, despite Deadly Hazards." July 17, 2020. https://www.rfa.org/english/news/myanmar/jade -scavengers-07172020181711.html.

———. 2020b. "Myanmar Leader Triggers Debate With 'Illegal' Reference to Dead Jade Scavengers." July 9, 2020. https://www.rfa.org/english/news/myanmar/jade -assk-07092020084300.html.

———. 2021. "Interview: Myanmar Police Take Unyielding Detainees in Handcuffs For 'Beatings and Torture.'" April 22, 2021. https://www.rfa.org/english/news /myanmar/shwe-yamin-htet-04222021181201.html.

Rajagopalan, Megha. 2012. "The Prisoners' Dilemma." *Foreign Policy*, January 30, 2012.

Ranciere, Jacques. 2004. "Who Is the Subject of the Rights of Man?" *South Atlantic Quarterly* 103, nos. 2/3 (Spring/Summer): 297–310.

Reddy, Malavika. 2022. "Wishful Performativity: Translation and the Linguistic

Structures of a Stalled Rights Imaginary in Mae Sot, Thailand." *Journal of the Royal Anthropological Institute* 28, no. 3: 993–1011.

Redfield, Peter. 2013. *Life in Crisis*. Berkeley: University of California Press.

Reid, Anthony. 1993. *Southeast Asia in the Age of Commerce*. Vol. 2. New Haven, CT: Yale University Press.

Reuters. 2021. "Myanmar Junta Warns Protesters at Risk of Being Shot in the Head—State TV." March 26, 2021. https://www.reuters.com/article/myanmar-cs-military -idINKBN2BI2GJ?fbclid=IwAR3EuPeoi8nKmA1nyAIfYRarSZ28oisFmgEgMcX fXbFPavrsPe5CGjYbWIY.

Rhoads, Elizabeth. 2018. "Forced Evictions as Urban Planning? An Historical Overview of Land Control and Forced Evictions in Yangon." *State Crime Journal* 7, no. 2: 278–305.

———. 2020. "Informal 'Justice' Brokers: Navigating Property Transactions in Yangon." In *Everyday Justice in Myanmar*, edited by Helene Kyed, 283–313. NIAS Press.

———. 2023. "Citizenship Denied, Deferred, and Assumed: A Legal History of Racialized Citizenship in Myanmar." *Citizenship Studies* 27, no. 1: 38–58.

Rigg, Jonathan. 1990. *Southeast Asia*. Boston: Unwin HMyan.

Riles, Annelise. 2001. *The Network Inside Out*. Ann Arbor: University of Michigan Press.

Rio. 2021. "Critical Juncture: Being a Soldier's Son in Burma's Ongoing Crisis." *Tea Circle Oxford*, April 12, 2021.

Roberts, Jayde, and Elizabeth Rhoads. 2022. "Myanmar's Hidden-in-Plain-Sight Social Infrastructure: Nalehmu through Multiple Ruptures." *Critical Asian Studies* 54, no. 1: 1–21.

Robinne, François, and Mandy Sadan. 2007. "Postscript: Reconsidering the Dynamics of Ethnicity through Foucault's Concept of 'Spaces of Dispersion.'" In *Social Dynamics in the Highlands of Southeast Asia*, edited by François Robinne and Mandy Sadan, 299–308. Leiden, NL: Brill.

Rozenberg, Guillaume. 2010. *Renunciation and Power: The Quest for Sainthood in Contemporary Burma*. Translated by Jessica Hackett. New Haven, CT: Yale University Press.

———. 2015. *The Immortals*. Honolulu: University of Hawai'i Press.

Rudy, Sayres. 2010. "Monistic Force at the End of the Line: Strategic De-territorialization after Sovereign Capture." *theory@buffalo* 14, 107–83.

———. 2014. "Fanon via Nietzsche toward the Post-sovereign Physical Subject." Paper presented at the Association for Political Theory Annual Conference, Madison, WI, October 16–18, 2014.

———. 2018. "Suicide against Death: Contesting Truth by Self-Immolation." Paper presented at the Western Political Science Association Annual Conference, San Francisco, March 29–31, 2018.

———. 2021. "'Human Rights,' 'Rule of Law,' and 'Violence.'" In *Rethinking Law and Violence*, edited by Latika Vashist and Jyoti Dogra Sood, 19–85. New Delhi: Oxford and ILI.

Ruel, Malcolm. 2008. "Christians as Believers." In *A Reader in the Anthropology of Religion*, edited by Michael Lambek. Malden, MA: Blackwell.

Sadan, Mandy. 2013. *Being and Becoming Kachin*. London: British Academy Press.

Saha, Jonathan. 2013. *Law, Disorder and the Colonial State*. New York: Springer.

Sahlins, Marshall. 2002. *Waiting for Foucault, Still*. Chicago: Prickly Paradigm Press.

Sai Aw. 2017. "4,000 Protest Coal Mine in Mong Kung." *Shan Herald*, April 11, 2017. http://english.panglong.org/2017/04/11/2000-protest-coal-mine-in-mong-kung/.

Said, Edward. 2014. "Traveling Theory." In *World Literature in Theory*, edited by David Damrosch, 114–33. John Wiley and Sons.

Sai Wansai. 2017. "Clarifying Myanmar's Complex Ethnic Makeup." *Asia Times*, December 7, 2017.

Sa Nay Lin. 2014. "Wan Bao and U Baing Companies Cursed for the 4th Time." [In Burmese.] *Irrawaddy*, May 24, 2014.

———. 2015. "Harn Win Aung's Views about LPT Issues while Fleeing and Avoiding." [In Burmese.] *Irrawaddy Weekly Journal* 2, no. 10.

San Moe Htun. 2016. "For Farmers' Downtrodden Lives When Will the Bridge to Prison be closed?" [In Burmese.] *Eleven*, June 14, 2016. http://news-eleven.com/opinions/20812.

Sanyal, Kalyan. 2007. *Rethinking Capitalist Development*. Abingdon, UK: Routledge.

Sardiña Galache, Carlos. 2011. "Interview: Aung San Suu Kyi." *ES Global*, September 19, 2011.

———. 2020. *The Burmese Labyrinth: A History of the Rohingya Tragedy*. New York: Verso Books.

Sarkisyanz, Emanuel. 1965. *Buddhist Backgrounds of the Burmese Revolution*. New York: Springer.

Sassen, Saskia. 2017. "Is Rohingya Persecution Caused By Business Interests Rather than Religion?" *Guardian*, January 4, 2017.

Saung U. n.d. "A life that has guarantees and/with authority that is just." [In Burmese.] *Worker Journal* 1, no. 7: 21.

Saw Wai. 2018. "An Open Letter to U2's Bono and Others." *Myanmar Times*, May 3, 2018.

Schissler, Matt. 2015. "New Technologies, Established Practices: Developing Narratives of Muslim Threat in Myanmar." In *Islam and the State in Myanmar*, edited by Melissa Crouch, 211–33. Oxford, UK: Oxford University Press.

Schissler, Matt, Matthew J. Walton, and Phyu Phyu Thi. 2017. "Reconciling Contradictions: Buddhist-Muslim Violence, Narrative Making and Memory in Myanmar." *Journal of Contemporary Asia* 47, no. 3: 376–95.

Schmitt, Carl. 1976. *The Concept of the Political*. New Brunswick, NJ: Rutgers University Press.

Schober, Juliane. 2011. *Modern Buddhist Conjunctures in Myanmar*. Honolulu: University of Hawai'i Press.

Schrank, Delphine. 2015. *The Rebel of Rangoon*. New York: Nation Books.

Scott, James C. 1972. "The Erosion of Patron–Client Bonds and Social Change in Rural Southeast Asia." *Journal of Asian Studies* 32, no. 1: 5–37.

————. 1976. *The Moral Economy of the Peasant*. New Haven, CT: Yale University Press.

————. 1985. *Weapons of the Weak*. University Park: Penn State University Press.

————. 1990. *Domination and the Arts of Resistance*. New Haven, CT: Yale University Press.

————. 1998. *Seeing Like a State*. New Haven, CT: Yale University Press.

————. 2009. *The Art of Not Being Governed*. New Haven, CT: Yale University Press.

Selth, Andrew. 2010. "Burma and the Politics of Names." *The Interpreter*, July 12, 2010.

————. 2015. "Myanmar's Coercive Apparatus: The Long Road to Reform." In *Myanmar: The Dynamics of an Evolving Polity*, edited by David Steinberg, 13–36. Boulder: Lynne Rienner.

————. 2019. *Secrets and Power in Myanmar*. Singapore: ISEAS.

Shah, Alpa. 2021. "For an Anthropological Theory of Praxis: Dystopic Utopia in Indian Maoism and the Rise of the Hindu Right." *Social Anthropology* 29, no. 1: 68–86.

Shange, Savannah. 2019a. "Black girl Ordinary: Flesh, Carcerality, and the Refusal of Ethnography." *Transforming Anthropology* 27, no. 1: 3–21.

————. 2019b. *Progressive Dystopia*. Durham, NC: Duke University Press.

Sharma, Meara. 2021. "Introduction." *ADI Magazine*, Flash the Coup/Stories from Myanmar, spring 2021. https://adimagazine.com/issues/flash-the-coup/.

Sharpe, Christina. 2016. *In the Wake: On Blackness and Being*. Durham, NC: Duke University Press.

Shwe Aung. 2015. "New Generation of Pro-Government Thugs." *Democratic Voice of Burma*, March 6, 2015.

Shwe Saw Thet (Shwebo). 2016. "Human Rights, Religious Rights, Myanmar's Rights." *Thagithway Journal* 3, no. 1.

Siddique, Haroon. 2013. "Burma Sectarian Violence Motivated by Fear, Says Aung San Suu Kyi." *Guardian*, October 24, 2013.

Silverstein, Michael. 1976. "Shifters, Linguistic Categories, and Cultural Description." In *Meaning in Anthropology*, edited by K. Basso and H. Selby, 11–55. El Paso: University of New Mexico Press.

————. 1993. "Metapragmatic Discourse and Metapragmatic Function." In *Reflexive Language: Reported Speech and Metapragmatics*, edited by J. Lucy, 33–58. Cambridge, UK: Cambridge University Press.

Simion, Kristina. 2021. *Rule of Law Intermediaries*. Cambridge, UK: Cambridge University Press.

Simmons, Erica. 2016. *Meaningful Resistance*. Cambridge, UK: Cambridge University Press.

Simpson, Audra. 2014. *Mohawk Interruptus*. Durham, NC: Duke University Press.

Si Thu Lwin. 2014. "'Nothing Has Changed': Land Activist Stages Solo Protest through Mandalay." *Myanmar Times*, November 21, 2014.

Slaughter, Anne-Marie. 2004. "Disaggregated Sovereignty: Towards the Public Accountability of Global Government Networks." *Government and Opposition* 39, no. 2: 159–90.

Sobo, Elisa. 2016. "Theorizing (Vaccine) Refusal: Through the Looking Glass." *Cultural Anthropology* 31, no. 3: 342–50.

Sojoyner, Damien. 2017. "Another Life Is Possible: Black Fugitivity and Enclosed Places." *Cultural Anthropology* 32, no. 4: 514–36.

South, Ashley. 2008. *Ethnic Politics in Burma*. Abingdon, UK: Routledge.

South, Ashley, and Marie Lall, eds. 2018. Introduction to *Citizenship in Myanmar*. Singapore: ISEAS.

Speed, Shannon. 2008. *Rights in Rebellion*. Redwood City, CA: Stanford University Press.

Spiro, Melford. 1977. *Kinship and Marriage in Burma*. Berkeley: University of California Press.

Spivak, Gayatri. 1988. "Can the Subaltern Speak?" In *Marxism and the Interpretation of Culture*, edited by Cary Nelson and Lawrence Grossberg. Champaign: University of Illinois Press.

———. 1996. "Bonding in Difference: Interview with Alfred Arteaga." In *The Spivak Reader*, edited by Donna Landry and Gerald MacLean, 15–28. Abingdon, UK: Routledge.

Swe Win. 2015a. "A Search for the Masters of Force." *Myanmar Now*, August 5, 2015.

———. 2015b. "Protecting Cows: A Buddhist Tradition Revived?" *Irrawaddy*, September 15, 2015.

———. 2015c. "Myanmar's Radical Buddhists Target Muslim Businesses, with Official Help." *Myanmar Now*, October 15, 2015. https://myanmar-now.org/en/news/myanmars-radical-buddhists-target-muslim-businesses-with-official-help.

Tahir, Madiha. 2017. "The Ground Was Always in Play." *Public Culture* 29, no. 1: 5–16.

Tar Yar Maung. 2019. "Governance in Myanmar's Jade Industry." Master's thesis, Australia National University.

Tate, Winifred. 2007. *Counting the Dead*. Berkeley: University of California Press.

Taussig, Michael. 1993. *Mimesis and Alterity*. New York: Routledge.

———. 1997. *Magic of the State*. New York: Routledge.

Taylor, Robert H. 2009. *The State in Myanmar*. Singapore: NUS Press.

Thakin Ohn Myint. 2013. Foreword to *A Taste of Prison*, 7–10. Edited by Thakin Ohn Myint. Yangon: Myanmar's Age.

Thamaga Thein Oo. 2014. "In Myanmar, Rights Are Not for Buddhism." *Thamaga News Journal*, December 5, 2014.

Thant Myint-U. 2001. *The Making of Modern Burma*. Cambridge, UK: Cambridge University Press.

Tharaphi Than. 2011. "Understanding Prostitutes and Prostitution in Democratic Burma, 1942–62: State Jewels or Victims of Modernity?" *South East Asia Research* 19, no. 3: 537–65.

———. 2015. "Nationalism, Religion, and Violence: Old and New Wunthanu Movements in Myanmar." *Review of Faith and International Affairs* 13, no. 4: 12–24.

Tha Sein. 2016. "A Lie Told Often Enough Becomes the Truth." *Global New Light of Myanmar*, November 3, 2016.

Thaung. 1959. "Burmese Kingship in Theory and Practice during the Reign of Mindon." *Journal of the Burma Research Society* 42, no. 2: 171–85.

Thawda Aye Lei. 2022. "Whose Footfall Is Loudest." In *Picking Off New Shoots Will Not Stop the Spring*, edited by Ko Ko Thett and Brian Haman, 125–31. Singapore: Ethos.

Thawnghmung, Ardeth. 2004. *Behind the Teak Curtain*. London: Kegan Paul.

———. 2019. *Everyday Economic Survival in Myanmar*. Madison: University of Wisconsin Press.

Thawnghmung, Ardeth, Su Mon Thazin, Moo Moo Paw, and Duncan Boughton. Forthcoming. "Water in One Hand, Fire in the Other: Coping with Multiple Crises in Post-coup Myanmar." *Critical Asian Studies* 55, no 2.

Thein-Lemelson, Seinenu. 2018. "Myanmar's Van Gogh Taken Too Soon, Leaves Legacy of Indomitable Beauty." *Irrawaddy*, January 16, 2018.

Thongchai Winichakul. 1994. *Siam Mapped: A History of the Geo-body of a Nation*. Honolulu: University of Hawaii Press.

Tilly, Charles. 1985. "War Making and State Making as Organized Crime." In *Bringing the State Back In*, edited by Peter Evans, Dietrick Rueschemeyer, and Theda Skocpol, 169–91. Cambridge, UK: Cambridge University Press.

Time. 2018. "President Donald Trump Just Delivered His First State of the Union. Read the Full Transcript." January 30, 2018.

Tin Htet Paing. 2015. "Burmese Cartoons Celebrate Centenary in Rangoon." *Irrawaddy*, December 31, 2015.

———. 2016. "Cartoonist Says Facebook Users 'Flagged' Him over NLD Gibe." *Irrawaddy*, January 11, 2016.

Toe Hla. 1987. "Money-Lending and Contractual Thet-kayits: A Socio-economic Pattern of the Later Kon-baung Period, 1819–1885." PhD diss., Northern Illinois University.

Tomasello, Michael. 2010. *Origins of Human Communication*. Cambridge, MA: MIT Press.

Tomasky, Michael. 2015. "President Obama's Challenge to Muslim Americans." *Daily Beast*, December 6, 2015.

Tran, Mai Van. 2020. "Resilience of Contentious Movements under Repression: The Role of Bystander Protection and Disruption." PhD diss., Cornell University.

Trautwein, Catherine. 2016. "Debt Trap Another Hurdle for Urban Poor." *Myanmar Times*, September 16, 2016.

Treadwell, Brooke. 2013. "Teaching Citizenship under an Authoritarian Regime: A Case-Study of Burma/Myanmar." PhD diss., Indiana University.

Turner, Alicia. 2014. *Saving Buddhism*. Honolulu: University of Hawai'i Press.

U Hla Win. 2015. "Whose Responsibility?" *Voice Weekly*, May 23, 2015.

UNOCHR. 2018. "Report of the Independent International Fact-Finding Mission on Myanmar," #A/HRC/ 39/64. https://www.ohchr.org/sites/default/files/Documents/HRBodies/HRCouncil/FFM-Myanmar/A_HRC_39_64.pdf.

VOA. 2021. "Those Who Are Unsatisfied with an Arrest in South Okallapa Gather to Protest." *Voice of America*, February 12, 2021.

Voice Weekly. 2013. "The Person behind Letpadaung Mountain." [In Burmese.] March 16, 2013.

Von Schnitzler, Antina. 2013. *Democracy's Infrastructure.* Princeton, NJ: Princeton University Press.

Wade, Francis. 2017. *Myanmar's Enemy Within.* London: Zed Books.

Walton, Matthew. 2012. "Politics in the Moral Universe: Burmese Buddhist Political Thought." PhD diss., University of Washington.

———. 2013. "The "Wages of Bamar-ness:" Ethnicity and Bamar Privilege in Contemporary Myanmar." *Journal of Contemporary Asia* 43, no. 1: 1–27.

———. 2017. *Buddhism, Politics, and Political Thought in Myanmar.* Cambridge, UK: Cambridge University Press.

Watanabe, Chika. 2015. "Commitments of Debt: Temporality and the Meanings of Aid Work in a Japanese NGO in Myanmar." *American Anthropologist* 117, no. 3: 468–79.

Wedeen, Lisa. 1999. *Ambiguities of Domination.* Chicago: University of Chicago Press.

Weiss, Erica. 2016. "Refusal as Act, Refusal as Abstention." *Cultural Anthropology* 31, no. 3: 351–58.

Whitehead, Neil. 2004. "On the Poetics of Violence." In *Violence,* edited by Neil Whitehead, 55–78. New Mexico: School for Advanced Research Advanced Seminar Series.

Whorf, Benjamin. 1956. "The Relation of Habitual Thought and Behavior to Language." In *Language Thought and Reality,* edited by L. Carroll, 134–59. Cambridge, MA: MIT Press.

Win Tin. 2012. *What Is That? Man-Made Hell.* [In Burmese.] Yangon: Red Star.

Wirathu. 2014. "Clarifications so That Those Who Oppose the Protection of the Race Law Can Be Known." [In Burmese.] Speech at Ahthawaddy playfield, North Okkala Township, May 11, 2014.

Wolters, Oliver. 1999. *History, Culture, and Region in Southeast Asian Perspective.* Ithaca, NY: Cornell University Press.

Women's Refugee Commission. 2018. *"It's Happening to Our Men as Well": Sexual Violence Against Rohingya Men and Boys.* New York: Women's Refugee Commission.

Woods, Kevin. 2014. "Political Anatomy of Land Grabs." *Myanmar Times,* March 3, 2014.

Worker Journal. n.d. "It Is Necessary to Give a Wage Salary That Will Be Sufficient for a Human Standard." [In Burmese.] Editorial, *Worker Journal* 1, no. 7.

World Bank. 2014. "Ending Poverty and Boosting Shared Prosperity in a Time of Transition." Report No. 93050-MM, November 2014. https://openknowledge.worldbank.org/handle/10986/23121.

———. 2015. "A Country on the Move: Domestic Migration in Two Regions of Myanmar." Qualitative Social and Economic Monitoring Project, January 2015. https://www.worldbank.org/en/country/myanmar/publication/a-country-on-the-move---domestic-migration-in-two-regions-of-myanmar.

Wortham, Stanton. 2005. "Socialization beyond the Speech Event." *Journal of Linguistic Anthropology* 15, no. 1: 95–112.

Ye Keh Pyay. 2014. "The Five Thaygone Farmers Who Cursed Have Been Charged under Chapter 505(b)." [In Burmese.] *Mizzima*, May 6, 2014.

Yuzana Khine Zaw. 2022. "An Ethnographic Study on Medicines, Care, and the Responsibility of Antimicrobial Resistance amidst Disorder and Decline in Yangon, Myanmar." PhD diss., London School of Hygiene and Tropical Medicine.

Ziv, Tali. 2022. "The Practice of Informality: Hustling, Anticipating, and Refusing in the Postindustrial City." *International Journal of Urban and Regional Research* 46, no. 5: 807–21. https://doi.org/10.1111/1468-2427.13134.

Zöllner, Hans-Bernd, ed. 2008. "Students, Society and Politics in Burma/Myanmar—Documents and Essays." Myanmar Literature Project, Working Paper no. 10:4.1.

Zuckerman, Charles, and John Mathias. 2022. "The Limits of Bodies: Gatherings and the Problem of Collective Presence." *American Anthropologist* 124, no. 2: 345–57.

Index

Figures, notes, and tables are indicated by f, n, and t following the page number.

Perpetrators

Antonius C. G. M Robben and Alexander Laban Hinton

2023

Reinventing Human Rights

Mark Goodale

2022

The Subject of Human Rights

Edited by Danielle Celermajer and Alexandre Lefebvre

2020

#HumanRights: The Technologies and Politics of Justice Claims in Practice

Ronald Niezen

2020

The Grip of Sexual Violence in Conflict: Feminist Interventions in International Law

Karen Engle

2020

When Misfortune Becomes Injustice: Evolving Human Rights Struggles for Health and Social Equality

Alicia Ely Yamin

2020

The Politics of Love in Myanmar: LGBT Mobilization and Human Rights as a Way of Life

Lynette J. Chua

2018

Campaigning for Justice: Human Rights Advocacy in Practice
Jo Becker
2012

In the Wake of Neoliberalism: Citizenship and Human Rights in Argentina
Karen Ann Faulk
2012

Values in Translation: Human Rights and the Culture of the World Bank
Galit A. Sarfaty
2012

Disquieting Gifts: Humanitarianism in New Delhi
Erica Bornstein
2012

Stones of Hope: How African Activists Reclaim Human Rights to Challenge Global Poverty
Edited by Lucie E. White and Jeremy Perelman
2010

Judging War, Judging History: Behind Truth and Reconciliation
Pierre Hazan
2010

Localizing Transitional Justice: Interventions and Priorities after Mass Violence
Edited by Rosalind Shaw and Lars Waldorf, with Pierre Hazan
2010

Surrendering to Utopia: An Anthropology of Human Rights
Mark Goodale
2009

Human Rights for the 21st Century: Sovereignty, Civil Society, Culture
Helen M. Stacy
2009

Human Rights Matters: Local Politics and National Human Rights Institutions
Julie A. Mertus
2009